SURVEY OF LONDON

MONOGRAPH 17

PREVIOUS MONOGRAPHS PUBLISHED BY THE SURVEY OF LONDON

1 Trinity Hospital, Mile End.
2 St. Mary, Stratford Bow.
3 The Old Palace, Bromley-by-Bow.
4 The Great House, Leyton.
5 Brooke House, Hackney.
6 The Church of St. Dunstan, Stepney.
7 East Acton Manor House.
8 Sandford Manor, Fulham.

9 Crosby Place.
10 Morden College, Blackheath.
11 Eastbury Manor House, Barking.
12 Cromwell House, Highgate.
13 Swakeleys, Ickenham.
14 The Queen's House, Greenwich.
15 The Church of St. Bride, Fleet Street.
16 The College of Arms, Queen Victoria Street.

Except for volumes 15 (available from the Survey of London *Department) and 16 (available from the* College of Arms) *all these monographs are out of print.*

PARISH VOLUMES OF THE SURVEY OF LONDON

I Bromley-by-Bow.*
II Chelsea. Part I.*
III St. Giles-in-the-Fields. Part I (Lincoln's Inn Fields).†
IV Chelsea. Part II.†
V St. Giles-in-the-Fields. Part II.†
VI Hammersmith.†
VII Chelsea. Part III (The Old Church).
VIII St. Leonard, Shoreditch.†
IX St. Helen, Bishopsgate. Part I.*
X St. Margaret, Westminster. Part I.*
XI Chelsea. Part IV (The Royal Hospital).*
XII All Hallows, Barking-by-the-Tower. Part I (The Parish Church).*
XIII St. Margaret, Westminster. Part II (Neighbourhood of Whitehall, vol. I).*
XIV St. Margaret, Westminster. Part III (Neighbourhood of Whitehall, vol. II).†
XV All Hallows, Barking-by-the-Tower. Part II.
XVI St. Martin-in-the-Fields. Part I (Charing Cross).†
XVII St. Pancras. Part I (Village of Highgate).*
XVIII St. Martin-in-the-Fields. Part II (The Strand).*
XIX St. Pancras. Part II (Old St. Pancras and Kentish Town).*
XX St. Martin-in-the-Fields. Part III (Trafalgar Square and neighbourhood).*
XXI St. Pancras. Part III (Tottenham Court Road and neighbourhood).†

XXII St. Saviour and Christ Church, Southwark (Bankside).*
XXIII St. Mary, Lambeth. Part I (South Bank and Vauxhall).†
XXIV St. Pancras. Part IV (King's Cross neighbourhood).*
XXV St. George the Martyr and St. Mary Newington, Southwark (St. George's Fields).
XXVI St. Mary, Lambeth. Part II (Southern area).*
XXVII Christ Church and All Saints (Spitalfields and Mile End New Town).†
XXVIII Hackney. Part I (Brooke House).
XXIX, XXX St. James, Westminster. Part I (South of Piccadilly).†
XXXI, XXXII St. James, Westminster. Part II (North of Piccadilly).
XXXIII, XXXIV St. Anne, Soho.
XXXV The Theatre Royal, Drury Lane, and The Royal Opera House, Covent Garden.
XXXVI St. Paul, Covent Garden.
XXXVII Northern Kensington.
XXXVIII The Museums Area of South Kensington and Westminster.
XXXIX The Grosvenor Estate in Mayfair. Part I (General History).
XL The Grosvenor Estate in Mayfair. Part II (The Buildings).
XLI Southern Kensington: Brompton.
XLII Southern Kensington: Kensington Square to Earl's Court.

*Original edition out of print. Photographic facsimile availiable from Survey of London, *RCHME, Fortress House, 23 Savile Row, London W1X 2JQ, or from AMS Press Inc., 56 East 13th Street, New York, and the agents of AMS Press.*
†Out of Print.

The Council Chamber as intended in 1911. From a watercolour by A. C. Horsnell, also signed by the architect, Ralph Knott (p. 77)

SURVEY OF LONDON

GENERAL EDITOR: HERMIONE HOBHOUSE

MONOGRAPH 17

County Hall

THE ATHLONE PRESS
Published for the Royal Commission on the
Historical Monuments of England
1991

Published 1991 by
THE ATHLONE PRESS
at 1, Park Drive, London NW11

for the

ROYAL COMMISSION ON THE HISTORICAL MONUMENTS OF ENGLAND

British Library Cataloguing in Publication Data
County Hall – (Survey of London monograph no. 17)
   1. London (England). Civic buildings. Architecture.
History
   I. Hobhouse, Hermione   II. Series
725.1309421

ISBN 0–485–48417–X

Library of Congress Cataloging-in-Publication Data
County Hall.
      p.   cm. — (Survey of London. Monograph : no. 17)
   Includes bibliographical references.
     ISBN 0–485–48417–X
   1. County Hall (London, England)   2. Knott, Ralph—Criticism and
interpretation.   3. Eclecticism in architecture—England—London.
4. London (England)—Buildings, structures, etc.
I. Royal Commission on the Historical Monuments of England   II. Series.
DA677.S87   no. 17
[NA4429.G7]
942.1 s—dc20
[725′.13′0942165]

Printed in Great Britain by Butler & Tanner Ltd
Frome and London

Preface

The Royal Commission on the Historical Monuments of England became responsible for the *Survey of London* on the abolition of the Greater London Council in 1986. *County Hall* is, therefore, the first major volume from the *Survey of London* to be published by the Royal Commission. It is also the seventeenth monograph to appear in the *Survey of London* series, marking the revival of a tradition, begun by the first Survey Committee, of publishing single volumes on individual buildings in parallel with the more substantial parish volumes. After 1945 the monograph series fell into abeyance, although studies of individual buildings, such as Brooke House and the Covent Garden Theatres, were published as part of the parish sequence. The earlier monographs were used to highlight the plight of some threatened building, as with those on *The Trinity Hospital in Mile End* of 1896, or *Eastbury Manor House, Barking* of 1917: both buildings were saved in consequence. Occasionally, as in 1937 with *The Queen's House, Greenwich*, the monograph celebrated what was seen as a triumphant restoration.

When the Greater London Council was abolished, it seemed appropriate to record the County Hall, built by the London County Council to house London's first elected government, and for over sixty years its centre, being both council chamber and administrative offices. This book discusses the history and architecture of the building which served the County of London as an Hôtel de Ville. Though not as ostentatious as some of its contemporaries and much less grand than some aspiring designers would have had it – as this volume reveals – it is still a very proud and important building, worthy of its prominent site. In view of the two London county councils' record of support and aid to the *Survey of London* it is very proper that it should be the *Survey* staff who have recorded their headquarters.

On behalf of the Royal Commission I would like to thank the many people who have contributed to the volume through their help and advice, most of whom are mentioned by name in the list of acknowledgements. It was begun under the Chairmanship of my predecessor, the Earl Ferrers. Various Commissioners have contributed advice and expertise, but particular thanks are due to Mrs Bridget Cherry and Dr Derek Keene for the interest they have taken in the progress of the volume.

It almost goes without saying that the book could not have been written without the help provided by past members and officers of the Greater London Council, whose names are noted elsewhere, and by the staff of the London Residuary Body.

As with all *Survey* publications, it is the work of a team of writers and researchers. The major part of the first draft, and much of the research has been contributed by Anthony McIntyre, with additional material from John Greenacombe, Derek Holdaway and Stephen Porter. Pat Reed and Gillian Duane were responsible for the early research, and additional work has been carried out by Ann Robey, Bridgett Jones and Colin Thom. The General Editor of the *Survey of London*, Hermione Hobhouse, was responsible for the concept of the book, and its editing, and has also contributed some original research and part of the text. The figures in the book were drawn by the *Survey* draughtsmen, Mike Clements and Ron New, while original photography was carried out by Derek Kendall of the Royal Commission's staff and the GLC Photographic Unit under the direction of Roy Ferriman.

PARK OF MONMOUTH

Commissioners

Acknowledgements

The *Survey of London* team has received help from many quarters in the preparation of this volume, and the names of persons and institutions to whom it is indebted are listed below. Particular thanks for support and assistance are due, however, to a number of past Members of the Greater London Council and of the London County Council, including Mr Tony Banks M.P., Mr William Bell, the late Lord Ponsonby of Shulbrede, Lord Plummer of St Marylebone and the Countess Spencer. Special thanks are also due to Miss Joan Coburn, Miss Eileen Cobb, Mr Chris Denvir and the staff of the Greater London Record Office and History Library, who made available to us the records in their custody with great efficiency and courtesy at a difficult time. Mr Ashley Barker, former Surveyor of Historic Buildings, GLC, and his staff at the London Division of English Heritage generously shared their knowledge of the fabric of County Hall. We are particularly grateful to Mr Andrew Saint for his specialist knowledge and advice on the early days of the LCC. Mr John Howes and his colleagues on the London Residuary Body were unfailingly helpful in providing information and access to the building.

The Royal Commission on Historical Monuments of England also acknowledges with gratitude the help given by the following: Mr Derek Addison; Miss Finch Allibone; Mr C. D. Andrews; the late Mrs S. Beattie; Mr P. A. Bezodis; Mr Neil Bingham; Mr Louis W. Bondy; Mr Keith Breathwick; Mr Kenneth Campbell; Sir Hugh Casson; Mrs Maxine Copeland; Mr Charles Corcoran; Baroness Denington; Mr S. T. J. Ford; Mr Derek Gill; Mr Francis Graham; Mr A. S. Gray; Mr T. J. Heard; Dr O. Wright Holmes; Mr Len Hudson; Mr E. P. Hyslop; Mr Walter Ison; Mr David Knight; Mr J. Anthony Leathart; Mrs H. Lusby; Mr Herman Ouseley; Mr David G. Moore; Mr Jerrold Northrop Moore; Mrs Josephine Parkhouse; Mr Ken Price; Mrs Betty Puddifoot; the late Lord Reilly; Mr Alastair Service; Dr Francis Sheppard; Mr John Smith; Sir John Summerson; Sir James Swaffield; Mr Robert Vigars; Mr David Walker; Miss Wendy West; Mrs Margaret J. R. White; Dr Clare Willsdon; Mr I. W. Wilson; Mr Thomas Woodcock (Somerset Herald).

Aaron Photographic Ltd; Actors' Charitable Trust; AEI Cables Ltd; The Architectural Association; The Architectural Press; BBC Hulton Picture Library; Bristol Central Reference Library; British Library; Bron y Garth Hospital, Penrhyndeudraeth; Library of the Chartered Institute of Bankers; Courtauld Institute; Crittall Windows Ltd; County Hall Development Group plc; Delta E.M.S. Ltd; Dorset County Council; Fitzwilliam Museum, Cambridge; Frome Museum; Guildhall Art Gallery; Gwynedd County Council; Inner London Education Authority; Donald Insall & Partners; London Library; Malvern Public Library; Museum of London; Stanley Peach & Partners; National Centre for Photography; Royal Institute of British Architects, Library and Drawings Collection; Skidmore, Owings & Merrill Inc.; Staffordshire Record Office; Surrey County Council; Waverley Borough Council.

Owners of photographs and other illustrations reproduced in this volume are acknowledged in the List of Plates.

Contents

	List of Plates	xi
	List of Figures	xiv
	Foreword	xvii
I	The London County Council and the Need for a County Hall	I
II	The Acquisition of the Site	6
III	The County Hall Competition	14
IV	The Final Design	26
V	The Building of County Hall 1909–1922	49
VI	Architectural Sculpture and Decorative Treatment	57
VII	London's Hôtel de Ville: The 1922 Building	70
VIII	The Northern Front	92
IX	The New County Offices – North and South Blocks	103
X	The Second World War and Post-War Development	110
XI	The Future of County Hall	120
	Appendix I: London County Council Hall Competition:	
	Instructions to Competing Architects	125
	Appendix II: List of Competitors and Published Designs	127
	Appendix III: List of Works by Ralph Knott	128
	Appendix IV: Select List of Major Contractors and Suppliers	129
	References and List of Abbreviations	133
	Index	143

Plates *at end*

List of Plates

All LCC and GLC photographs are in the possession of the Greater London Photograph Library

Frontispiece. The Council Chamber. *Perspective by A. C. Horsnell, 1911, from* Academy Architecture, *Vol.42, Dec. 1912, p.48a*

1. County Hall under construction, 1921. *Copyright Hunting Aerofilms (5603)*

2. (a) Old County Hall, Spring Gardens, in May 1939. *LCC photograph*
   (b) A meeting of the LCC at Old County Hall, Spring Gardens. *Oil painting by H. Jamyn Brooks, GLC Heritage Collection, courtesy of the Guildhall Art Gallery, Corporation of London*
   (c), (d) County Hall site in the early 1900s. *LCC photographs*

3. (a) Belvedere Road in 1909. *LCC photograph*
   (b) Westminster Bridge Road in 1905. *Sketch by Hedley Fitton from* Pall Mall Magazine, *Oct. 1905, p.403*
   (c) W. E. Riley's design for County Hall site. *From* The Building News, *21 April 1905, between pp.562–3*
   (d) The Assessors at work. *Watercolour by Joseph Finnemore, GLC Heritage Collection, courtesy of the Guildhall Art Gallery, Corporation of London*

4. Unsuccessful Competition Designs
   (a) River front elevation by H. Percy Adams & C. H. Holden. *RIBA Drawings Collection (AHP/AD [9], no.11)*
   (b) Belvedere Road front elevation by Salmon, Son & Gillespie. *From* The British Architect, *25 Oct. 1907, between pp.198–9*
   (c) River front perspective by Adrian Gilbert Scott. *From* The Builder, *12 Sept. 1908, between pp.282–3*

5. The Development of Knott's Design
   (a) Amended design of 1908. *Oil painting by Harold Wyllie, GLC Heritage Collection, courtesy of the Guildhall Art Gallery, Corporation of London*
   (b) Knott's Royal Academy design of 1909–10. *From* The Building News, *29 April 1910, pp.592–3*
   (c) Model of revised design approved in 1911. *LCC photograph*

6. (a) County Hall site in July 1909. *LCC photograph*
   (b) Foreshore in Feb. 1910. *LCC photograph*
   (c) Foundations of Section A under construction. *LCC photograph*

7. Laying the Foundation Stone in 1912. Marquee, Ceremony, and Ceremonial tools. *LCC photographs*

8. County Hall under construction, 1912–1920. *LCC photographs*

9. (a) Roof structure in May 1920. *Photograph in possession of Anthony McIntyre*
   (b) County Hall in October 1921. *Photograph by Bedford Lemere, RCHME*
   (c) North front in May 1930. *LCC photograph*

10. (a) Opening ceremony, 17 July 1922. *London News Agency photograph (Greater London Photograph Library)*
    (b) River front in 1922. *LCC photograph*
    (c) River front c.1933. *Photograph by Herbert Felton in possession of The Architectural Press*

11. Ralph Knott and the LCC Chairman and Chief Officers in 1922. *From* The Illustrated London News, *15 July 1922, p.105, courtesy of The Illustrated London News Picture Library*

12. (a), (b) Crescent and Members' Terrace in 1922. *LCC photographs*
    (c) The flèche in 1989. *RCHME photograph*

13. Belvedere Road front
    (a) In 1973. *GLC photograph*
    (b) Central bays in 1923. *LCC photograph*
    (c) Main entrance c.1930. *LCC photograph*

14. (a) Westminster Bridge Road front in 1988. *RCHME photograph*
    (b) Members' Carriage Drive c.1923. *Photograph by F. R. Yerbury in possession of the Architectural Association*
    (c) Knott's design for rainwater head, 1915. *GLRO, GLC Architect's Plan Room drawing (AD47/02)*
    (d) Members' Entrance in 1963. *LCC photograph*

15. Members' Carriage Drive in 1988. *RCHME photographs*

16. Members' Courtyard
    (a) Knott's design for the south elevation, 1912. *GLRO, GLC Architect's Plan Room drawing (BC7/02)*
    (b) Looking west c.1922. *Central News Limited photograph (Greater London Photograph Library)*
    (c) Knott's design for cast-iron lamps, 1922. *GLRO, GLC Architect's Plan Room drawing (AD16/01)*

17. Members' Courtyard
    (a) North side in 1929. *LCC photograph*
    (b) Members' Entrance c.1923 *Photograph by F. R.*

Yerbury in possession of the Architectural Association
(c) Memorial to Knott in 1937. *LCC photograph*

18. Northern Front
(a) In 1986. *GLC photograph*
(b) Vehicle entrance *c*.1933. *Photograph by Herbert Felton, RCHME*
(c) Heraldic carving in 1988. *RCHME photograph*

19. (a) Belvedere Road Entrance Hall in 1960. *LCC photograph*
(b) Ceremonial Staircase and Gates in 1990. *RCHME photograph*

20. (a) Ceremonial Staircase in 1922. *LCC photograph*
(b) 'Ambulatory' in 1990. *RCHME photograph*
(c) Entrance to Council Chamber in 1960. *LCC photograph*

21. Council Chamber in 1938. *Photograph courtesy of Times Newspapers Limited*

22. (a) Ayes Lobby in 1986. *GLC photograph*
(b) Room 177 in 1923. *LCC photograph*

23. (a) Members' Library in 1923. *LCC photograph*
(b) Room 168 in 1921. *Photograph by Bedford Lemere, RCHME*

24. (a) Room 129 in 1921. *Photograph by Bedford Lemere, RCHME*
(b-d) Rooms 128, 129 and 120, in 1922. *LCC photographs*

25. (a) Room 165 in 1936. *LCC photograph*
(b) Room 136 in 1921. *Photograph by Bedford Lemere, RCHME*
(c) Room 115 in 1923. *LCC photograph*

26. Principal Floor Corridors
(a) Design by Knott, 1913. *GLRO, GLC Architect's Plan Room drawing (AD4/07)*
(b) Carving on Lady Members' Staircase in 1986. *GLC photograph*
(c) Corridor in Block 12 in 1933. *LCC photograph*
(d) Postbox and pigeon-holes in 1986. *GLC photograph*

27. Fireplaces
(a) Room 115, *c*.1923. *Photograph by F. R. Yerbury in possession of the Architectural Association*
(b) Room 133, 1922. *LCC photograph*
(c) Belvedere Road Entrance Hall, 1922. *LCC photograph*
(d) Room 118, 1961. *LCC photograph*
(e) Room 188, 1922. *LCC photograph*

28. (a) Lamp-fitting and ceiling details in Council Chamber in 1986. *GLC photograph*
(b) Lift cage in 1923. *LCC photograph*
(c) Bronze doors inside Members' Entrance in 1990. *RCHME photograph*
(d) Radiator in Members' Entrance in 1990. *RCHME photograph*
(e) LCC coat-stand in 1986. *GLC photograph*

29. (a) Lunette painting. *From* The Architectural Review, *Feb. 1923, p.38, courtesy of The Architectural Press*
(b-d) Wood and stone carvings by A. H. Wilkinson, in 1990. *RCHME photographs*

30. Sculptural groups by Ernest Cole in 1990. *RCHME photographs*

31. (a) Horse's head chain-support on embankment wall. *From* The Builder, *8 Sept. 1911, between pp.274-5*
(b) Lion's head mooring-ring on Embankment wall in 1986. *RCHME photograph*
(c), (d) Sculptural groups by A. F. Hardiman, in 1990. *RCHME photographs*
(e) J. W. Singer & Son's Foundry, Frome, *c*.1910. *Photograph in Frome Museum*

32. (a) North Entrance lobby in 1990. *RCHME photograph*
(b) Staircase to Crush Hall in 1933. *Photograph by Herbert Felton, RCHME*
(c) D Staircase in 1990. *RCHME photograph*
(d) E lift lobby in 1933. *LCC photograph*

33. (a) Crush Hall *c*.1933. *Photograph by Herbert Felton, RCHME*
(b) Conference Hall *c*.1933. *Photograph by Herbert Felton, RCHME*
(c) Room 143 in February 1933. *LCC photograph*

34. (a) Room 153 *c*.1933. *Photograph by Herbert Felton, RCHME*
(b) Room 152 in 1933. *LCC photograph*
(c) Room 140 *c*.1933. *Photograph by Herbert Felton, RCHME*
(d) Room 142 in 1986. *GLC photograph*

35. (a) Education Library in 1933. *LCC photograph*
(b) Education Department Library and Sample Room in 1933. *LCC photograph*
(c) Medical Department Supplies, Room 35, in 1937. *LCC photograph*

36. (a) West Entrance Hall, Westminster Bridge Road, in 1988. *RCHME photograph*
(b) Second-floor corridor in 1990. *RCHME photograph*
(c) Third-floor corridor in 1986. *GLC photograph*
(d) Vehicle Licensing Hall in 1963. *LCC photograph*
(e) Luncheon Club in 1939. *LCC photograph*

37. (a) Main laboratory in 1954. *Fox photograph (Greater London Photograph Library)*
(b) Staff Chapel in 1965. *LCC photograph*
(c) Room 201 in 1990. *RCHME photograph*
(d) Octopus Room in 1921. *Photograph in possession of Anthony McIntyre*

38. (a) Roofscape in 1970. *GLC photograph*
(b) Area G in 1990. *RCHME photograph*

(c) Exterior of the Council Chamber in 1990. *RCHME photograph*
(d) Exterior of the Conference Hall and Education Library *c*.1933. *Photograph by Herbert Felton, RCHME*

39. New County Offices
(a) Drawing by G. Gilbert Scott. *RIBA Drawings Collection (ScGG, WhE & HiF [1]4)*
(b) Model of the new offices in July 1935. *LCC photograph*
(c) Window detail by Scott. *RIBA Drawings Collection (ScGG, WhE & HiF [1]49)*
(d) Perpective view of new offices at night by Stanley H. Smith, *c*.1937. *GLRO Print Collection*

40. New County Offices
(a), (e) Exteriors in 1939. *LCC photographs*
(b), (c) Carved panels in 1987. *RCHME photographs*
(d) Models for column capitals in 1938. *LCC photograph*

41. New County Offices in 1990. *RCHME photographs*
(a) Entrance to South Block
(b) Relief panel in North Block
(c) Entrance Hall in North Block
(d) M staircase in North Block

42. (a) War damage to County Hall in 1940. *Keystone Press Agency photograph (Greater London Photograph Library)*
(b) Riverside terrace in 1970. *GLC photograph*
(c) Members' Courtyard, infill block in 1986. *GLC photograph*
(d) Infill block in H Courtyard in 1990. *RCHME photograph*

43. Post-war Interiors. *GLC photographs*
(a) Infill offices in 1986
(b) Staff cafeteria in 1966
(c) Chairman's Reception Suite in 1970
(d) Room 448 in 1974

44. North Block extension
(a) Under construction in 1956. *Photograph by A. C. Halliday (Greater London Photograph Library)*
(b) L staircase in 1986. *GLC photograph*
(c) Exterior in 1957. *LCC photograph*
(d) Third-floor offices in 1960. *LCC photograph*

45. Post-war buildings
(a) Addington Street Annexe in 1989. *RCHME photograph*
(b) Island Block, interior in 1975. *GLC photograph*
(c) Island Block, escalator connexion in 1988. *RCHME photograph*
(d) Island Block, exterior in 1975. *GLC photograph*

46. (a) Memorial to Emma Cons in 1990. *RCHME photograph*
(b-d) *Portraits of Early LCC Chairmen from GLC Heritage Collection, courtesy of the Guildhall Art Gallery, Corporation of London:*
(b) Captain George Sitwell Campbell Swinton. *Charcoal drawing by J. Singer Sargent*
(c) Ronald Collet Norman. *Oil painting by Glyn Philpot*
(d) Sir John Lubbock. *Oil painting by the Hon. John Collier*

47. *Portraits of GLC Chairmen from GLC Heritage Collection, courtesy of the Guildhall Art Gallery, Corporation of London*
(a) Dame Evelyn Joyce Denington. *Oil painting by William Edward Narraway*
(b) David Thomas Pitt, Lord Pitt of Hampstead. *Oil painting by Edward Irvine Halliday*
(c) Thomas Archer Ponsonby, 3rd Baron Ponsonby of Shulbrede. *Oil painting by Carlos Sancha*
(d) Tony Banks, M.P. *Oil painting by Jane Murphy*

48. County Hall Redevelopment Proposals, 1989. *Photographs from the County Hall Development Group plc*

List of Figures

Note: Many of the figures are based on material formerly in the Greater London Council Architect's Plan Room at County Hall which is now in the possession of the Greater London Record Office. This source is indicated as GLC-APR

Material on the County Hall Competition reproduced from London County Council Hall Final Competition, *a Special Number of* British Competitions in Architecture, *edited by Alexander Koch, 1908, is identified as Koch*

1. Old County Hall, Spring Gardens: first-floor plan in 1905. *Redrawn from plans in GLC-APR (C1/03, C1/15, C1/18, C2/16, D/14)*   7

2. Old County Hall, Spring Gardens: site plan in 1902. *Based on the Ordnance Survey of 1893*   8

3. The County Hall site in 1905. *Based on the Ordnance Survey of 1893 and plans in GLC-APR (A2/03, A2/06)*   12

4. Suggested Plan of the Principal Floor, New County Hall, by the Superintending Architect, issued with the *Instructions for Competitors*, 1907. *Reproduced from Koch, p.2*   21

5. Ralph Knott's winning design for County Hall: perspective. *Reproduced from Koch, p.9*   24

6. Details of a design for a gateway, submitted by Knott for the Tite Prize. *Reproduced from* The Builder, *9 Feb. 1901, p.138*   25

7. Competition Designs for County Hall   27
   (a) Perspective by E. L. Lutyens. *Reproduced from Koch, p.34*
   (b) Perspective by G. Washington Browne. *Reproduced from Koch, p.43*

8. Competition Designs for County Hall   28–9
   (a) Ground-floor plan by H. T. Hare. *Reproduced from Koch, p.23*
   (b) Ground-floor plan by Jemmet & McCombie. *Reproduced from Koch, p.65*
   (c) Principal-Floor plan by E. L. Lutyens. *Reproduced from Koch, p.32*
   (d) Principal-Floor plan by Warwick & Hall. *Reproduced from Koch, p.88*

9. Competition Designs for County Hall   30
   (a) Perspective by Hinds & Deperthes. *Reproduced from Koch, p.97*
   (b) Perspective by Russell & Edwin Cooper. *Reproduced from Koch, p.83*

10. Competition Design for County Hall: perspective by Lanchester & Rickards. *Reproduced from* The Builder, *18 Jan. 1908, between pp.70–1*   32

11. Competition Design for County Hall: plans by Salmon, Son & Gillespie of Glasgow, 1907. *Redrawn from plans in* The British Architect, *25 Oct. 1907, pp.194–5*   33

12. Competition Design for County Hall: elevations by Nicholson & Corlette. *Reproduced from Koch, p.38*   34

13. Knott's winning design for County Hall: Ground- and Principal-Floor plans. *Reproduced from Koch, p.9*   36

14. Knott's winning design for County Hall: east-west section through Council Chamber. *Reproduced from Koch, p.10*   37

15. Postcard sent by Julian Leathart to Knott's office, 1911. *Reproduced from original in possession of Leathart's son*   39

16. Knott's winning design for County Hall: east and west elevations. *Reproduced from Koch, p.10*   40

17. Competitions Designs for County Hall   43
   Knott's winning design: elevation to Westminster Bridge Road. *Reproduced from Koch, p.10*
   H. T. Hare's design: elevation to Westminster Bridge Road. *Reproduced from Koch, p.24*

18. The development of the plan of County Hall, 1908–9   44
   (a) Knott's winning design plan, January 1908. *Based on Koch, p.9*
   (b) The amended plan approved in July 1908. *Based on Wyllie's elevation (see Plate 5a) and material in GLRO, AR/CB/2/124*
   (c) The 'waisted' plan, September 1908. *Based on a sketch in GLRO, AR/CB/2/125*
   (d) Knott's 'fan-shaped' plan, January 1909. *Based on material in GLRO, AR/CB/2/84*

19. The development of the plan of County Hall, 1909–10   46
   (a) Assessors' plan, March 1909. *Redrawn from a plan in GLRO, AR/CB/2/125*
   (b) Knott's published plan of 1910. *Redrawn from* The Building News, *6 May 1910, p.622*

20. Perspective sketch of C. H. Reilly's competition design for County Hall, May 1907. *Reproduced from original drawing in possession of C. H. Reilly's family*   47

21. Plan of County Hall buildings, showing relationship to existing properties in 1893. *Based on the Ordnance Survey of 1893*   50

22. Plan of County Hall showing division into Blocks and Sections for construction purposes. *Based on plans in GLC-APR (AC11/00, A1/05)*   52

23. Competition Design for County Hall by Matthew J. Dawson: detail of river front. *Reproduced from Koch, p.63*   58

24. Knott's winning design: detail of river-front pavilion. *Reproduced from Koch, p.11*   60

25. Drawings for panelling and fireplaces for Committee Rooms on the Principal Floor (Block 12), 1914 and 1920. *Reproduced from working drawings in GLC-APR (CD2/03, CD2/06)*   61

26. Detail drawings for metalwork, 1922. *Reproduced from working drawing in GLC-APR (AD46/08)*   62

27. Revised detail of river-front pavilions, 1912. *Reproduced from working drawing in GLC-APR (AD22/01)*   64

28. Entrance Hall, Belvedere Road, design for north wall, 1913. *Reproduced from a working drawing in GLC-APR (AD4/02)*   67

29. The flèche as designed in 1914 and as modified in 1921. *Redrawn from drawings in GLC-APR (AD23/01–02)*   72

30. Section through the Members' Courtyard and Carriage Drive. *Redrawn from a drawing in GLC-APR (C2/03)*   74

31. The Council Chamber, section looking west. *Redrawn from drawings in GLC-APR (AD2/01–03, AD36/10, AC9/05)*   78

32. Plans of the Council Chamber. *Redrawn from plans in GLC-APR (AD1/03–04)*   79

33. Members' Library: *Reproduced from a working drawing in GLC-APR (BD/01)*   82

34. London County Council Book Plate, 1903. *Reproduced from an original in possession of the Greater London Record Office*   83

35. Main Committee Room – Rooms 128, 129, 130
(a) Section looking north. *Based on drawings in GLC-APR (AD6/02, AC7/08) and survey*   84
(b) Section looking south. *Based on a drawing in GLC-APR (AD6/02) and survey*   84
(c) Plans. *Based on plans in GLC-APR (AD6/01, AD51/05) and survey*   85

36. Main Committee Room
(a) Section through Room 130. *Based on drawings in GLC-APR (AD6/02, AC9/05) and survey*   86
(b) Section through Room 129. *Based on a drawing in GLC-APR (AD6/02) and survey*   86

37. Typical panelling for a senior officer's room on the Principal Floor, 1920. *Reproduced from a working drawing in GLC-APR (BD2/07)*   88

38. Drawing for the Cashier's Office, ground floor, July 1913. *Reproduced from a working drawing in GLC-APR (BD4/05)*   89

39. Seating for Members in the Council Chamber. *Based on drawings in GLC-APR (AD31/01, AD33/06) and survey*   91

40. Northern Front (Section D), north-south section as built. *Redrawn from a drawing in GLC-APR (DC5/08)*   94

41. North façade of County Hall. *Redrawn from drawings in GLC-APR (DD11/01,04,07) and from photogrammetric survey*   96

42. Isometric projection of the 'Drum' in Section D. *Constructed from various plans and sections in GLC-APR (see folded drawing A, plus DD41/01–04) and from survey*   98

43. Designs for fireplaces for Committee Rooms in Section D. *Reproduced from working drawings in GLC-APR (DD25/03,06)*   99

44. Design for panelling and fireplace in Room 142, 1931. *Reproduced from a working drawing in GLC-APR (DD2/21)*   100

45. Conference Hall: drawing for a plaster capital, 11 January 1932. *Reproduced from a working drawing in GLC-APR (DD52/05)*   101

46. Education Library: plan at entrance level. *Redrawn from plans in GLC-APR (DD31/09, DD46/02,08)*   102

47. Education Library: plan of glazing in skylight. *Based on a plan in GLC-APR (DD52/02) and photogrammetric survey*   102

48. The New County Offices (North and South Blocks): outline plans showing alternative proposals, 1930–1. *Redrawn from sketch plans in GLRO, AR/CB/2/181*   104

49. The New County Offices (North and South Blocks): ground-floor plan as approved in 1936. *Redrawn from a plan in GLC-APR (AC1/02)*   107

50. Outline plan of North and South Blocks as built, 1936–1963. *Redrawn from plans in GLC-APR (G/3441/2, G/5588/22, AC11/03)*   112

51. The site of County Hall in 1986 showing phases of development. *Based on the Ordnance Survey revision of 1963*   115

SKETCHES

Sketch of the base of one of the bronze lamp-standards on the Ceremonial Stairs   48

Sketch of clock in the Main Entrance Hall, Belvedere
Road   56

Detail of radiator in the Members' Entrance   69

Sketch of the bronze-and-iron gates in the Main
Entrance Hall, Belvedere Road   109

FOLDED DRAWINGS

Folded drawing A – Plans of County Hall
(between pages 62 and 63)

I.   Typical office floor (fourth floor) as completed, 1922–
      33. *Redrawn from plans in GLC-APR (AC2/05,
      BC2/06, CC2/05, DC11/07, DC13/04, C5/07)*

II.   Ground floor as completed, 1922–33. *Redrawn from
      plans in GLC-APR (AC1/05, BC1/05, CC1/06,
      DC1/04, DC4/02–04, DC11/03, C5/03, C6/02)*

III. Principal Floor as completed, 1922–33. *Redrawn from
      plans in GLC-APR (AC1/07, BC1/08, CC1/07,
      DC4/05, DC11/04, C1/01, C4/04)*

Overlay. Principal Floor, northern section, as originally
      planned, 1912

Folded drawing B – Elevations and Section
(between pages 110 and 111)

I.   Elevation to the River Thames as originally built,
      1922–33. *Redrawn from drawings in GLC-APR
      (AC8/03, C2/02, AD22/01,04, AC11/12)*

II.   Section, looking north through the Crescent and
      Council Chamber. *Redrawn from drawings in GLC-
      APR (AC7/04, AC11/13, AD4/05, AD11/02,
      AD21/01, AD23/02, AD23/03–04)*

III. Elevation to Belvedere Road, central section.
      Redrawn from a drawing in GLC-APR (AC7/02)

Foreword

This book describes the history and architecture of the building which for sixty years served as the headquarters of Metropolitan government in London. In its design and in its extent it expressed the aspirations and responsibilities of a major local authority at a time when such authorities were the workhorses of government. The history of the building reflects the growth and importance of the London County Council, in a period when a visit to County Hall was part of the programme of visiting Heads of State, and when the income of the LCC was larger than that of some sovereign states. *The Times*, in reviewing the new County Hall, reminded its readers that, despite the very recent appearance on the metropolitan scene of both the County of London and the LCC, 'by virtue of the millions of people numbered in the one, and the millions in money with which the other has each year to deal, the human and economic interests under the Council's administration are unmatched for extent and complexity among the municipalities of the world'.

The building was judged not only as a functional centre, but also as a tangible symbol of London government. Its very site was a temerarious gamble: it had to stand comparison both with Somerset House and the Palace of Westminster, a challenge which was perhaps more successful architecturally than politically. Changing circumstances have made this more obvious. Its architect, Ralph Knott, could speak breezily of the unlikelihood of details being seen across a fogbound river, but the Clean Air Acts have allowed the building to be more fully appreciated than its designer could have hoped. In addition, it now stands in the company of other prestigious buildings, ranging from the Shell Centre to the National Theatre, instead of alongside a group of obsolescent warehouses and the Shot Tower.

Members of the Council and officers responded to the building. Kenneth Campbell, a senior architect with both the LCC and the GLC, recalled its effect:

it was the building itself which was important. It is a splendid city building and worthy of its position and its purpose. It held its own easily with the other three major Westminster [*sic*] buildings, the Palace of Westminster, New Scotland Yard and St. Thomas' Hospital, and being part of it gave me a sense of belonging to something which was the greatest of its kind nationally and second only to the Parliament buildings opposite . . . . It is difficult to put into words but I am sure it gave weight to our work.

Though like most buildings it became old-fashioned in its middle-age, later on County Hall came to exemplify the virtues of a lost age – 'good traditional materials firmly used . . . a civilised pile . . . appropriate for its purpose, worthy of its splendid position'. Its finest apartments were reserved for the Members, though also enjoyed by visitors. Hugh Casson recalled the heady years of preparing for the Festival of Britain when he visited County Hall:

it was a daily delight to pace those generously spaced and handsomely panelled corridors and to wonder at the diligence and detailed attention of the designers. Every corner beautifully turned, every cornice advancing and retreating in proper order, every door . . . giving a glimpse of well proportioned rooms, specially designed furniture and radiator casings. . . .

If it was the LCC's ever-increasing demand for space which led to the extension of the building, it is the meticulous record-keeping which enables the historian to trace the development of the design. A large number of interests were concerned with the creation and operation of the building, and these reflect not only the policies of the two major political parties, but also the interaction of Members' and officers' ambitions and schemes. Some saw the building merely as a shelter for LCC Members and officers, others as a magnificent headquarters for London, to be decorated with sculpture and works of art, complete with library and tea-room, and even a terrace which could rival that across the river. These differing objectives and ambitions are recorded in the LCC records, often in notes taken by officers, which amplify the drier official Council minutes. Equally cautious officers recorded the details of tenders and formal commissions to craftsmen and contractors so that the erection of the building is not only of interest in itself but throws light on the contemporary architectural profession and indeed the whole building industry.

Though relatively few of the unsuccessful competition drawings have survived, the researcher is almost overwhelmed by the number of contract and working drawings formerly stored in the Architect's Plan Room at County Hall. These throw an unusually detailed light on the changes made as the building progressed, the sources for the interior designs, and the names of the craftsmen.

The changes to the detailed design of County Hall were increased by the wartime break, when the great unfinished building stood on the embankment 'still partially scaffolded and enclosed by hoardings'. When work resumed, taste and economics had changed, and the building lacked some of its intended sculptural and decorative embellishments. Nonetheless it is a public building of great significance, designed not only to demonstrate the importance of London's municipality but also to enhance the lives of Londoners, both by inspiring a Renaissance of the South Bank riverside and by providing a public building whose interior and exterior would be of the best, superbly executed in choice materials. Though one of the most prominent public buildings in London, the carefully detailed and finely crafted interiors were not well-known, even to Londoners.

This is a record of the development of a building, important both architecturally and decoratively. As the book went to press, the future of County Hall was again uncertain, though the exterior of the main County Hall building has already been safeguarded.

It is also as a part of London history that County Hall is significant, as one of the last Conservative Chairmen of the Greater London Council recalled:

A great civic monument – yes, it was certainly that: the building and the reputation of the London County Council were somehow inseparable .... And how well Ralph Knott's classical exterior represented this vision – strong, serene, magnificent perhaps, but not grandiloquent.

CHAPTER I

The London County Council and the Need for a County Hall

County Hall was hailed as the 'Hôtel de Ville' of London in 1922 when it was officially opened by King George V and Queen Mary. For over sixty years it was the tangible expression of metropolitan government for Londoners of all political persuasions.

While it is no part of the scheme of this book to recount the history of the London County Council (LCC), or that of its successor, the Greater London Council (GLC), the story of County Hall is inextricably bound up with those Councils' duties and responsibilities and their Members' perceptions of their role in local government. In order to understand first the drive to build a headquarters and then the chronic inability of the LCC to house all its own staff in County Hall, it is necessary to look at the political and administrative movements which created and enlarged the LCC.

The London County Council was established by the Local Government Act of 1888 to meet the long-standing need for a centralized London government, an objective of reformers over the previous fifty years or so. It held its first meeting on 21 March 1889 in the board-room of the offices of its predecessor, the Metropolitan Board of Works (MBW), at Spring Gardens, Westminster. The Council's first Chairman, the Earl of Rosebery, recognizing the need for a new headquarters building for the Council and its staff, said 'We meet in a very small and in a very inadequate room, but that is not altogether unfitting. Our physical position at this moment resembles our political position. We shall go into greater premises, and we shall assume greater political power'.[1] Though the need was eventually realized in the construction of County Hall, this did not solve the LCC's immediate accommodation problem. As powers were piled on to the willing shoulders of local authorities in the early years of the twentieth century, so the LCC's need for space became increasingly acute. However, the self-confidence of both Members and officers grew with the breadth and extent of its responsibilities. This was reflected in the scale and appearance of the building, and in Herbert Morrison's description of it as 'the headquarters of the greatest municipality in the world ... almost the home of a parliament and a government rather than a municipality'.[2]

The Creation of the London County Council

There was no London-wide administration before the establishment of the Metropolitan Board of Works in 1855. Outside the City, local government was conducted variously by the Justices of the Peace, the Parish Vestries, innumerable Commissions for the paving, cleansing and lighting of the streets and seven separate Commissions of Sewers. Responsibility for poor relief was transferred from the vestries to district Boards of Guardians following the Poor Law Act of 1834, but in all other respects the administrative arrangements in the capital were untouched by the changes imposed upon other English urban authorities by the Whig administration of the 1830s, including the reforming Municipal Corporations Act of 1835.[3]

The changes in metropolitan administration which were effected in the mid-nineteenth century were made largely because of concern over public health. In particular, outbreaks of cholera, which first appeared in 1832, drew attention to the unsatisfactory state of the sanitary arrangements in most English cities, including London, and led to Edwin Chadwick's crusade for centralized authorities to tackle the health hazards caused by inadequate arrangements for sewage disposal and water supply. This campaign culminated in the establishment in 1848 of the Metropolitan Commission of Sewers, but the sewage-laden state of the Thames and the loss of life in the cholera epidemics of 1849 and 1854 clearly showed that a more powerful body was required.[4] In 1855 Sir Benjamin Hall's Metropolis Management Act established the Metropolitan Board of Works as the upper tier of London's government, with jurisdiction over the area which the Registrar General then treated as the capital for the purposes of the *Weekly Returns* of births and deaths, but excluding the City. The Board's members were elected indirectly, by the thirty-seven district boards of works and vestries which were constituted by the same legislation as the lower tier authorities.[a] The MBW was charged chiefly with the construction of a system of main drainage – a responsibility which it performed admirably – and it was entrusted with

---

[a] The local Board of Health for Woolwich brought the number of local authorities up to 38.

a number of other functions, including the embankment of the Thames, street improvements and the oversight of building regulations. Other duties were added later. In 1866 it took over the fire-fighting operations of the insurance companies and established the Metropolitan Fire Brigade; in 1874 it was entrusted with the regulation of slaughterhouses and in the following year it was designated as the authority for the implementation of the Explosives Act and the Artisans' and Labourers' Dwellings Improvement Act. It also developed responsibilities for parks and other open spaces, the Thames crossings and the regulation of places of entertainment.

Nevertheless, the Board's role was limited and its position was not strengthened by the creation of independent administrative bodies to operate within its area, such as the Metropolitan Asylums Board (1867), the School Board for London (1870), and the Port of London Sanitary Authority under the supervision of the Corporation of the City (1872). Nor was support for it increased by occasional imputations of corruption against some members of staff. Indeed, the period from 1855 to 1889 was to be dominated by the struggle over the shape of London's government, between the advocates of a stronger centralized authority and those opposed to the establishment of a potentially powerful metropolitan tier of local government.

The Government's intentions to follow up the 1855 Act with some reform of the Corporation of the City foundered, and none of the Private Member's Bills that were introduced into Parliament between 1860 and 1888, with the object of partial or complete re-organization of the system, reached the statute book. Such attempts at reform could not succeed without government support and the failure of Gladstone's Liberal ministry of 1868–74 to tackle the question slowed the impetus towards change.[5]

It revived during the early 1880s, however, stimulated by the creation in 1881 of the London Municipal Reform League, which absorbed the flagging Metropolitan Municipal Reform Association, founded in 1865. The League, under the presidency of the vigorous and skilful campaigner, J. F. B. Firth,[b] had considerable success in publicizing and co-ordinating the demands for a central municipal government for the capital. There were few who wished to retain the MBW, and revelations in 1886–7 that some of its officers had been guilty of corruption in the granting of contracts undermined what residual support the Board did have. On the other hand, attempts to alter the constitution of the City Corporation were likely to meet with stiff and well orchestrated opposition. Nevertheless, in 1884 Sir William Harcourt, Home Secretary in Gladstone's second ministry, introduced a Bill which proposed to establish a new arrangement for governing the capital by reforming the Corporation and greatly extending its jurisdiction, thereby creating a County of the City of London. Although the Bill was withdrawn before it reached the committee stage, its introduction had aroused the active opposition of the City and the vestries and the alarm of a considerable body of opinion which still viewed the centralization of London's government with strong suspicion.[7]

Following the failure of Harcourt's attempt to reform the City and introduce a metropolis-wide authority, and the fall of the Liberal ministry in 1885, it seemed likely that London government reform would be delayed for some time. In fact, it was Lord Salisbury's ministry which established the London County Council, as a part of its measures to reconstitute the administration of the counties and larger boroughs by creating county councils and county boroughs. Ironically, it was one of the leading critics of Harcourt's Bill and a prominent opponent of centralization in local government, C. T. Ritchie, who, as President of the Local Government Board, prepared and piloted through Parliament the Local Government Act of 1888 which created the LCC.[8] The solution to the problem presented by the City was to grant it a status by which it retained its autonomy, with a relationship to the LCC that was essentially the same as it had been to the MBW. Ritchie did not, however, develop his early ideas to set up district councils within the LCC area, to balance the powers of that Council, and so the vestries and district boards of works were left virtually untouched.[9] Thus the LCC came into being through the back door opened by the reform of county administration, rather than as a part of the complete overhaul of London's government so earnestly desired by the municipal reformers. It inherited the MBW's boundaries unaltered, together with its powers and the entire range of its administrative functions. In addition, it was given the right to oppose Bills in Parliament.

The arrangements made in 1888 did not satisfy everyone. The reformers wished to continue with their programme by widening the LCC's powers and area, particularly by bringing the City within its jurisdiction rather than by leaving it 'as an excrescence on the new system'. There was a proposal to this effect during Rosebery's Liberal ministry of 1894–5, but the Government fell before a Bill could be introduced. Once again, it was a Conservative Government which, by the London Government Act of 1899, carried through a reform of metropolitan administration by replacing the vestries and district boards with twenty-eight Metropolitan Borough Councils within the County of London. The powers of the LCC were not extended and the City was left untouched. The establishment of the Metropolitan Borough Councils was intended not only as a necessary reform of the lower tier of local government in London, but also as an administrative and political counterweight to the LCC.[10]

---

[b] J. F. B. Firth (1842–89) was M.P. for Chelsea, 1880–5, and for Dundee, 1888–9, and a member of the London School Board, 1876–9. His *Municipal London* (1876) was the most substantial of his numerous writings advocating the reform of metropolitan government.[6]

The first elections to the Council were held early in 1889 and the provisional Council's inaugural meeting took place at Spring Gardens on 31 January.[11] The Act allowed the MBW to continue for another two months, overlapping with the provisional LCC, but its rather mischievous intention to issue contracts for the construction of the Blackwall Tunnel, which would have been binding on its successor, were forestalled by advancing the date of its abolition slightly, to 21 March 1889.[12] Thus it was that the first meeting of the LCC was held on that date. The Earl of Rosebery was chosen as its first Chairman, for, although Firth was a strong candidate, his outspoken advocacy of centralization made him politically unacceptable; to have chosen him would have been 'a red flag to the City'.[13] Firth was given the salaried position of Deputy Chairman, but he died a few months later.[14] The Council consisted of 118 directly elected Members, who chose 19 Aldermen. In 1919, following the widening of the franchise, these numbers were increased to 124 and 20 respectively.[c]

Rosebery was not alone in hoping that it would not divide along party political lines, but two more or less coherent party groups were formed almost immediately, the Progressives and the Moderates.[15] The Progressives contained almost every shade of Liberal and Radical opinion, and attracted the support of a number of Fabians; the Moderates was the title adopted by the Conservative party in the LCC. Party discipline was relatively loose in the early years of the new Council and the whip was not strictly applied. Nevertheless, the organization of the parties soon came to resemble that of their Parliamentary counterparts, and, by the mid-1890s, both the Progressives and the Moderates operated with definite party leaders. It was not until the Standing Orders of 1934, however, that the positions of 'Leader of the Council' and 'Leader of the Opposition' were given official recognition.[16]

The Progressives took roughly two-thirds of the seats in the 1889 LCC elections and remained in power for the following eighteen years. Their success may have been partly due to the overhaul of the Liberal party organization in London following its poor results there in the general election of 1885.[17] The Conservatives responded in kind, making strong efforts in support of the Moderates' campaigns in the triennial elections to the LCC, and strengthening their organization in the capital by the setting up of the London Municipal Society in 1894.[18] In the 1895 election the Moderates and Progressives won equal numbers of seats and the latter retained control of the Council only because they had a majority among the Aldermen. At the elections of 1898 the Progressives re-established a comfortable majority. However, in 1907, their opponents, now known as the Municipal Reformers, won a majority of forty seats. The Progressives' efforts may have been weakened by the election to Parliament of a number of their most able members in the Liberals' general election victory in the previous year, but their defeat was also attributable to the shift in voting patterns in London, for, in electoral terms, the capital had become predominantly Conservative.[19] The Progressives never regained power. In 1925 they were replaced by Labour as the second largest party on the Council, a reflection of the general decline in the Liberals' electoral support and of the enlarged electorate produced by the extension of the franchise. In 1934 Labour came to power with a clear majority in a Council to which, for the first time, no Progressives were elected. The LCC remained under Labour control until its replacement by the GLC in 1965, when the system of local government established by the Acts of 1888 and 1899 was superseded.[20]

The Functions of the London County Council

As a county authority, the LCC discharged the administrative duties formerly carried out by the Justices of the Peace. It also took over the MBW's functions and developed them. It carried through a number of major street improvements, rebuilt six bridges over the Thames, constructed vehicular and pedestrian tunnels at Blackwall, Rotherhithe, Greenwich and Woolwich, continued the Board's work in maintaining sewerage and drainage systems and operating the fire brigade, added to the number of parks and open spaces under its control and acted as the authority for the implementation of legislation on building regulations, the storage of dangerous substances and the licensing of places of entertainment. Further duties were added, most notably the responsibility for education in London, which was transferred to the LCC on the abolition of the School Board for London in 1904. A range of welfare services formerly carried out by the Metropolitan Asylums Board and the twenty-five Boards of Guardians in its area, together with their hospitals, asylums, workhouses, infirmaries, dispensaries and residential schools, passed to the LCC in 1930. Between the two World Wars the Council obtained new powers respecting town planning and greatly expanded its operations in the provision of housing, both within the County of London and beyond it. By 1938 it had provided 86,700 new houses and blocks of flats, the vast majority of them within the previous twenty years.[21] On the other hand, the Royal ('Ullswater') Commission on Local Government in London of 1922–3 offered an opportunity to expand the Council's jurisdiction, which was not taken.[22]

The increasing range and scale of the LCC's duties added considerably to the size of its staff and budget. In 1891 the total number of its employees was 3,700, by 1938–9 the corresponding figure was 78,000, and its annual expenditure rose from less than £2 million in its early years to £37 million in 1937–8.[23] With this expansion

[c]In 1949 the number of elected Members was increased to 129 and the number of Aldermen to 21; six years later the number of elected Members was reduced to 126.

came growing self-confidence among its Members and officers, reflecting the current feeling in local government at the time. Indeed, the optimism and sense of purpose which characterized much of the work of the early County Councils probably reached its zenith in the mid-twentieth century. In a volume published in 1935 to mark the centenary of the passing of the Municipal Corporations Act, William Robson wrote that:

the local government service will grow substantially in size, in status, in *esprit de corps*, in professional excellence. Municipal officers will find themselves entrusted with great new responsibilities. They will have to develop qualities of creative leadership for preparing and carrying out the policy of the council beyond almost anything we now know. They will acquire new skills for the performance of new tasks. They will deepen their knowledge and broaden their outlook. They will have to strive to develop that imaginative insight into the processes of civilized life which is the true mark of the educated mind.[24]

Four years later Sir Gwilym Gibbon and Reginald Bell produced a history of the LCC to mark its Jubilee, summarizing its work and proudly declaring that 'What stands out above all ... is growth, and still more growth. The progress of the Council has been like that of a great river taking in tributary after tributary on its way'.[25]

Not all of the tributaries had flowed in to the LCC's river, however, for the control of the Metropolitan Police remained with the Home Secretary and a number of independent authorities had been created, such as the Metropolitan Water Board (1902), the Port of London Authority (1908), the London and Home Counties Traffic Advisory Committee (1924) and the London Passenger Transport Board (1933), which took over the Council's tramways. On the establishment of the National Health Service in 1948, the LCC surrendered some aspects of the health services which it had inherited in 1930 and had subsequently transformed, most notably the Poor Law hospitals. On the other hand, the Second World War had greatly added to the Council's work, both through the measures taken for civil defence during the war and, most significantly, because of the scale of the planning and reconstruction required in the aftermath of wartime destruction.

The long-term planning implications of reconstruction in London and south-east England were set out in two reports, the *County of London Plan* of 1943 – which was prepared under the auspices of the LCC – and the *Greater London Plan* of 1944, which covered a wide area around the capital. As well as the preparation and implementation of planning procedures, the LCC was also involved in the provision of new homes and the rebuilding and developing of new schools. Post-war redevelopment also provided the opportunity to reconstruct areas badly in need of improvement. One of these was that part of the South Bank close to County Hall, an area that had formerly been 'a large heap of rubble and a lot of semi-derelict buildings', which was transformed under the LCC and GLC into an arts complex.[26] Similarly, the development of the Council's Lansbury Estate in East London as a show place of 'living architecture' for the Festival of Britain expressed the self-assurance and energy of the Architect's Department. There was, indeed, no loss of confidence within the LCC in the post-war years. One young Council Member's impression in the 1950s was that the building and the reputation of the County Council were somehow inseparable: 'Twin bastions of democracy we thought – the Palace of Westminster and County Hall – equally imperishable ... Local Government was then a proper source of pride, and County Hall a visible embodiment of the pride'.[27]

The Greater London Council

The case for a regional planning authority in the London area had been made before the Second World War.[28] Post-war reconstruction was closely linked with this concept and the wider aspects of planning, such as the implementation of the Green Belt around the capital as set out in the 1944 *Greater London Plan* and the implications of the New Towns Act of 1946.[29] It was in respect of the emphasis upon regional planning in particular, that the organization of London's local government was questioned once again. The White Paper *Local Government in England and Wales during the Period of Reconstruction* (1945) stated that 'the problems ... of reconstruction, have made it clear that a reconsideration of the allocation of functions between the [metropolitan] boroughs and the county is overdue'.[30] There was, therefore, some pressure for change for practical administrative reasons, apart from political considerations. No changes were made during the immediate post-war years, however, for it was not part of Labour Government policy to alter London's system of local administration.[31] The Conservatives were more willing to countenance some change, partly because of their lack of success in elections in the capital since the mid-1930s, when both the control of the LCC and the majority of seats on the metropolitan borough councils had been won by Labour. An overhaul of the Conservative party's organization in London in 1945, when the title of Municipal Reform Party was abandoned, did not produce an electoral victory.[32] Indeed, it seemed that the migration from the LCC area to outer London by many amongst those sections of the electorate which consistently voted Conservative would make it difficult for the party to regain control of the Council. It did, however, appear that an extension of the LCC's boundaries would redress the electoral balance.[33] Thus, in the 1950s, the perceived need for a strategic planning authority coincided with the political will required for change, and in 1957 Henry Brooke, Minister of Housing and Local Government in Harold Macmillan's Government and a former Conservative Leader on the LCC, set up a Royal Commission to examine the local government arrangements in Greater London.

The Commission reported in 1960 and its essential recommendations were incorporated in the 1963 London Government Act. The London County Council was replaced by the Greater London Council consisting of one hundred directly elected Members and sixteen Aldermen: twenty-nine Metropolitan Borough Councils were created as the lower tier authorities. The area within the GLC's boundaries was 616 square miles, compared with the 117 square miles of the LCC's jurisdiction, and its electorate of almost 5,500,000 was double that of the LCC election in 1961.[34] Some of the outer areas included in the boundaries recommended by the Royal Commission were excluded from the GLC as actually established and, partly for that reason, its electorate did not contain an inbuilt Conservative majority. Labour won control in the elections for the first GLC in 1964, was replaced by the Conservatives three years later, and held power again in 1973–7 and 1981–6.[35]

The Powers of the Greater London Council

The GLC was established primarily as a planning authority for the London region having a wide brief with respect to planning, redevelopment, housing, highways and traffic. Other responsibilities were transferred from the LCC. Control of education within the former LCC area was allocated to the Inner London Education Authority, a new body separate from, although related to, the GLC. Outside the former County of London, education was administered by the boroughs. Amongst the initial proposals which did not come to fruition was one which would have included water provision within the GLC's responsibilities.[36] The most significant addition to the GLC's functions was made in 1970, when various aspects of transport in London were brought under its control.

Some of its responsibilities were subsequently removed. Those relating to main drainage, sewage disposal, the control of river pollution and the discharge of effluent were transferred to the newly established water authorities in 1973. This took away from the GLC the main purpose for which the MBW had been created in 1855. Similarly, also in 1973, the new regional health authorities took over from the Council the operation of the London Ambulance Service. Responsibility for the capital's public transport system was removed from the GLC's control in 1984, on the creation of London Regional Transport.

The Abolition of the Greater London Council

The removal of these various powers from the GLC, doubts about its success as a strategic planning authority for the London region, and continued political opposition to the upper tier of local government led to an examination of its position. In 1977 the Council, which was then under Conservative control, commissioned a review of London government from Sir Frank Marshall.[37] His report recommended that the GLC should be retained and strengthened.[38] No action was taken to pursue its recommendations in Parliament, however, either by the Labour Government then in office or by its Conservative successor that came to power in 1979. Following the Labour victory in the 1981 GLC elections, and that of the Conservative party at the general election two years later, it was the alternative of abolition of the upper-tier local authorities which was adopted and was effected in 1986. The Inner London Education Authority was not abolished with the GLC, but, by a separate measure, was dissolved in 1990.[39]

The Council has no permanent successor, although a temporary organization, the London Residuary Body, was created to operate during a transitional phase in which the GLC's functions were redistributed. The County Hall was designed and used as the headquarters of a London-wide administrative body, but that role necessarily came to an end when the Inner London Education Authority left the the building. Its future use is at present uncertain.

CHAPTER II

The Acquisition of the Site

The London County Council's first headquarters, inherited from the Metropolitan Board of Works, was its predecessor's board-room and offices in Spring Gardens, off Trafalgar Square (Plate 2a). Erected in 1861, on land leased from the Crown, this building had been designed for the MBW by its Superintending Architect, Frederick Marrable.[1] It was extended in 1878, to accommodate the growing staff of the MBW, but even so, was too small for the needs of the LCC. The board-room seated only forty-five, while average attendance at LCC meetings was eighty or ninety, and Members spilled over into the space formerly reserved for deputations to the MBW.[2] The strangers' gallery could hold only forty visitors and the LCC, mindful of the criticism levelled against its predecessor for secrecy,[3] wished to provide adequate space for both public and press.

The LCC solved these difficulties in the short term by deciding to meet at Guildhall, as the MBW itself had done in its early days.[4] However, one of the drawbacks of the City Corporation's relatively new Council Chamber – designed by Horace Jones in 1884 – was that, although there was enough space for the Members, the press were, in Rosebery's words, 'perched up in a gallery somewhere in the dome ... absolutely unable to hear any portion of our proceedings'.[5]

The problem for the LCC was not simply one of finding an adequate meeting place. Its Members were concerned, too, about accommodation for the growing numbers of staff, and also about the question of their public image. The comparison was inevitably drawn between traditional City splendour and the modest accommodation of the new County authority. This contrast was underlined by the cartoonists, and neatly summed up by Lord Farrer (1819–99) – an Alderman who had been a prominent supporter of the Municipal Reform League – in a letter to *The Times* in 1890:

Let our elder sister, dignified by age, flattered by the Press, and courted by society, give the entertainments to the Shah of Persia ... But until the good fairy, Mr. Ritchie [President of the Local Government Board], shall fuse our households, let poor Cinderella have, at the least, a well lighted and well ventilated scullery of her own, in which she can wash her plates and peel her potatoes for her mob of vulgar but hungry guests.[6]

Some Members thought that any plans at all for building

a new County Hall were a most extravagant proposition, and this split between those who wanted to build and those who did not was to remain until the Council was so far committed to a particular scheme that to retreat would have been more expensive than to go on.

The question of staff accommodation was a pressing one. Lack of space at Spring Gardens meant that Council staff were working in a number of scattered sites: in 1892 they occupied six different buildings. According to Sir John Lubbock, the LCC's second Chairman, several of these were 'very ill-suited for the purpose', and he urged the building of a new headquarters 'not only in the interest of efficiency, but of economy also'. By 1904 the staff was scattered through twenty-five separate blocks of buildings costing more than £34,000 per annum.[7] It became an LCC ambition, though one never fully realized, to house all central administrative staff on one site.

Early in 1889, shortly after the first LCC election, the Council appointed a Council Chamber and Offices Committee both to study the want of space at Spring Gardens and to solve the problems caused by the inadequate and scattered Council accommodation.[8] The pressing need, recognized by all, was for a bigger Council Chamber and extra committee rooms. These were provided in plans prepared by the Council's Architect, Thomas Blashill, which the Committee submitted to the Council in July 1889 (fig. 1).[9] Despite some opposition, a contract for the alterations, at a cost of £9,000, was signed in August 1889, and the Council's first meeting in the enlarged chamber took place on 22 April 1890 (Plate 2b).[a10]

A clause empowering the Council to raise a rate for the erection of a new headquarters had been inserted in the LCC Money Bill in 1889, yet choosing a suitable site and then selecting a design for the new building were to concern the Council for the next twenty years. The proposals and negotiations were often confused and decisions difficult to reach, not least because there was no clear division between the two emerging party groups on the Council on the matter. It can be said that the Moderates took an apparently conservative line on finance, and wished to limit the ruling Progressive Party's alleged tendency to extravagance with ratepayers' money, but the expression of Members' opinions and support was often individual, not to say idiosyncratic, rather than a strict following of party lines. Even a socialist like John Burns,

---

[a]This group portrait is symbolic rather than historically correct. It was painted in 1907–8 by H. Jamyn Brooks and shows the enlarged Council Chamber, but includes Aldermen and Members who had by then retired or died.

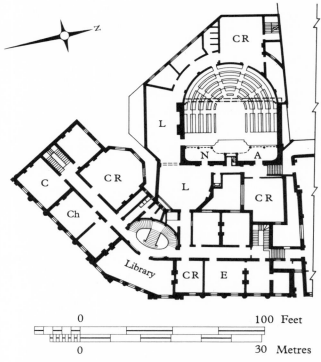

Fig. 1. Old County Hall, Spring Gardens, headquarters of the LCC from 1889–1922. Plan of the first floor, *c*.1905, showing the former Board Room of the Metropolitan Board of Works extended (beyond the dotted line) to create a horseshoe-shaped Council Chamber for the LCC, with Public Galleries over. Entrances to Ayes and Noes Lobbies (A, N) were provided either side of the Chairman's Dais, with a Press Gallery above.

a area, C Clerk, Ch Chairman, CR Committee Room,
E Engineer, L Lobby

the Member for Battersea, could appeal to his fellow Members 'to take an Imperial and Metropolitan view'.[11]

The Search for a New Site

The task of finding a site was initially entrusted to the Council Chamber and Offices Committee, which was re-formed after the 1892 election as the Establishment Committee. Towards the end of the decade the work was delegated to a Special Sub-Committee of the Establishment Committee. A considerable number of sites were considered before one on the Surrey side of the Thames was eventually chosen. As on all such occasions, the suggestions ranged from the practical to the fantastic, but they are worth reviewing briefly for the light they throw both on the attitudes and methods of Council Members and on conditions in London at the time.

The proposals included many historic or difficult sites available for re-development in the changing London of the 1890s. Those considered included the river-front site of Millbank Prison (where the Tate Gallery now stands),[12] Christ's Hospital, Barnard's Inn, St Paul's Churchyard, Newgate Prison,[13] and one on the Victoria Embankment between Horse Guards Avenue and New Scotland Yard. They were all in some way unsuitable – too small, too expensive or not sufficiently central.[14]

In 1893 the Committee reported that a possible site had been found on the west side of Parliament Street between Great George Street and (King) Charles Street (on which the New Government Offices, now occupied by the Treasury, were later built). It was recommended as the best site which had been considered so far, but was rejected, partly because some Members, including Lord Rosebery, did not like the idea of council offices close to the Houses of Parliament, although others were attracted by the idea.[15]

Meanwhile, pressure upon the existing accommodation continued to grow and the Council had to acquire offices in a number of buildings.[16] A possible solution was a further extension of the site in Spring Gardens. In June 1896 the Establishment Committee, under the chairmanship of the Moderate, Melvill Beachcroft (1846–1926), reported on a site between Spring Gardens and Trafalgar Square, including the Council's existing offices (fig. 2). The scheme that was proposed was not wholly popular, chiefly because the site was small, just under two acres, and costly. This was partly because of the length of important street frontages, which required expensive façades. Despite its cost, it attracted a lot of Moderate support, and the Council approved it.[17]

Parliamentary powers to acquire the land were sought during the 1897 session. That this too was not a strict party issue can be seen by the fact that the Bill's Second Reading in the Commons was moved by the Liberal M.P. and LCC Moderate, C. A. Whitmore (Alderman 1895–1901), and its rejection moved by another LCC Moderate, E. Boulnois (Member 1889–1901). The Bill also had several powerful petitioners against it, including the Duke of Devonshire, who lived nearby in Carlton House Terrace. It was defeated on its Second Reading.[18]

Another idea for a new County Hall was prompted by plans for a memorial to Queen Victoria. When it was suggested that the proposed 'memorial way' – The Mall – should terminate in a triumphal arch opening on to Trafalgar Square, Captain George Swinton (1859–1937), a future Chairman of the LCC, took up the cudgels (Plate 46b). He was one of the most remarkable Members of the Council at that time, and influenced its development in several important ways.[b] Well connected – his father being a Berwickshire landowner, and his mother the daughter of Sir George Sitwell of Renishaw – he was elected to

[b]Swinton wrote several books on town planning, dealing with traffic problems and related architectural issues like the Charing Cross Bridge project. Chief Whip of the Moderate, later Municipal Reform, Party 1903–12, he was made Chairman of the LCC in 1912 but resigned to become Chairman of the Town-planning Committee of New Delhi.

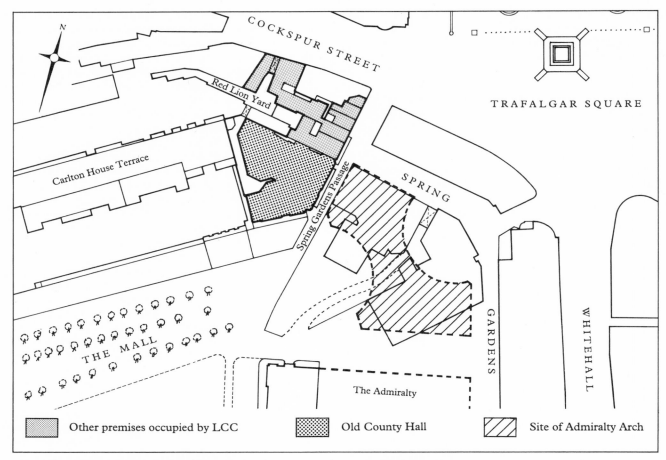

Fig. 2. Old County Hall, Spring Gardens. Block plan, *c.*1902, showing the additional buildings occupied by LCC staff in the vicinity. The proposals for The Mall in 1902 led Captain George Swinton to suggest building the new County Hall on the site where the Admiralty Arch (1910) now stands

the LCC in March 1901 as a Moderate and sat on the Establishment Committee from 1905 to 1909 – critical years for the new County Hall design.[19]

In a letter to *The Times* in May 1901, Swinton argued that 'nothing could be more unfortunate' than the idea of an 'arc de triomphe' at the end of The Mall. What was needed was 'a fine façade, high enough to make a terminal to the memorial way at one end as effectually as Buckingham Palace at the other', and herein lay an opportunity to build a new LCC headquarters spanning The Mall. He pointed out that though the LCC Members wished to remain on the Spring Gardens site, it was so small, cramped and awkward as to make this impossible, but that this could be remedied by his scheme, when everything between Carlton House Terrace and the Admiralty would be swept away. Would it not be possible, he asked, to combine upon this enlarged area, 'in one harmonious whole, three things, the terminal to the memorial way, the exits for the through traffic, and the County-hall?' He went on to describe the wonderful architectural result that might be expected, at no ruinous price, as grand as the LCC could possibly require, while even the most

ambitious of the advocates of municipal progress could hardly say that one face to 'the finest site in Europe', the other to the King's Palace, was not sufficient for the dignity of those 'whom the electors of London delighted to honour'.[20] Despite Swinton's advocacy this scheme came to nothing, and the idea of rebuilding on the Spring Gardens site gradually faded, though the old building actually remained in Council occupation until after the Second World War.

Other sites under consideration included the Holborn to Strand Improvement Scheme area (now Kingsway), Lincoln's Inn Fields, and the Royal Aquarium, Westminster.[21] However, nothing definite was done to promote any one of these locations, all of which were rather small and expensive. The Kingsway site was only on the list because it was an LCC development which was proving difficult to let. When the Council planned their Improvement Scheme in 1899, the Special Sub-Committee, which had taken over the search for a site from the Establishment Committee, suggested that the Council should take advantage of that development and incorporate their offices in it. However, the estimated cost of the Aldwych Crescent island site was £2,400,000, and proved too great for the Council to acquire for itself.[22]

The end of July 1902 saw the penultimate in the long line of suggested sites presented to the Council. The Adelphi was for sale, at a cost of £900,000. Its position on the Embankment between Somerset House and the Houses of Parliament was very suitable for an important public building, while the presence of County Hall there would in turn reinforce the claim of the Embankment to be the recognized quarter for such buildings. Some Council Members felt that the time was coming to an end when large sites in central London would be available for development, and that this could be the last opportunity to obtain a central site of large dimension facing the river.[23]

There was opposition to this scheme on the general grounds used against several of the others – that the expense would not be justified by savings in annual rental, that the present buildings were adequate, and that the new site would anyway accommodate fewer staff than the Council currently employed. One Member raised the further point that the Historical Records Committee would certainly oppose the destruction of the Adam buildings, and another objected that any building on this site would be overshadowed by 'such a hideous monstrosity as Charing Cross Station'.[24]

More imaginative, if hardly practical, were some of the suggestions emanating from outside official circles. In 1900 the architects N. S. Joseph, Son, & Smitham suggested building the new County Hall actually in the Thames, straddling old Waterloo Bridge.[25] Another proposal placed the building on an island opposite Charing Cross Station.[26] In 1904 an electrical engineer by the name of Alfred R. Bennett recommended the construction of a new bridge near the Temple, which would carry not only trams, carriages and foot traffic, but also a massive hall for the LCC.[27] Widely reported at the time, Bennett's scheme was illustrated as a Gothic building of considerable vulgarity (together with a Renaissance-style alternative). The *Architect & Contract Reporter* commented that it would 'blot out what is left of the perspective of the Thames with the callousness of a railway company', but was not worried about its chances of success since the LCC would 'never accept inspiration from outside sources'.[28]

Bennett's idea appeared when the Council was on the point of selecting a site on the south of the river, which although mooted several times in the previous decade, had not hitherto been formally put forward by the Committee.

The Choice of the South Bank Site

The LCC's involvement with the South Bank started in 1893, with the acquisition for its Works Department of

Bartram's Wharf, Belvedere Road, latterly in the hands of timber merchants who had gone bankrupt.[29] The freehold belonged to the Ecclesiastical (now Church) Commissioners, who were prepared to grant the Council a three-year lease at £1,500 per annum, with the option to purchase at any time during the tenancy for £39,000.[30] In March the Council approved the acquisition of this site, later known as No. 23 Belvedere Road, which had an area of some one-and-a-half acres and a river frontage of about 205 feet. The existing buildings included sawmills, workshops, and stables.[31] These were mostly rebuilt in 1895, at which time a river wall was also constructed, adding just under half an acre to the site.

It might have been expected that this purchase would have alerted the Council to the possibility of acquiring a large but relatively inexpensive site on the Surrey side of the Thames. In fact, this seems not to have been the case. The first person to suggest placing the County Hall south of the river was Lord Farrer, during a Council debate in 1896, though he did not specify the Belvedere Road site.[32] Two years later another Member, J. D. Gilbert (1864–1946),[c] suggested a site at Westminster Bridge, as part of a project for an embankment on the south side of the Thames from Westminster Bridge to Blackfriars Bridge, to be used either for an investment in commercial property or as a site for a new County Hall. The motion did not find even a seconder,[34] and another four years were to pass before this idea was again brought forward.

In the autumn of 1902 the Moderate Alfred Cohen drew attention to the advantages of the Lambeth site in a letter circulated to his fellow LCC Members. After summarizing the many objections to the Adelphi site, then under consideration, and, indeed, questioning the whole idea of centralized offices, he pointed out that if the Council was determined on a new building a four-acre site was available on the south bank of the Thames, between Westminster Bridge Road and the Works depot, which the Valuer thought could be purchased for £650,000. At a further cost of about £21,000 for the construction of an embankment wall in line with that of St Thomas's Hospital, and an estimated £10,000 payable to the Thames Conservators for the right to reclaim foreshore land, 1.3 acres could be added.[d] Thus a total area of 5.4 acres would be acquired for £681,000. The Adelphi site of 3.35 acres would cost more and provide less accommodation. Cohen urged that the Lambeth site be considered 'on grounds of economy, of beauty, and of great convenience of access'.[35] He was supported by Swinton, who thought that not only could the site house the whole of the Council's staff, but also that 'it would do an immense amount of good to the people of South London to have a fine municipal building placed among them'.[36]

Swinton's remark points to an LCC inheritance from

[c]Gilbert was one of two brothers who were LCC Members at the same time but sat on opposite sides. J. D. was a Progressive and an agnostic, the other, John, was a Municipal Reformer and an ardent Roman Catholic. It is said that they never spoke to each other.[33]
[d]In LCC records the acre is used as the measure of land area, but decimal notation is used when dealing with parts of an acre.

the Metropolitan Board of Works which extended to much more than their Spring Gardens headquarters. The great crusade of improvement was strongly alive within the LCC, and the South Bank was now perceived as an area long wanting reconstruction. The embanking of the river upstream from Westminster Bridge and the building of St Thomas's Hospital had been a start, and showed what possibilities there were for improvement along the South Bank downstream from Westminster Bridge to Black-friars.

No steps were taken to follow up either the Gilbert or the Cohen suggestion for several years, however. Yet the need for new and centralized offices was made more urgent by the passing in 1903 of the Education (London) Act, which gave control of the capital's education to the LCC and increased its office staff by nearly a third. In February 1904 the Council was forced to lease Nos. 56–60 The Strand.[37]

A number of late Victorian town planners had put forward schemes for the south bank of the Thames,[c] including the architect Arthur Cawston (1857–93). In a massive work suggesting a series of Haussmann-like improvements, he pointed out that the American tourist's first dispiriting view of London was from Waterloo Station, and his proposal for improving this included a new Waterloo Bridge and a new embankment with the re-location of Billingsgate Market opposite the Victoria Embankment.[38]

One of the most intriguing and comprehensive of these schemes appeared in the *Pall Mall Gazette*, and was said to be under consideration by the Council. The architect, Charles Mallows (1864–1914), suggested embanking the south side of the Thames between Westminster and London Bridges, and rebuilding the area behind as far back as Belvedere Road, Stamford Street and Southwark Street as 'a monumental terrace of public and other build-ings to balance in architectural effect those on the other side'. He suggested that river-based industry should be re-located in a series of basins or canals behind the new buildings, entered from the river by means of locks. These strikingly ambitious proposals remain one of the most thoughtful town planning schemes for the area.[39]

While some saw the South Bank in visionary terms, others thought only that it was the wrong side of the river and an expensive place to build, if cheap to buy. Under the heading 'Offices for the L.C.C. – An Almost Hopeless Search', the *Westminster Gazette* interviewed Melvill Beachcroft in November 1904. This article gave a fair summary of the predicament, and showed clearly the hardening attitude of the Moderates towards high rates, which was now becoming that party's main weapon against the ruling Progressives. For Beachcroft a central site was out of the question, and he included the Adelphi in that judgement since it would have involved an outlay of

£3,000,000, which, with interest rates at their current level, would have meant an annual liability of £75,000, more than twice what the Council were paying in rent at Spring Gardens. Beachcroft was no more optimistic about a site on the Surrey side of the river, where the land would be cheaper, but the building would cost much more because of the expensive foundations needed owing to the nature of the ground.[40]

In the event, it became obvious that the foundation problem had been greatly exaggerated by opponents of the South Bank scheme, including Beachcroft, for the raft foundation constituted only about seven per cent of the final site cost, including the expense of embanking. Amongst the various other charges was a payment to the Thames Conservators of £15,330.[41] Nevertheless, the South Bank site remained a relatively cheap solution, as a comparison with the other three major contenders shows:[42]

Date proposal submitted to the Council	Location	Cost £	Acreage	Approx cost per acre £
27 June 1893	Parliament Street	750,000	$2\frac{1}{4}$	333,333
14 July 1896	Spring Gardens	813,000	2	406,500
22 July 1902	Adelphi	900,000	$3\frac{1}{3}$	270,000
18 April 1905	Belvedere Road	600,000	$5\frac{1}{2}$ net	111,110

On 18 April 1905 the Council was presented with a definite scheme for what came to be known as the Bel-vedere Road site, stretching from Westminster Bridge on the south to the LCC Works Department on the north, with a river frontage of about 1,200 feet. Unlike some other sites considered by the Establishment Committee, this one was large enough to hold the whole of the Coun-cil's central staff while having room in hand for expansion. The cost of building, including that of embanking, was put at only £1,100,000. The area's rather run-down character, however, did not appeal to all Council Members. Andrew Torrance, the Progressive Member for East Islington, called the site 'cheap and nasty, unsavoury and inac-cessible', and quite unworthy of the dignity of a body like the Council. John Burns, on the other hand, saw it as an opportunity to 'lighten up a dull place, sweeten a sour spot, and for the first time bring the south of London into a dignified and beautiful frontage on the River Thames'.[43] The Establishment Committee recommended the Council to authorize them to proceed with the purchase of the site. In spite of a delaying amendment, proposed by H. P. Harris and seconded by Beachcroft, intended 'to avoid placing undue burdens on the ratepayers', the Council approved the recommendation by 83 votes to 21.[44]

The land the Council wanted was divided into three

---

[c]Between Westminster and Waterloo Bridges the Thames runs north-south, so that the 'south bank' at this point is in fact the east bank.

freeholds and a total of eleven tenancies. Of the freeholders, Simmonds and Morten and the Ecclesiastical Commissioners were prepared to sell, but Lambeth Borough Council was reluctant to do so. Although the negotiations to acquire the freehold of the Lambeth site proved to be protracted, there was no difficulty regarding a tenancy, for the land was occupied by the borough's own Works Department. The buildings along Westminster Bridge Road were occupied by small businesses and no problems were anticipated in obtaining possession, but the three tenancies on the Ecclesiastical Commissioners' land were more substantial, and the Council could be less certain of the tenants' willingness to leave. There was always the possibility that some tenants would not go by choice, and so application was made to Parliament for powers of compulsory purchase.

Ultimately, six petitions against the Council's Bill were presented in the House of Commons. The petitioners were the Conservators of the River Thames, Crosse & Blackwell, Peter Brotherhood, Holloway Brothers, the Borough of Lambeth, and the National Telephone Company. The telephone company did not occupy premises on the site but was worried that the works, involving the relocation of many of their cables, would be an unjustified interference with their customers' rights. Apart from the building firm of Holloway Brothers, who fought hard to remain on their site, the petitioners' objections were technical, designed to secure concessions or compensation rather than to prevent the Council from acquiring the land.[45]

The Council was able to demonstrate that some of the petitioners were making unreasonable claims, and reached agreement with others. The Bill was given its Second Reading on 13 March 1906, having been steered through the Commons by the Liberal M.P. and LCC Progressive Member, Sir Edwin Cornwall. When it was presented in the Lords only one petitioner remained – Holloway Brothers. A compromise was eventually arrived at and the Bill was given Royal Assent on 20 July 1906.

The South Bank Site

Once the decision was taken to build County Hall on the South Bank site negotiations were begun to purchase the properties. Their acquisition was to take some time; not until 1 January 1909 was possession of all of the freeholds obtained and settlement with some of the tenants of the premises in Westminster Bridge Road was not reached until 1911. In addition to the main site, the Council also decided to buy and demolish the buildings on the east side of Belvedere Road in order to widen the road, improving the approach to County Hall.

The short description of the County Hall site in volume XXIII of the *Survey of London* dealt mainly with its early history. That account is amplified here and a plan showing the freehold ownerships and the tenancies is given on page 12 (fig. 3). Some of the buildings and structures which stood on the site are shown in Plates 2c-d, 3a-b and 6a.

Simmonds and Morten's Property

The southernmost and smallest of the three separate freeholds was an area of 0.426 acres with a frontage to Westminster Bridge Road, once known as Float Mead. The owners were John Whately Simmonds and Frederick Morten, who had bought the property in 1881 for £38,000. Along Westminster Bridge Road were shops and houses dating from the middle of the eighteenth century, and the well-known Coronet public house (Plate 3b). They were held on seven tenancies, mostly on leases for 21 years from 1902, determinable by either party after 7 or 14 years.[46] Behind these buildings rose the substantial six-storey bulk of the Westminster Bridge Flour Mills (Plate 2c). This building was vacant and, to prevent the creation of a new interest, the LCC itself took the property for the remaining two years of the lease, using it as a stationery store for the Clerk's Department.[47] The LCC quickly came to a preliminary agreement with Simmonds and Morten and bought the freehold in October 1906 for £90,000.[48]

Property of the Lambeth Borough Council

The ground immediately to the north of Simmonds and Morten's property belonged to Lambeth Borough Council. This was an area of 1.032 acres, long known as Pedlar's Acre, which had been given to Lambeth parish sometime before 1639.[49] It included the sites of Acre and Vestry Wharves and of Nos. 3–9 (odd) Belvedere Road. For most of the nineteenth century the southern part of this land was leased by the engineering firm of Maudslay Sons & Field who used it for the construction of iron ships and the fitting of steam engines to hulls – the work for which the firm was perhaps most famous. Maudslays occupied this site until they became bankrupt in 1899.[50] In the following year Lambeth Council took possession of the ground for its Works Department. Maudslay's main building on the site was of considerable engineering interest as an early example of a 'masted' structure (Plate 6a).[51] It was demolished by the LCC in the summer of 1909.

Lambeth Council were, naturally enough, unhappy about the LCC's plans to displace them. They opposed the London County Buildings Bill in the House of Commons and put in a claim of £179,138 for the freehold and compensation. The settlement finally went to arbitration in 1909, when Lambeth were awarded £81,342.[52]

The Estate of the Ecclesiastical Commissioners

By far the largest piece of land bought by the LCC belonged to the Ecclesiastical Commissioners. This was an area of 2.542 acres comprising Bishop's Acre and part of a larger piece called The Four Acres, on which lay Soho Wharf, Belvedere Wharf and Nos. 15 and 17 Belvedere

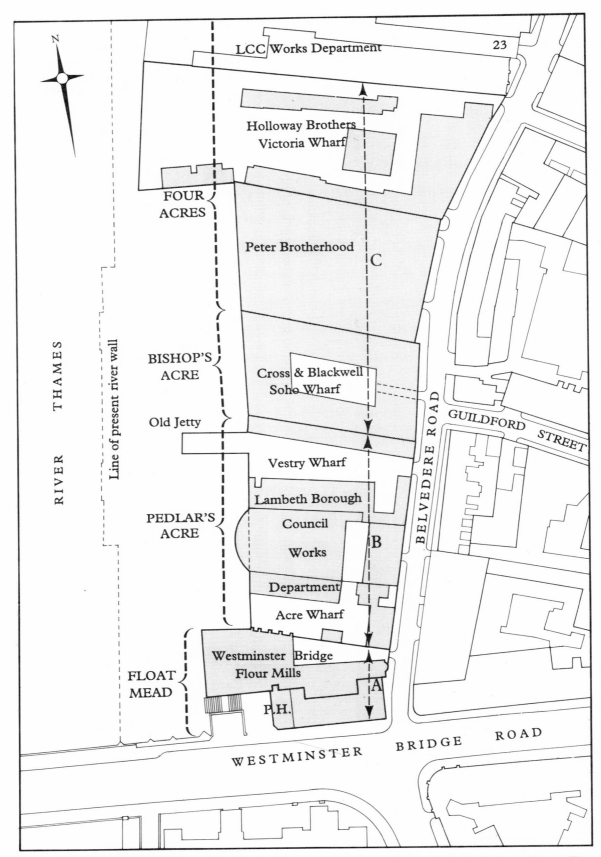

Fig. 3. The County Hall site in 1905. Plan showing the names of the properties acquired and existing occupiers. The northern boundary of Holloway Brothers' property was the limit of the County Hall site. The freehold owners were: A Simmonds and Morten (Float Mead); B Lambeth Borough Council (Pedlar's Acre); C Ecclesiastical Commissioners (Bishop's Acre and part of the Four Acres)

Road. The Commissioners' willingness to sell the freehold was the key to the whole site. Because the Commissioners also owned land on the east side of Belvedere Road, much of which was later bought by the Council, some time was spent negotiating a covenant to restrict the height of the LCC's proposed building and ensure an acceptable width for Belvedere Road. The Council purchased the site in 1906 for £125,000, excluding legal costs.[53]

The property was held under lease by three separate tenants. At the southern end, occupying 0.54 acres, was Crosse & Blackwell's jam and pickle factory. This had been built for the firm in 1882–3, to designs by Roumieu & Aitchison, and comprised warehouses, manufacturing premises and offices ranged around a central courtyard. The six-storey riverside and four-storey Belvedere Road elevations were composed of red brick with red-terracotta dressings (Plates 2c-d, 3a).[54] Crosse & Blackwell had a 999–year lease from Christmas 1896 at an annual rent of £1,246. They accepted £50,000 for their lease and £50,000 for fixtures, plus costs. They were allowed to remain as tenants until Lady Day 1908.[55]

North of Crosse & Blackwell and occupying 0.78 acres was the engineering firm of Peter Brotherhood, manufacturers of torpedo engines, who had a 79–year lease from 1897 at £1,300 per annum. Their site incorporated part of a yard lately occupied by Lucas Brothers, the builders. Brotherhood's premises were purpose-built, having been erected in 1881–2 to the designs of Hunt & Stewart.[56] After some attempts to relocate themselves on the Thames they moved to Peterborough, having received a total of £65,000 for the remainder of their lease and fixtures.[57]

The most determined opposition to the LCC came from Holloway Brothers, the builders, who occupied the northern end of the site. Known as Victoria Wharf, this area had previously formed the northern, and larger part of Lucas Brothers' yard.

Founded in Battersea in 1882, the firm of Holloway Brothers had enjoyed great success from the start. They agreed to take the lease of Victoria Wharf in 1889, but Lucas Brothers continued in possession until c.1896 and Holloways' occupation began in 1899. Theirs was one of the most sophisticated builder's yards in London, and the brothers took pride in the fact that many architects and other builders came to study and admire the works. Henry Holloway, one of the partners, described them as 'a model of what a builder's works should be'. The elevations were provided by the architects Read & Macdonald, several of whose buildings were erected by Holloways.[58]

Holloways was the only petitioner against the Bill to pursue its action through to the House of Lords. Their complaint is a familiar one in the history of compulsory purchase, a feeling that no payment could compensate for the upheaval and the loss of premises in a convenient and prominent position. Indeed, one of their chief reasons for wishing to retain the site was that the company's name, painted large on their works, was clearly visible to everybody coming across Westminster Bridge. Another of their claims was that the site was located in the 'building centre' of London. This was disputed, but contained an element of truth, for that section of the riverfront had long been occupied by a succession of stonemasons and builders, including the firm of George Myers.[59]

Holloways held out for reinstatement on a site in Belvedere Road with equal river frontage to their existing site, a virtual impossibility unless the LCC were to give up their Works Department land. Compromise was reached when the Council agreed to insert a clause into the Bill guaranteeing that Holloways 'should not without their consent be disturbed in the possession of their premises until three years after the date of service of notice to treat, and that they could have free access to their premises by road and by river so long as they were in occupation'. In 1908 an arbitrator awarded the firm £46,862 for its site, plant and fittings, and compensation of £50,512.[60]

The purchase of the premises on the east side of the Belvedere Road cost the Council a further £50,000. Legal and arbitration costs and a number of payments made to compensate those whose livelihoods were disrupted added to the final bill. The total cost to the Council of the acquisition of the site was later assessed at £617,032, only slightly more than the Valuer's 1905 estimate of £600,000.[61]

CHAPTER III

The County Hall Competition

With the passing of the London County Buildings Bill in 1906, the Establishment Committee was free to concentrate on the question of the design. The matter had, in fact, been engaging the attention of both LCC Members and outside commentators since the spring of 1905, when the decision to purchase the South Bank site had been taken.

The choice facing the Progressive administration was awkward: if they erected a fine building, the accusation of extravagance with ratepayers' money would be reinforced, while a plain building would be seen as unworthy to stand alongside not only Guildhall but the many provincial town halls being erected elsewhere in the British Isles. The Radical weekly *Truth* suggested that the Council should put up the cheapest building possible:

A big furniture depository is the sort of thing I have in mind, with a stock brick interior and cast-iron window frames. Possibly a good deal of the work might be done temporarily in corrugated iron sheds. I would provide in that way a council-room and offices for all the staff, showing that everything had been done on purely utilitarian principles.

The LCC's critics could then be left to complain at its parsimony.[1]

One of the first Progressive leaders to address the problem publicly was John Burns (1858–1943), who represented Battersea as M.P. (1892–1914) and as LCC Member from 1893 to 1907. One of the most active and colourful figures in the early years of the Council, and a socialist of Liberal sympathies, he had spent his early life employed in various engineering works, including those of Peter Brotherhood in Belvedere Road. He had had a hand in starting up the Works Department, was a great advocate of town planning, and always took an interest in the Council's activities from an artistic as well as a practical point of view.[2]

In an article in the *Pall Mall Magazine* for October 1905,[3] in which he called London 'the Cinderella of the cities in the matter of municipal recognition', Burns drew a sharp distinction between the offices occupied by the Council, and those of other authorities:

Compared with the Hotel de Ville in Paris, Spring Gardens is a slum. Contrasted with those of Berlin, Glasgow, Leeds, Birmingham or Liverpool, the London County Council offices are insanitary areas, costly, squalid, inconvenient – a reproach to London, a danger to the staff.

Even the London boroughs were now building themselves new town halls, and Burns suggested that the quality of work done by any organization was directly related to its environment. He contrasted the 'rabbit-warren habitation' of the War Office – 'responsible for the mazy conduct of that department, and the hazy sense of duty it has towards the country' – with the 'bold policy of banks, insurance offices and large commercial houses having prominent sites, adequate space, handsome exteriors and internal attractiveness' which stimulated 'a joy of work in staff, an order in business, and a supreme command of organisation impossible in low, mean and disorderly habitations'.

Turning to the question of style, Burns reviewed the fine parade of riverside buildings in London, and the improvements being carried out on Millbank between the Houses of Parliament and the Tate Gallery. He favoured 'a solid pile, less ornamental than Parliament – a massive building, yet withal fine to look upon – a structure that will fill with dignity and size ... one of the very best sites in South London ... an exalted and improving neighbour to St Thomas's Hospital; a worthy companion to the great Gothic mass that Barry has given to us in Parliament House, and to which the new County Hall in no sense should be an unworthy neighbour'.

Burns's interpretation of the principles of office planning and design was not shared by all Members of the LCC, nor by all Londoners, and many other points of view were expressed in the three years that were to elapse before the final choice of design. However, some of the problems that were to arise over the new County Hall turned out to be as much a matter of personalities and power as of concern for the design of the building.

The Architect to the LCC and his Department

By 1905, the LCC had an Architect's Department of growing experience and increasing self-confidence, headed by W. E. Riley. At a very early stage, Riley put forward the claim of his department to design and plan the new County Hall. He did this through the preparation of a design, based on the planning work for the brief as already carried out by his staff, and through overt lobbying of influential Members of the Council. Though running counter to the prevailing fashion for competitions, the claims of his department deserved to be taken seriously, and indeed in the later phases of the development of County Hall, the Architect's Department took over.

The Metropolitan Board of Works had had little need for an Architect in its early years. Its chief projects, the construction of sewers and embankments, demanded the skills of an engineer, and it was the Engineer who was the important MBW officer. This tradition persisted into the LCC, with the Engineer taking precedence after the Clerk of the Council over the heads of other departments until well into this century. The Clerk and the Engineer were traditionally knighted for their services. Not so the Architect. His work was mainly associated with the Public Control Department, whose responsibilities were those of checking weights and measures, and the licensing of places of entertainment: functions not demanding much from architecture.

Thomas Blashill (1831–1905) was appointed Architect to the MBW in 1887, and subsequently to the LCC. His department also had responsibility for fire-stations, and later designed some smaller jobs for the Works Department, such as the approach arches to the Blackwall Tunnel. But with the Housing of the Working Classes Act of 1890 empowering the LCC to redevelop slum housing, the Architect's Department was given a great opportunity. The creation of the eponymous Housing of the Working Classes Branch brought a number of high-minded and talented designers into the Architect's Department. Blashill's ability to recruit and organize these young architects was to create a great reputation for the department, and for the LCC, not only in the matter of public housing but in other branches of public architecture.[4] The Boundary Street Estate in Shoreditch, begun in the early 1890s, was the first project undertaken by the Council under the Act, and was followed in 1896 by the Millbank Estate.

Within his department, Blashill was respected and much loved. He retired in 1899, to be succeeded by William Edward Riley (1852–1937).[5] Riley was born in Yorkshire and educated at Batley Grammar School, and partly in France and Italy. He joined the office of William Critchley of Wakefield, and after five years in the office of Beck & Lee, moved to the staff of the Director of Engineering and Works of the Admiralty in 1877. There he was in charge of works in, among other places, Bermuda, Malta, Chatham and Devonport. He held the LCC post – the full title of which was Superintending Architect of Metropolitan Buildings and Architect to the London County Council – for twenty years, but because he was given a separate contract for his work on County Hall he was involved with it for a further ten years. A one time Council member of the Royal British and Colonial Society of Artists, and a member of the Royal Society of Artists, he was said to spend most of his spare time painting.[6]

Andrew Saint has pointed out the problem for the early LCC in reconciling the ambitions of Members who wanted to see London become a worthy 'imperial capital' with the drive towards working-class housing and other schemes of improvement for the London working man espoused by left-wing Members.[7] The contradiction had to be solved in the Architect's Department as elsewhere in the Council, and Riley proved very good at this. It has often been said that Riley was simply a 'good organizer' and 'brilliant administrator'. His close friend Frederick Hiorns, an architect working at the LCC from 1902 and for a long time Riley's right-hand man on the County Hall project, spoke of 'the almost ruthless force of his administrative control'. Indeed, he went further, saying that, possessed of an unusually forceful personality, it was almost inevitable that Riley should express himself by somewhat autocratic methods.[8] Yet Riley's artistic associations suggest, as the architectural production of his department demonstrates, that he was an excellent judge and positive advocate of good design. It is somewhat more difficult to assess his own merits as a designer, since, as Architect to the LCC, he headed a large department. After leaving the LCC he went into partnership with E. Glanfield, from 1919 to 1931, and they did some fine work, for example, the North Western Polytechnic, opened in 1929.[9]

The department Riley inherited was stocked with talented architects. As the housing projects begun in Blashill's time were completed, it was inevitable that Riley should get much of the credit rightly belonging to Blashill. But his department soon had work on a much larger scale than anything Blashill had handled.

1900 saw the beginning of the LCC's first cottage estate, Totterdown Fields in Tooting, and it is interesting that one of the architects most concerned with it was Ernest Stone Collins, later to work on County Hall.[10] In the same year a programme of fire-station building was begun, for which Riley reorganized his department. The resulting buildings are one of the great achievements of the Arts and Crafts movement. It was Riley who promoted and defended his architects in their efforts to improve the quality of London's streets. In 1915 he set out his views to an RIBA committee enquiring into the architectural work of public authorities, work which the RIBA felt they were incapable of handling in an artistic manner, and which should therefore be left to private architects. Riley told the Editor of the *Builder* that he challenged this claim absolutely, suggesting that the profession was 'overloaded by a sub-stratum of incompetent private members who could not obtain employment'. He continued, 'The routine through which an official must press his work is of such a character that feeble results ... cannot ensue. If outsiders had to encounter the same searching criticism and a tithe of the obstruction, their fees would only about half cover their requirements'.[11]

One of the most difficult problems faced by Riley greeted him in his first few years as LCC Architect, and shaped much of his response to later problems in Council service. The Holborn to Strand Improvement – the present-day Kingsway and Aldwych – had been under discussion for ten years, and was finally given the Parliamentary authority it required in 1899. This was by far the most ambitious improvement scheme undertaken by the LCC up to that time, and the problem of dealing with the elevations of this great street fell to Riley. The LCC Improvements Committee had agreed to a competition for elevations of the Strand-Aldwych part of the site, and Riley acted as assessor together with Richard Norman Shaw, then in retirement, but one of the grand old men of British architecture. It was a job fraught with difficulties since many of the firms rebuilding their premises had engaged architects of their own and designs had been prepared. Shaw proved a valuable friend both to the LCC and to Riley on this occasion, offering his work free of charge, and saving a situation which was potentially very embarrassing for the LCC by his skilful interventions with both architects and committees.[12]

Amongst Riley's staff were men who were to have an influence on the development and design of the new headquarters. One of these was Hiorns (1876–1961), the son of a Warwickshire man, educated in Plymouth, who joined the LCC in 1902, winning the Godwin Bursary in 1905, making apposite use of it to study 'Modern Town Halls in France'. He was interested in historic architecture, being a member of the Society for the Protection of Ancient Buildings, and a member both of the LCC Staff Arts and Crafts Society, and of the Art Workers' Guild. He was in charge of the general section from 1926 till 1935, then senior divisional architect responsible for all constructional work, becoming Architect to the LCC from 1939 to 1941. He was to play an important part as liaison officer between Riley and Knott in the construction of County Hall, and as the designer of the New County Offices in the 1930s (see page 106). A 'kind, quiet and retiring man who shunned publicity of any kind whatsoever', his work for the Council was not ostentatious. It included the South Eastern Technical Institute, the Weights and Measures Office in Euston Square, and major work on the LCC hospitals after 1930. He was to become an important member of Lord Reith's Consultative Panel for the post-war replanning of London.[13]

The office of Chief Assistant, General Constructional Section, was held by Percy Ginham (1865–1947), Richard Norman Shaw's former principal assistant. Ginham joined the LCC in 1902 at the time when Shaw was no longer taking on enough work to need an assistant, and came with the master's highest recommendations as an architect who knew the planning of buildings. His other referees were Ernest Newton and William Lethaby, both of whom he had known in Shaw's office. Lethaby, by now Professor at the Royal College of Art, had known Ginham for twenty years, and wrote of him:

He is an excellent architectural designer having taste and judgement in a high degree with a preference for refined simplicity ... If his influence could be exerted on public buildings, it would I am certain be to the great advantage of the streets.[14]

The appointment is an interesting one. The job carried responsibility for all building work done in the department except that for the Fire Brigade and for Working Class Housing, each of which had its own section. General Construction covered buildings from generating stations, park buildings, technical schools and homes for inebriates, to 'Schemes and Sites for the Council's Central Offices'.[15]

Ginham came into the department, where it was hoped he would be of help in future street improvement schemes, and where he was a direct channel of influence from Shaw to the department. It was Ginham, as head of the General Section, who was responsible for the early planning of the new County Hall, before the competition. The sketch plans which were prepared throughout 1905 and 1906, in order to show the Establishment Committee the possibilities of the site, were almost certainly his.[a] One of these was eventually to accompany the competition regulations, and was a fundamental influence on the way in which the competitors planned their schemes.

In-House Proposals

Riley's first reaction to the question of designing the new County Hall had been to make a bid for having it carried out by his own department. He himself prepared a perspective of a building on the site (Plate 3c), which was hung in Spring Gardens prior to the Council meeting on 11 April 1905, the week before it was decided to buy the Belvedere Road land.

This was widely published, and although the LCC Architect was careful to insist that the drawing was done merely to suggest the potential of the site, it is evident that he hoped to keep the work in-house, even if he thought it a remote possibility. He was later to say that the drawing was 'not even made from a plan, it was a mere sketch made in my own time at home ... done between Saturday and Monday'.[16] He claimed it was 'hastily prepared simply as a means of conveying the capabilities of the site in relation to its immediate surroundings in order that the members of the Committee and Council should have this information before them in considering the purchase of the site'.[17] Nevertheless, he felt not a little proud of his work, and kept the sketch hanging on the wall of his Spring Gardens office for some time. Whether or not he hoped to win over the Committee with his 'sketch', it must represent an effort to persuade them to let his department design the new building.[18]

The perspective immediately stirred up trouble. The *Building News* had to point out, a week after giving details of the scheme, that 'it by no means follows, of course, that this particular design ... will be adopted for execution'. But Riley had found his first ally, for the article congratulated the Council 'on the grasp of the possibilities of

[a]Copies of technical reports about County Hall which Riley presented to Committees generally bear the initials 'PNG' until 1915, when Ginham was retired because of ill health.

the site shown by its architect, and the certainty that if it commissions him to design the building, as it is quite justified in doing, it will secure a municipal hall worthy of London and the authority that, in spite of ignorant obscurantists, has done so much to improve and beautify it'.[19] In May Riley wrote to the Chairman of the Establishment Committee, J. W. Cleland, expressing alarm at the 'many symptoms of pressure being exercised to influence' the design of the new County Hall. His own 'earnest desire' was to obtain the best solution for the Council, over a building which he described as 'one of the most important ones for London which has been produced for the past 50 years or likely to be in the next 50'. He referred to the proposal for a competition, which he felt was an inherently unsatisfactory way of dealing with a building, since it would be necessary for the Council to hand over its authority to an assessor, supporting this view with a reference to other occasions. The Council would be unlikely to find 'the best architectural talent on the elevations and probably less ability still on the plans'. He reminded Cleland of Norman Shaw's 'magnanimous effort' in the initial stages of the Kingsway Improvement to give 'an artistic bent to the improvement'. Though Shaw was prepared to testify to the Committee that in his opinion Riley's office would be perfectly competent to design the new buildings, Riley himself was fearful that, 'where so many interests are involved, his [Shaw's] opinion in this direction would not be convincing to those outsiders who desire to obtain a foot-hold in such a large and remunerative scheme'. Riley ended by suggesting that if the Committee should decide not to entrust him with 'a complete tentative scheme', the best alternative would be for 'the work of construction, planning, and internal arrangement, which could concern no one but the Council and its staff', to be given to his department. Shaw should then be invited to become 'consulting Architect for the purposes of the elevation' – a role that Riley believed that he would undertake for 'a comparatively modest fee'.[20]

Riley continued to press the Council to choose an in-house architect, at the same time instructing his own department to prepare plans, presented to the Establishment Committee in February 1906.[21b]

In November 1905 William Lethaby, adviser to the Technical Education Board since 1894 and in close touch with the LCC Architect's Department, wrote to Sydney Cockerell:

As to L.C.C. I wish it were possible to get a Frenchman but that is impossible. I hardly see any way out: a comp. means the swashbuckler gang and the swashbucklest being taken. Probably the best thing obtainable now wd be the L.C.C. Office with Shaw as Consulting Archt ... The Shaw business wd work probably more or less, because after the main bulks were kept simple (which he wd do in two days) the office cd carry it out.[22]

The Move towards a Competition

There was a strong external lobby for a competition, mainly among RIBA members, who tended to view public architects as mere incompetent technicians, sheltering in the large offices of public authorities to avoid the competitive realities of the outside world, and, worse still, undercutting independent architects' fees at the taxpayers' expense. They knew that Riley had had Norman Shaw's architectural help on more than one occasion in LCC matters, and they knew too that Shaw disliked competitions almost as much as he disliked the RIBA itself.[23] As Riley had foreseen, they all wanted a chance at one of the decade's big commissions.

The subject of competitions was a source of much concern to the Institute in the early years of this century, following the peculiar outcome of the Liverpool Cathedral competition in 1903, won by the 24-year-old Giles Gilbert Scott. The youthful and inexperienced winner had been forced to accept G. F. Bodley (1827–1907), a competition assessor, as joint architect. This arrangement was widely criticized and in practice did not work well. The RIBA soon after formed a committee to establish approved guidelines for the setting up and running of future competitions. These 'regulations' were approved in the summer of 1905.

The RIBA wrote to the LCC on 3 April 1906 with their suggestion that a competition be held and sketching the basic lines they would like to see followed. Certain that 'the only way of securing a really broadly treated and fine work', was to get a 'strongly individualised personality', they were equally sure that the best way of attracting such a personality would be a competition. As Riley was quoting failed competitions at the Establishment Committee, so the RIBA mentioned the successes – among others, the Houses of Parliament and Foreign Office in London, the Opéra in Paris, the Reichstag in Berlin, and the New York Central Library. The Institute's suggestion was for a two-stage competition with six well-known architects invited into the second stage. There would be three assessors, one of whom was to be elected by the second-stage competitors, one appointed by the President of the RIBA, and one to be the Council's own Architect.[24]

When the Committee asked for Riley's opinion he reiterated the earlier arguments, but put forward his own suggestions for a competition. He proposed that 'he prepare plans showing fully the best possible utilization of the site, having regard to the functions of the various Departments, of the Committees, of the Council itself'. These plans 'when fully matured' would form the basis of the competition. He also proposed that the competitors should be told that they would have to work with him, and that he should have discretionary powers concerning

---

[b]His opposition to the idea of a competition was vindicated to some extent by a later comment of Halsey Ricardo, deploring the expense and effort generated by the competition (see page 41).

internal economy and construction. In commenting on the RIBA proposal, he suggested that two assessors, Shaw and himself, would be enough. He was not happy about the method of choosing the third, though he did finally accept the idea of a third assessor elected by the competitors entered for the second stage. Anticipating criticism, he cited the Liverpool competition as a precedent for his own dual role as assessor and collaborating architect.[25]

Riley lost his fight to have County Hall designed in his own department, but through the conditions for the competition he was able to retain a considerable influence over the development of the design. In the week following his report, Swinton proposed to the Establishment Committee that a public competition should be held for the design of the new building.[26] The deliberations of the Committee, together with much of Riley's advice, were presented in a Report to Council on 24 July 1906, setting out the case for a competition, and the most important of the regulations governing it. These were approved the following week, and the Establishment Committee instructed to go ahead with the arrangements.[27]

Framing the Competition

The main lines of the competition had been set out in the Establishment Committee's Report, though details remained to be clarified. A two-stage competition was proposed, the second stage being limited to no more than twenty-three competitors – the authors of between ten and fifteen designs selected by the assessors in the preliminary round, and up to eight leading architects invited by the Council to submit designs. Norman Shaw and Riley were recommended as assessors, to be joined at the second stage by a third, elected by the finalists. Riley's role in preparing the 'detailed particulars of the accommodation required by the Council' and his collaboration with the successful competitor, fortified by his 'discretionary power in all matters relating to the internal economy and construction of the building', were also clearly set out.

The Establishment Committee agreed to employ Shaw at an assessor's fee of one thousand guineas and instructed Riley to consult him on certain points of detail, among which was the fee to be paid to the third assessor. With typical modesty Shaw said that the third assessor should have a fee equal to his own, in spite of the fact that he would have less than half the work to do.[c] Shaw recommended that some of 'the younger talented architects' might with advantage be included in the list of those invited into the second stage of the competition, a suggestion with which Riley fully concurred. Shaw also thought

that some of those involved in the Kingsway Improvement might be invited.[28] These proposals were in general adopted by the Council on 31 July 1906.[29] The list finally presented to the Committee on 25 October contained nineteen names, and included all of the eight architects eventually selected – H. T. Hare, W. Flockhart, John Belcher, E. W. Mountford, T. G. Jackson, Ernest George, Sir Charles Nicholson, and Edwin Lutyens – plus those of Leonard Stokes, Aston Webb, J. J. Stevenson, Reginald Blomfield, Robert Lorimer, Horace Field, C. E. Mallows, Gerald Horsley, E. J. May, Mervyn Macartney, and Ernest Newton.[30] The last four clearly represented Shaw's idea of 'the younger talented architects': all were ex-pupils or assistants of his. Hare, Flockhart, Macartney, Mountford, George, and Blomfield had been involved in the Kingsway competition. Stevenson, at 75, was the oldest by ten years, and Lutyens, who took the competition very seriously, at 37, the youngest of a handful under 45.

Preliminary letters of invitation were sent out on 6 November 1906, and these included the information that the winner would have to collaborate with Riley. The eight invited architects originally selected included Blomfield and Webb, but Blomfield declined, saying he had too much work on. Aston Webb, after a havering correspondence with the Clerk, also turned it down, because of the association of the Council's Architect with the successful competitor, which he felt raised 'several difficult and important points'. Flockhart and Ernest George took their places.[31] The suggested list was submitted to the Council on 18 December 1906, and approved on 22 January 1907.[32]

Webb's objections raised the matter of Riley's shared responsibility for the design of the building, soon to become a bone of contention with the RIBA.

At the same time the Establishment Committee put forward the conditions for the competition, later issued as the *Instructions to Competing Architects*, which were also approved by Council on 22 January 1907, as were the fees of 1,000 guineas each, payable to Shaw and the third assessor.[33d]

The RIBA Protest

Several of the conditions were unusual and proved to be contentious. The first was the suggested plan discussed below, the second was the invitation to the eight selected architects to join at the second stage, which was felt to be unfair, and was castigated as 'unbusiness-like'.[34] The third, and most disliked, was Riley's role. He was to be

[c]It had originally been intended to pay Shaw 2,000 guineas and the third assessor 1,000 guineas, but the Committee talked Shaw into accepting the lower figure.

[d]The *Instructions* were published (*inter alia*) in the *RIBA Journal* for 9 February 1907, pp. 225–7. For a selection of the more important conditions see Appendix I.

given a separate and personal appointment by the Council as their 'Official Architect', working with the winning architect, and receiving one-tenth of that architect's commission for the building.[35] In the words of clause 8 of the *Instructions*, it was laid down that 'Mr W. E. Riley, the official architect, shall have discretionary power in all matters relating to internal economy, building construction, and stability'.

Exception was taken to this clause by the RIBA. After the *Instructions* had been published, and in spite of their broad conformity to the Institute's proposals of April 1906, the Institute sent a belated protest to the LCC, both about this condition, and about a report of LCC proceedings which had mentioned the *Instructions* as 'approved by the RIBA', whereas, in fact, they had 'never been submitted to their consideration'. The latter point was countered by Shaw's claim that the draft had been available in the RIBA library for inspection.[36]

The Institute interpreted Riley's role as 'official architect' as an appointment as 'joint architect' for the work, and their letter pointed out that there was 'a well established principle of the Royal Institute, *binding on all its members*, that no Assessor shall accept the appointment or act as Architect to carry out a building, on the design of which he has to adjudicate'.[37]

This reference to Riley's position led the Clerk, Laurence Gomme, to ask Shaw's advice in the matter. Shaw reiterated his approval of the clauses 8 and 9, setting out Riley's position and emoluments: 'I have always felt that the object of a competition is to get the very best building that can be had, and that any means (short of injustice) towards the attainment of this end is not merely legitimate but desirable'. He cited the Liverpool Cathedral competition, as Riley had done in a report of 1906.[38]

The climax of the RIBA protest was reached at a special meeting on 28 May 1907, called by several outraged members (including J. S. Gibson, C. E. Mallows, H. V. Lanchester, Herbert Read, R. Falconer MacDonald and Herbert Wills), when a resolution was tabled banning Institute members from taking part in the LCC competition.[39] It was proposed by Gibson, Chairman of the RIBA's Competitions Committee, who had given evidence in the House of Lords on behalf of Holloway Brothers against the London County Buildings Bill. His chief objection was that the invited architects, six of whom were past or present members of the RIBA Council, had, by accepting the invitation, tacitly consented to the LCC's conditions, thereby breaching the Institute's own regulation prohibiting an assessor of a competition from himself competing or acting as architect for the proposed work. Colcutt replied that the regulation was intended to prevent an assessor being subsequently appointed as the architect, but that this did not apply in the County Hall case, which was an exceptional one. He referred to the by now familiar precedent of the Liverpool Cathedral competition, only for A. W. S. Cross to point out that Sir Aston Webb, then President of the RIBA, had stated on

that occasion that such a situation 'would never occur again'. Gibson's comments implied that Riley could not act fairly in the dual role of assessor and joint architect, but practically all of those who spoke at the meeting disputed the insinuation and several members of the older generation begged Gibson to withdraw his resolution, although he stood firm.

Riley was at the meeting, he said only to observe, but now rose to speak. He first pointed out that there had been plenty of time to make this complaint before the conditions for the competition had been finalized, and then denied that he had written them. This was not the entire truth. The Establishment Committee had asked Riley and Shaw together to prepare the *Instructions*. The implication of Riley's remark is that Shaw prepared the conditions on his own, which is a little hard to believe. Certainly it was Riley who proposed his own association with the competition winner, and even though the RIBA suggested him as an assessor, he did nothing to dissuade the Committee, seconding the Institute's recommendation virtually as soon as it was made.[40]

Riley may have thought he was acting in the best interests of the LCC and of architecture in general. His impatience with what he saw as the RIBA's narrow self-interest was evident, but events were to prove that his responsibility for 'internal economy, building construction and structure' was wide enough to hamper the competition winner to a considerable degree. Of his own position as an assessor, he said, somewhat disingenuously, that the Institute Council had not consulted him before suggesting him to the LCC as an assessor. It could be a very barren honour, as he had discovered when he was appointed one of two assessors on the Kingsway competition in 1900, and he thought that any endeavour to ascribe undue importance to his being an assessor on the County Hall competition was insincere. Gibson's resolution was defeated by 50 votes to 29 and the matter stopped there.[41]

Riley was later to propose to the Establishment Committee that he serve as an assessor without vote, merely as a consultant to the others, but this suggestion was rejected.[42]

Another condition caused no immediate acrimonious controversy but is equally revealing of contemporary preoccupations. Schedule C of the *Instructions* dealt with the drawings to be presented – plans of each floor, elevations of the three principal façades and two sections – but at the end there is a specific prohibition against the submission of perspectives in either stage of the competition. This was no doubt one of Shaw's interventions, reflecting his latter-day belief that perspectives were drawn in an attempt to make architecture 'more pictorial', appealing to those who understood little of the subject but being not especially useful to those who did.

The idea that perspectives were false and misleading had been developing for some years. In a series of pieces in the *Architectural Review* about the sorry state of the architecture room at the Royal Academy, Shaw (who had often had the responsibility for hanging that room), Halsey Ricardo, John Belcher, and others tried to establish what architectural drawings were and why the general public, as well as other artists, found them so uninteresting. Belcher was quite clear what the problem was:

The pretty sketch or suggestive drawing dashed off in an hour or so cannot properly represent architecture. It is by the geometrical plans, elevations, and sections, and half-inch details that it can best be understood. It is these which show the real thought bestowed upon the work and the knowledge possessed by the author.

There seems to be a tacit assumption here that it is not only the public which is deceived, but also the architect himself. Shaw was less outspoken, as befitted the man who had done so much to generate the problem with the magnificent perspectives of his younger days. He set out a definition of 'what I should call architectural drawings, viz., plans, sections, and elevations (especially sections) drawn to a good scale, with some detail drawn to a larger scale'. This he thought would create 'a good exhibition, pure and simple'.[43] Shaw's words foreshadow the drawings requirement for the County Hall competition, right down to the phrase 'drawn to a good scale', which translated into sixteenth-scale plans and elevations – a size many of the competitors felt to be excessive.[e]

This new distaste for perspectives invited a more critical analysis of the plan, and, to a lesser extent, the section. The increased importance attached to the plan made Riley's role, particularly concerned as it was with the plan, more significant. That is why some RIBA members could say that whoever won the competition would be reduced 'to the level of a sub-official of the Council under the control of the Superintending Architect', despite that official's claim that his role was merely to assure the rational ordering of the building's internal spaces. The new spirit did not consider this to be a minor item by any means.[44]

At the same time we find architects less willing to accept the opinion of men who judged their elevations as 'works of art', a matter of taste, rather than as 'good plans', a matter of rational determination. An *Architectural Review* article of 1906 shows how these attitudes were blended and how the problem of perspectives was seen to affect the outcome of competitions:

Even supposing the really best design to gain the premium (which again is not always the case) it becomes a question whether the plan should be considered of the first importance or the elevations ... and as the best plan does not postulate the best elevation, and *vice versa*, the door is open for comparative failure in one or other direction.[45]

Architects in later years were to attempt a solution by giving greater importance to the plan, which Shaw and others thought the area least susceptible to deceitful presentation. It is interesting that many of the entrants in the County Hall competition, particularly those experienced in competitions, prepared showy perspectives to amplify their plans and sections,[46] and the moment the competition was decided the first thing the Members of the Council wanted was a nice perspective to show what the building would look like.[47]

The competition had been tarnished at its outset by the RIBA's objection to Riley's appointment as Official Architect. Moreover, Riley's misgivings about this method of choosing an architect were being confirmed. He was later to claim that the RIBA's involvement and the resulting competition delayed progress on the County Hall for nearly two-and-a-half years, and that the total competition expenses amounted to over £8,000.[48]

He had foreseen these problems in 1905. In the same year he had tried to turn the RIBA's arguments against themselves, pointing out to the Establishment Committee that in March 1899, the Council of the RIBA had recommended to the LCC that Shaw should be consulted 'as to the architectural treatment of Vauxhall Bridge', and that in the following September, the RIBA's Standing Committee for Art had congratulated the LCC on the design of Embankment Gardens Generating Station.[49]

Convinced that a competition was unnecessary, Riley had fought hard to have Shaw selected, and failed. The two thought they had 'saved' the Kingsway competition, and may have felt that competitions in general were bound to fail without their intervention, and that they could not allow this one, once decided upon, to proceed without them. Convinced from the outset that the idea was misconceived, they were not perhaps the best people to ensure its successful execution.

The Terms of the Competition

The competition was first advertised in *The Times* and a selection of British professional and technical journals at the end of February 1907. Advertisements were also placed in three Continental Journals – one French, one German and one Italian – the competition being open to architects of any nationality despite an attempt by some Members to restrict it to British citizens.[50f] Competitors were given six months to produce their designs, which had to be with the LCC by 27 August 1907.

Much of the information given in the *Instructions* was necessarily conventional – schedules of accommodation, drawings required of the competitors, as well as a budget for construction, in this case £850,000. In addition, a plan for the guidance of competitors was issued, drawn up by Ginham on Riley's instructions. From the time when they began considering the project in 1905, Riley's department

[e]The plan of a building 720 feet long – roughly the length of County Hall – drawn at a scale of one-sixteenth inch to one foot would measure 43 inches. The competitors therefore had to draw on sheets 52 by 30 inches.
[f]Riley had suggested advertising in some American journals.

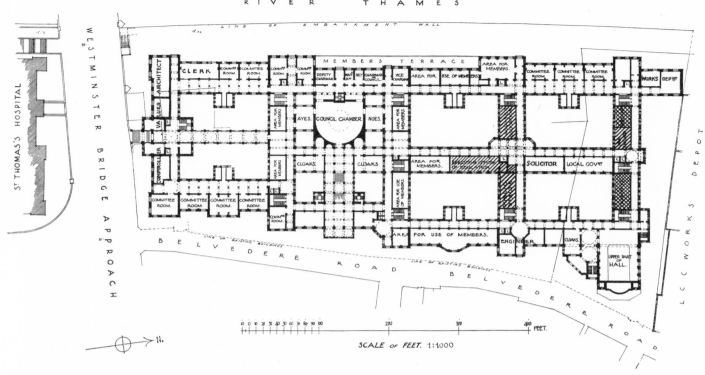

Fig. 4. Suggested Plan for County Hall by the LCC's Superintending Architect, issued in 1907 as part of the *Instructions* for competitors. As well as indicating positions for the Council Chamber and Public Hall, the plan also shows suggested locations for the Members' and Chief Officers' accommodation

had never stopped working on plans, at sixteenth-scale.[51] By February 1906 a plan, symmetrical on the river front, had been developed with many features that were incorporated in the *Instructions*. Chief of these were a first floor reserved for the use of Members and department heads, with public access rooms on the ground floor, and the vertical stacking of departments. This plan (fig. 4) emerged in the *Instructions* as 'a sketch plan ... which shows a suggested arrangement of the accommodation ... to be regarded as merely a suggestion which competitors may modify in any way they desire'. Despite this, many competitors may have felt a certain inhibition about altering the general plan drawn up by an assessor, particularly as that assessor was to be responsible for the internal arrangements of the building.

The *Instructions* and the plan together defined the site for competitors. This was curtailed by a 50–foot set-back on the west side of Belvedere Road, but extended by a proposed embankment to be built out into the Thames, raised some 18 feet above datum, the face of which was to be clad in granite to the architect's design.

The building was to comply with the London Building Acts, but little else was stipulated about construction or materials. Services were to include central-heating radiators and a system of mechanical ventilation, though fireplaces were to be provided in the principal rooms.

The LCC's main requirements for the building were quite specific in certain areas, but left a number of other matters unclear. For instance, no detailed instructions were given about vehicular access for Members, or indeed for 'cart access' to parts of the basement. In his special volume on the competition published in 1908, the Swiss architect Alexander Koch, himself an unsuccessful competitor, commented that the first thing that any architect did upon entering for a competition, was to look out in the programme what principal rooms were wanted, so that he might express them in the elevations. He complained that in the County Hall conditions, 'while, so to say, every little corner required for a broom-stick was enumerated in the programme, the representative rooms were put under one head:- "Suitable accommodation, amounting ... to 16,000 square feet, for the general use of the members"'. Thus the Members' Terrace which appeared in all the designs was not even mentioned, and was only taken by all the competitors from the suggested design of the Council Architect.[52]

Lutyens must have expressed the feelings of many competitors when he later complained to Herbert Baker:

The L.C.C. I feel sick of – bruised with. One was so in the dark as to what was wanted. The site so lovely, the conditions so difficult.[53]

Most attention was paid to the first floor, which was to be for the use of Members, with offices for the heads of departments where possible.[g] Schedules of accommodation were provided for the floor: there was to be a Council Chamber of 4000 square feet, two lobbies, a public gallery for 150 persons with direct access from outside, and a gallery with separate circulation for the press. There was also to be an Assembly or Public Hall to accommodate 800, complying with the LCC Theatre Regulations, and a library 'as conveniently situated to the Council Chamber as possible', with accommodation for a librarian and twelve staff. Muniment and record rooms, strong room and storage were to be provided in the basement. The description of the areas intended for Members seems particularly vague in comparison with that requested for Council staff; the brief called for 'suitable accommodation' for some 200 Members, together with facilities easily accessible from the Council Chamber and lobbies, including an 'ample cloak room', fitted with lockers and telephones. Also called for were a Members' reading-room, restaurants, a possible smoking-room for gentlemen, and a cloakroom for ladies. These provisions, not dissimilar from those provided in the Houses of Parliament, reflected the same view of the Council's position which led it to model its Standing Orders on Erskine May rather than on the usual standing orders for local councils.[h] In addition, some twelve committee rooms, varying in size from 600 to 1,200 square feet, were to be provided, the way in which they were specified betraying that they had been taken off the sketch plan (fig. 4).

The specifications for 'Rooms for Heads of Departments' on the first floor, which with waiting rooms varied from 350 to 500 square feet, were supplemented by detailed schedules of respective accommodation for their departments elsewhere. The special requirements of each branch pay eloquent tribute to the care with which the Clerk and his colleagues had drawn up their lists. Some departments, like Housing and Asylums, needed to be accessible to the public, and 'on one floor if possible', a request echoed by the Local Government and Statistical Department, for which 'a quiet portion of site' was essential. The Public Health Department needed room for a bacteriological laboratory on the top floor, and also two bedrooms and sitting-rooms for medical officers' use 'during epidemics'. The Chemical and Gas Department also required laboratory space, while Public Control needed to test gas meters. The newly joined Educational Department was very precise in its requirements: 'Essential qualifications – Good light, quiet, easily accessible to the public, 100 of whom are seen daily for weeks at a time'.[54]

The Effect of the Municipal Reform Victory in 1907

Less than a month after the competition was first advertised, the Progressives were defeated and the Municipal Reformers took office as the majority party on the LCC. The new administration at first tried to cancel the competition but soon decided to leave things as they stood. This meant that competing architects were designing a County Hall for a body which, while still answering to the name of LCC, had a quite different character from the client that had sponsored the competition.

A major overhaul of the Moderate political machine had been a key element in the victory. A few months before the election, the Conservative London Municipal Society, formed in 1894, had persuaded the Moderates to change their somewhat uninspiring name to that of Municipal Reformers. During this election, said to have been 'contested with a vigour and violence of emotion unmatched in the history of the Council', the Moderates – never themselves in power at the LCC – used their campaign to pillory the ruling party as 'the Wastrels'. It was perhaps this which did most damage, combined with a brilliant series of cartoons and posters designed by E. Huskinson. These were works of political satire far more potent than any which had appeared in earlier elections. There is little evidence that the County Hall project, expensive as it was to be, was cited in the campaign, though the subject appears as a makeweight in some cartoons. The main targets were the tramways and the accident-prone steamboat services, but of course, the Municipal Reform platform was built on economy and value for money.

The Progressives were furious at what they regarded as the hijacking of a name to which they had a historic claim as direct political descendants of the London Municipal Reform League. In addition, they found themselves embarrassed at having to defend an eighteen-year period of government which had seen much reform and improvement, but which had also seen rates rise from 1s. 9¼d. in 1889 to 3s. 0d. in 1906, against a party which seemed to be laying claim to a kind of radicalism. The municipal debt had gone from £18 million in 1893 to £23 million in 1903, and, after central government had moved the London School Board and its debt to the LCC, to £48 million in 1907.[55]

The previous year's parliamentary election was doubtless another factor. Progressives and Moderates had long been affiliated with the national political parties, but the election in 1906 to the House of Commons of no less than thirty LCC Progressives as members of the Liberal

[g]Clerk, Comptroller, Engineer, Architect, Solicitor, Medical Officer of Health, Valuer, Statistical Officer, Chief Officer of the Fire Brigade, Manager of Works, Chief Officer of Tramways, Educational Adviser, Executive Officer, Chief Inspector of Education, in that order.
[h]The penultimate Director-General of the GLC, Sir James Swaffield, made the point that the Council Members saw themselves as in the same league as Members of Parliament, and much enjoyed the occasional all-night sitting.

parliamentary majority brought this fact clearly before the public eye. It was not lost sight of by campaigning Municipal Reformers, who averred that the Progressives were using the LCC to subvert Parliament.[56]

Immediately after the 1907 local government elections the Municipal Reformers put their policies of economy into practice, cutting the steamboat service and winding down the Works Department. They also called into question the new County Hall, a project which the Progressives hoped they had taken too far for reversal, and in spite of the fact that the need for a new headquarters was recognized by all parties.

Only two 1906 Establishment Committee members were re-appointed to the 1907 Committee: Edward Smith and Captain George Swinton. Richard Robinson (1857–1923), a previous member from 1896 to 1904, replaced Cleland as Chairman. Within a fortnight of the election Robinson had asked Riley what the LCC's liability would be if the architectural competition for the design of the new County Hall were to be abandoned. The Finance Committee met to establish the consequences of giving up the site altogether and the Engineer, Architect and Valuer were instructed to look again into alternative sites in the Westminster Improvement Area and Kingsway.[57]

The Establishment Committee's report on the County Hall situation, twice deferred, was presented to the Council on 18 June 1907. After summarizing the Council's commitments to the Belvedere Road site and the architectural competition, the Committee reported that there was only one possible alternative site, the Westminster Improvement Area, of which the cost per acre was 50 per cent higher than the Belvedere Road site. The report concluded:

having regard to the stage which has been reached in the acquisition of the site and to the large sum of money which would be lost if the Council did not proceed, and also to the fact that the competition ... has been in progress for ten weeks, the best course ... is to go on with the scheme with all possible dispatch in order that the staff may be housed in the new building at the earliest moment.[58]

Calling off the project altogether would have cost the Council £200,000. Once this was known Members stopped agitating to have the scheme cancelled and turned their attention towards hastening its completion and making substantial economies. In some respects the two aims were contradictory. Speeding the works along meant having to buy up the leases of the premises fronting Westminster Bridge Road, which the Council had intended to let run until their expiry in 1923–4, foregoing the rents. These tenancies were acquired in 1910–11.[59]

On the other hand there was still a hope of getting out of the agreement to take over Holloways' property at the north end of the site. The Establishment Committee consulted Riley about the possibility of using the Belvedere Road site without Holloways' holding. Riley estimated that it would accommodate some 450 people, and

that to fit the extra number on the reduced site was not practical, particularly since the Council now planned to house a further 500 staff in the new building, making a total of 2,738.[60] A suggestion that the London School Board offices on the Victoria Embankment be kept, to reduce the necessary size of the new building, brought the comment from the Clerk, that to do this 're-creates a difficulty that New County Hall was meant to remove'.[61]

It was soon recognized that the purchase of the northern part of the site was inevitable, not least because the Council had served a notice to treat. However, the Council decided to defer development on this part of the site until 1914 at the earliest, leasing it back to Holloways immediately for 21 years with break clauses at 7, 10 and 14 years.[62]

The Result of the Competition

Despite its contentious *Instructions* and austere requirements for large plain geometrical drawings, the first stage of the competition attracted 99 designs. The competitors numbered 152, eight of them, the assessors noted, of foreign birth, and, individually or jointly, they produced a total of 1,199 drawings. Within a month of the closing date, 27 August 1907, fifteen designs had been selected for the final stage (see Appendix II, page 127).[63] Together with the eight invited architects, the first-stage winners elected Aston Webb to join Shaw and Riley as third Assessor (Plate 3d). After three weeks' scrutiny of the final 23 schemes – 346 drawings – the Assessors presented their Report to the Establishment Committee on 30 January 1908.[64]

This brief and laconic document was doubtless meant to reassure all parties concerned. But its few paragraphs hedge the Assessors' decision to a great extent, and render unsurprising the long process of change and interference that was to follow. As they observed, the competitors' schemes were at this moment little more than sketch designs, and some modifications were inevitable:

Under these circumstances, we have selected the design which, in our opinion, shows the greatest promise of a worthy result, and best deals with the problem set.

We find, unanimously, that design No.106 is, on the whole, the best, and we therefore recommend it for acceptance and execution.

It is a forcible and artistic suggestion which conveys to us the purpose for which it is to be erected, and is almost entirely without costly and unnecessary features: moreover, we are of opinion that the estimated cost is a fair one, and that the building could probably be erected within the sum named in instruction No.34 ... There are other points in the plan that require modification, but the brilliant qualities of the design far outweigh, in our opinion, these and other comparatively unimportant defects.

This report was accepted by the Council on 4 February 1908, despite some fierce criticism of the design from the Rev. Frank Hastings, the Progressive Member for East St Pancras.[65]

Fig. 5. Ralph Knott's winning design for County Hall, 1908. Perspective view from the south-west across Westminster Bridge

The Winning Design (figs 5, 13, 14, 16, 17a)

The design chosen by the assessors was that submitted by Ralph Knott (1878–1929), a 29-year-old assistant in Aston Webb's office. No stranger to the world of the public building competition, Knott, jointly with his friend and future partner Ernest Stone Collins (1878–1942), had previously entered the Bristol Reference Library and Malvern Free Library competitions of 1902 and 1904, coming second in both, and the Lambeth Municipal Buildings Competition of 1905. Although not premiated, their Lambeth entry was commended by the assessor, H. T. Hare, but others found its generally restrained mixture of baroque and mannerist styles 'probably rather too severe for a building of this nature'.[66] At the time of winning the County Hall competition, however, Knott had designed very little that was actually built – the *Building News* credited him with 'some good country domestic buildings, principally in Sussex'.[67]

Born in Chelsea, the eighth child of a prosperous tailor in Pont Street,[68] Knott had been educated at the City of London School, and had served his articles in the architectural practice of Woodd & Ainslie. About 1900 he had joined Aston Webb's office, where he worked on the Admiralty Arch and the Victoria and Albert Museum. In 1901 he was placed second in the Tite Prize, with a design for a gateway in which elements of County Hall can be recognized (fig. 6).[69]

Though some critics thought the winning design to be one of the duller entries – 'cold, grim and soulless' was the Rev. Frank Hastings's description – it was in fact a workmanlike and impressive scheme, which fulfilled the demands of a difficult brief. Innocent of the domes and baroque grandeur which were a feature of so many competitors' designs, it nevertheless dominated the site and made full use of the riverside. The main element of the river front was a square portico with double columns projecting on to the embankment. Office wings on either side were cleverly handled, with rusticated ground and first floors and two attic floors in a mansard to conceal the sheer bulk of the building. Central features punctuated the Westminster Bridge Road and Belvedere Road fronts, a subsidiary entrance on the former and an ingenious circular Public Hall set in a deep recess on the latter. Pavilions at each corner of the building were intended to contain baroque sculpture groups, and decorative carved and moulded architectural features enriched pediments over doors and windows. Tall chimneys increased the domestic impression given by the double rows of dormer windows, and enlivened the skyline, together with a flèche topped by a weathervane bearing a ship in full sail.

Considerable re-working of the design was to take place over the next three years, and though Knott suffered in the process, as other young and inexperienced designers have done on similar occasions, much of the change was beneficial. For Riley the experience of judging the designs had been nearly as distressing as the Kingsway competition. Shortly after the result was known he wrote to Belcher:

In the progress of the work, as each scheme went out of further consideration, I am bound to say that I experienced the deepest feeling of sympathy with those whose efforts and hopes were alike disappointed by the decision though of course this was inevitable. I am not used to the experience and I hope I shall not be called upon again to go through such an ordeal. I am henceforth an advocate of selection in works of such magnitude.[70]

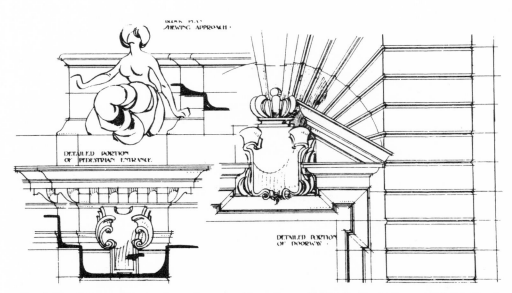

Fig. 6. Detail from a 'Design for an Entrance Gateway to a Public Park' which earned Ralph Knott second place in the Tite Prize, 1901

CHAPTER IV

The Final Design

The Assessors (Plate 3d) presented their final report on the competition to the Establishment Committee on 28 January 1908. The drawings for the twenty-three final stage designs were exhibited in the Medical Examination Hall on the Victoria Embankment. A good deal of professional and public comment followed, as was to be expected for what the *Building News* called 'the most important competition since the Law Courts . . . on one of the finest sites now available in Europe'.[1] The unsuccessful entries deserve study, not least because their authors included some of the most famous names in the profession, and one critic declared that there was 'finer architecture amongst [them] than can be recognised' in Knott's scheme.[2] In fact, some of their ideas were to appear in the final design for County Hall, including some elements from the first stage designs.

The Competition Entries

The *Instructions to Competing Architects* set out the main requirements of the brief, and in addition the competitors were provided with a plan of the site, incorporating a sketch plan of the first floor showing the allocation of accommodation as suggested by the Architect's Department (fig. 4). A series of *Replies to Competing Architects* amplified these (see Appendix I).[3]

The competitors must also have been aware of Riley's sketch design (Plate 3c), which had been published in 1905, and which more than one commentator thought had induced most of the competitors to add 'cupolas, towers and such features'.[4] Taken together with the prominence of the site and the scale of the plan, Riley's grandiose perspective must have gone far to convince competitors that a building of civic splendour rather than municipal utility was required. Certainly, they do not seem to have taken too seriously the Municipal Reform Party's intention, if they won the election, to reduce expenditure on the building by 40 per cent – from the £850,000 to £500,000.[5] London as the head of empire and the world's great city was a common image at the time, and few can have thought that such a city would not look for the very finest of buildings for its administrative headquarters.

From the limited number of competition plans available today – generally only ground and first-floor plans – it seems that hardly anybody questioned the suggested plan-ning of the building. Competitors concerned themselves instead with circulation and architectural style, which goes a long way to explain the similarity of so many of the designs.

Much of what we know about the competition drawings we owe to Alexander Koch (1848–1911), who had worked in Semper's office, studied in Berlin and practised in Zurich before coming to London in 1885. He published *Academy Architecture* and *Architecture Review* and later *British Competitions in Architecture*. His volume on County Hall illustrated the twenty-three final entries in the competition and six others. Koch himself entered the competition but was not selected for the second stage.[6]

The plan provided by the LCC gave a suggested layout of cross blocks and internal courts adapted to the irregularly-shaped site. It clearly influenced the competitors, many of whom opted for a similar solution, incorporating a central north-south corridor connecting the cross blocks. One, that of Alexander Marshall Mackenzie (1847–1933), was boomerang-shaped with a stepped-back crescent towards the river, another, that of the well-established Edinburgh commercial architect, G. Washington Browne (1853–1939), had an apsidal northern end, while maintaining a frontage parallel with the river (fig. 7b). Some competitors provided a major feature on the Belvedere Road frontage. Arthur & Walter Reid & East designed a deep crescent with a parade for the use of Members and a high tower reminiscent of those being built on town halls in Germany at the time.[7]

The Council Chamber was placed by most competitors in a central position, sometimes with an external feature to mark its situation. The Anglo-French firm of R. A. Hinds & Jules Deperthes identified the Members' area by a higher mansard roof with a small dome at each corner (fig. 9a). Other competitors, such as the Scot, Hippolyte J. Blanc (1844–1917), well-known for his Edinburgh churches, crowned the Chamber with a dome.

Lutyens, indeed, provided domes at either end of an axial corridor which linked the Members' Library and the approach to the Public Hall with a central Council Chamber (figs 7a, 8c). These twin domes, closely modelled on those at Greenwich, rose out of the octagonal halls, which were the main organizational element of his plan. They provided a link between brick upper storeys and the heavy rusticated stone levels below. Some thought that he had not done enough building on a large scale to justify inclusion in the list. His design, on the other hand, expensive as it undoubtedly would have been to build, showed

a Design by E. L. Lutyens. River-front elevation showing the three dock entrances. The arcades on either side enclosed the public embankment walk under the wings of County Hall

b Design by G. Washington Browne. Perspective view from the north-west showing the apsidal northern end and the dome over the Council Chamber

Fig. 7. Competition Designs for County Hall, 1908

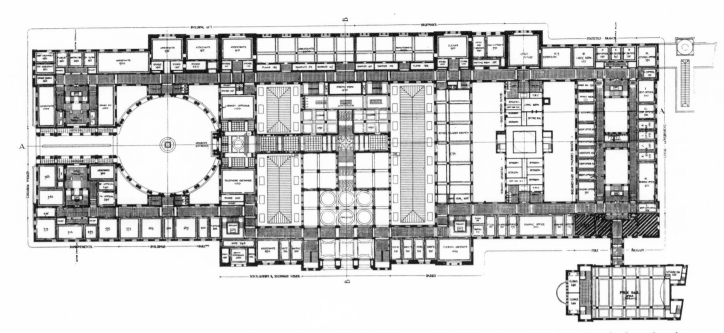

a Design by H. T. Hare. Ground-Floor plan showing the Members' Entrance from Westminster Bridge Road to the large interior courtyard, the entrance from Belvedere Road (with a staircase up to the Council Chamber on the floor above), and the almost-detached Public Hall. The shape and position of Hare's courtyard doubtless influenced Knott's own, revised, design for a Members' Courtyard

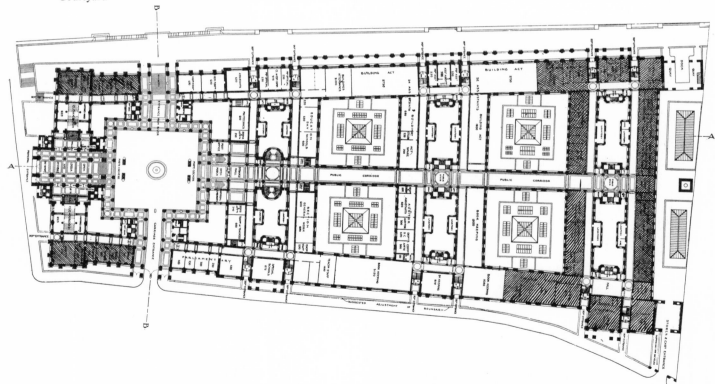

b Design by Jemmet & McCombie. Ground-Floor plan showing the carriage entrance leading from Belvedere Road into a large square 'Members' Courtyard'. The carriage entrance is flanked by covered passages for pedestrians, an arrangement afterwards adopted by Knott for his own Carriage Drive from Westminster Bridge Road

Fig. 8. Competition Designs for County Hall, 1908: Plans. The hatching indicated the allocation of space to different Departments

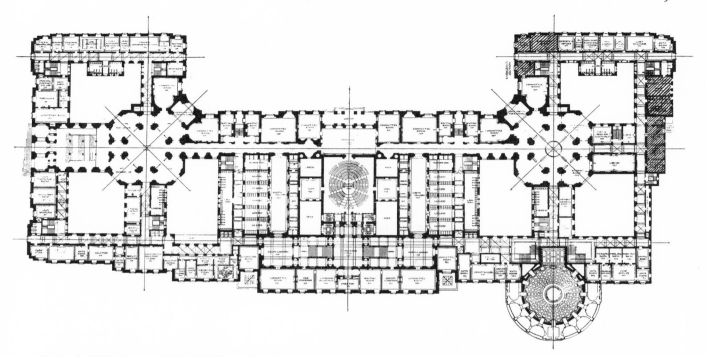

c Design by E. L. Lutyens. Principal-Floor plan, showing the long transverse corridor (linking the North and South Halls, under the two domes), the central Council Chamber, and the Public Hall at the north end of Belvedere Road

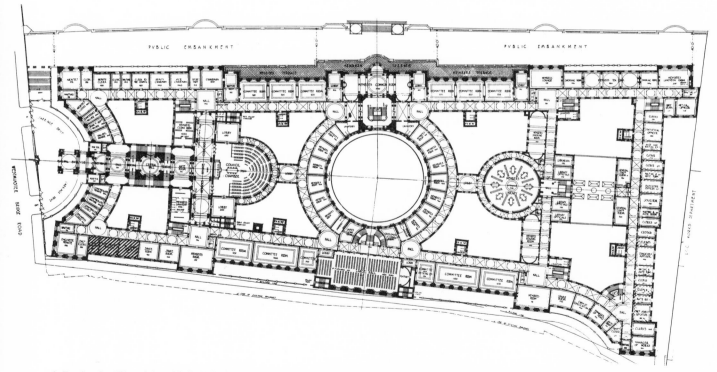

d Design by Warwick & Hall. Principal-Floor plan, showing the entrance from the Westminster Bridge Road via a 'Central Hall' to the horseshoe-shaped Council Chamber. A tall campanile was placed over the 'Central Hall' and a lower tower, crowned with a dome, over the staircase in the centre of the river front. To the north of the great central light-well, ringed with offices, a circular Members' Library balanced the Council Chamber on the south, while the Public Hall was accommodated in the central portion of the Belvedere Road front

a Design by Hinds & Deperthes, 1907. Perspective view from the south-west. The Members' accommodation was grouped below the mansard roof

b Design by Russell & Cooper, 1908. Perspective view across the River Thames

Fig. 9. Competition Designs for County Hall, 1907–8

a better integration of plan and elevation than most of the others. Lutyens' failure to secure the commission, which he saw as an important part of the 'high game', was a source of real chagrin to him – 'All my nine months' work is lost ... All my little bits of work seem dull'.[8]

The various entrances required for Members, public and staff, were treated by competitors in a wide variety of ways. Some, like E. W. Mountford, John Belcher, and R. Frank Atkinson, placed the main entrance on the east with a grand parade for Members into the Council Chamber. Others, like the veteran town hall architect, Henry T. Hare (1861–1921), provided a Members' Entrance on the Westminster Bridge Road, a feature commended by the *Building News* as a plan of 'great dignity ... with its main entrance beneath a boldly designed archway' (figs 8a, 17).

Hare, trained in Yorkshire and Paris, had already designed a number of municipal buildings, including those at Oxford and Southend. He had been invited into the second stage, justifying 'his reputation by submitting a design of great simplicity and dignity, combined with originality'. The *Building News* went on to say that it had been 'rumoured that this design was one which nearly achieved selection, and, as an addition to the architectural beauties of London, it is to be regretted that it did not do so'.[9] Its plan was developed from the south, where a carriage entrance on Westminster Bridge Road led into a circular courtyard and Members' Entrance. Hare did not continue his series of important rooms farther north on to Holloways' land. There is an impressive clarity about the scheme, and some clever planning. To gain two handsomely proportioned courts surrounded by well-lit offices, he set his cross-blocks with single-sided corridors back-to-back. Hare must indeed have been very near to victory with this scheme, for it is hard to believe that it was a more expensive proposition than Knott's, and his elevations were considerably plainer. The scheme was to have its effect on the final version of Knott's design.

The question of natural lighting posed considerable problems for the competitors, in view of the large number of corridors and circulation spaces. Corridors with rooms on one side only provided better and more agreeable lighting, but double-sided corridors with borrowed lighting were more economical, and most competitors included both types in their solutions.

One of the requirements was for an assembly hall for public use, and therefore, like a theatre or concert hall, subject to the LCC's own licensing regulations. This was treated in a number of ways: one or two schemes integrated it within the main block, but in many it was detached from the building, often placed on the northern end of the Belvedere Road front, as the LCC plan had suggested, thus taking advantage of the broader northern dimension of the site. Lutyens, together with Flockhart, Hare, Ernest George, and Mountford, left it as a slightly unhappy projection, which might have looked rather curious when built.

As Halsey Ricardo observed in the *Architectural Review*,

little advantage was taken of the grandeur of the riverside site – only one competitor, Matthew J. Dawson (1875–1943), is known to have provided a Main Entrance from the river (fig. 23). This had a carriage road on the embankment, below a loggia, from which a gallery and vestibule led to the grand staircase and thence to the Council Chamber and Assembly Hall on the Principal Floor.[10] Lutyens' scheme had three dock entrances under the building, other schemes had somewhat ambiguous arches under the embankment, or, like those of S. B. Russell & Edwin Cooper (fig. 9b), and Knott himself, contained elevations which implied that river craft could land passengers on steps leading to the terrace.

Different aspects of the internal planning exercised different contemporary critics, and because it was a building of such a composite nature, being both grand Hôtel de Ville and workaday office block, an effective critique was almost as much of a problem for the critic, as was the design for the competitor. Thus Lutyens was praised by the *Builder* for 'a very symmetrical and architecturally effective interior', but he was criticized for providing a circuit of 160 feet for Members returning to the Council Chamber from the voting lobbies.[11] Both Hare and Warwick & Hall were generally praised for their planning, and both were 'tipped' as winners in press gossip.[12]

There was some surprise that the latter partnership, also specialists in town hall design, was not invited directly into the second stage of the competition; yet they won their way through by producing a plan of some sophistication (fig. 8d). Beginning with a crescent carriage entrance facing Westminster Bridge Road, their plan develops northwards into the Council Chamber, Members' rooms organized around a circular court, and a Members' Library in a corresponding position to the Council Chamber.

There were press criticisms of the way in which some first stage schemes had been rejected, and the *Builder* reproduced that by Lanchester & Rickards with the frank comment that it was better than at least one of the second stage designs (fig. 10).[13]

Despite the prohibition of perspectives, most of the professional criticism, as well as the comment from the general public, was based as much on style and the view from the river as on sophisticated questions of internal planning. However, two, at least, of the more avant-garde designs did break away from the mechanical and somewhat unimaginative layout of the 'Suggested Plan'. Both Adrian Gilbert Scott (1882–1963) and Salmon, Son & Gillespie of Glasgow, rejected the central block flanked by two courtyards either side for a more open arrangement. 'The main idea', wrote Scott, in the *Builder*, 'was to take advantage of the size of the site, provide fine courtyards, avoiding, of course, all well-holes ... inexcusable on a site of this magnitude'.[14] His scheme provided a grand arched entrance from the Westminster Bridge Road leading into the south court, with a comparable space on the north of the Council Chamber block. Salmon's plan (fig. 11) was

Fig. 10. Lanchester & Rickards' competition design for County Hall, 1907. Perspective view, drawn by E. A. Rickards, of the central portion of the river front

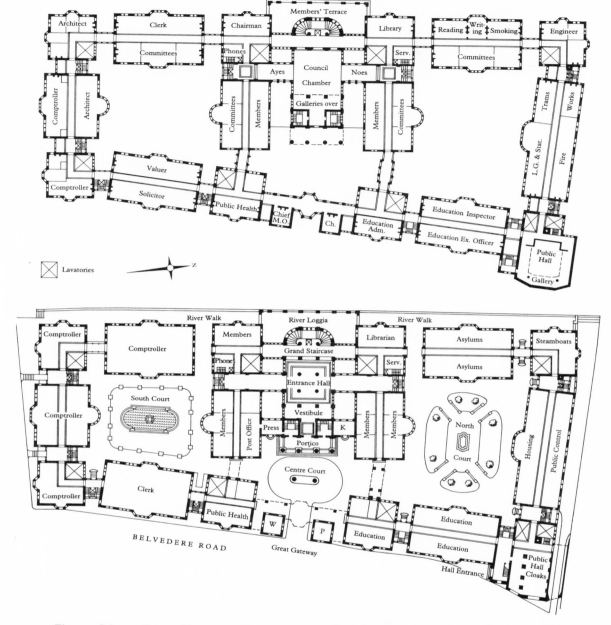

Fig. 11. Salmon, Son & Gillespie's competition design for County Hall, 1907. Ground-Floor (below) and Principal-Floor plans, showing the blocks linked at first-floor level and the generous landscaped courtyards. Ch. Chemist; K Keeper; P Porter; W Watchman

one of the 'freest' and most original of those plans which have survived. Entered through a 'Great Gateway' from Belvedere Road, the site was ringed with a series of individual blocks linked at and above the Principal-Floor level, each one dedicated to a different department. A central E-shaped block with the base resting on the embankment contained the Council Chamber flanked by Members' accommodation and committee rooms. Most of the embankment front was given over to Members, but Architect, Clerk and Engineer were also to enjoy river-views. In addition, the central courts contained gardens and fountains. This ingenious and adaptable scheme was elevated in what reads today as Post-Modern *avant la lettre*, but which may at the time have had overtones of industrial dwellings: a series of gables complete with dormer windows and the occasional 'Queen Anne' pepper-pot,

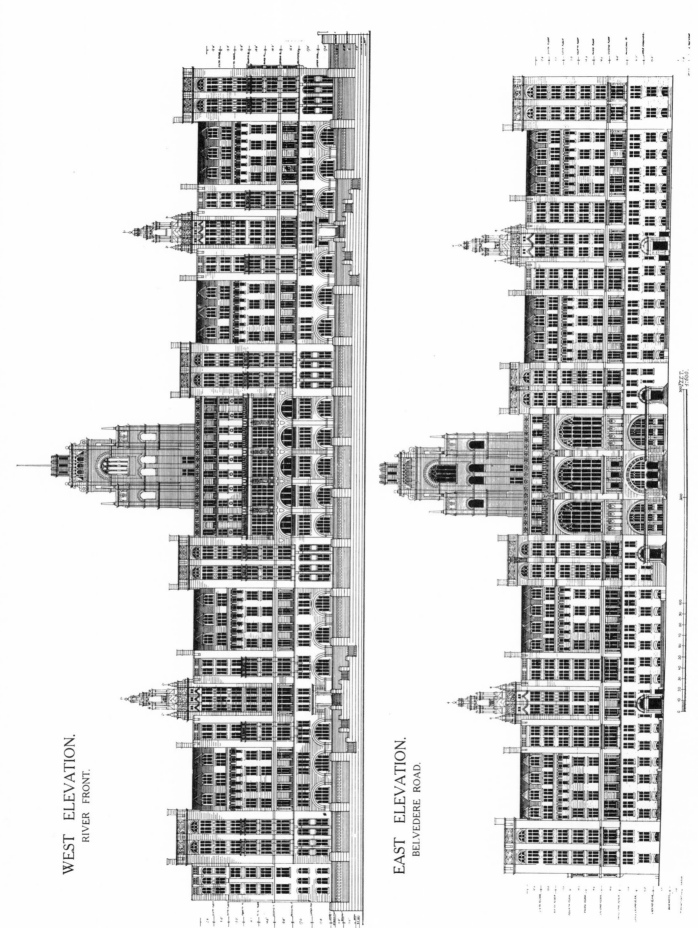

WEST ELEVATION.
RIVER FRONT.

EAST ELEVATION.
BELVEDERE ROAD.

Fig. 12. Nicholson & Corlette's competition design for County Hall, 1908. Elevations. The three tall round-headed windows over the main entrance on the Belvedere Road front would have lit a three-storey 'County Hall' (Public Hall) on the Principal Floor. The tower was raised over the principal staircase and contained offices

were presided over by a highly ornamented version of a Wren City steeple (Plate 4b).[15] Scott's skyline was dramatically plain and simple, depending for effect on a row of gigantic chimney-stacks and dormers above an impressive leaded roof (Plate 4c). His elevation to the Thames was necessarily high to 'tell across the river', but equally without central emphasis; a lower but still substantial 'loggia' on the river front provided accommodation for Members. C. H. Reilly of Liverpool University also designed a lower block on the river front (fig. 20), with the deliberate intention of making the building more impressive from the other side of the river, as well as providing details of a more sympathetic scale than a single monolithic building would have necessitated.[16]

That Riley's 'sketch' elevation (Plate 3c) had been taken seriously by many of the competitors is clearly shown by the preponderance of classical designs with one or more domes. These varied from the 'simple and charming design' by Thomas Davison to the lofty and characteristically overblown one set between four lantern towers from Clyde Young & W. Poley. Even Stanley Peach, better known for his power stations, followed the Riley format, and provided a Capitol-like design.[17]

However, not all the competitors were seduced. The detailed but repetitive, almost curtain-wall, treatment of (Sir Charles) Nicholson & Corlette was criticized as unsuccessful Gothic, 'mixing Elizabethan and even commonplace Renaissance detail' (fig. 12).[18] Frank Atkinson's 'immense central tower reminiscent of the Palais de Justice at Brussels' brought a flavour of the Beaux Arts training to the competition,[19] as did that of Lanchester & Rickards, while Russell & Cooper's scheme presaged their monumental Port of London Authority building in Trinity Square. H. Percy Adams & C. H. Holden, well-known for their hospital designs, produced an interesting plan with a large number of courtyards – though not the twenty-two 'well-holes' held up for censure by A. G. Scott[20] – and an elegant stripped classical façade with two towers, which foreshadow that of the London University Senate House (Plate 4a).[21]

The Prize-winning Design

Ralph Knott's scheme stands out amongst the others for its relative simplicity. In the words of the *Architect & Contract Reporter*, he was the only finalist who entirely omitted 'any attempt at grand halls or staircases or fine architectural effect, such as were suggested by the typical plan supplied'.[22] It is notable that Knott, who had seen plenty of opulence in Webb's office, was among the first to produce designs which modified the English Renaissance in such a way that it conformed more with what Inigo Jones would have called 'masculine' architecture. Here was a design which managed to unite interior with exterior to a high degree, while using the great size of the building for quietly dramatic purposes.

Knott's plan was extremely straightforward; a central block flanked by courtyards, then by transverse east-west blocks with central corridors and rooms on either side, two further courtyards, and finally by single-sided ranges at the north and south of the building (fig. 13). There was an entrance from Westminster Bridge Road, and a modest one on the north side, but the main axis was east-west through the building. On the river front the main feature was a massive five-bay open arcade between full height rusticated blocks (fig. 5). This projected over a public embankment walk with a flight of steps leading down to the water. The Belvedere Road frontage was dominated by a deep crescent, almost entirely occupied by a circular block containing the Public Hall. The main entrance was behind this building under a *porte-cochère*. Knott's skyline lacked domes, or the Germanic watch-towers of Warwick & Hall and Hinds & Deperthes, the only features being an extremely modest flèche, two stories of dormers, and a very uncompromising row of chimneys. The *Builder* would rather have liked a dome – 'one does feel that a grand and monumental architectural character, with something of the dignity which a central feature like a dome can impart, even when not carried to an unreasonable and unpractical height, is what might be looked for'.[23] However, in Halsey Ricardo's words, the new building was 'to be mainly a beehive and a workshop rather than a palace – Somerset House should be the model rather than the Houses of Parliament'.[24]

The *Building News* found little real enthusiasm for the scheme, commending its simplicity but criticizing the double-sided corridors, and the planning of the Ayes and Noes Lobbies, and the lavatories and messenger's boxes. It recognized the convenience of the siting of the Public Hall, since it could be so easily omitted from the final scheme. The 'numerous dormers' would have 'a fidgety effect, by no means redeemed by the tall chimneys. But of all these things', it concluded, 'our readers can judge for themselves'.[25]

Alexander Koch, in an open letter to the Members of the LCC, was as critical of the interior as of the exterior:

Considering cheapness to be the first consideration, I will not dispute great merits in the chosen design, but ... this cheapness has been obtained especially by interior arrangements which cannot be tolerated for a moment, and will certainly have to be altered.[26]

Amongst other improvements, he instanced the need for better corridors, a proper Members' Terrace 'in connection with the Restaurant', and a grand Members' Entrance from Westminster Bridge Road. It is interesting to see how many of his suggestions were later incorporated in the final designs.

The architectural plainness of the scheme would, of course, have commended it to the new Municipal Reform administration, with its anxiety not to be seen to be extravagant. The very absence of domes and other features

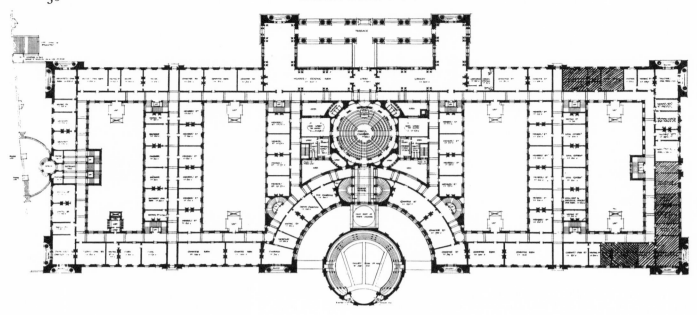

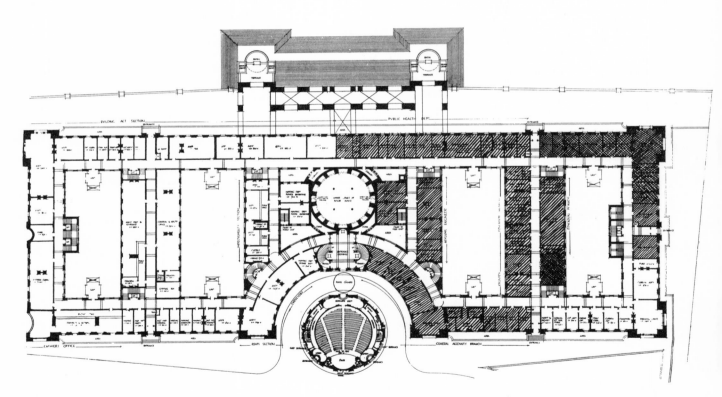

Fig. 13. Ralph Knott's winning design for County Hall, 1908. Plans of the Ground Floor (below) and Principal Floor showing the symmetrical layout with equal-sized courts. The hatching indicated the allocation of space to different Departments, which were intended to be 'stacked' vertically, the Chief Officers being on the Principal Floor.

    There were entrances on all sides of the building, including one at the north end, two from the embankment, and an impressive one for pedestrians on the Westminster Bridge Road front. On the Belvedere Road front a *porte-cochère* between the main building and the detached circular Public Hall gave access to both.

    The Members' accommodation was located in the centre of the Prinicpal Floor. The riverside portico contained their Reading Room and Library, and enclosed a Members' Terrace under an arcade. Private rooms for the Chairman and other dignitaries were placed in the crescent, overlooking the Public Hall

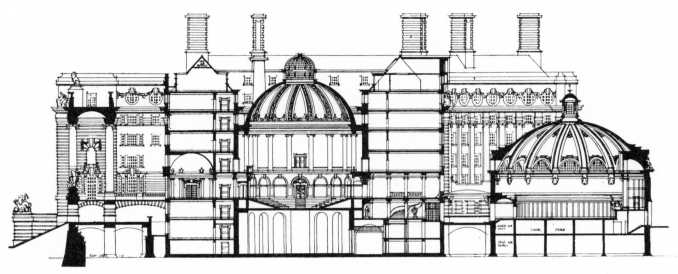

Fig. 14. Ralph Knott's winning design for County Hall, 1908. Section, looking north, showing, from left to right, the embankment, the arcade under the portico, the Council Chamber and the Public Hall

which critics looked for to grace such an important site was desirable from the Council's point of view. Knott's plan owed more than that of many other competitors to the plan circulated, being, if possible, even simpler. There were, however, two other elements in his plan which would have been appreciated by the Assessors. One was the possibility of detaching the contentious Public Hall, something which other competitors had also provided for, the other was that nothing of significance stood on the northern part of the site, to be occupied by Holloways for some time to come.

A question of a more personal nature was raised about Knott's involvement with Aston Webb, from whose office he took leave of absence in June 1907 to work on the County Hall competition, returning after the second stage submission on 30 December 1907. It is sometimes said that Webb was reluctant to award Knott first place, fearing that this would be interpreted as an act of favouritism, but there is no evidence of any such reluctance. In fact, Webb agreed to take on the job of third Assessor fully aware that two of the finalists were currently or had been assistants of his. But the letter he wrote at the time to the Clerk, disclaiming any prior knowledge of their designs, shows he was sensitive on this issue:

I may say to prevent any misunderstanding that I am informed that two of my old assistants, one still with me, have been successful in the Preliminary Competition but that their designs were not prepared in my Office nor have I seen them or been consulted about them in any way, indeed I have not seen any set of the designs successful or otherwise.[27]

More interesting questions are raised by the economical nature of Knott's scheme. Its simplicity was perhaps no coincidence. At least one architectural periodical said quite baldly that the reason was Knott's being in a 'position to

obtain the best information as to the working of the Council's business'.[28]

Almost certainly this is an allusion to Knott's association with E. Stone Collins, his partner in the Bristol and Malvern libraries competitions, who was then employed as an assistant in Riley's own department. The two had been at school together, though Collins was the older by four years, and they were fellow students at the Architectural Association. After training with George Kenyon and E. W. Mountford, Collins joined the LCC's Architect's Department, where he worked on the Totterdown estate. Knott and Collins wanted to enter the County Hall competition together, but Riley had ruled that no-one in his department should work on it without first relinquishing his post, and the newly married Collins was understandably reluctant to give up a permanent appointment.

Thus Knott entered the competition on his own and Collins retained his position with the LCC. When questioned about a connexion with Knott which had possibly influenced the outcome of the competition, Collins feigned innocence. They had jointly entered competitions before, he said, but when the conditions for County Hall were issued they had decided that as he was an officer in Riley's department, it was not advisable for him to be associated with Knott in the competition – though presumably this did not preclude him from giving Knott hints or advice. Collins then fell ill with appendicitis and was laid up for two months, and it was while he was on sick leave, late in July 1907, that he became directly involved with Knott's design. In his own words:

Mr Knott showed me his scheme which was well advanced, but informed me the strain of the work was beginning to tell on him and it would be necessary to obtain assistance to do the repetition work & drawing out of some of the upper floor plans and I assisted him to complete the drawings in my spare time, my services were given gratuitously as a friend.[29a]

Twenty years later Collins gave the Clerk a differently turned version of these events:

Knott showed me his scheme, with which I was greatly impressed, [and] he expressed grave doubts as to whether he could get the drawings done in time and asked me if I could give him a hand. I had 4 weeks holiday leave due and decided to spend that time helping him.

Before sending in the drawings we discussed whether they should be sent in under the joint names which Knott was willing to do. The inception of the scheme being entirely Knott's, I decided it was not fair to expose him to the risk of disqualification owing to my position on the Staff ... Knott then promised to take me into Partnership should anything eventuate.[31]

Although in both versions Collins is careful to limit his role to that of helping to draw out an already matured scheme, as a First Class Assistant in the Constructional Division he had more than a vague idea of what Council and Committee were thinking. The head of this division was Percy Ginham, who was running the County Hall business day-to-day, being briefed by Riley and preparing reports for him to present to Committee. It is difficult to imagine that any other competitor can have had an equal understanding of the drastically altered wants of the Council after March 1907. The Knott-Collins connexion was to be a source of friction with Riley, who referred to Collins subsequently, perhaps ironically, as Knott's 'chief draughtsman'.[32]

Knott's Office

Shortly after winning the County Hall competition Knott set up an office in Adelphi Terrace House (Nos. 1–3 Robert Street), where he was soon joined by Collins, who resigned from the LCC at the end of April 1908. This was effectively a partnership, although not formalized as such in law until 1919, and from 1908 non County-Hall work emanating from the office was credited jointly to Knott and Collins. At County Hall the situation was different. There Knott's *locus standi* was personal, as the 'Selected Architect', and Collins, though he was deeply involved with the County Hall work, had no official standing, even after 1919. When Knott died in 1929, before County Hall was finished, Collins, as his partner and long-time colleague, was the obvious person to succeed him. But he had to be appointed to the post; there was no automatic right of succession to Knott's role inhering in the firm.

Up to the time of Knott's death the signed drawings for County Hall carry his signature, over the designation 'Selected Architect'; after 1929 the drawings are signed E. Stone Collins, above the name 'Knott & Collins'.

The scale of the design drawings required the services of a number of draughtsmen, and by the summer of 1911 there were at least seven assistants working in the office (fig. 15).[33] The most distinguished were Arthur Gordon Shoosmith (1888–1974) and Julian Leathart (1891–1978). Shoosmith, a pupil of Goodhart Rendel and Burnett, went on to become Lutyens's representative at New Delhi between 1920 and 1931.[34] Leathart, who had studied under Beresford Pite, joined the office about 1909, having previously worked for W. D. Caröe, and Nicholson & Corlette. He left Knott in 1915 and after completing his war service worked for Morley Horder and then for Henry Tanner, before setting up his own practice in 1921 with another of Knott's assistants, William Frazer Granger (1888–1969). In 1921 Granger was still working for Knott on County Hall. The Leathart and Granger practice was noted for its 'kinemas' and schools.

Though Knott's career was almost entirely absorbed by the County Hall project, he did carry out a number of smaller jobs, and in 1913 he and Collins found the time to enter the Devonport Guildhall competition. Their entry gained third place, but the standard of draughtsmanship attracted criticism.[35] Among Knott's smaller works were a house in a modified County Hall style in Upper Grosvenor Street, Mayfair (1908–9), and Mallord House, Chelsea, completed in 1911. The Chelsea house, designed for the painter, Cecil Hunt, shows Knott working entirely successfully in a sort of free-style architecture, a brick and tile building containing one or two exaggerated classical elements. It is frequently true that small buildings bring out the best in architects, but these two projects in particular show in Knott an architectural skill which is evident only in one or two parts of County Hall, such as the Members' Entrance and Carriage Drive.[b]

All through its construction, County Hall involved two architectural offices, Knott's office and one representing the LCC. The relations between them were involved and need some clarification. Knott was the 'Selected Architect', Riley the Council's 'Official Architect', and their duties were set out in the Rules of the Competition. Further complication was added by the fact that Riley held a personal appointment for his work on County Hall, distinct from his post as Architect to the Council, which was to mean that when he reached the official retiring age as a Council employee, he could continue as architect for County Hall.[36c]

---

[a]It is hardly surprising that Knott was under pressure, for besides the County Hall drawings he was also working on an entry for the Bethnal Green Municipal Buildings competition, which had to be submitted by 2 September 1907, less than one month after the closing date for County Hall. His entry for Bethnal Green was credited to 'Knott and Round', the latter name unidentified but presumably someone who had assisted Knott with the drawings.[30]

[b]A list of Knott's known works is given in Appendix III.

[c]Riley owed his independent role as Official Architect for County Hall to Knott's insistence on being given a contract. This inspired him to follow Knott's example and ask for similar treatment.

Fig. 15. Postcard sent by Julian R. Leathart in July 1911 to his colleagues in Knott's office, which gives some clues to the number and identity of Knott's assistants: D. Dennington; H. unknown; G. W. F. Granger; Sgn. unknown; Shoo. A. Shoosmith; T. F. T. unknown. The drawing on the obverse shows Leathart himself and 'Old Collard'

If the economical nature of Knott's scheme commended itself to those who were representing a frugal administration in County Hall, the relationship between Riley and any successful competitor must have also been significant. As Riley had reminded the Establishment Committee in 1907, he was to have considerable control of the building's design:

It may not be realised that the conditions make it quite explicit that I am to interpret for the architect who may be selected the planning and internal arrangement of the building, and ... it was the main object of the Establishment Committee who recommended the competition, that an endeavour should be made to unearth a genius who would be able to *elevate and ornament* a building of these pretensions.[37]

This role would be easier with a younger man, without his own standing and reputation. Since by the second stage even the anonymous first stage competitors would have been known by name, if not by design, to the Assessors, the temptation to Riley to avoid experts on municipal buildings, like Warwick & Hall or H. T. Hare, would have been very great.

Changes to Knott's Design

The Assessors' Criticisms

The Assessors had made it clear in their Report that they anticipated that changes would be needed:

As is usual in a competition for a building of this magnitude, all the designs (which after all can be, at this stage, little more than preliminary or sketch designs) show certain discrepancies and irregularities, sometimes in plan, sometimes in elevation ... and any of the designs ... would need modification before being executed ... we wish to record our opinion that the great

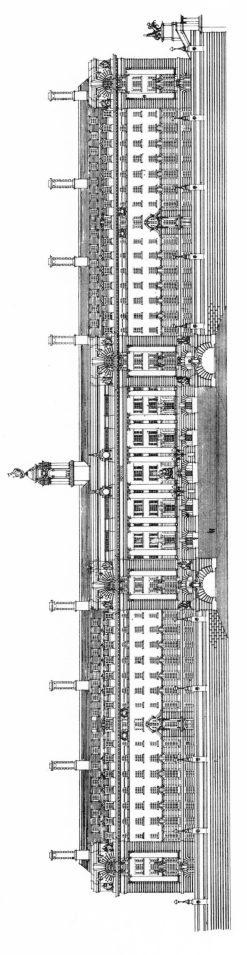

a Elevation to the Thames, showing the central square portico and the steps down to the river

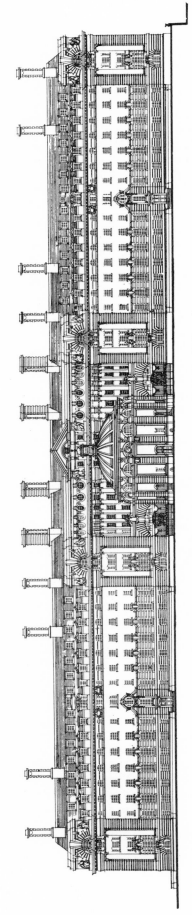

b Elevation to Belvedere Road, with the quasi-detached Public Hall set in a recess

Fig. 16. Ralph Knott's winning design for County Hall, 1908

projection of the centre portion of the river front requires modi-fication, and that the fine flight of steps into the river ... should be omitted.[38]

One can only assume that in Knott's design they felt they had discovered, in Halsey Ricardo's phrase, 'the best conception of how to treat the problem given'. In 1909 Riley told J. D. Gilbert that the winning design was 'a masterly one, owing chiefly to its great simplicity'.[39] If so, the simplicity was perhaps deceptive, and later changes which were forced upon it largely sacrificed that quality.

Halsey Ricardo had concluded that Knott's design could only be called a beginning, 'a counter wherewith to win the competition ... we know ... that it must be re-designed'. He went on to point out how futile such a proceeding made the expense of the competition, in words that must have been welcome to Riley:

an enormous set of conditions, regulations, statements about areas, and the rest of it, is compiled, a suggested plan ... and an actual expenditure of £7,000 in cash ... in order to discover talent. To this expense must be added the expenditure of the ... unsuccessful competitors, which ... comes to close upon £10,000. Had the Council been strong enough to have selected an architect at the first instance, all this labour, this anguish of invention, and ... this expense – had been saved.[40]

In fact, a considerable further 'anguish of invention' was to take place before the Council could approve a final design. Inevitably, it was a long and tedious process, played out as it was between the Selected and Official Architects, the other Assessors, Aston Webb and the increasingly ill and literally jaundiced Norman Shaw, and finally, of course, the Members. Of these the most import-ant was the Chairman of the Establishment Committee, R. C. Norman (1873–1963). Norman (Plate 46c) was an LCC member from 1907 to 1922, Chairman of the Council in 1918–19, and, according to his political opponent Percy Harris, 'by far the ablest man on the Municipal Reformers' side ... always a difficult man to reply to, because he never left a weak spot in his armour'.[41] Brother of the Governor of the Bank of England, Montagu Norman (1871–1950), he was nephew to the conservationist and well-known antiquarian, Philip Norman (1842–1931), also connected with the LCC through his editorship of the *Survey of London*. Norman took over the Chairmanship of the Estab-lishment Committee from March 1908 to March 1910 and remained on the Committee until 1913. He had not thought the Belvedere Road site a good buy, either financ-ially or in terms of the prestige of its location. Nor did he like the fact that compulsory purchase had been resorted to. In his opinion it would have been better for the Council to have bought land in the area by agreement and as it became available, building the county offices piece by piece as need arose. But, as he pointed out, these were questions that 'should have been raised three years ago'.[42]

Once convinced of the quality of Knott's design, Norman was to become one of its principal defenders.[d]

The changes canvassed, both to the external features and the plans, were very extensive, but the very reticence of the scheme presented problems for the Assessors, who considered themselves charged with cutting it down to fit the new Council's brief. Figures 18 and 19 show the way in which Knott's original concept went through several metamorphoses to emerge a very different building from that which won the competition.

Knott proposed a rectangular plan, more or less sym-metrical about its short axis, except for the entrance at Westminster Bridge Road. The most striking feature of the design (figs 13,16) was his treatment of the Belvedere Road front. Here Knott scooped out a great crescent embracing in its centre a free-standing, shallow-domed, circular Public Hall projecting forward of the front line of the building. This was the assembly hall called for by the *Instructions*. Between the hall and the crescent a semi-circular carriage drive, guarded by wrought-iron gates under ornamental arches, led to a *porte-cochère* and the principal entrance. In the view of the *Builder* this was the one point of Knott's design 'which, architecturally considered, may be called a stroke of genius'.[44] The prin-cipal feature on the river front was a massive loggia rising straight from the embankment's edge, and comprising two full-height pavilions joined by an open colonnade of coupled columns. From this loggia down into the river ran the contentious flight of steps which the Assessors in their report said should be done away with. There was not a great deal of floor area within the pavilions as planned – on the Principal Floor they held about half the Members' Library and Reading Room. What they did do, architecturally speaking – as did the Public Hall with its projection eastward from the Belvedere Road front – was to lengthen the building along its short, east-west axis. Knott had chosen this axis for the alignment of all his main spaces, but there was not really room for the many functions required along this route without the employ-ment of some such device. Many competitors, Lutyens and Hare among them, had produced plans organized along the north-south axis, relieving the monotony of that long route with varied spaces, but also 'trespassing' on to the Holloway site. Knott's solution was in fact a very clever one: he could not only fit in a generously sweeping carriage drive which penetrated to the heart of the build-ing, but he could still give comfortable room to the Council Chamber which stood at the centre of his plan. It was all very compact planning, and was given due expression in elevation, as recognized by the *Architect & Contract Reporter*:

Mr Knott is undoubtedly aesthetically right in the elaboration he has bestowed upon the centre of his river front and of his Belvedere Road elevation as compared with the almost brusque

[d]There is a story that when asked by Norman for his frank opinion of Knott's scheme Shaw called it 'the best thing since Wren'.[43]

simplicity of his wings; for the former expresses the existence of the council chamber and the administrative part of the Council's functions, and the latter that the building is mainly the workshop of a numerous staff of employés.[45]

Development of the Design

What such a plan could not tolerate was a lot of whittling down in the length of its principal but shorter axis, and unfortunately this is what it was immediately to suffer. For if the Assessors had felt that the riverside steps were excessive, the Establishment Committee were just as certain that the Public Hall was unwanted, a piece of information Knott received officially on his first visit to see Riley and Norman after winning the competition. During this meeting, on 7 February 1908, Norman told him that there was not the slightest chance of the Public Hall ever being wanted, and that it would strengthen the Committee's hand if they could prepare a plan showing that a building on the site without Holloway's land could accommodate the present staff. Riley made a number of suggestions: that the Council Chamber be moved nearer to Westminster Bridge Road, that it ought to be horse-shoe shaped rather than round, and that the whole plan ought to be wedge-shaped, with the eastern front following the line of Belvedere Road, and the Westminster Bridge Road front having similar angles with both long façades. Knott was given a new schedule of accommodation, and, in Riley's words, 'agreed to take the new schedule and plan away to prepare some sketches and see me again in four days time'.[46] Even if forewarned by Collins, Knott must have felt keenly the rapid transition he had made from fêted artist to servant of the LCC.

In these circumstances, when the brief was being radically altered, major changes in the design of the building were being proposed, and in the light of the Assessors' reference to his winning project as a 'sketch design', it is understandable that Knott felt at liberty to re-design the elevations as well as the plans. At any rate he did so, and difficulties were to arise between himself and the Assessors during the next few years as a result.

Already by the middle of February 1908 the plan was considerably changed, and Knott had added a crescent entrance on the Westminster Bridge Road front. As Riley pointed out, this was 'nearly the same as that shewn on Warwick & Hall's plan' (fig. 8d), and the charge of plagiarism might be levelled at him if this change became known, but Knott responded that 'the disposition to drop the public hall on the Belvedere Road front had robbed him of the reason for such a feature'. While plagiarism was obviously not something Riley wished to encourage, he thought a few hints from other plans would not be amiss, and concluded their second meeting by advising Knott to have a look at the schemes of Hare (fig. 8a), Flockhart, and Jemmett & McCombie (fig. 8b), where he might pick up some useful bits of planning.[47]

Later the same month Riley began his long series of direct interventions, presenting Knott with a plan that his department had prepared which showed a building extending not only over the competition site, but also over the Works Department land to the north.[48] Nothing came of Riley's suggestion, which was obviously strategic and not a proposal intended for immediate execution, but it does raise again the question of building style.

None of the competitors had thought their plans through as extendible, in this or any other direction, even though it was well known that the LCC owned the land north of Holloways, and experience had shown that local authorities had a constantly growing need for accommodation. Had they done so, it is possible that one of them might have thought of producing a more flexible, or at least a less monumental building, to which extensions could be made. The competitors' choice of style is largely explained by the fact that the LCC, like all local government bodies of the time, was expected to prefer monumental architecture. Within the LCC were some of the finest 'Free Style' architects of their generation, and the suspicion must remain that had Riley's department been given the job, perhaps without Shaw's help, they could have produced a fine building and one capable of later extension.

At the same time that Knott was revising his plan, a report by Knott and Riley was before the Finance and Establishment Committees with suggestions for possible savings on the building. On the assumption that the prize-winning scheme could be built for the original sum, it was thought that £48,000 could be saved by omitting the Public Hall, and £128,000 by erecting only so much of the building as would reach the boundary of Holloway's site, leaving an expenditure of £674,000.[49] These attempts at saving money continued for some time. It was hoped that by widening Belvedere Road, and at the same time moving it eastward and enlarging the Council's site, it would be possible to omit Holloway's site from the calculations. At this point the Committee still believed that Holloways might release the Council from their obligation to proceed with the purchase of their lease, and even when it became clear, in March 1908, that they would not do so, the Council decided to lease the site back to them for a number of years. They would build only three quarters of the scheme immediately, 'finishing off the . . . building short of the premises of Holloway Brothers so that it will not present an unfinished and distasteful appearance'.[50] In the event County Hall stood lop-sided on the South Bank for eleven years (Plate 10b).

By 2 July 1908, Knott and Riley were ready to present the Committee with a new plan and elevation, and a perspective by Harold Wyllie (Plate 5a, fig. 18b). They reported that the modifications to the elevations were those proposed by the Assessors:

The central projecting features have been reduced, and are now connected by a segmental shaped colonnade which forms a covered terrace for the use of members approached from rooms devoted to their use on the Principal Floor.

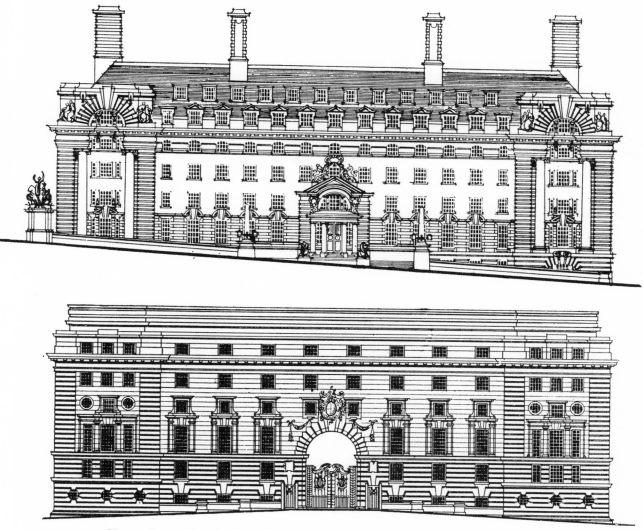

Fig. 17. Competition elevations for the Westminster Bridge Road front of County Hall, 1908, by Ralph Knott (above) and H. T. Hare (below)

The large flight of steps leading from the embankment to the river front of the central bay of the design has been omitted and substituted therefor are the slight projecting segmental bay and flight of steps parallel to the embankment which were adopted by the Committee on the 21st May, 1908.[51]

An attic storey had also been added to the central section, and the much criticized turret or flèche had gone.

These changes were approved by Council in mid-July, but not without debate and minor dissent. The Rev. F. Hastings had thought the earlier design dull and considered the new attempt no better. He had looked at Wyllie's picture of the new façade in the lobby, and thought that if the splendidly drawn barges and the colouring were taken away, the design itself was 'very poor'. Though many Members thought the building less than inspired, Norman, as Chairman of the Establishment Committee, urged the Members not to turn themselves into a 'Committee of Taste'.[52]

The new design was criticized in a letter to *The Times*, in which the pseudonymous correspondent claimed that the altered design, published in July, had occasioned 'much painful surprise and consternation' in art circles. Knott's design had been hailed on all sides as promising, and worthy of the long line of monumental architecture, of noble bridges and palatial buildings, dignifying the Thames from Greenwich to Westminster:

Now, it appears, . . . the river frontage of the selected design is to be shorn of its characteristic motif – the very architectural effect by which . . . the successful competitor triumphantly carried off the blue ribbon of the concours . . . .

As proposed to be altered the design gives place to effects suggestive of two linked cotton-mills with an apologetic architectural feature, apparently appliqué, to form something central . . . A more disastrous result of meddling interference, frustrating an art work of national importance for the frontage of our noble river, can hardly be conceived.[53]

Shaw was upset by this letter, as was Norman, who proposed to write to *The Times* in his own and the Committee's defence. Riley told Knott that he had 'personally received a strong hint to advise [him] to stick to the main features of the successful scheme', and that if he did it might be possible to forestall further correspondence to *The Times*.[54] This presented some difficulties since so much of Knott's work had been criticized by the Assessors.

It is true that changes had been demanded, and possibly an unreasonable number of them. Yet Knott himself had gone far beyond the modifications asked for by the Assessors in altering his design, in many cases entirely on his own initiative. Thus in August 1908 he presented a scheme which had two crescents, one on each long façade, and a dreadfully pinched system of circulation, described by Riley as 'reducing the already narrow site on the waist to something verging on an impossibility' (fig. 18c).[55]

Riley then suggested — and had a drawing ready to illustrate the idea — that Knott's original Belvedere Road feature of a circular hall sitting in a semi-circular recess be shifted to the river front, where the hall would serve as a Council Chamber.[56] He was later to claim that he always considered this part of the winning design to be its most convincing element, and certainly the one which had influenced his vote.[57] When Knott said he liked the idea but could not see how to treat the elevation of the Chamber, Riley produced a photograph of the baroque church of the Madonna di Vico in Piemonte as an exemplar. Knott remained unconvinced, however, and Riley then suggested a crescent on the river front, but without any buildings in it. This idea had emanated from Shaw, as Knott was embarrassed to learn after he had disparaged it.[58e]

Despite the doubts expressed at this October meeting, Knott re-worked his scheme to accommodate the Council Chamber situated in a riverside recess. On 5 January 1909 he presented Riley with a complete set of floor plans except for the basements, which were intended largely for storage. These plans have not survived, but Riley made extensive notes on the scheme, shown in outline in figure 18d. The revised plan had so many entrances and features that it made impossible demands on the site: a shallow recess on the Belvedere Road front remained to contain the main entrance, which was housed behind a *porte-cochère* of 'open columns' forty-three feet high; there was a pedestrian entrance in Westminster Bridge Road, while on the river front was the additional 'very deep recess' some 137 feet across and 103 feet deep. In this recess Knott had placed an elliptical Council Chamber and over it the Members' Library, located, however, as Riley observed, some five floors above the rest of the Members' accommodation. A row of coupled columns across the front of the Chamber and recess provided a Members'

'Shaw's responsibility for the eventual siting of the crescent on the river front was acknowledged by contemporaries like Clough Williams-Ellis.[59]

a Knott's winning competition plan, 1908, with the circular Public Hall in a recess on the Belvedere Road, and the square portico on the river

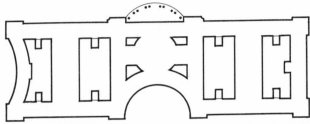

b The amended plan approved by the Council in July 1908, incorporating changes asked for by the Assessors and the Establishment Committee, which included the omission of the Hall and the reduction of the portico

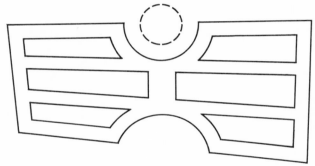

c The 'waisted' plan proposed by Knott in August 1908. The dotted circle indicates the position for the Council Chamber suggested by Riley

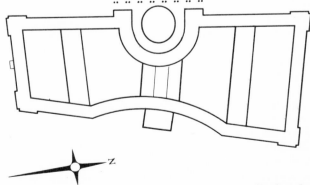

d Knott's 'fan-shaped' scheme of January 1909, showing the Council Chamber on the river front, and the *porte-cochère* entrance on the Belvedere Road front

Fig. 18. The development of the plan of County Hall, 1908–9

Terrace some seventeen feet in width. The circulation for Members was not well planned, while the sheer bulk of the Chamber made it impossible to light the surrounding rooms properly. Riley also had some criticism of the 'radial' or 'fan-shaped' arrangement of the cross-blocks, the irregular courtyards, and the lack of light.[60]

The plan of the County Hall as eventually built seems to have emerged from the meeting of the three Assessors held, without Knott, on 2 February 1909, to consider Knott's plans in the light of whether they complied 'reasonably with the elevations and plans as they intended they should be modified when the award was made'. Under discussion was Knott's revised scheme (fig. 18d). The radial plan was particularly disliked, Shaw going so far as to say afterwards that had it featured in Knott's competition entry he would not have won through to the second stage. The Assessors felt that if the crescent was to be moved from the Belvedere Road front to the river side then a screen of columns should be carried across the front of it, to preserve the 'rectangular disposition of the building on the river front'. They also wanted the Council Chamber to go back 'practically to the axial position on the plan', and the courts 'squared up'. Shaw and Webb both 'expressed the strongest possible desire' for a Members' Entrance in Westminster Bridge Road.[61]

These views were put to Knott two days later, when the main points of discussion were the siting of the Council Chamber and the treatment of the river-front. It was now Riley's turn to be embarrassed, for Knott had produced a clay model of Riley's own suggestion for placing the Chamber in the crescent, and was, in Riley's words, 'somewhat tenacious' in his defence of this arrangement. But the meeting ended with an agreement to take the Chamber out of the crescent. It was also agreed that the crescent itself would be widened and raised and the roof above it lifted up two storeys, the intention being to 'make the heightened central composition unmistakeably the feature of the river front'.[62]

Throughout February and March 1909 these and other points were discussed at meetings involving all the protagonists, in combinations of almost Machiavellian complexity. The Assessors met privately, and together with Knott; the Royal Academicians met individually with Riley, sometimes relaying messages through Percy Ginham; and Norman, as Chairman of the Establishment Committee, had separate meetings with both Knott and Riley.[63]

A plan was produced by Riley to demonstrate the Assessors' ideas, and this was discussed with Knott, though Riley was not allowed to show it to the Establishment Committee.[64] This 'Assessors' plan' (fig. 19a) shows the essential features of County Hall as built, though with two equal-sized courtyards to the south of the centrally placed Council Chamber and a crescent screened by a single row of coupled columns along the river front. Knott made a stand on the question of the 'southern courtyard', where he wanted a smaller court immediately behind the

Westminster Bridge Road front to make room for a large Members' Courtyard to the north, but he accepted in principle the suggestions for the treatment of the river front.[65]

As to the treatment of the colonnade itself there was some disagreement. Knott himself wanted a double colonnade of coupled columns, thus re-instating in a slightly different form a feature which was present in his original design. His two rows of columns were set twenty feet apart, making a covered walkway or Members' Terrace between the pavilions at the ends of the crescent. Shaw did not like this: apart from the question of light he thought the effect in perspective would be a 'jumble' of columns. Webb would have preferred two rows of single columns. Even less did Shaw like Knott's alternative, which dispensed with one of the two screens but doubled up the columns into groups of four. Tempering his criticism with some judicious flattery, Shaw told Riley that the crescent was 'a most delightful piece of design and *entirely* Mr. Knott's!' which it would be 'a pity' – even 'a sin' – to hide behind a screen of columns.[66] At his own Piccadilly Hotel the purpose of the screen of columns had been only to conceal 'a mass of cheap work'.[67]

Another area of disagreement between Knott and the Assessors was the design of the 'angle blocks', that is the pavilions at the corners of the building, where Knott had replaced the original columns with 'massive rustications'. Apart from being 'most unfair' to the Assessors, Shaw felt this change had been 'all in the wrong direction', and he urged the reinstatement of the original, 'very masterly', design.[68]

Neither the design of the angle blocks nor the exact form of the colonnade had been resolved when the Council was asked on 6 April 1909 to approve the revised treatment of the river front. The drawing presented to the Council (and subsequently reproduced in the *Building News*) was an elevation, leaving it unclear whether the screen of coupled columns indicated was single or double.[69] In spite of a protest from the Rev. F. Hastings, who wanted the Council to commission a 'model in a cheap material' before agreeing to any changes, the Council approved the new elevation.[70] Towards the end of the year, however, a far from cheap $\frac{1}{4}$-inch scale model (costing £400) was ordered from the well-known sculpture and modelling firm of Mabey to help settle the still unresolved features of the design (Plate 5c).[71] Knott, meanwhile, was working up a perspective of the river front for exhibition at the Royal Academy, which clearly showed his intended treatment of the double colonnade (Plate 5b). Knott's perspective was reproduced in both the *Builder* and the *Building News* in 1910, the latter also publishing a plan in which the Members' Courtyard and the organization of Members' accommodation appear virtually as built (fig. 19b).[72]

Following the delivery of Mabey's model in July 1910 the Establishment Committee was asked to decide on two 'outstanding points' – the design of the 'angle blocks', and the screen of columns across the crescent, both features

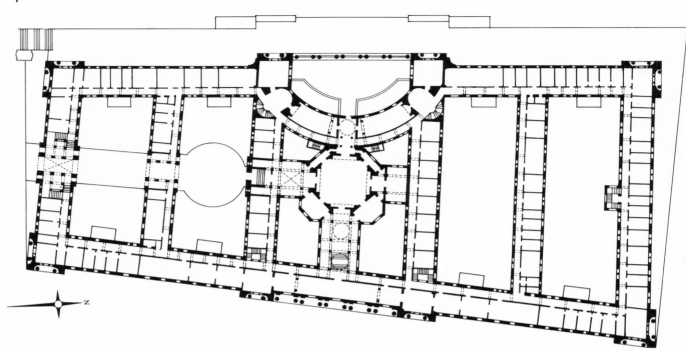

a The Assessors' suggested plan of March 1909, showing the Westminster Bridge Road entrance and Members' Courtyard, and the riverside Crescent screened by a single row of columns

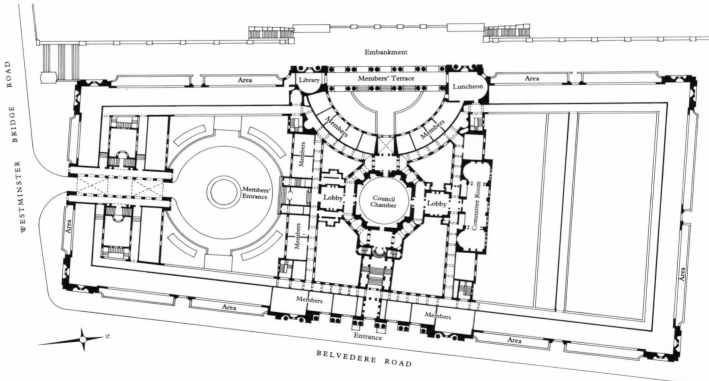

b Knott's plan published in 1910, showing a double row of columns across the Crescent, Carriage Drive and enlarged Members' Courtyard. The planning of the central Section A is shown virtually as built

Fig. 19. The development of the plan of County Hall, 1909–10

having been made removable on the model.[73] Knott's revised treatment of the pavilions was allowed to stand, but the question of the colonnade was a more difficult matter. Discussions, with visits to Mabey's studio to view the model, continued throughout the summer and autumn, culminating in an Assessors' report to the Establishment Committee in October 1910 which suggested either reducing the colonnade to a single screen of columns or omitting it altogether and carrying 'the Order round the segmental crescent'. The Assessors' preference was for leaving out the colonnade as this would give 'a far more valuable architectural treatment and get rid of all objection to the destruction of light'. Knott still favoured the double colonnade, but preferred to lose this feature completely rather than see it reduced. The Assessors called for a new 'part-model' to show the 'architectural treatment' of the crescent without the colonnade.[74] In April 1911 a photograph of the revised model (Plate 5c) was shown to the Council with a recommendation from the Establishment Committee that the Council should approve the omission 'of the cross colonnade in the centre portion of the river front', and the carrying of the 'order' round the crescent. The Committee reported that the Assessors thought the modified design was 'a considerable improvement on that approved on 6th April 1909'. Knott had acquiesced in the modification, expressing the opinion that the amended design would form 'an entirely satisfactory elevation'. The 1909 design was accordingly rescinded and the new one approved.[75]

Though 'consequential adjustments' were necessary, the main lines of the County Hall design were at last settled, at least as far as the southern three-quarters of the building were concerned, on which construction had already in fact begun. In its final form the crescent with its attached columns was not unlike C. H. Reilly's unsuc-cessful entry (fig. 20), published in November 1907,[76] which Shaw and Riley would have seen at the first stage of the competition. It is said that Reilly was convinced Knott had stolen the design of the crescent from his elevation, and was so outraged he never spoke to Knott again.[77]

The building which emerged from this long and many-faceted revision was a more sophisticated and interesting one than Knott's original competition entry (folded drawings A and B between pp. 62-3 and 110-11). The planning, which originally had been very close to the 'suggested plan', had been refined to provide a Members' Entrance and Carriage Drive into the heart of the building, the embankment had been retained, but the Members' Terrace had been set back and a public thoroughfare provided along the river. The residual 'docks', which led Riley to assume that coal would come into the building by barge,[78] had disappeared, and vehicular access was to be from the northern side of the building. The design of the two fronts of the building had been virtually reversed – the square colonnade which had been the most striking feature on the river front had become the main element on the Belvedere Road front, while the deep circular entrance on the east had been transmuted into the shallower crescent of the river front. The elevation had become plainer and simpler: not only did much of the rich baroque decoration of the original design never materialize (fig. 24) but the pavilions, with the exception of those in the centre, lost their columns. The decision not to build immediately on the northern quarter of the site was to open the way to further variation of the original design in the late 1920s when the northern front was finally put in hand.

Early on in his struggles Knott gained an ally in Norman, who began to make frequent visits to Knott's office, where they would discuss the Committee's views and require-

Fig. 20. C. H. Reilly's competition design for County Hall. Perspective sketch of May 1907

ments out of Riley's earshot. The two men, only five years apart in age, seem to have formed a friendship outside the LCC job, with Knott spending some time in Norman's country house, Moor Place, at Much Hadham in Hertfordshire.[79] These informal meetings were an added source of friction with Riley. 'My present impression', he noted in November 1908, 'is that all the matters he [Knott] brings to me have been settled between him & the Chairman of the Establishment Committee before he comes'.[80] A certain stiffness developed between the two architects, not least because of what Riley must have seen as a

vindication of his earlier advice against a competition. As Ricardo had written in his review of the competition, 'the public, ignorant of what architecture really is, naturally underrates the value of experience, and is ready to back youth and liveliness against practice and resource'.[81] Whether youth and liveliness were not being to a large degree stifled by practice and resource is another question. An equally important point is that all this took time, pushing the start of building work back to a period when it would be seriously affected by economic difficulties in the building trade, and by the First World War.

Sketch of the base of one of the bronze lamp-standards on the Ceremonial Stairs which were made by the Bromsgrove Guild

CHAPTER V

The Building of County Hall 1909–1922

Work began on the construction of County Hall in 1909, before either elevations or internal planning had been finalized. Considerable delays resulted, partly because of the clumsy dual responsibility of the architects, and partly through unforeseen problems over the construction of such a massive building on the riverside site. However, not only the river wall and foundation slab, but to some extent the substructure, were sufficiently independent of the superstructure to allow construction to begin before the design of the latter had been fully thought out.

The general plan of construction (fig. 21) was to erect a coffer dam up to the boundary with Holloways' premises, behind which the embankment wall could be built, and then to clear the site of made ground and Thames mud by excavation – about 19 feet in all – and lay a five-foot thick concrete foundation 'raft' on top of the ballast which underlies the area. Over and above the structural advantages of this scheme on a piece of littoral with uncertain bearing strength and stability, the slab gave complete flexibility for the planning and setting out of the building (Plate 6).

The immense task of constructing the building presented problems of its own. These were made more serious as the process of designing fell far behind in relation to site works. Riley suggested to Knott in the summer of 1909 that the contract for the construction of the building itself might be split into two sections: the first to cover substructure and the building up to ground floor level (including foundations and two basements); and the second to cover superstructure - the remaining, more complicated and contentious part of the building. Knott immediately acknowledged the advantages of this idea, and there is no doubt that the building was completed more quickly as a result of this separation of contracts.[1] In addition the building was divided vertically into Sections and Blocks (fig. 22), on which work started progressively.

The Embankment Wall

The contract for building the embankment wall was won, in October 1908, by Price & Reeves, of Waterloo Place.[2] They began by erecting the coffer dam, starting work on this in January 1909. The dam was closed on 10 September and the area behind it cleared of water during the following week. It was a single-pile construction, consisting of a row of 600 tongued-and-grooved timber piles, 14 inches square, driven through 4 feet of mud and 11 feet of ballast into the clay, 'until their points were 9 feet below what would be the bottom of the new wall'.[3]

The wall itself, on which work began in September 1909, is an impressive structure, similar in its main features to the embankment wall in front of St Thomas's Hospital (Plates 8b, 9b). Built of concrete founded on clay, it is faced with ashlar work of Aberdeen and Cornish granite and surmounted by a granite parapet. The engineering work and overall design of the wall were the responsibility of the LCC's Chief Engineer, Maurice Fitzmaurice, who also supervised its construction, Knott's contribution being limited to designing the architectural features of the central section.[4] The massive ornamental bronze mooring-rings of lions' and horses' heads (Plate 31a,b) were modelled by the sculptor Gilbert Bayes on Knott's recommendation (see page 59).[5] The wall was completed in September 1910 at a cost of £58,090, some £4,500 below the contract price.[6]

Foundations and Substructure

The contract for the construction of the raft foundation had been awarded to F. & H. F. Higgs in April 1909.[7] The late departure of Lambeth Borough Council from the site delayed demolition work, and further problems arose because of friction with Price & Reeves over access. A technical problem arose too. Behind the coffer dam a deep foundation trench was dug, and the gap strutted on to the unexcavated foreshore. When Higgs began their excavation at this point, they faced the prospect of a collapsing coffer dam (Plate 6a,b). These problems were eventually overcome, but, together with flooding of the excavation, they increased the original contract sum of £46,900 by nearly £5,000.[8]

The work was also considerably delayed. The contract had divided the raft into two sections, from Holloways' boundary to the southern boundary of the Lambeth site, and from there to Westminster Bridge Road. The intention was to build the centre section of County Hall first, and to gain time by dividing up the foundation and substructure work. Although Higgs's whole contract was finished only four months late, on 3 October 1911, Section A was delayed by 13 months – from 7 June 1910 to 5 July 1911.[9]

Discovery of the Roman Boat

During excavations for the raft, in May 1910, the sub-

Fig. 21. Outline plan of County Hall, and the New County Offices (North and South Blocks), showing the relationship to the existing street plan. Much of the east side of Belvedere Road (Narrow Wall) was demolished for road widening after the building of County Hall

stantial remains of a Roman boat were uncovered on the foreshore. Theories about its origin have varied, from the initial one of a galley, sunk in a battle between Allectus and Constantius, AD 296, to a ferry boat holed in old age by her own mooring post. The modern view is that it is an authentic Roman 'round-bottomed ocean-going' boat with a 'protruding keel'.[10]

The discovery was apparently made by F. L. Dove, a former Chairman of the Establishment Committee. In January 1910, while inspecting the excavation for the concrete raft with R. C. Norman, Dove noticed a dark curved line in the face of the excavation, which the workmen suggested was a sunken barge, but he realized that it must be of considerable antiquity, and should be treated with care. Removal of the soil revealed the 'remains of a Roman boat, carvel-built of oak, lying N.E.-S.W., its bow towards the shore', 19 feet below high water. It measured approximately 38 feet in length, and about 18 feet in beam.[11] The vessel was protected *in situ* and then stored by the Council, eventually finding its way into the Museum of London.

Progress of the Building Programme

The delay to the contract caused by Higgs's late finish was more theoretical than real as there were other problems. A major difficulty was that the design details and even the method of construction were not yet finalized, partly due to the activities of the Assessors, and partly to a fruitless attempt by Knott to persuade Riley to adopt new methods of construction. Knott expended months of effort attempting to convince Riley of the wisdom of using a reinforced-concrete floor structure. Riley, being responsible for this part of the design, was extremely critical of Knott's proposal to use a patent flooring system. He argued so strongly, always backed by structural and cost calculations, that Knott eventually gave in and a system of steel joists with concrete casing and infill was adopted.[12]

The only stanchions and girders of heavy construction are in Block 2, the area occupied by the Main Committee Room, where the upper floors are built above large clear spans over the boiler room. Because the architectural style is of a massive nature, load-bearing brickwork seemed the obvious choice and the idea of using steelwork generally for vertical structure was ruled out virtually from the beginning. The roof, however, is steel framed, with plate girders built up in curved sections from the top of the brickwork at fifth-floor level to form the structure of the sixth floor as well as the roof slope (Plate 9a). Walling is generally of London stock brickwork, with blue engineering bricks set in sand and cement where loading demanded higher strength. The clearest sense of how County Hall is built is to be felt in the sub-basement, where the heavy solidity of the building is apparent in the massive piers visible in corridors of painted brickwork.

Drawings for the substructure were by no means ready for sending out to tender in the middle of 1910. Although Riley complained in the autumn of 1909 that Knott's revisions to the design had already held up the works by nine months,[13] it will be seen from events described in the last chapter that many design changes were still to come. But in mid-June 1910 Riley's schedule still foresaw Knott's drawings coming into his office at the end of August. These would be checked by Riley, given to the quantity surveyors at the end of October, and work would begin at the end of March 1911. Allowing fifteen months for substructure works, it was estimated that the whole building (Sections A, B and C) would be completed towards the end of 1915. To save time, Riley recommended the procedure, eventually adopted, of asking contractors for both sub- and superstructure contracts to quote for Section A, and to agree the construction of Sections B and C at the same rates, thus saving the time and expense of preparing new bills of quantities and getting tenders for those parts of the building.

While Riley undoubtedly hoped that the 1915 completion date would be met, the Establishment Committee were warned in June 1910 that this might have to be modified because of unexpected difficulties.[14] A major problem was Knott's slowness in providing drawings, compounded by the cumbersome method by which they were then checked in Riley's office.

Knott had originally promised to deliver drawings of the whole building by October 1909. Two firms of quantity surveyors, John Leaming & Sons and J. Rider Hunt & Company, were chosen by tender in February of the following year, but still had nothing to work on. At the beginning of June 1910 Knott was only promising substructure drawings at the end of that month. Steelwork drawings were of particular importance, and although some of these were being delivered, subsequent changes meant that many, having been checked and sent to the quantity surveyors, were rendered useless, because of altered loadings. Riley complained at the end of November that he still had not received small-scale plans of the building, dealing with drainage, ventilation, water supply, means of escape, and so on. He warned that dealing with matters of detail before more general questions were settled, 'involves considerable risk of alterations being required . . . later on'.[15]

Plans and sections of the whole building were finally delivered by Knott on 20 January 1911,[16] nearly fourteen months after they had been requested by Riley. Nevertheless, changes were still required, some of them substantial. Thus the height of the Council Chamber – 100 feet in Knott's original scheme – was only reduced to its eventual height of about 50 feet in March 1911.[17]

Substructure tenders for Section A were presented to the Council on 25 July 1911. Charles Wall Limited won the contract with the lowest tender of £47,738, considerably below Riley's estimate of £56,000, and at the same time it was agreed to award them the contract for Sections B and C as well, at an estimated cost of £104,000.[18] By early December the brick piers beneath the Council Chamber were built up to a height of 12 feet and some steel joists and girders were being fixed at basement-floor level. The average number of men on the site was 68, most of whom were bricklayers.[19]

The Establishment Committee were very concerned about the delays. At a meeting in December 1911, Isidore Salmon, the Vice-Chairman, complained that it would be nearly three months before the working drawings for the Council Chamber block would be ready for the contractor. Both Riley and Knott were asked to explain the delay, the former blaming the latter, and the latter the changes made by the Assessors and the illness of Norman Shaw.[20]

A few months later a revised completion date – the end of 1917 – was put forward,[21] and the matter was discussed at length in Council. Edward Smith, a Progressive Member of the Establishment Committee, declared that the present condition of affairs was a crying scandal and the LCC was the laughing-stock of London. He referred

Sections: B   A   C   D

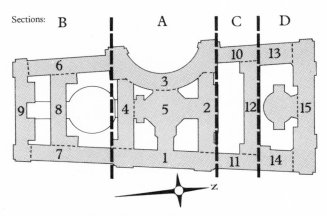

Fig. 22. Plan of County Hall showing the division of the building into Blocks (numbered) and Sections (lettered) for construction purposes

sarcastically to the arrangement by which Riley had responsibility for checking Knott's steelwork drawings, and the inevitable delays and disagreements which arose as a result.[22]

If in public Riley did nothing to diminish the feeling that Knott was to blame, in private he said it outright. However, with a growing feeling that adverse criticism of one architect would reflect badly on both, or that Knott might snap back, Riley began to find other reasons for the lack of progress on the building. He made the point that there had been a coal strike, preventing the manufacture of bricks, and in early June 1912 a dock strike began, stopping delivery of any materials. He was also quick to point out the value of his suggestion to split the contract into sub- and superstructure, contrasting it with Knott's delays over various points, like the 'extension of the Crescent' or the construction of floors.[23] When comparisons were made with other sites, Riley provided Salmon with ammunition about other London buildings which were behindhand including various government contracts, such as the War Office, which took over six years to build.[24]

In June 1912, dissatisfaction at the lateness of the drawings led Edward Smith to threaten to move the adjournment of the Council if the complete superstructure drawings were not delivered as promised on 9 July. This date was met, though Knott delivered only the complete general drawings, saying that he had always meant to supply only those and not the details as well. He got away with this, though the Council rather felt they had been deceived by the qualification.[25]

Confidence was partly restored, however, and at the Council meeting on 16 July, when Smith asked facetiously if any steps were being taken to secure the erection of the new County Hall within the next 10 years, Salmon, now Committee Chairman, was ready with a revised schedule. Tenders for the first section of the superstructure would be invited in January 1913, construction would begin in April, and it was hoped to complete the whole building by midsummer 1916,[26] an improvement of roughly eighteen

months on the completion date given only four months earlier.

There is no obvious reason for Knott's slow progress with the drawings. If we had any record of his version of events, to oppose or balance Riley's detailed records, the reasons might become clear. It seems evident, however, that Knott was spending a disproportionate time in redesigning the scheme, and doing so in an unsystematic way. Riley pointed out on several occasions that Knott was working out detailed arrangements of groups of rooms without reference to what was happening elsewhere in the plan. The problems could well have been caused by his inexperience. He had virtually opened his career with one of the largest commissions of the Edwardian period and could hardly have been expected to deal efficiently with such a complex problem. It was here that Knott needed, but did not always welcome, the help which Riley's experience and technical skill could provide. The friction between the two men was seized upon by some politicians and sections of the press as an important factor contributing to the delay, Knott and Riley being seen as more interested in quarrelling than in getting on with the job in hand.

The question of who was to blame for the delay was to simmer on as a political issue long after it had ceased to have any practical significance. In 1913 Salmon defended the Municipal Reformers' record over the new County Hall, blaming the Progressives, and claiming that the greatest delay had taken place because of the competition and the three years taken to find, select and appoint an architect. Norman, too, was inclined to put the blame on the competition and on the choice of a young and inexperienced architect.[27] The Progressives were held to be responsible because they had devised the 'system of the two architects', an implication vigorously repudiated by Percy Harris and Edward Smith, who implied the real reason for delays was that the two architects did not get on, and that this in itself was, 'a crushing condemnation of the Moderates' business capacity'.[28]

The Laying of the Foundation Stone

By March 1912 the works were sufficiently advanced for King George V, accompanied by Queen Mary, to lay the foundation stone. There was some discussion about where the ceremony should be held. It was suggested that the stone might be laid in a convenient place and relaid in a prominent one at a later date, but the idea was rejected as unconventional. So a permanent location had to be chosen, one that was visible either on the outside of the building or on the Principal Floor inside it. The latter seemed the only practical solution, and the stone – a large block of Iona marble – was laid in the north-east lobby adjacent to the Council Chamber (fig. 31) on Saturday 9 March 1912 (Plate 7a,b). Edward White, Chairman of the Council, and Maurice Fitzmaurice, the Chief Engineer, were knighted on the occasion. The ceremonial tools used for laying the stone are among the finest artefacts commissioned by the Council. The trowel was designed and made by students of the Central School of Arts and Crafts, and the mallet, plumb-rule and spirit-level by the Bromsgrove Guild of Applied Arts (Plate 7c–e).[29]

The Erection of the Superstructure

Shortly after the foundation stone was laid, the Council considered ways of speeding the works along. It was hoped to time things so that the superstructure could be begun immediately the substructure was complete – estimated as mid-April 1913. One suggestion was to invite contractors to submit alternative tenders for three- and two-year periods of construction, with a bonus for each week saved on the contract time. However, no contractor was interested in such an arrangement so, as with the substructure, bills of quantities were prepared for Section A only, and tenderers were asked on what conditions they would be prepared to take on the work for Sections B and C. While other firms submitted lower prices for Section A, Holland & Hannen and Cubitts agreed to do all three sections at the same rates and this brought their overall price below the rest, at an estimated £968,211.[a]

The contract with Holland & Hannen and Cubitts was signed on schedule in April 1913. Knott made such good progress with the drawings for the other two sections that these were issued to the contractors in mid-June.[31] Moreover, completion of the substructure was sufficiently advanced by the end of August 1913 to allow Holland & Hannen and Cubitts to make a start.[32]

While construction was under way, minor changes were being made to the internal organization of County Hall. Many suggestions were offered, the most ambitious and romantic coming from R. M. Sebag-Montefiore, a Municipal Reformer, who wanted the Establishment Committee to consider 'the advisability of providing a roof garage for the use of members' aeroplanes'. F. L. Dove, the Committee Chairman, replied that, as aviation was not yet an 'exact science', the river would make a safer landing place.[33] More mundane but more practical were Salmon's efforts to organize staff restaurants and locate committee rooms where they would be most useful.

Isidore Salmon (1876–1941) was Chairman and Managing Director of the well-known caterers J. Lyons, who were at the time expanding rapidly. Their Strand Palace Hotel had opened in 1909, and both the Regent Palace Hotel and Strand Corner House were to open in 1915. These projects made him well qualified to superintend catering arrangements for the new County Hall.

The building of County Hall was dogged by bad luck, as well as by unfortunate politics. Having missed their chance to build during the last years of a period of stable prices before 1895, the LCC held their competition just as costs began to rise at an increased rate after 1906. By the time a start was made on construction, widespread strikes and lockouts prevailed, making progress slow and erratic. The coal and dock strikes of 1912 have already been mentioned; two years later came the so-called Triple Alliance of miners, railway men and transport workers, each agreeing to support the others in strike action. 1914 also saw the famous strike and lockout in the building industry brought about by employers' use of non-union labour. A principal reason for union solidarity, and of this strike in particular, was the growing numbers of tradesmen who were being put out of work by new processes and methods of construction.[34] The employers, the Master Builders Association, reacted to the strike by locking out all workers who were unwilling to sign a document which would bind them to ignore blackleg labour. This ploy, designed to lure blackleg workers and often used successfully in previous disputes, was less successful on this occasion; few competent workmen would sign, and the strike dragged on.[b]

In addition to the waste of public money involved, and the political embarrassment, Council staff were increasing at a rate unforeseen when building work began, and space was urgently needed. Between 1908 and 1911 there had been an increase of 16 per cent from 2,100 to 2,441; Sections A, B and C would hold only 2,270.[36]

The strike hurt. After years of underspending on the capital vote for County Hall, the beginning of 1914 had seen the job moving ahead at last. From the 68 men employed on site in December 1911, the number had risen to 560 in January 1914, with 139 at work on the substructure and the remainder employed on the super-

[a]Tenders were submitted for Section A, Section A with some work omitted (A*), and Sections A, B and C. The six lowest of the thirteen received were:-

	A	A*	A,B,C
Holland & Hannen and Cubitts	£542,870	£518,871	£968,211
W.E.Blake Ltd	£543,000	£516,646	£978,069
Chas. Wall Ltd	£537,000	£519,756	£979,422
Trollope & Colls	£535,602	£516,314	£986,672
Holliday & Greenwood	£545,500	£527,784	£988,755
G.E.Wallis & Sons	£549,849	£528,136	£988,981

The overall prices reflect the conditions stipulated by the tenderers for undertaking Sections B and C; e.g. Trollope & Colls wanted an extra five per cent for this work over the rates for Section A.[30]

[b]Holland & Hannen and Cubitts were reluctant to employ blackleg labour at County Hall, partly because they were afraid of getting such a large contract 'blacked', but also because of the poor quality of blackleg labour.[35]

structure contract, 250 of them on site and 171 in outside yards.[37] Now all that came to a halt. Settlement of the strike was being slowly worked out when the declaration of war in August 1914 ended all strikes practically overnight. However, the County Hall schedule had slipped by some four months.

Extension of the County Hall Site

In the autumn of 1912 the Committee had decided to take possession of Holloway Brothers' site for building Section D. The Council were bound to give two years' notice of their intention to end Holloways' lease, and 1914 was one of the optional years for acquisition.[38] Early in 1914 Salmon had told Riley that he wanted to be ready to begin Section D (fig. 22) 'the moment Holloway Brothers vacate'. Riley assumed that the working drawings for the raft foundations were well forward, and that Knott's sub- and superstructure drawings for the section were also ahead of schedule.[39] Knott provided drawings for the preparation of bills of quantities in July, and a contract for the river wall extension was signed towards the end of the month with Morrison & Mason of Glasgow, for £23,000, although work began only after war had been declared, on 17 August.[40c]

The Effect of the Great War

The war's initial impact was not on manpower but on supplies, and the County Hall job was fairly well stocked in many areas. As late as March 1916 there were still 400 men at work,[42] though the northern extensions of the embankment wall had fallen behind schedule. Because of military demand for the railways, moving granite up from Cornwall for the wall was proving difficult and only about 20 per cent of the contract value had been executed.[43]

Even so, work to the building was progressing as never before, and in December 1915 the contractors were estimating that the roof would be on by the following June. But this optimism was misplaced: when an expenditure of £200,000 on the building in 1916 was suggested, the Comptroller pointed out that there was a Treasury objection to spending on building because it tied up scarce labour needed for the armed forces, and competed with projects needed for the war, and that work would probably have to stop once the building was covered in.[44]

The Council was of course in direct competition with the Ministry of Munitions, which wanted builders in great quantity for the construction of factories. The Ministry had been formed in the early part of 1915 under Lloyd George, and County Hall, as one of the largest office developments in London, was not to escape its attentions.

The building first suffered when the contractors took men off because the supply of materials dwindled. Holland & Hannen and Cubitts had written to the Council in March 1915 proposing suspension of works, but were told that they must continue as best they could and that the architects would consider claims for an extension of time.[45] The contractors argued that there were insufficient materials to continue the job properly, and negotiations went on until, on 24 January 1916, Riley caught their men dismantling a crane without the Council's permission. He was told that they had been ordered to do this by the Ministry of Munitions. Riley ought to have known that with Henry Holloway in that very Ministry, busily earning his knighthood, he was unlikely to get very far. His protest was met by a Ministry letter ordering a complete stop to the works under the Defence of the Realm Act.[46]

Wartime occupation of County Hall

There is little doubt that the move to stop work at County Hall was ill-timed, although there is some reason for believing the LCC view that the Ministry was influenced to act by Holland & Hannen and Cubitts, if not by Holloway.[47] It can be argued that the completion of the building would have served the war effort as well as complete cessation. Besides wanting men and equipment to build munitions factories, the Ministry needed somewhere to house its burgeoning administrative staff, which was to grow from nothing to 65,000 by the end of the war. The Government had already taken over and occupied many London buildings. The new County Hall would make an ideal place for the Ministry for exactly the same reasons that it suited the LCC; but it was unfinished. There were no doors, no windows, no partitions or plastering. It was a shell, and there was no question of its being immediately habitable.

After necessary work had been done to close the contract, the building stood idle for almost a year. Knott's office was running down as his staff enlisted.

> The office is like the ten little nigger boys, one by one they disappear, & I think the final end of the County Hall stint will be a mass of drawings, mostly torn, & every one in the wrong drawer, possibly a skeleton of a bulky person will be lying near (tho' not near enough to be of use) supposed by its bulkiness to be Collins. If any survivors are found, they would of course be redrawing the seating in the Council Chamber.[48]

Knott himself joined the Royal Flying Corps at the end of 1916, and spent the war designing 'shops' for them. However, he was stationed in London and hoped to visit his office in the evenings to take care of the little business there was to be dealt with.[49]

In February 1917, the Principal Architect to the Office of Works had a look around the partly completed building,

---

[c]Henry Holloway took advantage of the wartime emergency to frustrate the Council's intentions by writing a personal letter to Lloyd George, informing him that their business was moving out of the riverside works, and suggesting that the premises could be used for munitions.[41]

and was critical of the Ministry of Munitions' decision to stop work on County Hall.[50] Early in March Riley reported that the Office of Works wanted to take over Sections A and B from basement to third-floor level, and works were soon in hand to fit up these areas.[51]

Next in line was the Food Controller, who wanted various rooms on the Principal Floor for a Food Economy Exhibition, which took place in the summer of 1917 – the first public function to take place at the new County Hall. Many government departments and other organizations contributed. As *The Times* reported:

the new L.C.C. Hall will be given over to working exhibits, practical demonstrations and lectures dealing with every phase of national economy and welfare. The Council chamber is to be transformed into a French market where London housewives may study the shopping methods of our allies. A war economy restaurant conducted by the Savoy Hotel management will be installed in a series of rooms and terraces overlooking the Thames and in the Great Courtyard, where the Ministry of Munitions occupies the Central Stand; open air concerts will be given by bands of the British Army.[52]

By November 1917 the Army Council was fitting up the rest of the building for occupation by up to 1,900 Ministry of Food staff.[53]

To mark the end of the war, fireworks were launched from the roof of County Hall on Saturday 16 November 1918, provided naturally enough by the Ministry of Munitions.[54d]

If the LCC thought they would get all this back when the war ended they were badly mistaken. Not only was the Ministry of Food staying put in the spring of 1919, but having given up occupation of Grosvenor House, Mayfair, to the Ministry of Pensions they were concentrating their forces at County Hall.[56] In May of that year 134,400 square feet were occupied as government offices and a further 112,900 square feet used as storage.[57]

Construction work could, of course, continue while the building was part occupied, and an arrangement was made for Holland & Hannen and Cubitts to complete their contract at cost plus a fixed profit. Building operations resumed in mid-May 1919 (Plate 8c), despite the wartime removal of plant and scaffolding, and by the end of the month 110 men were back at work.[58] However, the LCC itself was desperate for office space and wanted to transfer its own staff there. During the war the Government had taken over other Council premises, and because of a staff depletion during the war, the leases of yet other buildings had not been renewed. Now the staff was growing again. Further, as the Clerk, James Bird (Plate 11), pointed out, the LCC was under pressure to contribute to post-war reconstruction: 'the Ministry of Labour [was] pressing us to go on with the New County Hall; the Local Government Board pressing us to begin Housing; and the Ministry of Education probably looking for an early resumption of the 40 and 48 suspended schemes'.[59] The staff of the LCC

was to grow now much more rapidly than had been foreseen before the war, indeed, to a large extent as a result of it.

Repossession of County Hall

During the war elections had not been contested, and the Progressives under the Rev. J. Scott Lidgett and the Municipal Reformers under Norman formed a coalition administration on the lines of that at Westminster. The first post-war election was held in March 1919. The Progressives had agreed not to contest many seats if the Municipal Reformers would incorporate certain Progressive material in their manifesto. At the last minute this agreement was cancelled, and the election went ahead on party lines. A Municipal Reform victory resulted, but at the same time the first significant Labour group of fifteen Members was elected.

One subject united both major parties. They were demanding an extension of the geographical area under Council control, as well as higher government grants for such work as housing, and a generally strengthened central local authority for London. The Government was hesitant even to discuss these matters, the Prime Minister Lloyd George refusing for some months to receive an LCC delegation headed by Norman and Lidgett. The Ministry of Health, which had replaced the Local Government Board in 1919, later set up a Royal Commission – the Ullswater Commission – to consider if any changes were needed, but its report in 1923 did not advocate any.

The Municipal Reformers' 'centralist' phase was to last until 1922, when the London Municipal Society challenged for the right to make Municipal Reform policy, and won. Thereafter the LMS ideal of a weak central authority in London combined with strong local boroughs would be Municipal Reform doctrine.

This was an uneasy period in relations between the LCC and central government, partly because of the LCC's demands for reform and the government's resistance to it. There was also pressure on the LCC to deal with the urgent post-war issues of housing and education. The tension engendered did not help the Council in its struggle to repossess its partly completed headquarters.[60]

The Ministry of Food were understandably hesitant to quit premises on which they had spent £100,000, but of which they had had little use.[61] The Council's patience was nevertheless wearing thin. At the beginning of June 1919, they sent a deputation to meet Sir Alfred Mond (1868–1930), the First Commissioner of Works. An extremely successful manufacturer in the chemical industry and one of the founders of ICI, Mond had been responsible for the building during the war, but now he came to the LCC's aid, promising a gradual reduction of the 1,000 Ministry of Food staff over the next few months, with complete withdrawal by the end of September.[62]

d County Hall itself had been a minor casualty of the war, suffering slight damage in an air raid in September 1917.[55]

With this problem finally resolved the Council could plan the completion of County Hall.

Knott had been discharged from the Royal Air Force in January 1919. It seems the war had a softening effect on the previously brittle relationship between himself and Riley and the job proceeded smoothly thereafter. Riley, who had been due to retire as Architect to the Council in 1918, had been kept on for an extra year because of the war.[63] Amid protests from the Department, his post went to George Topham Forrest (1873–1945), a Scot, who had worked in the North and for Essex County Council. He was Architect to the Council from 1919–1935 (Plate 11).[64] Riley's retirement did not affect his involvement in the County Hall project, for which he retained his personal appointment. Although this was an anomaly, no-one could have foreseen in 1907 that the building would still be unfinished twelve years later. He was given administrative assistance and a room at County Hall, a reasonable one at first and later a small and viewless one – room 524a, on the crescent, behind the cornice.

County Hall now began to take on the image of an important public building. By July 1919 349 men were working on the contract, a number which kept steady through the autumn. In October it was reported that over 6,000 cubic feet of Portland stone had been fixed, together with a large number of marble columns, plinths, pilasters and wall linings in the Council Chamber and lobbies. In other areas, structural work was being disrupted by lack of steel due to coal and rail strikes. The building had reached fifth-, and in some places, sixth-floor level.[65] Other decisions were being taken over the decorative finishes of the Principal Floor, where a large number of rooms were under completion. In this area, some pre-war decisions on finishes and decoration were revised, the whole floor not being completed until well after the official opening date in 1922.

The Establishment Committee were able to meet in County Hall, the first committee to do so, in July 1919, though it must be said that they resumed meeting at Spring Gardens immediately after.[66] Staff from the Architect's Department started moving in the summer, and by early September the whole department was in the new building.[67]

By March 1921 over a thousand men were on the job, the highest number ever. The roof structure was up, windows were being fixed, and the marble work to the Ceremonial Staircase was nearing completion.[68] By October the *Evening News* could report the installation of the Education Department from their offices on the Embankment, to be followed by part of the Comptroller's Department, and before Christmas by the Librarian:

But it has been a long business. It is now thirteen years since the plans were accepted. During that time Londoners have grown weary of watching the slow progress of the great new structure.

The present generation has grown up to believe in an incomplete LCC hall, and it will take years to change their convictions.[69]

Nevertheless, County Hall was being completed at a time of growing optimism, the beginning of 'normal times' after the years of war and post-war hardship. The official opening in July 1922 was to be a royal occasion which gave Londoners an opportunity to see their long-promised Hôtel de Ville.

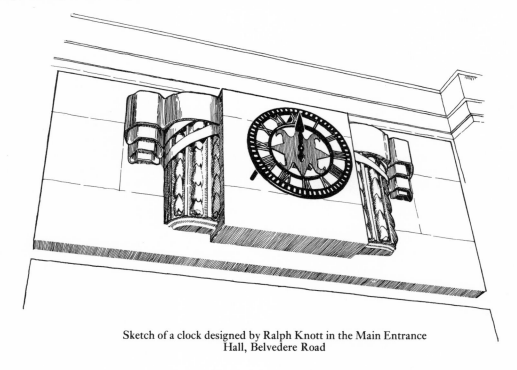

Sketch of a clock designed by Ralph Knott in the Main Entrance Hall, Belvedere Road

CHAPTER VI

Architectural Sculpture and Decorative Treatment

The general decorative treatment of County Hall evolved in a very different manner from that intended in Knott's original design. This was due partly to the changes made between 1908 and 1911 under the aegis of the Assessors, but mostly to the delay caused by the 1914–1918 War, which led to changes both in public taste and in the wealth available for public display.

General schemes of decoration had been drawn up before the war, and some were already in hand when work on County Hall was suspended in 1916. The contracts for the external stone-carving and statuary and for the interior wood-carving were allowed to stand, but others had been postponed in 1915 on the grounds that the Government wanted the LCC to cancel all non-essential expenditure. In the changed post-war climate few of the latter were re-instated.[a]

Knott's original design for County Hall, like those of many of his competitors, was liberally decorated with architectural sculpture, and he also proposed a number of large free-standing sculptural groups (figs 23, 24). All this could have been expected from the man who had been responsible in Aston Webb's office for the detailing of the prize-winning scheme for the Victoria and Albert Museum and for the Victoria Memorial.[2] Contemporary schemes by other architects followed the same pattern; the most notable of these was Cardiff City Hall and Law Courts (1898–1904) designed by Lanchester, Stewart & Rickards, with magnificent baroque figures by P. R. Montford (1868–1938). Knott's design for the Council Chamber (*Frontispiece*) had included heroic figures under the windows, and similar baroque groups appeared as late as 1912 in drawings for the Members' Courtyard (Plate 16a). In the event, the statues which appeared on the face of County Hall were far less ebullient, the majority emanating from the hand of Ernest Cole (Plate 30), a sculptor more comparable with Epstein than with Pomeroy or Brock, who appear to have been the inspiration for Knott's own groups.

Another fashionable form of decoration for public buildings which Knott had originally intended to use at County Hall was mural painting. In fact the planning of one scheme – for the Ayes and Noes Lobbies – was quite well advanced, and had the war not intervened would certainly have gone ahead. There were, of course, some celebrated Victorian precedents for this type of decoration, of which Ford Madox Ford's series of historical scenes at

Manchester Town Hall (1876–88) is a notable example. In Birmingham, under a scheme proposed in the 1890s, students from the local School of Art were employed to paint panels below the windows in the Town Hall,[3] and although only six were completed, this may well have inspired the LCC's later plans to use students for some of the decorative work at County Hall (see below). Bristol and Liverpool were among the English cities with contemporary schemes for civic buildings, and exchange visits with the City of Paris would have given LCC Members the chance to see the new murals in the Hôtel de Ville and the individual Mairies.[4] Swinton, through his friendship with John Singer Sargent, probably knew of the decoration of McKim, Mead & White's Boston Library, while at home there was the example of the 1911 competition for decorating Chelsea Town Hall, where Sargent, Wilson Steer and E. A. Rickards formed the jury.

Among the paintings proposed for County Hall before the outbreak of war were murals for the eight lunettes in the Ayes and Noes Lobbies, which were to have been executed by Frank Brangwyn, who had taught Knott etching. Although Brangwyn offered to do the work and accept payment later, this was one of the commissions postponed in 1915 and never taken up again.[5] The lunettes in the Main Committee Room (room 129) were also intended to be filled by painted decoration (fig. 36b).[6]

Another element in the early design of the important rooms on the Principal Floor was the fashion for re-using panelling and other decorative elements from demolished historic buildings; this was seen as some atonement for demolition. A precedent had been set by central government, and the Council already had a collection of salvaged historic features, some of which had been re-used at Spring Gardens. This was an important interest of the Historical Records Committee, the predecessor of the Historic Buildings Panel, and the Members played their part in influencing early schemes for the interiors.

A list drawn up by Riley in December 1908 of 'articles of historic interest' for possible re-use in the new County Hall was long and various, and included sections of staircase and moulded ceilings as well as panelling, and chimneypieces, in particular those from houses on the west side of Lincoln's Inn Fields demolished for the making of Kingsway. In response to protests from Knott, with some support from Riley, only the panelling and chimneypieces were considered for re-use, and in the end no old panelling

---

[a]Among the casualties were a pair of granite lions for the balustrade of the Members' Terrace.[1]

SECTION
THRO' CENTRE OF A BAY

INSCRIPTION ALONG THE FRIEZE

ANNO·DNI·MCMX

NVOVS

METROPOLITAN·BOARD
OF WORKS·MDCCCLVI·AD.
LONDON·COUNTY·COUNCIL
FOUNDED·MDCCCLXXXVIII·A.D.

PART ELEVATION OF CENTRE PORTION

Fig. 23. Matthew J. Dawson's competition design for County Hall, 1908. Detail of the river-front elevation showing proposed statuary
and inscription

was installed in the new County Hall.[7] In 1914 Knott designed new and appropriate panelling for the rooms where it was proposed to put the old chimneypieces (see fig. 25),[8] but he was never very happy about using these imported pieces, later telling Riley that he did not wish his County Hall to become a salvage heap of architectural oddments.[9] In the event, the long delay in the furnishing of County Hall due to the war led to second thoughts, and in 1919 the Establishment Committee decided not to use the old chimneypieces. In 1920, therefore, Knott was able to replace most of them with new ones of his own design.[10]

The reasons for this change of heart were educational rather than aesthetic. It was considered that the 'most instructive use to which the majority of the mantelpieces could be put would be to place them in such a position that the public would have intimate access to them'.[11] Exhibition at the Geffrye Museum rather than removal to County Hall was thus deemed more appropriate, and the only chimneypiece from Lincoln's Inn Fields to be installed at County Hall – the 'Bear and Beehive' in room 118 (Plate 27d) – was placed in a waiting-room used by the public. However, three other old chimneypieces, from Furzedown House in Streatham, were re-fixed in rooms occupied by Chief Officers.[12]

There is, therefore, very little 'architectural salvage' in County Hall and most of the internal decoration is new work designed by Knott and executed by craftsmen chosen by him and Riley. The most elaborate decorative treatment was concentrated on the Principal Floor, and very large areas were involved. Most of the walls here were panelled in hardwood, marble being used in the ceremonial areas. All the chief rooms on this floor have fireplaces with carved overmantels, in stone, plaster or wood. An important part of the decorative scheme is the elaborate art bronze-work of the entrance doors, gates and railings throughout the building (see Plates 14c, 16c, 19b, 28a,c,d). Knott was fortunate in being able to call on a number of specialist firms experienced in high quality work for Victorian and Edwardian churches and public buildings. These included Farmer & Brindley, the marble specialists; G. P. Bankart, famous for their lead and plasterwork;[13] the bronze founders J. W. Singer & Sons of Frome (Plate 31e); the Bromsgrove Guild (fig. 26a,b); and the William Morris Company (Westminster) Ltd. of Lambeth.[b] Equally, there were carving and modelling firms (like the Mabey family firm or the Indunis), who were able to carry out designs in wood and stone, and had trained on public monuments. In the 1920s many of these firms were forced into liquidation or amalgamation.

Most of the wood carving on the Principal Floor, as well as much of the detailed design of the bronze decoration, is the work of the Edinburgh-born carver George Alexander (1881–1942), the person above all others who contributed

to the high artistic quality of the building's interiors. Alexander was both a modeller and carver, with a reputation for 'sympathetic collaboration with architects'. Although well-known as a wood-carver, he had made his name as a designer in metal, collaborating with a firm of Sheffield iron-workers and with the Crittall Manufacturing Company. The contemporary critic, Kineton Parkes, wrote of his work as 'some of the finest applied sculpture of the revival inaugurated by [Alfred] Stevens, a monument of plastic decoration worthy of comparison with those of the later Renaissance in England and on the Continent' (Plate 26b).[15] At County Hall Alexander was responsible both for the wood carving in the most important committee and chairmen's rooms, and for designing the Members' seating in the Council Chamber. He also modelled the manganese bronze enrichments and ornamental work in the Council Chamber and on the ceremonial doors.[16]

Architectural Sculpture: the work of Gilbert Bayes, C. H. Mabey and Ernest Cole

The first architectural sculptures to be commissioned for County Hall were the ornamental bronze mooring-rings of horses' and lions' heads on the embankment wall (Plate 31a,b). As has already been mentioned, these were modelled by the sculptor Gilbert Bayes (1872–1953), brother of Walter John Bayes, the Principal of the Westminster School of Art. Bayes, who worked extensively for the Lambeth firm of Doulton, was an exponent of the 'New Sculpture' and interested in the use of mixed media. Knott had suggested him for the embankment wall job, and in October 1909 he was one of three artists invited to submit models for the mooring-rings or 'dolphins', the others being Courtney Pollock and Hubert Paton. Not surprisingly, Knott preferred Bayes's model.[17] The casting was carried out by J. W. Singer & Sons, who regularly worked for Hamo Thornycroft and other prominent sculptors (Plate 31e). In 1911 the *Builder* published a drawing by Knott's assistant, J. R. Leathart, of one of the two horse's heads (Plate 31a). In 1910 Bayes exhibited his 'Sigurd' at the Royal Academy, and it was bought by the Chantrey Bequest and is now in the Tate Gallery. Later on he was commissioned to execute the eleven foot figure 'The Queen of Time' on the Oxford Street façade of Selfridges.[18] He was also the designated sculptor of six bronze groups for County Hall which were one of the commissions postponed in 1915 and never reinstated,[19] and in 1931 he modelled the memorial plaque to Knott in the Members' Courtyard (Plate 17c).

Most of the architectural sculpture on the exterior of the building, including the northern front, was entrusted to Charles H. Mabey Junior (1867–1965), a cadet member

[b]Singers later lost both trade and some of their men to the Morris Art Bronze Company, of Dorset Road, Lambeth, founded in 1921, with the backing of the William Morris Company. Formal amalgamation of the Singer art bronze work section to form Morris Singer took place in 1927.[14]

Fig. 24. Ralph Knott's competition design for County Hall, 1908. Detail of one of the river front pavilions showing proposed statuary and carvings

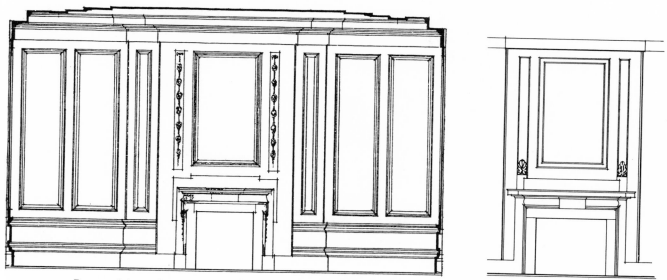

a Room 138 (committee room), designed to incorporate a fireplace from No. 29 Millbank Street, Westminster

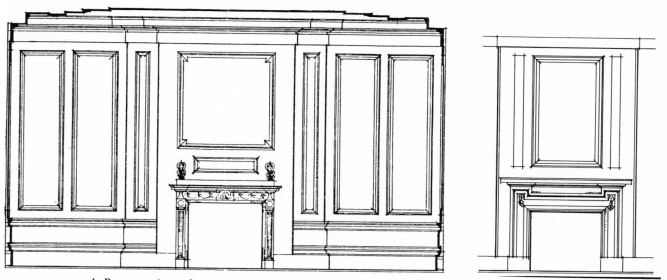

b Room 139 (committee room), designed to incorporate a fireplace from No. 25 Millbank Street

Fig. 25. Working drawings for panelling and chimneypieces for rooms on the Principal Floor in Block 12. The panelling was designed, in 1914, to complement old fireplaces salvaged from historic buildings, which are shown in the left-hand drawings. These, however, were never installed, and in 1920 new chimneypieces designed by Knott were substituted (shown on the right)

of a family well known for its carving and modelling. His uncle, James Mabey (d.1883), appears to have worked under the sculptor John Thomas on the Palace of Westminster, and his father, Charles Henry Mabey (d.1912), worked at Todmorden Town Hall (1870) and on the Temple Bar Memorial.[20] Mabey's firm had provided the model of the new County Hall building in 1910, and commissions for models based on Knott's drawings of architectural details for carving in stone and wood followed from this. These included not only the heraldic shields on the Crescent frieze, but also the caskets, torches

and other details round the various ceremonial entrances to the building, a full-scale model of the main cornice, and models for the treatment of various elements in the Council Chamber.[21] The best examples of Mabey's workmanship in architectural stone-carving can be seen above the Members' Entrance on Westminster Bridge Road and in the Members' Courtyard behind it (Plates 14d, 17a), over the doorway to the Members' Terrace (Plate 12b) and in the heraldic panels on the Crescent frieze (Plate 12a).

Knott's intention to decorate the frieze around the

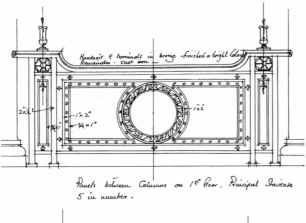

Panels between Columns on 1st floor. Principal Staircase
5 in number.

Elevations of Panels over Staff Entrances.
in cast & wrot iron — 2 in number —

a (above) Balustrade in cast-iron and bronze for the Ceremonial
   Staircase
b (below) Window-guard, in 'cast and wrot iron', for the first-
   floor windows over the staff entrances on the Belvedere Road
   and river fronts

Fig. 26. Working drawings for metalwork to be made by the
Bromsgrove Guild, 1922

Crescent with the arms of the London Boroughs did not
at first find favour with all the Members. In 1916 (Sir)
Cyril Cobb challenged the idea on the grounds that only
twelve boroughs were officially armigerous, and he proposed that the arms of other cities, such as Birmingham
and Manchester, should be used instead.[22] Sir John Benn
then suggested having medallion portraits of famous Londoners, such as Chaucer, Dryden, and Macaulay, but
Knott objected that these would be even more difficult to
make effective from a distance than heraldic designs. Many
Members appeared to think that a plain frieze would be
best of all.[23] When, in 1919, the decoration of the frieze
became a matter requiring a decision, models were made

of both the coats of arms and the medallions and shown
to Members, who selected the former.[c]

Another difficulty over the use of heraldic decoration
occurred on the Westminster Bridge Road front, where
Knott was proposing to place a head of Minerva over the
central portal of the Members' Entrance, flanked by the
arms of the City and of Westminster. When the LCC was
granted its own coat of arms in 1914, this was used to
replace Minerva, but then Sir Ernest Debenham complained that the use of the arms of these other authorities
was not popular with a number of Members. Ultimately
they were replaced by a decorative treatment of the LCC's
mural crown (Plate 14d).[25]

The most prominent sculptures on County Hall are the
figure groups by Ernest Cole and Alfred Hardiman, which
embellish ten of the twelve pavilions on the four façades
(Plates 30, 31c,d, fig. 27). In 1915 it had been intended
that Cole should execute all the groups, starting with those
for the eight pavilions on Sections A, B and C.[26] But he
failed to complete the contract, the two central pavilions
on the Belvedere Road front being left figureless as a
result, and the four groups on the later northern end
(Section D) were entrusted to Hardiman.

Ernest Cole (1890–1979) was only twenty-four when he
began working at County Hall. He had been educated
at the Art School at South Kensington, where he was
discovered by Charles Ricketts and Selwyn Image when
they were judging art work there.[27] He later found one or
two patrons, but the County Hall sculptures formed by
far the largest commission that he was ever given. His
studio was at the Old Bus Stables, just off Sirdar Road in
North Kensington, and it was there in April 1915 that he
set to work. In the following October he enlisted in the
army, but continued to employ an assistant and to work
himself at weekends until he was sent to France towards
the beginning of 1917. He made considerable progress,
finishing five-and-a-half groups in some eighteen months,
for twelve of which he was in the army.[28]

Cole spent little time in France. His joining up had
caused much anguish in the artistic community, and it
seems the authorities were persuaded to transfer him to
the safer world of military intelligence. In his efforts
to obtain special treatment for Cole, 'whose loss in the
trenches I would consider a national disaster', Charles
Ricketts compared him to Alfred Stevens.[29]

Cole was sent to the United States, and on his way
there met his future wife, Laurie Manly, a widowed lawyer
who was to have such an influence on his career as virtually
to end it.[30] Cole was never to rejoin the artistic circle he
left in 1916. He had, it appears, become a convert to
'modern art nonsense' and his old friend Ricketts could

[c]The sixteen coats of arms on the frieze are, from north to south, those of the LCC, the City of London, Hammersmith, Bermondsey,
Islington, Camberwell, Kensington, Wandsworth, St Marylebone, Westminster, Paddington, Southwark, Chelsea, Greenwich,
Holborn, and the LCC. The arms of the City and the boroughs are arranged in order of acquisition, starting at the northern end.
Although the Council had agreed that the arms of the Metropolitan Borough of Lambeth should be among those displayed this was
not done, apparently because these arms, too, were unofficial. They were later included in the frieze on the north façade and also used
in the decoration of room 153.[24]

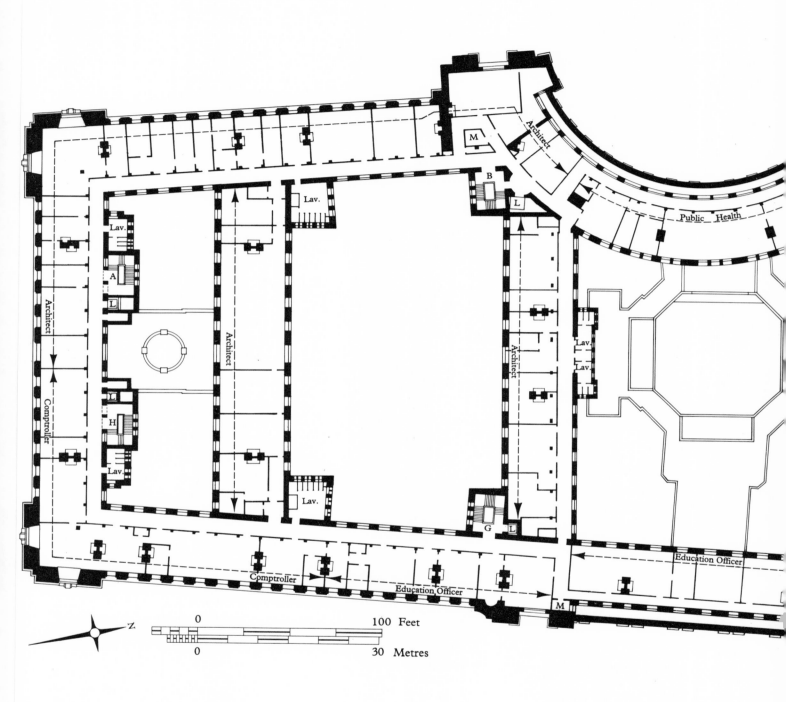

Lav.

Lav.

Architect

Lav.

Architect

Comptroller

A

H

Lav.

Comptroller

M

B

L

Architect

Architect

Public   Health

Lav.

Lav.

G

L

Education Officer

Education Officer

M

Z

0   100 Feet

0   30 Metres

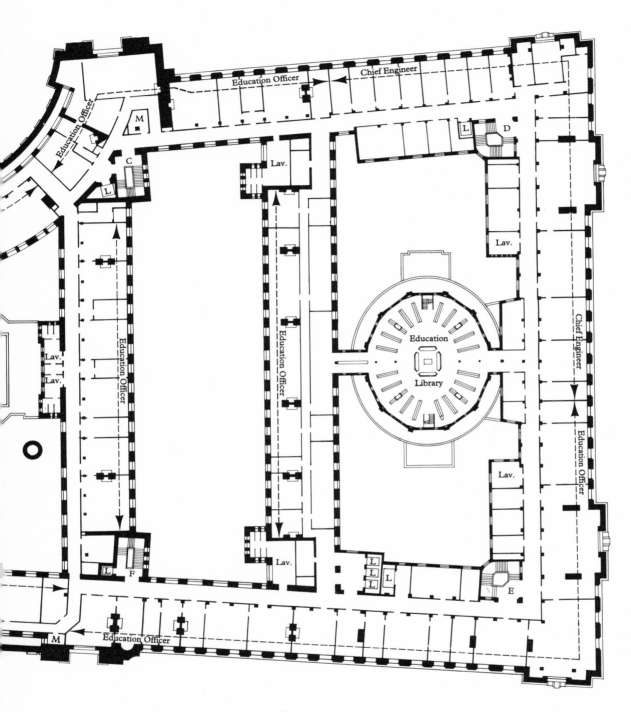

I. Typical office floor (fourth floor), showing original allocation of office space between Departments

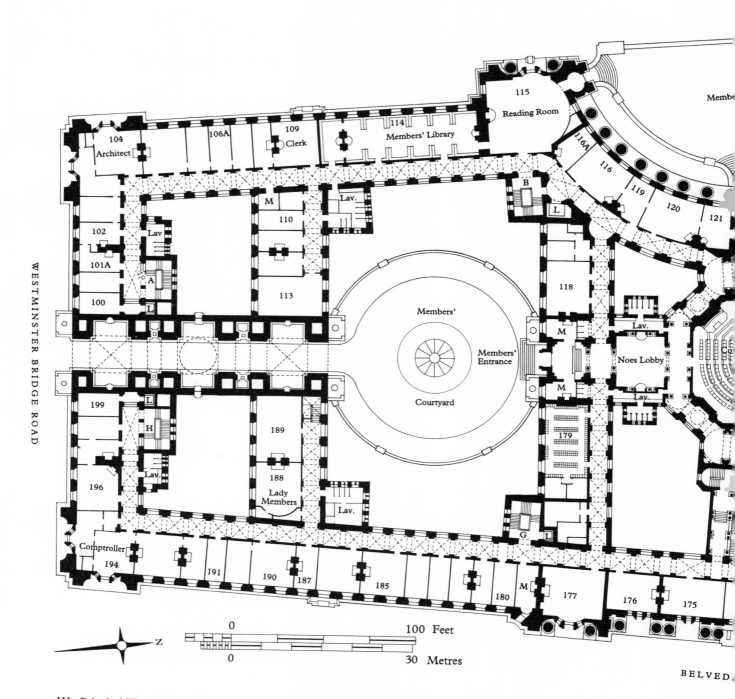

WESTMINSTER BRIDGE ROAD

104
Architect

106A

109
Clerk

114

Members' Library

115
Reading Room

Memb

116A

116

119

120

121

102

101A

100

Lav

A

L

M

110

113

Lav.

Members'

Members'
Entrance

Courtyard

B

L

118

M

Lav.

Noes Lobby

Co

199

196

H

Lav.

189

188

Lady
Members

Lav.

179

M

M

Lav.

G   L

Comptroller
194

191

190

187

185

180

M

177

176

175

0   100 Feet

0   30 Metres

Z

BELVED

III. Principal Floor as completed 1922–33, showing numbering and original allocation of rooms.
   Overlay shows the northern section of the Principal Floor as it was originally planned in 1912

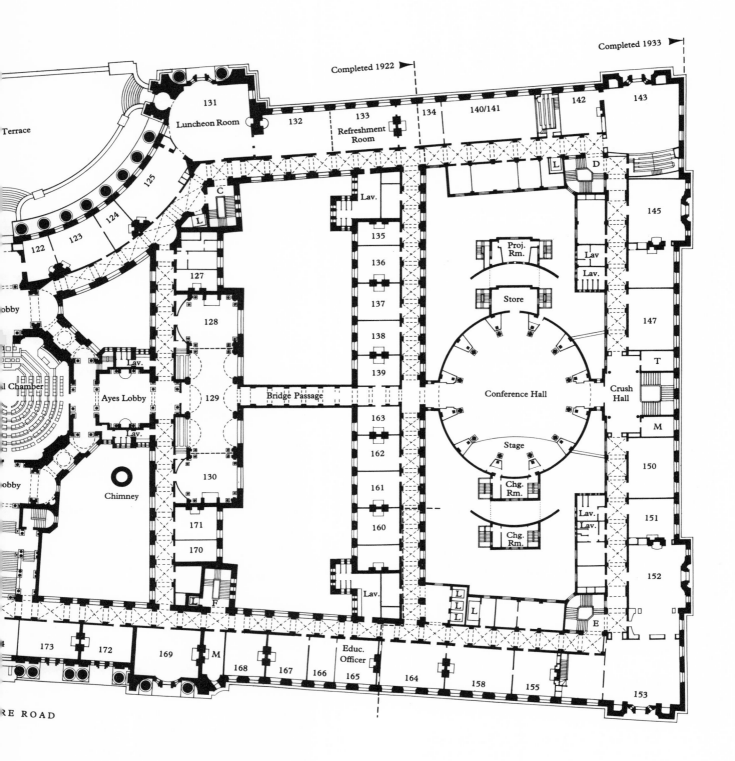

Terrace

131
Luncheon Room

132

133
Refreshment Room

134

140/141

142

143

125

124

123

122

C

L

127

128

Lav.

135

136

137

138

139

Lav.

Proj. Rm.

Store

L

D

145

147

T

Lobby

Lav.

Ayes Lobby

Lav.

129

Bridge Passage

Conference Hall

Crush Hall

M

l Chamber

Chimney

130

171

170

163

162

161

160

Stage

Chg. Rm.

Chg. Rm.

Lav.

Lav.

150

151

152

Lobby

L
F

Lav.

L
L
L

L

E

153

173

172

169

M

168

167

166

Educ. Officer
165

164

158

155

RE ROAD

Completed 1922 ►

Completed 1933 ►

never thereafter refer to Cole without 'a sort of rage possessing him'. Cole had, in his phrase, 'gone over to the enemy'.[31]

This new Cole was to have a good deal of trouble with his old patron, the LCC. When he was discharged from the army, eight months after the end of the war, the sculpture work was as he had left it, with-five-and-a-half groups completed of the initial eight required. Quite understandably he wrote to the Committee asking for an increase in his fee. Prices and costs had after all risen quickly during the immediate post-war years; George Alexander had put some of his prices for oak carving up by ninety per cent. Knott recommended that the Committee grant an increase of £1,600 to finish the outstanding work, which they did.[32] Unfortunately Cole's rate of progress fell dramatically. He seems to have had trouble finding a new studio, but this hardly explains the fact that twenty-one months after approval for his increased fee, he had only carved one-and-a-half groups, and still had one to finish. Worse than that, Knott rejected one group, which Cole had already had carved in stone without previous approval of the plaster model. This was the 'Motherhood' group intended for the Belvedere Road front: Knott thought it 'unsuitable in scale and finish'.[33d]

After this long delay Cole asked for a further £1,000, in March 1921. Although the architects were prepared to recommend this to the Committee, their report was debated by the Members with mounting impatience. Riley concluded that the Members were not impressed with the value or suitability of Cole's work, and that 'more than one Member indicated that they regarded his work as a positive eyesore, and by no means an artistic advantage to the building'. The Chairman then agreed to see Cole and to indicate that 'the present was not a good time to consider granting any increase'.[35] Relations deteriorated further when the following week a postcard, addressed simply to 'New County Hall', and including a request for £600, arrived from Cole's wife: 'Mr Cole is unwell from the strain and worry ... I am taking him away for a bit to cheaper places'.[36] Cole was paid an additional £200.

As Knott bravely set about collecting artistic opinions of Cole's work, the Committee made it plain they considered it irrelevant what other artists thought.[37] The opinions Knott eventually received, from excellent authorities, were favourable to Cole's work. The poet and art-historian Laurence Binyon (1869–1943), then Keeper of Prints and Drawings at the British Museum, wrote:

If you had Michelangelo to do the groups for you, the LCC would I expect be disgusted with his work ... what public building in London has statuary as interesting? There is sincerity and imaginative intention so manifest in the sculptures that they ought to be judged with generosity and goodwill ....

I firmly believe that no other English sculptor living would have produced groups to match Cole's for bigness of conception and style.

Binyon also told Knott that the American sculptor Paul Manship had told him that he thought 'the groups on your fine building the most interesting things in sculpture that he had ever seen over here'.[38] Another artist who wrote in support of Cole's work was the painter (Sir) George Clausen.[39]

The Committee Chairman, Hubert Greenwood, sent Knott to Paris to find out whether Cole was prepared in principle to continue the work. He was, for a price, and Knott wrote a report for the Committee, supported by the Binyon and Clausen letters, recommending that Cole be allowed to continue. Riley, most unusually, dissented from this report, stating that he did not 'concur with the opinions expressed as to the value of the *recent* work executed by Mr Cole'.[40]

In October 1921, the Solicitor wrote to Cole asking him to honour his contract or consider his employment at an end. By this stage many Members were happy to do without the two unfinished groups for the Belvedere Road front, and the letter merely provoked one final outburst from Laurie Cole, writing from Florence. She was particularly scathing about Knott, the sculptor's last real defender on the project. She contrasted him, as 'an architect collecting, throughout the war double fees, part from Government for sitting in an architectural office, and part from the Council and other clients', with Cole, as 'a sculptor unique in England who had done great works for the Council with his own hands and who had volunteered and served as a private soldier and then in the French trenches, thrown away three and a half years out of his twenties – not sitting warm and comfortable at home drawing – but out soldiering'.[41]

Predictably, Cole's employment at County Hall came to an end, and the Belvedere Road front was left as we see it today, without the proposed groups in its central section.[e]

Striking though some of Cole's statuary undoubtedly is, the subject matter is not easily identifiable. Various themes, most of them having no obvious connexion with

---

[d]The stone carving had been carried out by Induni, an Italian sculptor who 'regularly carves a large quantity of the Royal Academy sculpture exhibits' and worked on the Victoria Memorial. A photograph of the 'Motherhood' group taken in 1921 survives among the County Hall photographs in possession of the London Division of English Heritage.[34]

[e]In the 1920s Cole and his wife settled at Kingston, near Canterbury, where they lived a reclusive existence in a house which Cole commissioned, and claimed was the first steel frame bungalow ever built. It had no electricity until the 1970s.

At the beginning of the 1939–45 war they spent five days in gaol under suspicion of being sympathetic to the enemy. This was not entirely surprising. For several years Cole had been receiving a daily copy of the Italian fascist newspaper *Il Popolo* – for the sculpture, he claimed – and it seems his wife corresponded with Mussolini, for whom she had a tremendous admiration.

Laurie Cole died in 1957. Ernest lived until 1979, and would often be found in bed surrounded by wood chippings, carving away and oblivious to all else. Throughout his life Cole appears to have destroyed most of his work soon after he finished it.[42]

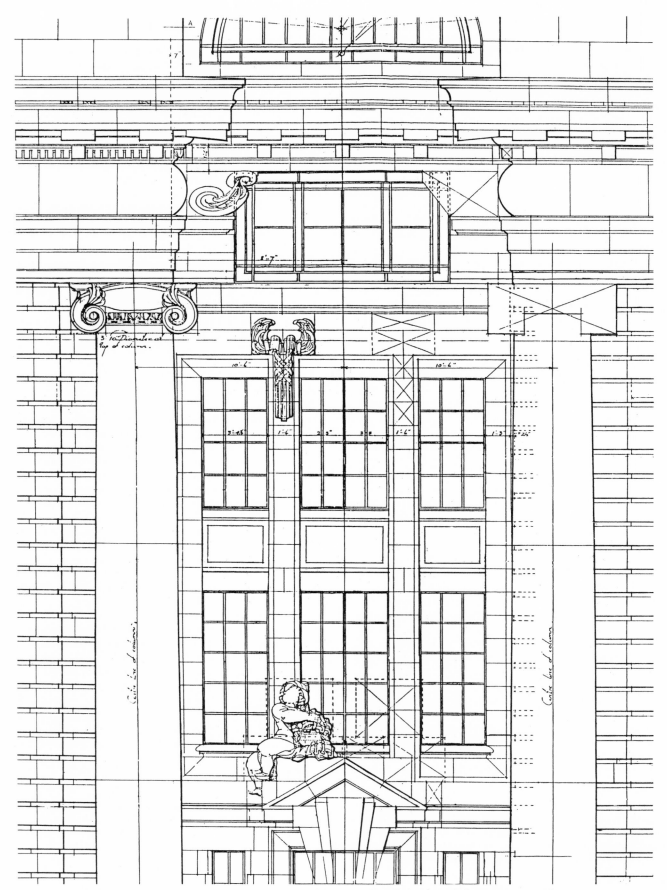

Fig. 27. Working drawing for the river-front pavilions, 1912. Detail showing window treatment and statuary

the world of local government, are mentioned in the Committee papers, but there is no definitive list of the completed groups and the allegorical treatment precludes a straightforward correlation with any of the subjects mentioned. An attempt to discover what the statues represented was made in 1920 by one of the LCC Aldermen, (Sir) Evan Cotton, who tabled a series of facetious questions to the Council.[f] The questions were disallowed by the Clerk, but not before a reply had been drafted stating that Cole's work was 'a sincere attempt to embody the representation of beauty in stone', and venturing explanations for some of the groups.[43] In 1923, however, Riley himself confessed that neither he nor Knott had ever been clear about what the statues represented.[44] However, it cannot be assumed that this style of work was not at first well regarded by the Committee, since the rejected group 'Motherhood' is very much more representational in treatment than any of the accepted works.

Mention is made of some nine different groups either modelled or carved by Cole – 'The Creation of Eve', a 'Hero Group', a 'Love Group', the 'Expulsion from Eden' and 'The Good Samaritan' (both bronzes), a 'Thames Group', 'The World Beyond', 'Motherhood', and 'Sacrifice', the last intended as a substitute for 'Motherhood' but never carried out.[45] The 'Creation of Eve' was originally meant for the north central pavilion on the Belvedere Road front, and 'Motherhood' for the corresponding south pavilion. When neither this nor 'Sacrifice' were forthcoming or acceptable, the 'Creation of Eve' was moved to the river front, and the central part of the Belvedere Road front left unadorned.

The statues executed by Cole are as follows:

Belvedere Road front: south end – 'Hero Group'. In 1920 the archer figure was said to embody the idea of striving to achieve a definite purpose.

Westminster Bridge Road front: east pavilion – 'World Beyond Group', humanity supporting the world (Plate 30c); west pavilion – untitled group. In 1920 it was said to represent 'Benevolence and Humanity'.

River front: south pavilion – untitled group (Plate 30b); south central pavilion – 'Thames Group'; north central pavilion – 'Creation of Eve' (Plate 30a).

Except for the 'Creation of Eve' and the 'Thames Group' they are all signed by Cole. Some, at least, were carved *in situ*.

The contemporary opinions of Cole's County Hall work already quoted were garnered specifically in their defence, and contemporaries were by no means unanimous in their praise. Writing in 1924, Charles Marriott (1869–1957), the successful novelist turned art critic of *The Times*, felt that Cole's sculptural groups were a mistake, not because they were badly done in themselves but because they

needed 'a much more florid architectural context to support them'. He thought that the proper style of ornament for County Hall was that of Mabey's work in the crescent.[46] The justice of this remark is hard to deny. Cole's work, large in scale though it is, is not well 'set off' by the building, which manages to make it less significant than it merits.

When work on the northern front was put in hand in the late 1920s, the Council decided to continue with figure sculptures in the pavilions, but they employed Alfred Hardiman (1891–1949), with whom relations were considerably easier than they had been with Cole (see page 97 and Plates 31c,d). Hardiman was a former student in the Artistic Crafts Department at the Northampton Polytechnic, Clerkenwell, where he won an LCC Senior Art Scholarship to the Royal College of Art. In 1920 he won a Prix de Rome scholarship in sculpture, and throughout his life was a regular exhibitor at the Royal Academy. Among his works are the bronze figure of St George, now at Eltham Palace but originally fixed to the front of No. 13, Carlos Place, Mayfair, and the memorial to Field-Marshall Haig in Whitehall. His fee for the work at County Hall was £4,100.[47]

Work by London County Council Students

In 1912 the Edinburgh town planner Patrick Geddes organized an exhibition of Designs for Mural Painting for the decoration of schools and other institutions, in which the LCC participated, Riley serving on the Committee.[48] The exhibition was intended to encourage the kind of decorative work which Geddes had pioneered, and the LCC co-operated by making space available for murals in LCC schools.

The following year, Swinton led a movement to have students employed on some of the decorative work. Halsey Ricardo put the case for student involvement in a letter to William Garnett of the Educational Adviser's Department. Arguing that the standard of technical education in the LCC schools was high, indeed not inferior to that in Germany, and that Members were unaware of the quality of their own schools, he attacked the LCC for not making practical use of its own teaching. As trustees of public money, the LCC trained students to be good craftsmen, but how often, he asked, were these principles put into practice:

They train the student, for instance, to appreciate and practise fine lettering – whilst they permit, on the public buildings and street corners, lettering that is a venomous eyesore. They train him to discriminate the various stiles of fine metal work and surround their open spaces with railings of cheap commercial manufacture . . . .

[f]Cotton asked whether the figures were unclothed as a protest against the 'monstrous price of clothes' and whether their positions 'crowded on precarious perches outside the windows, indicates the lack of housing accommodation'. He wanted to know what was the message to the masses these groups were meant to convey, and why the 'two muscular citizens' in the group nearest Westminster Bridge had such despairing looks on their faces and 'appear to be preparing to hurl a bomb at the Houses of Parliament'.

The LCC is building itself a County Hall. How many of its students will be invited to do the ornamental carving of the stone and wood – how many to do the decorations in paint and plaster – how many the metal work, the cabinet work, the seats, the lettering? Why are we, as ratepayers, debarred from getting any dividend from our investment? And, think, how it would hearten our students to be allowed to do some real work.[49]

Knott came down firmly against this idea. He felt very strongly that the carving on such an important building should be in the hands of experienced professionals. It was 'rather hard on outside sculptors' that such an opportunity should be given to students. The Committee should follow the lines they had already laid down and allow him a free hand in such purely aesthetic matters. But Knott had a nice course to steer between unskilled innocence and skilled artistry, explaining that he did not want 'sculptors of big reputations' because of the 'difficulty in inducing them to merge their very pronounced individualities into mine'.[50]

Both Knott and Riley were worried about the way artists or student artists might be selected:

it would be intolerable to carry out a building on which an architect's reputation may be judged, the decorative details of which would be settled or even influenced by a Committee of men who have not been educated on strictly architectural lines.[51]

In 1916, in response to pressure from the Education Committee, Knott agreed that 'some small portions of wood-carvings – overmantels and that sort of thing might be found' for students from LCC-supported art-schools, and that they might 'try their hand at colour decoration on the large plaster spaces of the Staff Refreshment Room ceiling'. If this proved unsuccessful it 'could be lime-whited out'.[52]

Riley's reservations about employing students were sceptical rather than snobbish, practical rather than artistic. When it was suggested by the Establishment Committee after the war that students from the Central School of Arts and Crafts be given a chance, he pointed out that there was £120–worth of work that they might do, but they thought this was too small. Riley continued:

I then pointed out that a very large number of relief panels were wanted for the Central School of Arts and Crafts, the very home of these students, and that they had been invited to look into this question long before the war, but the result so far is nil. This seemed to impress the Chairman very much.[53].

The uncarved panels can be seen along Southampton Row to this day.

Between Knott's vigorous defence of artistic principles, Riley's scepticism and the Committee's indecision, almost nothing came of the suggestion for student decoration of the building. Knott might have felt that by banning

student work he was opening the way for professionals, whose work he knew would be of a higher standard. But a Municipal Reform administration which grudged money to build their immense headquarters was not about to pay established artists to decorate its walls.

The only student to work extensively at County Hall was the Birmingham-born sculptor, Alfred H. Wilkinson (1884–1958), who won a competition (held within the Central School) for carving on the Ceremonial Staircase. This was never carried out, but it led to Wilkinson being employed to execute the stone-carving in the Belvedere Road and Westminster Bridge Road entrance halls and on the Members' Library chimneypiece (Plates 27c, 29c,d), for which he was paid £670.[54] Wilkinson was later commissioned to carry out the wood-carving in the northern section of County Hall (Plate 29b).[55]

A second competition was organized in 1921 for the decoration of spandrels in the Principal Floor corridors. Each of four art schools – Royal Academy, Slade, Westminster, and Royal College of Art – was to submit two lunette cartoons, on the subject of 'Life in the London Parks controlled by the LCC', a theme possibly inspired by the example of Stockholm Town Hall. The paintings were to be experimental, not in positions of prominence, and the intention was that each year the Committee should choose from a new selection, so progressively decorating the building. The first series of eight was prepared and installed for inspection in December 1922, together with a further unsolicited six on 'Railways'.[g] Five of the cartoons were exhibited in the following year at the Royal Academy Decorative Art Exhibition, when that by H. Weaver Hawkins of 'The Vale of Health' was highly praised (Plate 29a).[57] Others were reproduced in the *Architectural Review*.[58] Knott was happy with them and recommended that they be left in place for a year to give Members a chance to judge them properly.[59]

However, having viewed the cartoons *in situ* the Committee decided that no murals should be installed at County Hall 'unless they are of undoubted artistic merit',[60] thus closing the door on an enterprise which might have been the long-term influence for good in the art schools that many saw as its purpose. It would certainly have put the corridors of County Hall on a different level of enjoyment. So ended Swinton's vision of the County Hall as a work of art embodying the principles and practice of the LCC arts-and-crafts educational system.

The whole affair caused an uproar in the schools concerned, whose Principals – Henry Tonks, Charles Sims, W. Rothenstein, and Walter Bayes – wrote to the Chairman of the Establishment Committee on 17 November 1923. They objected very strongly to the Committee's rejection of the works as un-artistic, offering to submit them for opinion to a committee of experts, including the

---

[g]The artists were: Henry J. Lee and J. Cosmo Clark (Royal Academy); R. C. Guthrie and Rodney Burn (Slade); William Liley, Miss Braden and R. V. Pitchforth (RCA); and a group from the Westminster School of Art led by Norman Howard and H. Weaver Hawkins.[56]

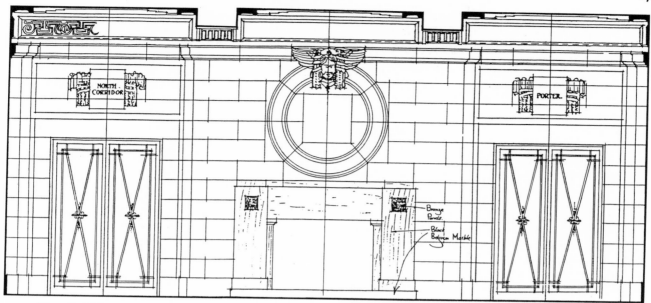

Fig. 28. Main Entrance Hall, Belvedere Road. Working drawing for the north wall, showing the fireplace, carved enrichments and bronze doors as designed in 1913

Directors of the National Gallery and the Victoria and Albert Museum, and the Slade Professors at Oxford and Cambridge. Needless to say, the LCC did not take up this challenge to its artistic judgement.[61]

The controversy spilled on to the correspondence pages of *The Times*. The irony is that for once Knott and Riley had supported the proposed decoration by students. Swinton, who had not been on the Establishment Committee since 1909, but always kept an eye on matters of art connected with County Hall, offered his regrets and an explanation:

In the first place the members adjudicating wished the train drawn as they see a train, and the crowds besporting themselves on Hampstead Heath clothed as they know them, not fancifully in all the colours of the rainbow. Then our corridors are new and clean, and look very well as they are. But the real trouble was that, while in all probability these cartoons were designed and worked out in wide studios, these corridors in which they were shown – and rightly shown because they would have to hang there – are only nine feet wide. We were too near them. Hence the tears.[62]

Two of the lunettes, those from Westminster Art School showing Hampstead Heath, were bought shortly after by the management of the underground railways for the entrance to their Westminster station.[63h]

The Italian Government Gift

In 1920 the Italian Government, having heard that the LCC was erecting a new headquarters, offered to give the

Council two blocks of Italian marble for the building, since 'Most of the great buildings of London are associated with Italian Art, either in architecture, material or decoration'.[64] Knott was asked what type of marble he wanted and the size of blocks required, and, with the chimneypieces in the Belvedere Road entrance hall in mind, ordered 'Verdi di Prato' (Verde Prato). Though told that 'Breccia Paonazzetta' was 'held in higher esteem' by Italians, Knott adhered to his first choice, and when it was found that this could not be supplied in the sizes required he proposed to redesign the chimneypieces, but seemingly did not do so (see Plate 27c, fig. 28).[65]

The Council Portrait Collection

In addition to the sculpture and carving commissioned for the building itself, the Council also owned a number of paintings and works of art, many presented by Members or by the public, but others specifically commissioned. As the paintings were largely hung in the ceremonial and official parts of the building, it is appropriate to consider them briefly here.

The LCC, as the first London-wide local government body, inherited works of art and other property from a number of predecessors, most notably the Metropolitan Board of Works, and the London School Board, and later on the Metropolitan Asylums Board and the Boards of Guardians. Finally, the GLC became heir to the Middlesex County Council, as well as the LCC. Together these

---

[h]The cartoons are said to have been returned to the Westminster School of Art just before the outbreak of the Second World War. The school closed for the duration and never re-opened.

collections provide a record of the individuals who played an important part in the management of London, and also some indication of the esteem and affection in which many of those bodies were held by their members. Not all of these objects were displayed, but many of them found homes in lobbies and corridors, and in Committee Rooms and offices, doing a great deal to soften the austerity of the Edwardian panelling.[66]

The most important single collection is that of the portraits of Chairmen of the London County Council and of the Greater London Council, not least because of the interesting manner in which it started, and the unusual personality of its originator, Captain George Swinton. All but one of the Chairmen are depicted in this collection of eighty-eight portraits (Plates 46b-d, 47).[i]

Swinton had embarked on an army career, but resigned to study painting under Sir Hubert Herkomer. His interest in painting was second only to his enthusiasm for town-planning, and he was a personal friend of some of the leading painters of the day.[67] As he later recalled, the portrait collection began as a compliment to an acting Chairman:

his brother Councillors, in grateful recognition of work well done, inviting him to have his portrait painted – at their expense, and presented to him, but with a thoroughly-understood arrangement that he should give it back to them in order that it may be hung on the walls of the County Hall as a pleasant remembrance.[68]

The collection includes works by some of the most outstanding artists working between 1889 and 1986. It is also a record of the men and women who for ninety-seven years played a part in the history of local government in London and their patronage of the arts. The majority of the Chairmen were extremely busy in public life, a proportion were M.P.s, one became Prime Minister, all without exception held a variety of public offices outside the LCC and the GLC. No history of County Hall can ignore the contribution the portrait collection made to its decoration; in addition, the motives behind its creation throw a lot of light on the attitudes of the generation which created the building, and the way in which they intended to enrich the lives of Londoners.

During the move to the newly opened County Hall in 1922, the Council's collection of portraits of all its past Chairmen was brought over and hung, experimentally, in various parts of the Principal Floor, though there were relatively few areas thought to be entirely suitable. The Establishment Committee agreed guidelines for hanging the portraits, deciding that as they were by eminent artists they should be displayed in the 'best possible positions from the artistic point of view'; they should be hung in positions visible to members of the public visiting the building, and they should as far as possible be hung together.

In view of the 'considerable diversity of opinion' among Members on the matter, the Committee sought the advice of the President of the Royal Academy, and other RAs as to the best way to hang the collection. They recommended that the portraits should be varnished, put under glass 'as a preservative from the effects of the London atmosphere' and re-framed in a uniform manner in a type of frame which they personally recommended. Sir Richard Llewellyn and Richard Jack also generously offered to advise on the hanging and arranging of the portraits. It was decided to hang one portrait in each of the twenty panels in the Ayes and Noes Lobbies and display the remainder elsewhere (Plate 22a).[69]

The small collection on which so much thought and time had been expended was remarkably representative of leading contemporary portrait painters. That the collection was of such quality was almost entirely due to Swinton's vision and persistence. He left a vivid description of the way in which he built up a collection of portraits by the best-known painters of the day at an extremely modest figure through a mixture of cajolery and mild social blackmail.[70] His tough and unscrupulous approach in what he felt to be a good cause, combined with his social standing and his own artistic knowledge, enabled him to secure some outstanding works in the early days of the collection.

He moved from the fairly obvious names for painters of the early sitters, to finding more 'up and coming' artists for later Chairmen. Thus the portrait of the first Chairman, the Earl of Rosebery, was a copy 'after and touched by G. F. Watts, O.M.'. Rosebery was followed by Sir John Lubbock, M.P. (1834–1913), afterwards Lord Avebury, a City banker and scientist, and a prominent early campaigner for the preservation of historic buildings, who was painted by the Hon. John Collier (Plate 46d). Collier (1850–1934) was a fashionable figure, connected to the Council through his brother, Lord Monkswell (1845–1909), Chairman 1903–4, whom he painted, together with several other Progressive Chairmen – W. H. Dickinson, later Lord Dickinson of Painswick (1859–1935), Chairman 1900–1, Sir Andrew Torrance (d.1909), Chairman 1901–2, and Sir Edwin Cornwall (1863–1953), Chairman 1905–6. Indeed, as Swinton pointed out, Collier and 'Mr. Leonard Watts, who painted Sir John Hutton, Sir Arthur Arnold and Mr. McKinnon Wood, were for a time almost Painters in Ordinary to the Council, though relieved at intervals by Mr. Herman Herkomer, who painted Sir William Collins, Sir William Richmond's Lord Welby, Mr. Spencer Watson's Sir John McDougall, and Sir George Clausen's Sir John Benn'.

The collection was growing steadily, and although 'not very exciting', Swinton thought it worth while to try and put it on a safer footing. The main problem, of course, was financial. Public funds could not be used and Swinton could never count on more than £100 in contributions from Members – in his own words, 'A pittance!'. In

---

[i]On the abolition of the GLC, the Portrait Collection passed to the Corporation of London and is held by the Guildhall Art Gallery.

1907 and 1908, however, the Council was able to secure portraits of Sir Evan Spicer and Sir Henry Harris from the young William Orpen, at a time 'when the meager sum which we were able to offer our painters was sufficient recompense'. Spurred on by this success, Swinton approached Sir William Orchardson (1835–1910), 'the doyen, and perhaps the most honoured of our portrait-painters living at that moment', and a brother Scot indebted to one of Swinton's relatives. On being told of the financial constraints, Orchardson readily agreed to 'give a present to London, and paint us a picture for £100', in this case a portrait of Sir Richard Robinson, Chairman 1908–9.[71]

Where Orchardson led, other painters could be persuaded to follow, and the plea of 'we take no money from the Rates, will you give a present to London and paint us a portrait for £100', secured pictures from Alma-Tadema, Edward Poynter, Llewellyn, Strang, Nicolson, Ouless, Britton Rivière, Ambrose McEvoy, Glyn Philpot (Plate 46c), Hacker, Walter Russell, Fiddes Watt, Jack, Frank Dicksee, Solomon, Harcourt, and Sir John Lavery.

Swinton had hoped to persuade his close friend Sargent to contribute to the series, and did indeed approach him, but at a time when the artist was 'overwhelmed with work'. One of Sargent's most successful portraits was of Swinton's wife, painted in 1896–7, and Swinton always had it in mind that if the Council had chosen a Chairwoman, and Sargent had lived longer, 'he might have been asked more easily to do something that no other had done'. There is, however, one Sargent in the collection. This is a charcoal sketch of Swinton himself, made in 1906, which the sitter later presented to the Council (Plate 46b).[72]

Despite his other concerns, Swinton retained an interest in the portrait collection. He secured its future by an arrangement with the Royal Academy by which the President would assist the Council in choosing an artist annually.[73] It was not until 1940 that the Council obtained powers under the Annual LCC Act to spend money from the rates on the Portrait Collection.[74] The tradition of having the Chairman's portrait painted was continued by the GLC, its last Chairman, Tony Banks, commissioning a group portrait (Plate 47d).

Detail of a radiator in the Members' Entrance

CHAPTER VII

London's Hôtel de Ville: The 1922 Building

County Hall was opened formally on 17 July 1922 by George V, accompanied by Queen Mary and the Duke of York. They were met at the Belvedere Road entrance at noon by the Chairman of the LCC, F. R. Anderton, the Home Secretary and various other national and London dignitaries. Standing on the Members' Terrace steps, the King replied to an address made by the Chairman of the Establishment Committee and declared the building open (Plate 10a). After a flourish of trumpets the King descended the steps and met some of the people involved in the project, including the site foreman and other workmen, all of whom had been given the day off with full pay.[1]

The King and Queen then inspected the Council Chamber, where Ralph Knott handed the King the key with which the room was officially opened. Though there were some 52 rooms for the use of the public or Members on the Principal Floor, not all of these were finished.[2] However, the royal party toured the Main Committee Room, two committee rooms on the Belvedere Road front, and the Members' Refreshment Rooms, Reading Room and Library. They left by the Members' Entrance, which was thronged by council staff and building workers (Plate 11).

Though parts of the building had been occupied by government staff during the war, and LCC employees were working in the building from 1919, photographs show that large sections of the riverfront were still under scaffolding in October 1921, as was the whole of the first and ground floors of the Westminster Bridge Road front (Plate 9b). Unfinished areas had to be disguised 'so that on the opening day it should not be in any way obvious that parts of the building were incomplete'. Crittall's bronze doors on to the Members' Terrace were only fixed during the weekend before the opening.[3]

Contemporary Comment on the Building

On the whole architectural opinion was favourable, though after the battles over the competition, it was difficult for critics at the time of its opening to find anything new or very original to say. As early as 1908, the *Architectural Association Journal*, reviewing Koch's book, had recommended it to 'anyone not heartily sick of the competition and all pertaining to it'.[4] The half-finished building had become familiar to Londoners during the

war, and even now it lacked the northern quarter postponed by the LCC, leaving, in Clough Williams-Ellis's words, 'certain shameful and hinder parts unfairly exposed on the north-eastern flank' (Plate 9c).[5]

The Times thought the building was 'in every way worthy of the great municipality which has grown up round the historic capital of the Empire'. It also saw significance in its location, reiterating the hopes of the Establishment Committee which selected the site, by suggesting that it might 'foretell the coming of a new and brighter era for the people of South London'.[6]

Newspapers were uncritically enthusiastic, while the architectural press tended to be restrained but polite, with the exception of the *Architectural Review*, which carried an effusive article by Aston Webb's son, Maurice, a close friend of Knott.[7]

Much comment on the building was concerned with the question of architectural style. Knott himself said that it 'may perhaps be best described as a free treatment of English Renaissance'.[8] Not everybody agreed. Professor C. H. Reilly (himself a competitor in 1907), writing in *Country Life*,[9] felt that Knott had broken with English precedents, and 'shown great courage' in doing so:

His building belongs neither to the English classical tradition nor to the English Gothic. If one had to assign it an ancestry one would say it came from the Low Countries by way of Mr. Norman Shaw.

The *Architect*, too, detected the influence of Norman Shaw, whose late work, and that of his followers, it felt to be a 'true advance' towards building up a living English tradition of architecture. County Hall was seen as a 'late example of this movement', leading to the rather surprising conclusion, that for this reason, 'we think [it] a more valuable contribution to contemporary architecture than has yet been recognised'.[10]

The *Builder*, in one of the more detailed reviews,[11] recognized the complexities of such a building, pointing out that County Hall combined 'some elements of the palace and the Parliament House, with the functions of a depository, a studio, and laboratory'.

Its correspondent commended the chief materials used externally – Cornish granite and Portland stone, bronze panels, and red 'Roman' tiles for the roof; these, he felt, were materials that had proved their worth in the 'exacting climate' of London, and which would 'improve in colour and texture as they weather and mellow under its influence', particularly if spared the action of the 'steam cleaner'. He did, however, criticize the way in which some other materials were used, notably such contrasting materials as white glazed bricks and granite, placed in positions where both could be seen, as in the Members' Carriage Drive (Plate 38b). Conceding both the utility and costliness of white glazed brick, the writer complained that its juxtaposition with the granite and the stonework raised 'the question as to which is the real standard of sound construction – the white, clean, flat expanses of the brick, or the heavily rusticated and ribbed greyness of the "architectural" portion below?'. In this comparison the fine architecture was found wanting, because it was made to appear a 'cleverly and elaborately constructed sham, not an added grace blooming directly from the main stem of practical convenience and good sense'.

Another criticism was of the lack of structural logic in many of the highly decorated parts of the building. Just as the white glazed tiles pointed up a contradiction externally (Plate 38c), the vaulted spaces internally could not be understood except as indications of confused architectural thinking. The vaulting of the Main Committee Room (Plate 24a, fig. 35) was found unconvincing because the ceiling of the press gallery which overlooked it was flat, and the corridor vaulting on the Principal Floor had a contrived look, again because it was decorative rather than structural.

C. H. Reilly was strongly critical of the treatment of the great Crescent, despite the fact that in 1907 he had included a similar crescent in his own unsuccessful design (fig. 20):

It seems to me that a central feature which is to command a very long front must come boldly forward or go boldly up. It cannot come forward and then retreat in the middle. By doing so it becomes a weak feature where a strong one is needed.

He felt that viewed from the Westminster Embankment 'the building – to use a somewhat rough simile – seems to have had its centre feature knocked in' (Plate 10b). The *Builder* too was disappointed with the Crescent, finding the use of columns on the curved front rather less than happy:

Just as the roof surface scored by its simplicity, the wall below might have been made to count as a great cylindrical expanse left free for the play of shadow and reflected light.

That opinion showed the changing sensibilities of the times, but it was in these new times that County Hall was judged. Indicative of this attitude was the *Evening Standard*'s retrospective comment that when the sculptor Ernest Cole had occupied a room in the partially completed building for a studio, 'the unfinished hall in its naked purplish brick was more impressive than it will ever be again'.[12]

The *Builder* did not go as far as this, and chose to end its criticism on a polite note, uninterested perhaps in pursuing arguments against an outdated architectural style:

While one detail or another may be open to criticism there is not the faintest doubt that the main effect is altogether right. It is to Mr Ralph Knott's credit, as an artist, that he has done the great things greatly and has created a work of architecture in harmony with the spirit of the city of which the County Hall is a representative building.

Architectural Description

County Hall was remarkable for its complex planning, and the way in which it was designed to channel several different types of user along different routes. This was achieved by a series of different entrances and severe stratification.

The Plan

The 'wedge-shaped' plan of County Hall as finally completed is in outline an elaborated trapezium, whose long axis runs north-south through the Members' Entrance in Westminster Bridge Road, a distance of some 750 feet (folded drawing A, between pages 62–3). At the heart of this plan lies the Council Chamber, centred on the intersection of the long axis and the short east-west axis, the latter passing the middle of the Belvedere Road front and the riverside crescent. The two long north-south sides of the building are not parallel to each other but to the river on the west and to Belvedere Road on the east. Consequently the short east-west axis which is at right angles to both the long sides has a bend in the middle. The east-west cross-blocks are all parallel to each other.

Within the envelope formed by the four outer ranges of the building the space is divided up by the cross-blocks into courtyards and light-wells. In Knott's competition plan these were to provide light to the offices – those offices which lay on either side of the much-criticized central, and therefore dark, corridors. With the addition of a Members' Entrance from Westminster Bridge Road, the courtyard next to the Council Chamber block was enlarged to create a grand formal space, while that next to the Westminster Bridge Road front was reduced proportionally. When the northern section (Section D) was replanned in the late 1920s the Conference Hall and Education Library were added to the northernmost courtyard, and while this did not become in any sense a formal space, it largely lost its original function as a lighting area.

The Principal or Ceremonial Entrance to the building is situated in the centre of the Belvedere Road front (Plate 13, folded drawing BII, between pages 110–11), where there are also a number of everyday entrances for staff and visitors. From Westminster Bridge Road a carriage entrance of great architectural drama, with inconspicuous doorways for staff, leads straight into the Members' Courtyard where the Members had their own separate entrance. In the original 1908–12 scheme a roadway along the northern front was intended to provide access for those whose job it was to maintain the huge building. As built in 1930–3

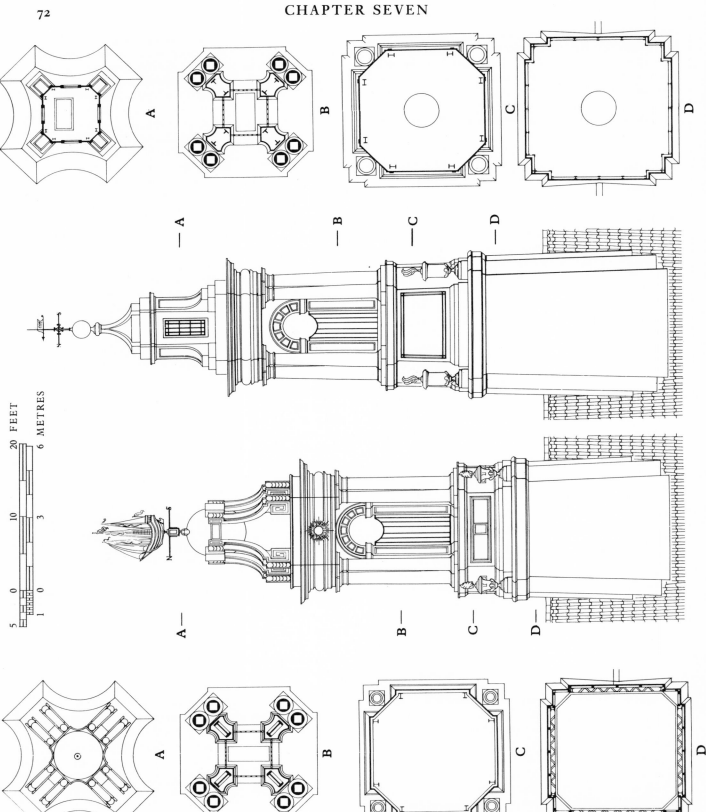

Fig. 29. The flèche. As designed in 1914 (left). As modified by Riley and Knott c.1921 (right); the weathervane shown here was replaced by a dolphin

this was retained, but in addition a formal, though relatively little-used, entrance to the Conference Hall was also provided. Although the river front is generally thought of as being free of entrances, there were in fact two staff entrances here, one in the centre of each wing, north and south of the central crescent. These entrances were closed sometime after 1931, and railings built across them.[13]

The Exterior

The building stands on a plinth of grey Cornish granite which is adjusted in Westminster Bridge Road and Belvedere Road to take account of the sloping site. On this rugged base sits Knott's great composition in Portland stone (Plates 10c, 13a, 14a). The ground floor has heavily rusticated banding, finished by a plain stringcourse, from which rise the Principal Floor window surrounds and the plain rusticated panels between them. The first or Principal Floor is treated as a *piano nobile*, with a range of segmentally pedimented windows, expressing externally the use of that level by Members and department heads. Above two further storeys in plain ashlar is one whose windows, equal in width to those below, sit within a rudimentary frieze. The wall is topped by a deep moulded cornice.

The Architects themselves admitted that the steep-pitched roof – 'the prominence of which is emphasised by the Italian roofing tiles, of rich red colour' – was 'unusual in this country'. The use of bright red tiles may have been an attempt to introduce some colour into the building, something that was held to be lacking in London.[14a] In some quarters it was felt that the new roof was altogether too red, though as Sir Aston Webb pointed out, 'we can depend upon our climate to put that right soon enough'. In the nationalistic atmosphere of post-war England it was stressed that the so-called 'Italian' tiles were, of course, of 'British Manufacture'.[16]

Within the roof are two further floors of offices, lit by copper-clad dormer windows. The fifth-floor windows correspond with those in the lower floors, while on the sixth floor they occur in alternate bays. Large chimney stacks in Portland stone punctuate the roof on all sides of the building, although Knott abandoned the idea put forward in his competition design to carry them around the roof of the Crescent (fig. 16a). Each stack has a door in its base at roof level, and handrails around the tops of the stack to protect the sweeps when cleaning the flues (Plate 38a). The sweep would enter the door, climb to the top, and lower his brush from above, weighted by a large iron ball.

The flèche in the centre of the Crescent is a steel-framed wooden structure sitting on a platform within the tiled roof (Plate 12c, fig. 29). Like the dormers, it is clad in copper. The design of this feature went through many modifications from its original appearance in Knott's competition entry. It had been intended as a smaller and more delicately detailed element, the final changes to its design, emanating from Riley but readily adopted by Knott, coming in 1921.[17] These modifications concerned the general scale of the flèche, including larger mouldings which would read better from a distance, as well as a change from a round top to a pointed one. Knott's competition design had shown a ship as weather-vane; as built the vane is topped by a dolphin.

The Crescent itself on plan is an arc whose centre lies roughly on the middle of the embankment promenade (Plate 12a,b). In place of the grand portico with its double row of paired columns, the actual building has the sweep of sixteen Portland stone Ionic columns following the curved face of the Crescent, for which Shaw had fought so hard. The order is repeated on the *in antis* columns within the pavilions which flank and give visual support to the recess. The capitals, with their pronounced upper curvature, are a variant of those on the temple of Apollo Epicurius at Bassae, and were fashionable at the time.[b] The order differs from the classical original in having volutes set parallel rather than diagonally, unfluted column shafts of squatter proportion and quite different bases, and a pulvinated or cushion frieze in the Roman style of Piranesi, which Wren used occasionally.

The crescent has a high stone parapet – a wall with a central oval window and then alternating circular windows and framed panels carved with the arms of London boroughs. Behind and above this, the sixth floor is lit by a strip of windows largely concealed by the parapet. The great depth of the entablature in the Crescent means that the accommodation behind on the fourth and fifth floors is starved of light. To alleviate this Knott transposed the relative positions of the offices and the corridors hereabouts, the latter being brought to the front of the building where they are lit, indirectly, by the circular windows in the parapet wall (see folded drawing B11, between pages 110–11).

The Westminster Bridge Road front (Plate 14a) is a more compact and dramatic composition – the most successful of the three completed in 1922, in the opinion of more than one contemporary critic. It may have been consideration of this elevation that led Knott to change the design of all the corner pavilions. Originally these were to have followed the same design as central pavilions, with columns *in antis* (fig. 17a). But on this front the pavilions

---

[a]A suggestion along these lines had been made in 1910 by a Mr F. C. Clarke, recently returned from Dresden, where he had seen the New Town Hall, and was forwarded to Knott. Clarke pointed out how much more effective either red or light green would be 'in preference to the dull and dead slate colour tiles prevalent in England'.[15]

[b]They were used by Belcher & Joass at Electra House, No.84 Moorgate (1900–3), and by Beresford Pite at the Amalgamated Approved Societies Building in Euston Square (1907).

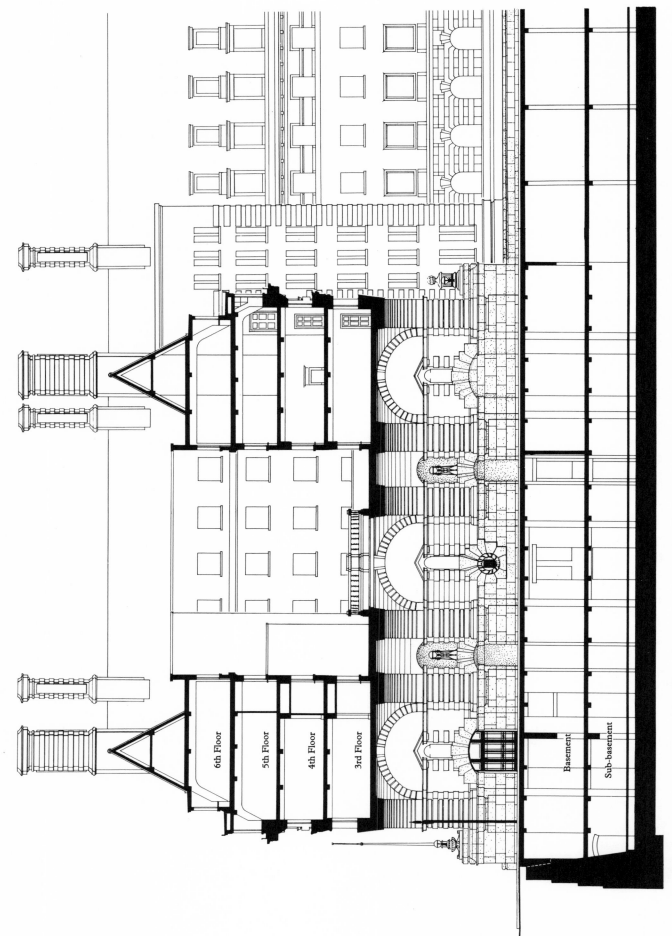

Fig. 30. Westminster Bridge Road front (Block 9). Section looking west, showing the Members' Carriage Drive leading from Westminster Bridge Road (on the left) to the Members' Courtyard

are relatively close together, and he might have felt that his dominating original design would have thrown the façade out of balance by being repeated in such a short space. The revised version has the same jagged voussoirs above arched attic windows, but in place of the columns, a greater expanse of rusticated stonework.

The focus here is concentrated about the lofty arched entrance to the Members' Carriage Drive (Plate 14d), its keystone rising into an oval window framed with excellent stone carving by C. H. Mabey. The carriage entrance is guarded by tall wrought-iron gates – made by Strode & Company – and flanked by granite 'sentry boxes' serving as entrances for pedestrians. The latter were designed as pedestals for equestrian groups – similar to those planned for the internal courtyard (Plate 16a) – which were never executed and are today surmounted by bronze lighting standards made by Strodes.

The great vaulted tunnel of granite and rusticated Portland stone which leads from the Westminster Bridge Road entrance to the Members' Courtyard is the most overtly dramatic architectural sequence at County Hall – Pevsner calls it 'frankly operatic' (Plates 14b, 15, fig. 30). Although foreshadowed in several of the competition entries, among them Lanchester & Rickards', Jemmet & McCombie's and H. T. Hare's (fig. 8a,b), this was a late addition to Knott's design and it plays havoc with the circulation in the cross blocks. Nevertheless, this feature, with its suggestion of great and dramatic architecture, is very skilfully handled.

The tunnel is 140 feet long and only 17 feet wide and is divided into three bays. The central bay contains an open saucer dome surmounted by a balustrade, while the other two finish in groined vaults supported by six massive piers on each side of the road. The bays have pedimented aedicules at high level, those in the central bays having a circular opening beneath them giving glimpses of the white-tiled light-wells beyond. There are staff and public entrances at the south end (Plate 15a) and an independent entrance to the Lady Members' accommodation at the north end.

Emerging from the carriage drive into the Members' Courtyard (Plates 16,17), the visitor has almost the impression of arriving within a fortress. The apparently low block on the north side containing the Members' Entrance, with its attic storey surmounted by rows of dormers, and the massive central feature of a rusticated doorway crowned by a winged trophy, has the look of the *corps de logis* of a French château (Plate 17a). This is the only internal court to be given the full-blown Portland-stone-and-granite architectural treatment of the exterior, the effect of which has now been spoilt by the curtain-wall infilling of 1972–4. Although the courtyard itself is rectangular the roadway is circular, formed by the upper surface of a drum-like structure which housed the basement record office (Plate 16b). Outside this drum the walls of the court rise from the basement level. At the four corners of the court prominent square lavatory-towers

with well-handled stone detailing reach almost to the top of the roof. In 1922 C. H. Reilly had felt that the 'fine appeal to the imagination' made by the covered approach was 'a little dissipated' when 'you walk through the arch and find the circular court suggested is not really circular'. The cast-iron lamp-holders on the granite wall surrounding the central enclosure were made by the Bromsgrove Guild (Plate 16c). On the north side of the court a short flight of steps leads to the bronze doors enriched with ornaments modelled by George Alexander (Plate 17b). The two flanking granite plinths are surmounted by stubby stone columns each carrying a pair of illuminated glass spheres.

The second long frontage faces Belvedere Road (Plate 13a,b, folded drawing B1), and here the central feature is a broad and massive attached 'portico', projecting only slightly from the main body of the building. Set between pavilions similar to those flanking the riverfront Crescent, it corresponds with the Crescent in width, as Aston Webb suggested it should, to distinguish externally the 'county hall' part of the building from the 'county offices' part. In its design this portico virtually reproduces the river-front colonnade for which Knott had fought so tenaciously, but unsuccessfully, in 1910, and which was itself a development of his original scheme (Plates 5b, 13a). Thus it gives the clearest idea of Knott's architectural style at the time of the competition, being almost identical to his prize-winning river-front elevation, albeit expressed as an attached feature rather than extending forward as he originally intended.

On the ground floor five wide doorways, each fitted with pairs of heavy bronze doors, interrupt the rusticated banding and granite plinth. The tall central opening, which cuts through the stringcourse and is dressed with a pediment decorated with anthemion acroteria, is the Ceremonial Entrance (Plate 13c). The ground-floor storey provides the base for the five-bay colonnaded screen, whose pairs of columns, rising through three stories, carry a plain entablature surmounted by a deep windowless attic. The latter consists of a large plane of stone, relieved only by a stringcourse near the top supported on four lion's-head brackets, and a bronze fitting for the flag-pole (Plate 13b). Like the parapet wall in the Crescent, this huge panel deprives the accommodation behind of most of its light, a defect which Knott here alleviates, as in the Crescent, by reversing the positions of the offices and corridors.

The northern front was, of course, not completed until 1933, and is discussed in Chapter VIII.

The Principal Floor

The completed County Hall was a happy blend of materials, of which many Londoners could be proud. Reginald Blunt visited it soon after it opened:

Internally, the impression is chiefly one of finely proportioned chambers with oak wainscotting carried up to the frieze, in spacious panelling relieved about the mantels and doorways by some suggestive carving; of the use of dark Ashburton marble and Hopton Wood stone for pillars and fireplaces; of inverted electric light which gives an excellently even illumination reflected from the ceilings; of floors of teak and oak, and, in passages, of inlaid rubber composition, quiet, easily cleaned and wonderfully durable.[18]

But however impressive the building, its very size and the diverse nature of the accommodation make it a confusing place. The inherent problems of finding one's way about in its miles of corridors are further compounded by the interruption to the circulation caused by the Members' Entrance, and the absence of completely consecutive room numbering, inevitable in a building planned with cross blocks.

The arrangement of the accommodation within the building generally follows the principles set out in the 'Suggested Plan' of 1907 (fig. 4). On the Principal Floor were concentrated all the committee rooms, and offices for the Chairman and other important Members, and for the Chief Officers. The distinctions between minor committee rooms and important offices were blurred, and these rooms often changed their uses. However, there were certain zones which were dedicated to Committee use or office use almost throughout County Hall's occupation as a centre of local government. Thus the rooms overlooking the Crescent were all for the use of Members, either as public rooms or offices, as was the range to the north. The southern end of the riverfront and Westminster Bridge Road front was occupied by officers. The central section of the Belvedere Road front housed some of the most finely finished committee rooms of the 1922 building, with smaller rooms on either side, whose use seems to have varied over time between smaller committee rooms, and offices for either Chairmen of Committees or Chief Officers.

The Belvedere Road Entrance and the Ceremonial Staircase

County Hall's Belvedere Road entrance (Plate 13b,c) had two functions: as a ceremonial entrance and as the main staff and public entrance. From Belvedere Road one enters a wide hall with a low coffered ceiling, which sits below the committee rooms on the Principal Floor (Plate 19a). The floor is of grey marble mosaic (by Art Pavements and Decorations, Limited)[19] with decorative banding and the LCC coat of arms at its centre, and the walls are lined with Roman marble. The decorative stone carving above the ten doorways and over the fireplaces was carried out by A. H. Wilkinson.[20] It was for the two chimneypieces here that the Council used the gift of Verde Prato marble

from the Italian Government (see page 67). This replaced the black Belgium marble which Knott had intended in 1915,[21] but without any significant change to the somewhat Art Deco-ish design (Plate 27c, fig. 28).[c] The room was intentionally austere, but a fine one, and makes a fitting prelude to the more elaborate ceremonial route beyond. At the same time the restrained decoration avoids too jarring a contrast with the ground-floor offices ranged along utilitarian corridors to which the hall also gives access by steps rising out of it to left and right.

Elegant bronze and wrought-iron gates, designed by Knott and made by Singers of Frome for £295, guard the entrance to the Ceremonial Staircase leading to the Council Chamber and the Principal Floor (Plate 19b).[22] An amusing insight into the Council's view of its own popularity comes in a letter concerning these gates from Knott's office to Riley, in October 1921. Riley had earlier written suggesting that the gates ought to be reduced in height. Knott replied that he gathered from the discussion in the Committee, when the gates were originally proposed, that they should be of 'such a nature that they could not easily be scaled by an angry mob', and, he added, he did not feel that 'the idea of merely suggesting that ingress is forbidden to the public at that point is what was intended by the Committee'.[23]

Doorways either side of these gates lead to the public galleries in the Council Chamber. Since 1955 the right-hand passage has also led to the Staff Chapel (see page 90).

The marble-lined walls of the Ceremonial Staircase support a colonnade of coupled columns carrying a barrel-vaulted ceiling, which is intersected by the groins of semi-circular windows which light it from above (Plate 20a). The staircase balustrade and the railings guarding the opening on to the stairs from above were made in cast iron and bronze to Knott's design by the Bromsgrove Guild (fig. 26a). To Charles Marriott this staircase recalled the 'classical reconstructions' of such artists as Alma Tadema.[24] The lobby at the top of the staircase forms part of the marble-lined corridor or 'ambulatory' which surrounds the Council Chamber at Principal-Floor level (Plate 20b,c). Most of the marble used here is white Pentelic, from the old Athenian quarry, relieved by bands of Sienna or Cipollino. The many columns in this part of the building are of black Belgian, Bleu de Savoie, or Ashburton marble.[25] The white marble walls provided suitable spaces for the LCC's War Memorial, and for lists of Council office-holders.

Knott had hoped to use marble for the flooring of the 'ambulatory', to correspond with the rich marbling of the walls, but the Establishment Committee felt that it 'might tend to wear slippery', and at Knott's suggestion a non-slip patent linoleum product called 'Ruboleum' was selected.[26]

The location of the Council Chamber illustrates one of

---

[c] In 1968 the Belvedere Road entrance hall was remodelled, and, it was thought, the chimneypieces covered up by false-work. Only when this was removed, ten years later, was it discovered that they had, in fact, been torn out. They have never been found.

the problems created by the wedge-shaped plan. The short east-west axis is 'bent' in the middle to make a right angle to each façade and the Chamber has its centre on the intersection of this bend with the north-south axis. Consequently the centre line of the Ceremonial Staircase aims towards the centre point of the Chamber rather than towards the Chairman's seat opposite. One commentator thought 'a pair of attendants in gorgeous uniform, standing ready to open the bronze doors, might compensate for the lack of the vista'.[27]

The Council Chamber

The octagonal Council Chamber (*Frontispiece*, Plates 21, 28a, figs 31, 32) provided accommodation for 200 Members, rather than the 144 actually elected to the Council, in order to allow for possible future increase. The plan adopted here is foreshadowed not only by the 'Suggested Plan' for the new County Hall (fig. 4), but also by the extended chamber at Spring Gardens (fig. 1). There the LCC had replaced the MBW's 'House of Commons' style face-to-face seating plan with a horse-shoe arrangement of benches, while also installing press and public galleries, and Ayes and Noes Lobbies (with entrances on either side of the Dais). These features are all incorporated in the larger Chamber at County Hall where benches are arranged in tiers. Four galleries overlook the Chamber, that behind the Chairman's Dais being for the press and the others for the public. Doors leading to the Ayes and Noes Lobbies are on the north and south sides of the Chamber respectively.

The centre of focus within the Chamber is the Dais and the Chairman's seat, the latter elaborately carved, and veneered in black oak from a tree dug up at Villiers Street.[28] The Chairman's bench, and the officials' bench immediately in front of it, are decorated with lions' heads and enriched mouldings carved by George Alexander, who was also responsible for the carved ends to the Members' benches.[29]

The lower parts of the Chamber are faced with marble. For the plinth, the capping of the dado and the framing of the doorways, black Belgian marble is employed, and for the filling of the dado, greenish-grey Greek Cipollino from the island of Euboea, which has a very pronounced vein structure. This was a fashionable marble at the time, used to best effect in Bentley's Westminster Cathedral, but also found in Mountford's Central Criminal Court. Veine Dorée, a beautiful marble from the Italian Alps, is used for the columns and pilasters supporting the lintels of the gallery openings. The capitals and bases are made of manganese bronze, as are the elaborately patterned gallery fronts and the radiators (Plate 28d), all of which were modelled by Alexander and carried out by a number of specialist foundries.[30]

Natural lighting is provided by four tall clear-glass windows, one at each of the splayed corners. In front of these windows are empty plinths, each decorated with a boldly modelled festoon in bronze, and originally intended as bases for statuary groups symbolizing Progress, Prudence, Education and Guardianship. Though these were rejected by the Establishment Committee as early as 1913, an idea of the effect Knott had in mind can be had from a perspective published in the previous year (see *Frontispiece*).[31]

To contrast with the green of the Cipollino and the black Belgian marble, a bright blue carpet was laid and the oak seats were upholstered in orange-red leather.[32] This richness of colouring is another indication of Knott's move away from the polite style shown in the 1912 perspective to a more individual and highly flavoured manner.

There were a number of technical innovations, and Members' benches had an elaborate ventilating system from the beginning (fig. 39, see also page 90), though a loudspeaker system was only added later.

The upper part of the walls and the ceiling of the Chamber are finished in plaster, while in an attempt to anticipate the acoustic problems so easily foreseen, and indeed so early revealed, the circular central panel of the ceiling is of felt.[33] In this respect the room was regarded as a failure from the outset. The *Daily Express* dubbed it 'The L.C.C.'s Hall of Murmurs', and observers were unanimous in finding the acoustics dreadful. Knott's original design had put its height at a hundred feet, and although he had been persuaded by Riley to reduce this to fifty-five, it was not low enough, being still about twenty-five feet higher than Spring Gardens.[34] The difficulty precipitated numerous letters to *The Times*, each recommending a different solution, as well as one to the Chairman of the Council, which blamed the speakers rather than the room, a theory welcomed by Knott.[35]

This is a problem which, despite various attempts to overcome it, has never been solved. Reports were prepared by the Building Research Station, and some of their recommendations were tried, but with little apparent effect. In November 1951 the Council decided to install a Tannoy amplification system, operated by a controller who would switch on a microphone in front of each speaker in turn and adjust the amplification level. The system was never entirely satisfactory, being prone to silent lapses and sudden surges of feedback.[36]

The responsibility for this problem was Knott's, for insisting on a high octagonal ceiling, and blame cannot be attached to either the Municipal Reformers' economical approach, or to the grander ambitions of the Progressives.[d] In fact the brief initially called for a 'conversational chamber', and this instruction was never altered.[37]

Contemporaries seem to have been generally impressed by the new Chamber. Clough Williams-Ellis saw it as 'octagonal, domed and lofty – where red leather, grey oak

---

[d]The Building Research Station told the Council in 1929 that the acoustical problems were inherent in the shape of the chamber.

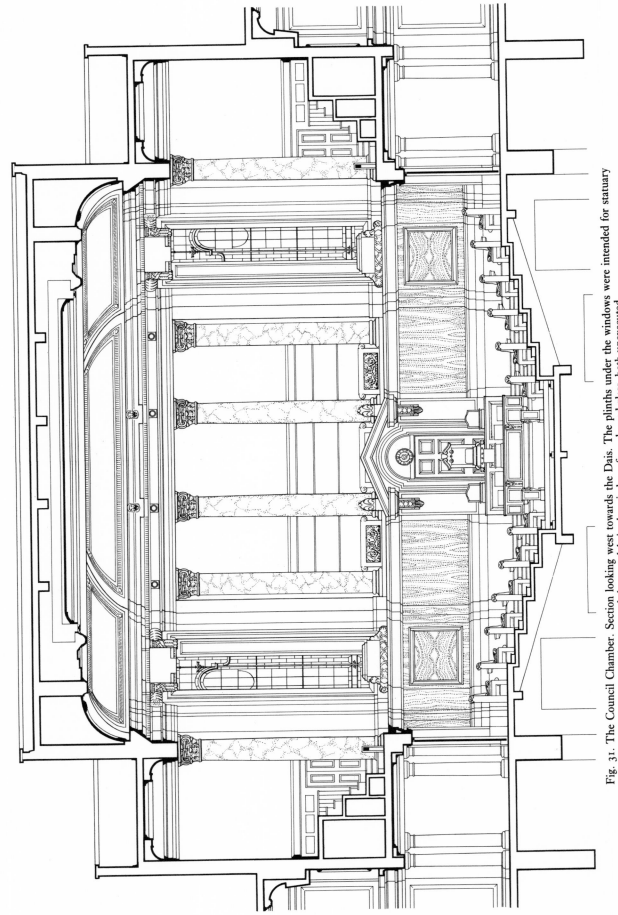

Fig. 31. The Council Chamber. Section looking west towards the Dais. The plinths under the windows were intended for statuary groups and the roundels in the windows for coloured glass, both unexecuted

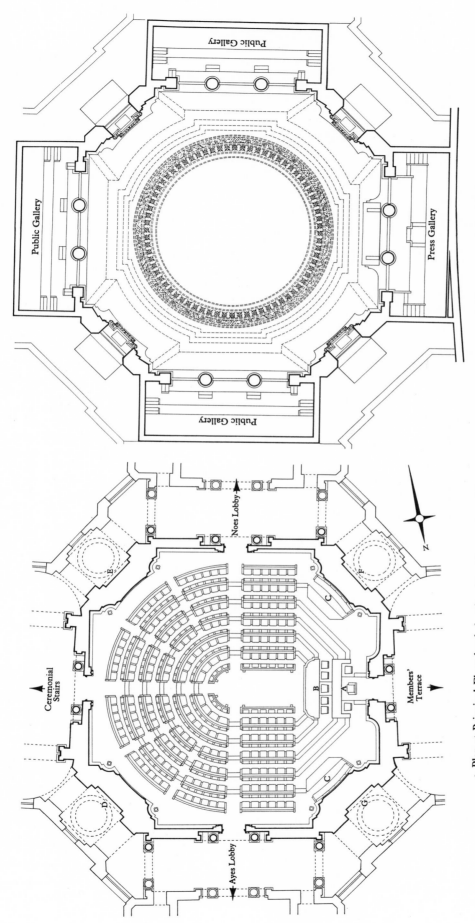

Fig. 32. The Council Chamber and the surrounding 'ambulatory'

a Plan at Principal-Floor level showing horseshoe seating of Members, the Dais occupied by the Chairman (A) and the Clerk (B), and seats for officers and distinguished visitors (C). The letters in the 'ambulatory' show the positions of the Foundation Stone, 1912 (D), the Staff War Memorial and Book of Remembrance, 1939–45 (E), the Arms of No.601 (London) Squadron R.Aux.A.F., 1955 (F) and the Inscription commemorating the completion of County Hall, 1963 (G)

b Plan at Gallery-level with reflected ceiling plan. The Press and Public Galleries were reached by separate staircases from the Belvedere Road Entrance Hall

and quiet coloured marbles, softly lit by four tall windows, combine to produce an effect of calm grandeur unusual in a secular building'.[38] But it did not completely eclipse memories of the 'old panelled chamber' at Spring Gardens, which although smaller and less convenient, had a 'homely atmosphere', as Gibbon and Bell recalled in 1939:

The new chamber, even after nearly twenty years, remains a rather aloof personality: it is not exactly unfriendly, but ... it ... does not, as the old room did, prompt the features to relax into an affectionate and reminiscent smile. It is business-like, has an air of dignity and conveys an impression of expense rather than richness.[39]

The Voting Lobbies

The two top-lit voting lobbies (Plate 22a) are located on either side of the Council Chamber, between the 'ambulatory' and the cross corridors to the north and south. Columns of black Belgian marble with white Pentelic caps screen the lobbies from the 'ambulatory' and corridors, and flank the two chimneypieces within each lobby. The chimneypieces themselves are also made from black Belgian marble, inset with a central panel of coloured marble – lapis lazuli in the Ayes (north) Lobby, red Skyros in the Noes. Both rooms are panelled in highly figured and polished Indian laurel wood, the panelling above the chimneypieces being enriched with carving by C. H. Mabey.[40] This scheme of decoration was arrived at only after several attempts. The earliest drawing for these lobbies (1913) shows raised-and-fielded panelling – probably in oak – and larger chimneypieces more in the style of those in rooms 169 and 177. A drawing of 1914 has the walls lined with panels of 'Enriched Leather'. In 1919 Knott wanted to use 'greywood' for the panelling, but when this proved impossible to obtain Indian laurel was substituted.[41] It was for the lunettes in these lobbies that Frank Brangwyn was to have provided murals, and it was here that part of the Portrait Collection was hung.[42]

The Members' Entrance

Members arriving by carriage from the Westminster Bridge Road, through the rusticated and vaulted tunnel leading to the Members' Courtyard, enjoyed a completely different approach to the Council Chamber and Principal Floor (Plates 14, 15). Here there was no question of an entrance being made to serve two classes of user. The Members' Entrance, in the centre of the north side of the Members' Courtyard, leads directly to the Principal Floor and the Council Chamber. The bronze doors at the top of the steps in the Members' Courtyard open into a small marble-walled vestibule (Plate 28c), where a further short flight of steps leads into a corridor.[e] From here the Members had direct access to all their accommodation: to the cloakroom and lavatories, themselves the subject of admiring comment in the press,[43] through the Noes Lobby and across the 'ambulatory' to the Council Chamber, eastward to the committee rooms along Belvedere Road, or westward to the Members' Library and to refreshment rooms along the riverfront.

The Westminster Bridge Road Entrance Halls

On either side of the Westminster Bridge Road end of the Carriage Drive doors and steps lead down into squarish low-ceilinged entrance halls (Plate 36a). These are at 'ground-floor' level, communicating directly with the corridors through bronze-and-glass doors in the fireplace walls: on the north side partially screened staircases lead to the upper floors and basements. Although primarily intended for staff use, the two halls are nevertheless finished in the same grave manner as the main entrance hall in Belvedere Road. The walls are lined with the same conspicuously jointed Roman marble, and the ceilings are deeply compartmented. The floors are of terrazzo, laid – by Art Pavements and Decorations, Limited – to a pattern which Knott had designed originally for the Belvedere Road hall.[44] Above the fireplaces are stone-carvings by A. H. Wilkinson denoting the attributes of good government. That in the west (riverside) hall includes the scales of Justice and the wheel of Nemesis, 'representing the impartiality of the guidance of Administration' (Plate 29d), while the carving in the east hall shows 'the winged helmet of Mercury suggesting Rapidity, Power and Wisdom'.[45][f]

As in the Belvedere Road hall, Knott uses the combination of expensive materials and austere design to mitigate a steep drop in emotional temperature between one part of the building and another, here between the Piranesian grandeur of the Carriage Drive and the severely utilitarian corridors.

Principal Floor Corridors

The long oak-lined corridors of the Principal Floor are for many visitors one of the more enduring images of County Hall (Plate 26a,c). The receding tunnel-like vistas of white plaster vaults, the dark high-quality panelling with its reiterated emphatic mouldings, over-scaled pedimented doorcases and pervasive acanthus ornament, and

[e]The plan as originally built has four risers from the vestibule which lead to a landing in the corridor. Three risers led left and right up to the corridor and three more straight ahead to the Noes Lobby. The impracticality of putting this landing in the middle of a corridor must have been soon apparent, for before the building was opened the depression was boarded over and a further three risers added to the flight leading up from the vestibule. This piece of false flooring can be detected by ear.

[f]The taste for decorating municipal buildings with 'civic allegory' was evidently widespread. Compare, for example, the groups depicting 'Control' and 'Accounting' on the Municipal House in Prague (1909–11).

the polished parquet flooring, are almost hypnotically powerful. The dominant element in this was not, however, intended originally. At first the walls were meant to be given a Keen's cement dado, the change to oak panelling, which added a further £9,000 to the cost, being advocated by Knott as a way of saving on maintenance.[46]

The corridors were furnished with oak benches – twelve were ordered in 1922.[47] Also to be found there was a set of pigeon-holes for the Members' mail, an older-looking piece perhaps salvaged from Spring Gardens, over which a uniformed messenger presided (Plate 26d).

River-front Crescent Rooms (116A, 116, 119–124)

The Crescent and the areas on either side were the exclusive province of Members. Rooms for the Chairman, Deputy and Vice-Chairmen, and for the Whips and the Leader occupied the Crescent, with reading and refreshment rooms for Members on either side. These rooms were decorated with enriched plaster ceilings, often with substantial cornices, oak panelling and carved oak and marble fireplaces of great elaboration. Though the rooms were re-ordered and re-decorated under the GLC in the late 1960s and early 1970s,[48] the original drawings and contemporary photographs indicate that the standard of design and workmanship was very high. Most of the drawings date from 1912–1915,[49] but like much of the interior decoration the work was only carried out after the war. Indeed, these rooms were excluded from the royal tour because the panelling was still unfinished in July 1922. This part of County Hall suffered considerable damage in the Blitz, and drawings for reinstatement were prepared but not executed.[50]

Although in the later years of the Council the allocation of rooms became more flexible, in 1922 the three largest (rooms 120, 123 and 116) were allotted to the Chairman, Deputy-Chairman and Vice-Chairman respectively. The Whips occupied the two rooms on either side of the central lobby (121 and 122), and the other smaller rooms were allocated first to the Chairman's staff, and Chairmen of Committees, and later to the Leaders of both parties.

All the rooms were lined with raised-and-fielded oak panelling, enriched with carving by George Alexander, with mantelpieces decorated, as elsewhere in County Hall, in a strictly hierarchical manner. In the Chairman's Room (Plate 24d), entered through a pedimented and pilastered oak doorway, was an oak fireplace with a mantel supported by substantial consoles ornamented with lions' heads, with marble slips and a fine steel grate. At the wall angles on the mantelpiece were two carved owls; above was a panel, and the room was decorated with an acorn and leaf frieze. The Vice-Chairman's Room was treated in a similar way, but there the owls were replaced by eagles. Other fireplaces were lighter in feeling, those in the Whips' Rooms had bolection mouldings round the fireplace, with floral festoons sculptured in limewood above.[51]

The domed central lobby leading to the Members' Terrace was treated as an extension of the 'ambulatory' and lined with marble – white Pentelic inlaid with pale Siena for the walls, Ashburton for the pilasters and columns, and black Belgian for the pedimented doorcases which dressed the two entrances into the Whips' rooms.[52]

The Members' Terrace itself lies within the segmental space enclosed by the Crescent and bounded towards the river by the balustrade overlooking the embankment (Plate 12a). It was here that the Opening Ceremony took place in 1922 (Plate 10a), and throughout County Hall's existence as a public building it was used for both formal and informal entertaining, being recalled by many Members with as much affection as the equally famous terrace on the opposite bank (Plate 47c). To Reginald Blunt, visiting County Hall with the London Society in 1922, it was, together with the Members' Courtyard, the most impressive element of the building:

Approached by three broad curved flights of descending steps from the Council Chamber Lobby, the Luncheon and the Reading Rooms, and commanding northward over the river the fine sweep of the Victoria Embankment, with the perspective of Westminster Bridge and the Houses of Parliament to the south, one can imagine the attraction of this spacious pavement on a summer afternoon; and could predict . . . that heated Councillors will prefer the discussion of the future of their Metropolis over tea and cakes by Father Thames to even the self-regulated ventilation of their Council Chamber behind.[53]

Refreshment Rooms (131, 132, 133)

Along the river front, north of the Crescent, rooms 131–3 were designed as refreshment rooms, with serveries to the north and south in rooms 134 and 125. The refreshment rooms were panelled in oak, with enriched plaster ceilings and oak or marble chimneypieces, decorated with varying degrees of elaboration. The chimneypiece in the Members' and Visitors' Refreshment Room (133) was remarkable for its great scroll-and-ram's head pilasters carved in oak by George Alexander (Plate 27b). This room was divided from the Members' Room to the south (132) by a moveable partition. There was an intention in 1915, apparently never carried out, that room 132 at least should have had a 'decorative frieze in colour'.[54] In 1933, room 134, one of the serveries, was extended and converted to a retiring-room, and in the 1960s room 133 was divided to make an office for the Chairman and a secretary's room.

The large Members' Refreshment Room (131) was housed within the northern Crescent pavilion. It has a bay window on the west overlooking the Thames, and in the south-west corner a lobby and door with outside steps leading on to the Members' Terrace. Knott designed a pair of very handsome marble chimneypieces for this room and the corresponding room (115) in the south Crescent pavilion (Plate 27a), but neither have survived post-war redecoration. Above the chimneypiece was a panel carved with a rose and leaf design, while round the top of the

Fig. 33. Members' Library. Working drawing of 1913, showing the proposed treatment of both internal and window walls. Neither the portraits nor the busts were ever installed

panelling is a frieze of carved bosses, all the work of Alexander. As part of the post-war refurbishment this room and the adjoining refreshment room (132) had their ceilings lowered, but the original panelling was allowed to remain.

Reading Room (115) and Library (114)

The Reading Room (Plate 25c) occupied the corresponding position on the other side of the Crescent to room 131, looking out on to the river and the terrace. It was originally decorated in a similar manner with an identical chimneypiece (Plate 27a) and identical carving above and on the walls and pilasters. This room, too, was altered in the 1960s, but more radically, to make the Chairman's Reception Room (Plate 43c). A door in the south wall gave access to the Members' Library.

This was one of the most gracious and successful of the public rooms created by Knott at County Hall (Plate 23a). It is furnished with oak bookcases, in the manner of an eighteenth-century gentleman's library, as the original drawings depicted (fig. 33). There are two chimneypieces, that at the south end being decorated with a carving by Wilkinson showing 'Truth reading aloud, the second figure recording, with the plumed helmet of Minerva, Goddess of the Arts' (Plate 29c). With its comfortable tables set between the handsome bookcases, and the river before the windows, the library was a room where not only Members and officers but London historians could appreciate the civilized objectives of visionaries like Swinton. Beyond the south fireplace is a small galleried librarian's office complete with oak spiral staircase.

The Members' Library at County Hall housed a publicly available collection of works about London topography and local government, which was one of the most complete holdings on that subject. From 1891 the LCC began to collect works on local government matters for the use of Members, and by 1907 it was responsible for two additional libraries, the Education Collection, and the Horniman. The Harben Collection followed in 1910, and the collection of London material built up by John Burns, M.P. and LCC member for Battersea, was presented by the newspaper proprietor, Lord Southwood, in 1943. One of the requirements of Lord Southwood's gift was that the 'premises and surroundings in which it is housed should be conducive to the comfort of members of the public who want to consult and examine it'.[55]

By 1901 the collection had grown so much that the Historical Records and Buildings Committee decided to hold a student competition for a bookplate for the Council's Library. The results were adjudicated by G. J. Frampton, but none were judged good enough, and on Frampton's advice the commission was offered to Robert Anning Bell (1863–1933). He favoured 'a rather severe treatment – perhaps an architectural frame with the Council's coat of arms and any figures which might be introduced rather subordinated to the set of the design'. A different design (fig. 34) was finally chosen by the Council, described by Bell 'as adapted to the ideas of the Committee ... The seated figure is of course the London County Council – the sturdy tree beneath which she sits may be taken to typify London itself, the scars of old wounds and the fact that it bears fruit and flowers at the same time are obvious metaphors'.[56] In 1944, W. Surrey Dane (1892–

1978), the printer and publisher, was commissioned to design a bookplate for the Burns collection incorporating the Council's arms, together with a plan of Battersea Park.

Rooms 118 and 179

To the east along the corridor in Block 4, the oak-panelled Waiting Room (118) was given one of the finest old marble chimneypieces in County Hall (Plate 27d). Originally intended for the Large Conference Room (171), it came from a rear room at No. 59 Lincoln's Inn Fields. The carved central panel, representing Aesop's fable of 'The Bear and the Beehive', is by William Collins, the eighteenth-century statuary who specialized in modelling reliefs for chimneypieces, and follows a design by Francis Barlow first published in 1665-6.[57] This room, too, has been divided.

Room 179 was originally allocated as part of the Members' cloakrooms, and dressing-rooms, needed in a more spacious age. It was later converted to offices.

The Main Committee Room (128, 129, 130) and Conference Rooms (170 and 171)

North of the Council Chamber was the Main Committee Room, originally intended for Education Committee meetings and equipped with galleries for press and public (Plate 24a-c, figs 35-36). It can be divided into three separate rooms by means of two large screens housed in boxes beneath the floor. These partitions are extremely well designed, and fit so subtly into the panelled interior, that when fully open or closed, a spectator finds difficulty in perceiving that the room is possible of such transformation. Though the original drawings date from 1912, only the structural work and the minimum of panelling was completed before the Council had to stop work (Plate 24a), and the enrichments, the fireplaces, and the fitting out of the public gallery were added in 1921. The original scheme had called for decorative painting in the lunettes at either end of the main room.[58] Each compartment is treated separately, with a barrel-vaulted ceiling in the centre, and at the ends lower ceilings having a wide cove and a deeply moulded central wreath of flowers and fruit. The panelling itself is relatively simple, with a richness of detail given by the carving on the cornice and over the fireplaces by George Alexander. The ceiling and galleries are supported by oak columns with Ionic capitals set on the diagonal. There is a complete carved acanthus cornice, carved swags are placed at the springing of the ceiling vault at the ends of the room, and the gallery ends are marked with carved pine-cone finials. At either end of the room is a large marble fireplace with a carved oak tympanum – in one symbols of the industrial arts in a floral setting, and in the other an open book garlanded by large naturalistic leaves. A suite of removable oak seating and desks was commissioned for this room from the Bath Cabinet Makers' Company, at a cost of £1,700, together

Fig. 34. The London County Council bookplate, designed in 1903 by R. Anning Bell

with horseshoe-shaped Committee tables and sets of chairs for the two end rooms.[59]

In the Large and Small Conference Rooms to the east, (rooms 171 and 170 respectively) oak panelling gives way to painted softwood. Both these rooms were designed in 1915, but whereas in 171 the panelling is of the traditional full-height raised-and-fielded variety, that in 170 is composed of narrow panels of a more modern cast. Knott's striking black-and-purple marble chimneypiece in 171 was a late substitution. He had originally intended to place here the well-known 'Bear and Beehive' chimneypiece now in room 118.[60]

Committee Rooms 169, 172-3, 175-7 and Waiting Room (174)

Knott designed a fine sequence of committee rooms for the central block and pavilions on the Belvedere Road front – 'such vistas of Committee Rooms, great and small' as Reginald Blunt observed. The six which lie either side of the narrow central waiting room (room 174) are handed. They are fitted with elaborate oak and marble fireplaces, raised-and-fielded oak panelling, often with a low dado, and moulded plaster ceilings. The two pavilion rooms (169 and 177), which have central curved window

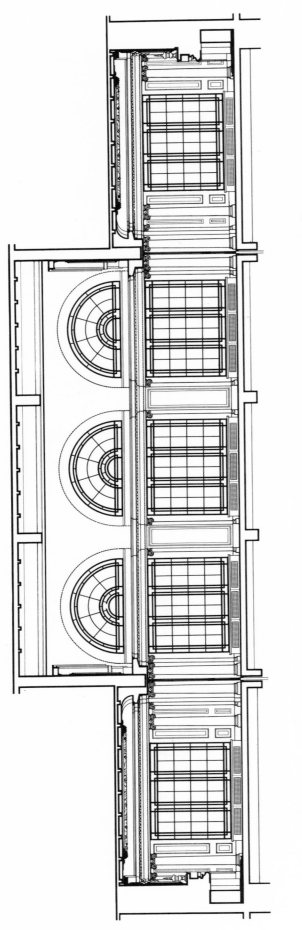

a Section looking north. The central window was replaced in 1932 by doors into the new Bridge Passage leading to the northern section of County Hall

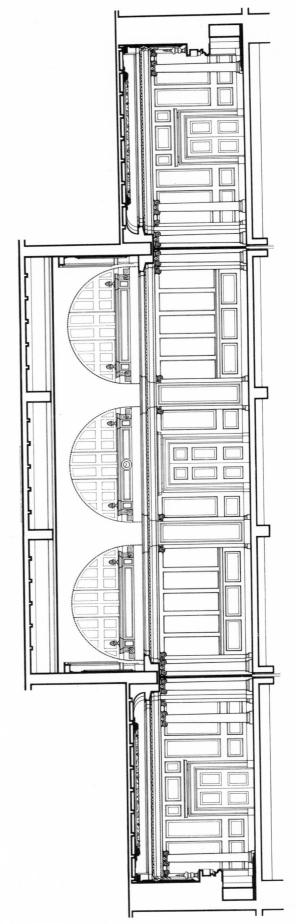

b Section looking south showing the Press Gallery and Public Gallery above

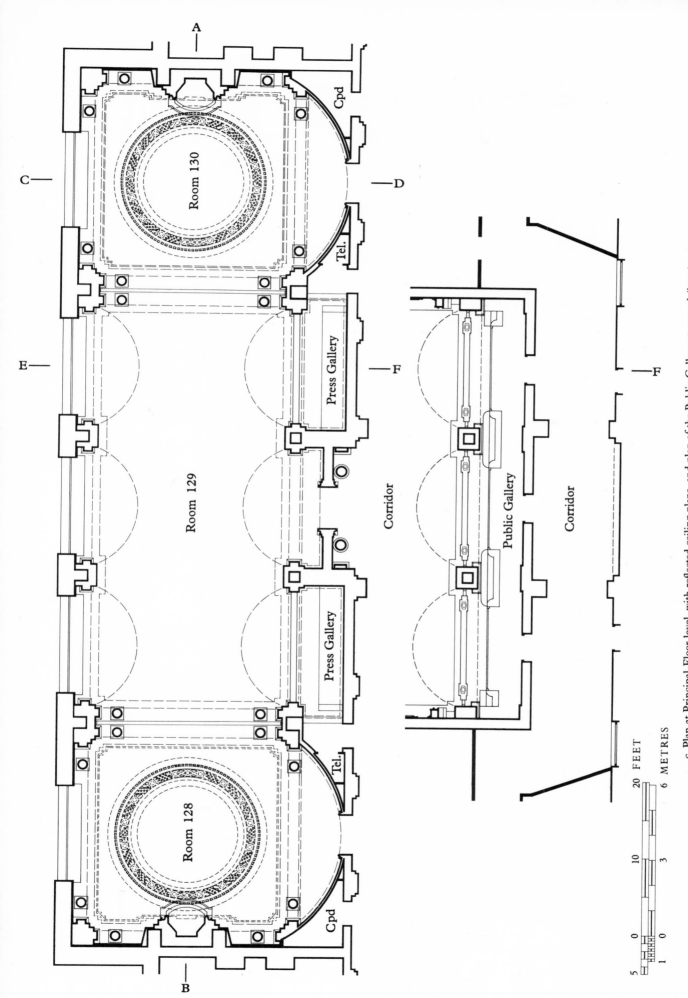

Room 130

Room 129

Room 128

A

B

C

D

E

F

F

Cpd

Tel.

Press Gallery

Press Gallery

Corridor

Public Gallery

Corridor

Tel.

Cpd

FEET

METRES

20

10

5

0

6

3

1

0

c Plan at Principal-Floor level, with reflected ceiling plans, and plan of the Public Gallery at second-floor level

Fig. 35. Main Committee Room – Rooms 128–130 – as built. The room is capable of sub-division by means of sliding partitions housed in slots in the floor. In the two sections the partitions are shown raised

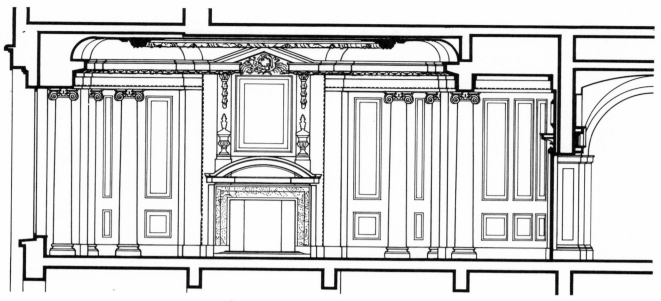

a Room 130. Section (C-D) looking east, showing treatment of chimneypiece wall

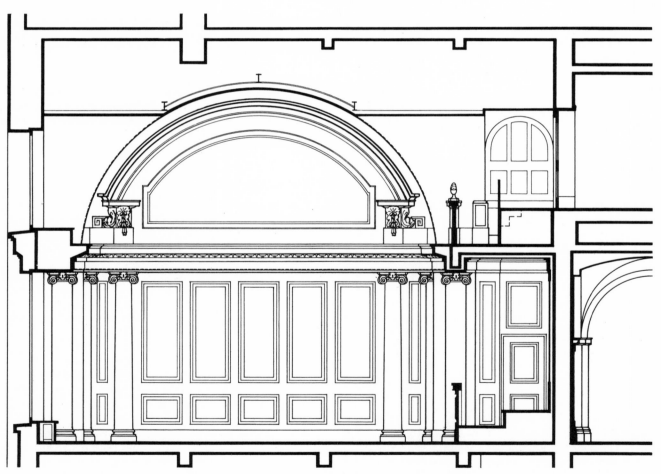

b Room 129. Section (E-F) looking east, with the sliding partition separating room 129 from room 130 raised

Fig. 36. Main Committee Room – Rooms 128–130

bays, are the most important (Plate 22b). Their coffered ceilings are decorated with interconnecting circle and key bands, the panelling has recessed panels with bead-and-reel cornices punctuated by rosette capitals similar to those in rooms 131 and 133, and very handsome red, yellow and white marble fireplaces designed in Knott's office. Rooms 172 and 176 are slightly smaller and more plainly finished, with segmental pediments over the fireplace in which are set clocks salvaged from Old County Hall. The ceilings have scrolled heart bands filled with floral ornament. The inner band has a layered acanthus-leaf border on the outer edge only, giving it a slightly disquieting unfinished appearance. Rooms 173 and 175, on either side of the waiting room, also have elaborate ceilings ornamented with plaster bands, and pedimented oak and marble fireplaces. The waiting room (174) has a deeply undercut circular ceiling and another of the clocks from Old County Hall, set into the oak panelling, but no fireplace.

Some at least of the oak panelling in the committee rooms and offices was originally treated with potash, 'giving it a deliciously soft and cool effect', but this seems to have worn off in the intervening years, or the treatment has been reversed.[61]

Rooms 167–168 and 180–184

On either side of the central range of committee rooms along the Belvedere Road front are other oak-panelled rooms which were first occupied by chairmen of committees. To the north, rooms 167 and 168, intended originally as committee rooms, were allocated to the Chairmen of the Education Committee and the Education Sub-Committee. Similar, though not absolutely identical in appearance, both rooms have full-height raised-and-fielded panelling, plain plaster ceilings, and wooden chimneypieces with marble slips framed by carved elongated consoles. The panel over each fireplace – square in 167, oval in 168 – has carved enrichments (Plate 23b).

The four narrow rooms to the south of the central range form a handed sequence – room 180 being paired with 184 and room 181 with 182. All four have two-thirds-height panelling and moulded plaster cornices. Rooms 182 and 183 also have decorative plaster friezes and integral oak chimneypieces with green-veined marble fillets.

Lady Members' Room (188) and Lady Members' Visitors' Room (189)

A suite of rooms in the eastern half of Block 8 was set aside for women Members of the Council and given its own separate entrance from the Members' Carriage Drive. In its early years, the LCC did not have women Members

as such. Those who had been elected to the first Council were debarred by the courts, through legal action taken by two Moderate Members, B. T. Beresford-Hope and Sir Walter de Souza, and no women sat on the LCC until after the passing of the Qualification of Women (County and Borough Councils) Act in 1907.[62]

Possibly as some sort of *amende*, the suite provided was particularly elegant. The separate Lady Members' Entrance comprised a small panelled hall with an inlaid marble floor, whence a short oak staircase led up to cloak-rooms and to the Lady Members' Room (188) and Lady Members' Visitors' Room (189). The staircase has turned balusters and a flamboyant newel, carved by George Alexander, in the form of a vase supported by two satyr's heads, with flowers and fruits (Plate 26b).[63g]

Knott's original design for rooms 188 and 189, dated 1915, had made use of old onyx columns from Avery Hill Training College in south-east London to frame the chimneypieces; but in 1920, before the work was put in hand, new wooden columns were substituted (Plate 27e).[64] Both rooms were finished in oak with panels of silk tapestry and silk. In the Lady Members' Visitors' Room there is a white marble chimneypiece with a coloured marble slip and an overmantel decorated with a plaster wreath, and a clock originally intended to be surmounted by a statuette. The Lady Members' Room, which has a bowed east end, was finished in similar style.[65] By the 1980s both rooms had lost their wooden columns, and the silk tapestry had been replaced by flock wallpaper. They had long ceased to be used exclusively by women Members, and room 189 had been divided in two.

Rooms 135–139 and 159–163

This range of rooms along the south side of the cross-corridor in Block 12 was originally designed for the use of committees and committee chairmen, but was first occupied as offices. Handsomely finished, they have full-height raised-and-fielded panelling of softwood, painted 'ivory or light stone colour', and enriched plaster ceilings (Plate 25b). Knott had originally intended to use old chimneypieces in these rooms – the reason softwood panelling was used instead of oak – and he varied the design of the overmantel to complement the individual pieces (fig. 25).[h] In the event these were not used, the rooms being furnished instead with wooden chimneypieces of Knott's own invention.[67] (The eighteenth-century chimneypieces now in rooms 160 and 161, were installed only in 1932 on their removal from Old County Hall in Spring Gardens: they came originally from houses on Millbank.)[68] In 1933 rooms 139 and 163 were reduced in size when the bridge passage connecting room 129 with the Conference Hall was driven through them.

[g]This was removed in 1986; it is to be hoped that it will be replaced when the building is refurbished.
[h]The intended chimneypieces were from Lincoln's Inn Fields, Millbank, Upper Marylebone Street, Goswell Street and Peckham.[66]

Chief Officers' Rooms

The more important Chief Officers and their deputies were located on the Principal Floor, and offices also had to be provided for their immediate support staff. To some extent the decoration of the rooms allocated to the Council's officers reflects the hierarchical structure of the organization, although this is not always rigorously pursued. At the top of the tree, so to speak, are the four fully oak-panelled offices, three of them fitted with 'historic' chimneypieces, which were originally occupied by the Architect (104), the Clerk (109), the Chief Education Officer (165) and the Comptroller (194). The marble fireplaces in the Architect's, the Clerk's and the Comptroller's rooms came from Furzedown House, Streatham, bought by the Council in 1908 for redevelopment as a school and training college.[69] In dignity and finish these rooms are comparable to the Members' accommodation, and the Architect's room, in the south-west corner pavilion overlooking the Thames, was perhaps the best. The chimneypiece here has a central panel of putti leading a goat to the sacrificial altar; down the sides are representations of musical instruments. In the days of the GLC this room was occupied by the Director General and the names of the holders of this post are inscribed above the chimneypiece. The corresponding room in the south-east corner pavilion overlooking Belvedere Road (194) was taken by the Comptroller. The chimneypiece in the former Clerk's room (109) has a sculpted frieze with a cupid and figures representing the arts.

In a class by itself is room 165, which Knott designed for the Chief Education Officer. This is finished in accordance with Knott's drawing of 13 September 1915,[70] but being the northernmost room of the 1922 building on the Belvedere Road front it may not have been fully fitted out until Section D was built in 1930–33. Like the other Chief Officer's rooms it has full-height oak panelling but of a much more 'moderne' cast, consisting of narrow vertical planks having only the simplest of mouldings at top and bottom (Plate 25a).

The next step down from the fully oak-panelled office was one with painted raised-and-fielded deal panelling and a large apsidal ended panel above the chimneypiece (fig. 37). The best office of this type is the former Deputy Clerk's room (105), which is no smaller than the Clerk's own room further north along the river front, and retains its original light fittings. Other examples are room 196, where the apsidal-ended panel has had to be shortened to fit above a corner chimneypiece, and the much smaller room 192.

Another typical treatment found in both large and small rooms on this floor is a panelled dado and a very characteristic chimneypiece which incorporates a narrow apsidal-ended panel. Examples of this type are rooms 108, 185, 187, 190, 193 and 197. Not all these rooms were originally occupied by officers, several on the Belvedere Road front being allocated to Chairmen of Committees; however, rather surprisingly, the large room 193 was originally occupied by the Deputy Comptroller. Variations on this theme are rooms with a dado but no chimneypiece (e.g.

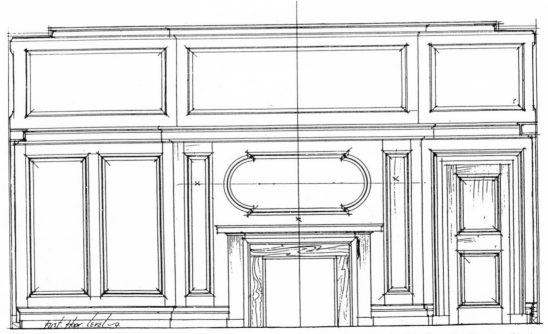

Fig. 37. Working drawing for panelling in the Deputy Clerk's room, 1920. At this date the Deputy Clerk was to have occupied a small room (108) next to the Clerk, but was subsequently allocated a larger room (105) which was panelled in the same style, as were rooms 192 and 196

Fig. 38. Cashier's Office on the ground floor. Working drawing of July 1913 showing typical 'officer's fireplace'

103A, 107, 184, 195), rooms with chimneypieces but no dado (112), and rooms with neither (e.g. 106A, 113, 198, 199).

The oak panelled interiors were seen as too sombre by some: as soon as the Clerk, Sir James Bird, was installed in his room (109), he called in Frederick Hiorns, Riley's former assistant and now architect with responsibility for County Hall under Topham Forrest, to complain. Not only did he want the 'balcony' outside his window removed, but he also objected to the 'somewhat sombre effect of the panelling of his room', and wondered if some sort of additional staining or colouring could be carried out to 'make the effect somewhat more cheerful'.[71]

Furniture

Furnishing these vast headquarters presented problems. To design and manufacture furniture specially was ruled out as too expensive, and it was felt initially th᷈ to install the Spring Gardens furniture would lead to a scrappy appearance undesirable at least on the Principal Floor. In the spring of 1921 the Establishment Committee discussed the possibility of buying secondhand furniture at auction, which Knott, to Riley's surprise, thought an excellent idea, as did Swinton. The sum of £1,000 was approved for a trial purchase so as to be able to compare the results of buying at auction with buying new.[72]

But this was obviously not the answer, or at least not the cheap answer that the Moderate Reformers were looking for. In the autumn it was decided that any suitable furniture from Spring Gardens or elsewhere in the new County Hall be renovated and moved to the Principal Floor, and replaced by standard office furniture.[73] As the Builder reported at the time the building opened:

The furniture already placed in some of the minor committee rooms leaves much to be desired, but for this the architect was not responsible. It seems that, after having designed the panelling and the fireplaces in accord with what (despite these criticisms) is a masterly and thoroughly artistic scheme, he was superseded by the Supplies Department, which stepped into the breach and produced the one thing missing, in the traditional British way.[74]

Some furniture designed by Knott, mostly for the Principal Floor, was made during the war at the behest of Debenham, who was trying to keep the failing cabinet-making industry alive. In 1914 Knott had four vacancies in his office, due to men signing up, but filled these and began designing the furniture straight away.[75] As well as seating and desks for the Council Chamber, with their elaborate folding and unfolding, and incorporation of warm air ducts and outlets, he also designed the removable seating made by the Bath Cabinet Makers' Company for the Main Committee Room (Plate 24c).

Office Floors

The central administrative staffs of the majority of the departments, some 2,300 officials, were housed in the new building. Three departments – Valuation Estates and Housing, Fire Brigade, and Tramways – and parts of those of the Chief Engineer and the Stores, with a staff of about 800, had to await accommodation in Section D. Until the completion of that section rooms were provided in the completed building for only the heads of those departments.

The ground and upper floors were largely given over to offices with lightweight partitions between the rooms to facilitate amalgamation and sub-division. Offices next to the chimney stacks had their own fireplaces (Plate 37c, fig. 38). The partition separating the offices from the corridors has a continuous 'frieze' of borrowed lights with a characteristic pattern of glazing bars, alternating vertical bars with a saltire cross in the light over the doors (Plate 36b,c). An iron mechanism for opening the door-light was provided and has in many cases survived. Equally typical of the simple but effective style found in the corridors are the unadorned wooden door architraves, relieved only by two flat discs where the upright members meets the horizontal member (Plate 36b) – a device also found on the Belvedere Road front. The walls of the corridors were originally distempered 'a pleasant French grey' and the woodwork painted cream.[76]

The floors generally, except in the basements, are laid with English and Japanese oak blocks, stained and polished on the Principal Floor, originally polished with beeswax in humbler parts of the building.[77]

Several of the rooms were fitted up for special purposes, emphasizing the building's varied functions. On the ground floor of Block 12 were the Education Library and sample room (Plate 35b), the Medical Supplies room (Plate 35c), and on the third floor the medical examination rooms. Laboratories were placed on the top floor of Block 12, where it was hoped that the products of chemical experiment would be least obnoxious to other users of the building (Plate 37a). The staff restaurant (Plate 36e) was also on the sixth floor, on the riverside Crescent, and kitchens serving both that restaurant and the Members' Refreshment Rooms on the Principal Floor were located on the seventh floor. The organization and fitting up of these spaces was largely supervised by Sir Isidore Salmon of J. Lyons and Company, Member for West Islington (1907–10) and Hammersmith (1910–25).

The Record Room below the Members' Courtyard (B21) was the only room in the basement to receive special treatment, having plaster panelling to its walls. Most of the other rooms here and in the sub-basement were used for storage. An exception was the miniature rifle range in the sub-basement of the Crescent. Requested by the LCC Staff Association, it was fitted up at the Council's expense in 1924,[78] and remained in use until 1989.

Staff Chapel

In 1955, in response to a request from the Staff Christian Union, the Council allocated part of the octagonal-shaped corridor surrounding the heating and ventilation compartment beneath the Council Chamber for use as a Staff Chapel.[79] This oddly shaped space was hardly ideal for the purpose (see folded drawing A, ground-floor plan), but accommodation in a central position in County Hall was scarce. Dedicated in October 1955, the chapel is furnished with a number of 'historic features'. Linen-fold panelling from a house in Wandsworth, 'demolished for open space purposes', lines the walls behind and to the sides of the dais, and fronting the dais is a richly carved

rail of seventeenth-century Flemish oak formerly in the basement of County Hall whence it had been transferred from the Geffrye Museum (Plate 37b). Both the panelling and the rails were restored by craftsmen in the LCC Architect's Department.[80] In the passage leading to the chapel from the main entrance hall are two large majolica panels, in the style of della Robbia, of groups of choristers framed by borders of fruit and flowers.

Heating and Ventilating

While the Architects had responsibility for all work relating to the heating and ventilation of the building, G. W. Humphreys, the Council's Engineer in succession to Maurice Fitzmaurice, acted as consultant.

The heating and ventilating installation is best described in terms of the three sub-contracts under which it was constructed. The first was for the manufacture of six multi-tubular boilers designed by Humphreys. Each was seventeen feet long by eight feet in diameter, four being fitted to operate as hot water boilers and two as steam boilers. These occupied an area in the sub-basement directly below the Main Committee Room. The contract was awarded to Davey, Paxman and Company.

The second sub-contract, carried out by the Buffalo Forge Company, dealt with the installation of the combined system of heating and ventilation of the Council Chamber and the Main Committee Room. A supply of air was drawn in from either of two alternative positions at the fifth-floor level and passed through a spray chamber where it was completely saturated at a pre-determined temperature, controlled by automatic means, and filtered through a series of eliminator plates. Thermostats in the Council Chamber and Committee room determined whether the air leaving the washer required further heating and automatically opened or closed the steam valves and air dampers. Temperature and humidity were thus controlled. An individual supply of air was provided to each Council Chamber seat, and the direction of the air current could be regulated by a lever placed in front of each seat (fig. 39). Stale air was mainly extracted through ceiling grilles and a lesser amount through gratings at floor level, which were connected to separate fans. All this produced beneath the Council Chamber a room full of ducting which soon became known as the Octopus Room (Plate 37d). A modern architect might have given more prominence to this technical element rather than to the classical orders which enfold the building, but Knott has nested it unobtrusively below the chamber it serves. It is no less remarkable for being hidden away.[81]

The third sub-contract provided for heating arrangements throughout the building, the hot water supply to basins and sinks, the supply of warm air to the sub-basement, and the steam services for cooking and air warming. The hot water system of heating was adopted, using forced circulation, the water being pumped through the four boilers to seven control chambers situated in various positions, and thence to the radiators. Riley claimed proudly that, 'control is so complete that, although the boilers and pumping plant are centralised, the radiators in the most remote parts of the building are effectively heated'. The hot water for lavatories was supplied by storage calorifiers heated by the steam boilers, and circulated through the building by centrifugal pumps.[82]

Three separate sets of fans and air-heaters with a series of distributing trunks were provided for warming and ventilating the sub-basement. Most of the rooms were ventilated mechanically by exhaust fans. Fresh air entered the rooms through inlets behind radiators (or through open windows) and was removed through gratings connected to the fans by means of air ducts over the corridors. There was some discussion about the effectiveness of this method at design stage, but in the event it seems to have worked adequately. There were, it was estimated, over 2,000 radiators and skylight coils, over 6,000 valves of various kinds and some 30 miles of piping. This contract was carried out by J. Jeffreys & Company Limited, in association with R. Crittall & Company Limited, G. N. Haden & Sons Limited and Norris & Dutton Limited.[83]

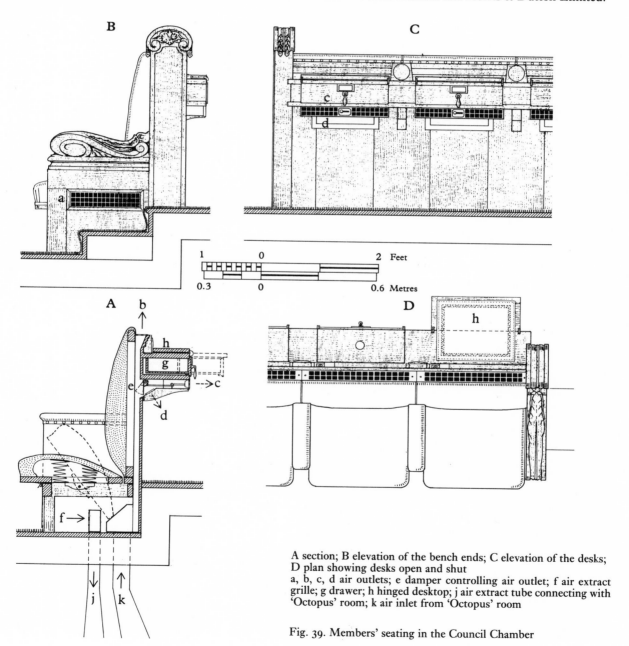

A section; B elevation of the bench ends; C elevation of the desks; D plan showing desks open and shut
a, b, c, d air outlets; e damper controlling air outlet; f air extract grille; g drawer; h hinged desktop; j air extract tube connecting with 'Octopus' room; k air inlet from 'Octopus' room

Fig. 39. Members' seating in the Council Chamber

CHAPTER VIII

The Northern Front

The northern quarter of County Hall (Section D) was not completed until eleven years after the opening of the building. Although the Municipal Reformers had postponed the construction of Section D in 1908, work on the design had not been stopped and in May 1914 the Council authorized the Establishment Committee to make preliminary arrangements for putting the building in hand. Drawings and bills of quantities were prepared in readiness for the inviting of tenders before the war brought a halt to all such work.[1]

After the war the high cost of building inhibited any further progress towards the construction of Section D and the subject was not raised again until 1920, when changes to the plan were discussed. Over a year later the Establishment Committee was still putting off a decision on whether to proceed.[2] One argument urged for going ahead as soon as possible was the perennial need for space. A less obvious reason was that the northern edge of the foundation raft was not properly sealed. Maintaining a dry building required continuous pumping, and there were fears for the structure if the projected extension was not completed soon. Independently of any decision about the superstructure of Section D, therefore, the Committee decided late in 1922 that this raft and the retaining wall should be finished. The work was carried out between 1923 and 1925 by Holloway Brothers at a tendered price of £58,126.[3]

In this period of post-war recession the Municipal Reformers had maintained their stance as the party of thrift, but by 1928 the economic situation had improved and completing County Hall no longer seemed an extravagance. A more urgent and compelling reason for proceeding, however, was the greatly increased volume of work likely to fall on the Council as the result of Government legislation, then in preparation, to reorganize the Poor Law administration in London. Under proposals which passed into law in 1929, the twenty-five Boards of Guardians, the Metropolitan Asylums Board, the four Boards of School District Managers, and the Central Unemployed Body, were all to be abolished and their work transferred to the LCC. With this in mind the Establishment Committee strongly recommended that the completion of Section D 'should be effected at the earliest possible date', and in July 1928 the Council decided to go ahead.[4] Bills of quantities were being prepared by September 1929, and in the following May contracts for the superstructure were signed.[5] British building materials and British oak for the Principal Floor panelling were stipulated, and the Council also wanted the stone to be worked and the joinery prepared 'within the London district (i.e., a radius of 15 miles from Charing-cross)'.[6] In spite of severe limitations on all public spending imposed by the National Government in the early 1930s, the LCC was allowed to complete the building.

Development of the Plan and Changes to the Design

In the years between 1920 and 1929 the design was considerably modified, partly because the Council was constantly trying to fit more accommodation on the site, and partly to take into account the experience of using and working in the building.

Knott's original design had projected Section D as a range of offices, although on the Principal Floor most of the rooms along the northern front were left unallocated (folded drawing AIII, overlay, between pp. 62–3). The absorption of additional bodies and the growth of the Council's responsibilities meant that there would have to be more committee rooms, while the absence of any large room suitable for meetings or conferences gave rise to a campaign, initiated in 1920 by the Progressive Member, Percy Harris, for the reinstatement of the 'Public Hall', which the Municipal Reformers had shorn from the original competition design in 1908. It was now proposed that this should be built in the central courtyard of Section D and made directly accessible from the northern roadway. The Establishment Committee, dominated by the Municipal Reformers, confirmed the feasibility of this suggestion, but declined to give the matter further consideration until a decision had been made to proceed with Section D itself.[7] It was, however, revived in 1922 when Riley showed the Committee a sketch plan with a public hall in the central courtyard,[8] but was seemingly laid to rest in 1924 when the Committee formally instructed the newly constituted sub-committee for Section D to exclude the public hall from its deliberations.[9]

A different tactic was then employed by Knott and Riley to get the public hall back into the scheme. Thanks to the efforts of Captain Swinton, the LCC's collection of Chairmen's portraits was increasing, and indeed proving an embarrassment to the Architects, who could not find a suitable space in which to hang it. At the same time the Architects wanted to alleviate what was generally regarded as the tiresome and wasteful corridor system round the perimeter of the building by introducing some kind of central corridor running north from Block 12. In the summer of 1924, therefore, Knott and Riley came up with a scheme in which the public hall was superseded by a picture gallery at ground-floor level, with room for up to two hundred portraits, arranged in an unusual manner around a large open circulation space.[10] This was the decisive factor, and although the sub-committee was still clinging to the idea of omitting the gallery altogether in 1927, it was reinstated in 1928, now even more strongly justified as an aid to circulation because of the Establishment Committee's decision to pack additional offices into Section D by putting them on both sides of the corridor.[11] This 'double banking', as it was called, gave an increase of about twenty-five per cent over the single-sided layout used generally in Sections A, B and C.[12a] In July 1928 the Council formally agreed that the construction of the picture gallery should proceed concurrently with the rest of Section D, though the final designs had still to be worked out.[13]

The revisions to Section D were not confined to the plans; some important and telling changes were also made to the design of the northern façade. This had always been regarded as the least important of the four elevations, fronting only on to a narrow road and in any case obscured by other buildings to the north. In 1907 the competitors had not even been required to submit an elevation for this front, and in Knott's design the only important features here were the two corner pavilions, matching those on the south front. By the 1920s, however, there were plans to clear the area to the north of County Hall as part of the proposed scheme for a new Charing Cross road bridge. If carried out this would expose the northern elevation of County Hall to full view from the proposed new bridge, and Knott was concerned about the effect of the great expanse of featureless walling between the two pavilions. He therefore re-designed this front, moving the pavilions away from the corners nearer to the centre, and extending the rustication from the pavilions round to the east and west fronts. The Council approved the amended elevation in October 1928.[14]

During the late summer and autumn of 1928 the so-called 'picture gallery', initially rectangular, evolved into a large elliptical Conference Hall ringed with spaces for hanging pictures (fig. 40). It was raised to Principal Floor level in order to make the space below available for a Licensing Hall for the Road Fund and Motor Car Driving Licences Section of the Public Control Department. The urgent need for additional space for Licensing had been discussed by the Section D sub-committee in 1927, when it was decided to transfer the department to the northern end of the building,[b] but the earliest reference to the Licensing Hall being beneath the Conference Hall is in September 1928. The cost of this change was not an issue because the building work would be paid for by the Ministry of Transport.

The evolution of the Conference Hall shows the close working relationship and more relaxed collaboration which had developed between Knott and Riley since the war. Towards the end of November 1928 Knott sent a revised plan for the hall to Riley, who retained responsibility for 'matters relating to internal economy'. This plan, which has been lost, was described as circular, consisting of a Conference Hall with radiating bays around its edge for the Picture Gallery. The round form was an innovation, Knott's previous rectangular plan being now dismissed by him as 'boring'.[15] Riley welcomed the change but saw that where the circular plan met the rectangular blocks, there was an awkward junction, and he suggested a 'slightly elliptical' plan, reducing the north-south axis and giving more generous access to the hall. He sketched his suggestions and sent them to Knott, who adopted them without hesitation.[16]

Knott evidently intended to have a skylight in the centre of the hall roof, and to light the gallery bays, which were to match the hall in height, by means of fully glazed roofs. Riley suggested changes here as well: why not, he asked, lower the gallery roofs and use clerestory lighting instead to light the hall, thus giving the galleries better proportion and more effective lighting.[17] Again Knott saw the sense of these proposals and agreed immediately.[18] It was this alteration which facilitated the later development by which the Education Library was placed above the Conference Hall (fig. 42).

Change of Architects

In the early days of 1929 Knott was busy working on the revisions. But on 25 January 1929, three days after writing his last letter to Riley, he unexpectedly died after a short illness.[19] He was only 50 years old. In 1931 the Council ordered a bronze plaque to be set up in his memory in the Members' Courtyard, on the east side of the Members' Entrance. Designed by Gilbert Bayes and made by Morris Singer, it has a profile of Knott in low relief and was unveiled in June 1932 (Plate 17c).[20]

E. Stone Collins's partnership with Knott (see page 38) provided continuity while the Council considered what to do. As Knott's contract with the LCC had been a purely personal one, Collins had no automatic right of succession. In the event, however, the Council chose to employ him, but decided that the time had come when Riley's services could be dispensed with, partly because his continued presence was seen as an arrangement which involved 'considerable administrative difficulty and is at

---

[a]In Sections A, B and C only limited use is made of 'double-banking', thus facilitating the 'infilling' in the larger courtyards during the 1970s (see page 117).

[b]According to Gibbon and Bell, the number of vehicles registered by the Council rose from 8,268 in 1904 to 37,939 in 1919, and in 1937 reached 74,423. In 1904 the Council issued 18,000 driving licences, in 1937 nearly 361,000.

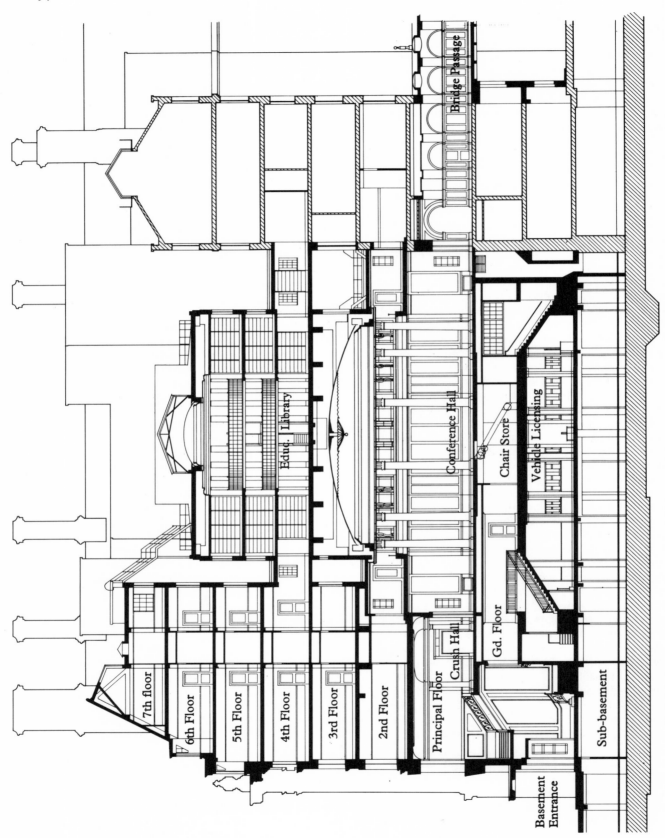

Fig. 40. Northern quarter of County Hall (Section D). Section through the building looking east, showing, from left to right, Block 15 (the northern front), with Entrance Hall and offices above, the 'Drum', containing the Education Library, Conference Hall and the Vehicle Licensing Section, and Block 12 (the northern end of the 1922 building). The Bridge Passage at Principal-Floor level was built at the same time to connect with the former Main Committee Room (Room 129)

times the cause of some embarrassment'. As Architect to the Council he had been succeeded ten years earlier by George Topham Forrest, with whom his relations were strained. It is reasonable to assume that Topham Forrest felt uncomfortable with the older man prowling the corridors and peering over his shoulder. The Council provided a substantial *douceur* for Riley, who retired on 11 June 1929, the day that Collins's appointment as Knott's successor officially began.[21]

The Re-siting of the Education Library

The final major change to the planning of Section D was made in the summer of 1929, following Knott's death. It came quite unexpectedly, and was quickly agreed upon and incorporated into the design and bills of quantities. This was the Education Library, one of the more unusual pieces of design in the whole complex of County Hall.

In 1889 the School Board for London had formed a small circulating library for the use of teachers in infants' schools. Known as the Pedagogical Lending Library, it was originally accommodated in a committee room of the London School Board Offices on the Embankment. As the library grew it developed into a lending library for teachers, as well as a 'circulating library scheme supplying books to secondary schools and literary institutes for the use of pupils taking advanced courses, etc'.[22]

In 1922 the library moved to County Hall, where it had been allocated space on the ground floor of Block 12 (Plate 35b). Under the management of G. H. Gater, the Council's Education Officer from 1924 to 1933, the borrowing system was re-organized and the circulation rocketed. By 1926 the premises in Block 12 were no longer adequate and books were spilling into the corridors outside. In 1929 Gater appealed to the Establishment Committee for a purpose-built library in Section D, to hold between 70 and 80,000 volumes.[23]

Gater's appeal came long after the other departments had claimed their share and there seemed to be nothing left to give away. Yet it appears that he went to the Committee with a plan already formed to place his library on top of the Conference Hall. The records which trace the development of this scheme are so slight as to make any definite conclusions about its origins impossible. The idea could have originated with Collins, or even with Knott. It is strongly reminiscent of the latter's abortive scheme of January 1909 in which he proposed placing the Members' Library above an oval Council Chamber (see page 44).

The Establishment Committee, meeting in July 1929, thought the idea excellent, and a sum of £25,000 was allocated. Collins confirmed that it was technically feasible, and the job was immediately put in hand by the architect and the structural engineers, Whitaker, Hall & Owen.[24]

Construction

In 1928 Knott had proposed a steel-frame structure clad in stone as being a quicker and lighter building method than the load-bearing brickwork used for the first three sections, and although Riley thought this might lead to cracks appearing where the two constructions met, it was the method adopted. When the construction of the earlier sections was being discussed Riley had objected to steel framing, and indeed to innovative construction techniques generally, partly on the pretext that the Model Bye-laws were under review, but by 1928 he could hardly stand in the way of what had by then become standard methods.[25]

Construction work began in the early part of May 1930, delayed somewhat by the late inclusion into the plans of the Education Library, and went ahead regularly, if a little slowly. The main contractors were Gee, Walker & Slater, while the steel frame, designed by Whitaker, Hall & Owen, was built by A. D. Dawnay.[26c] The total cost of the building was approximately £1 million.

The riverside block was ready for occupation in the middle of February 1932, the northern block late in the same year, and the whole section was opened on 27 January 1933. The general economic gloom meant that a lavish formal opening was out of the question and the occasion was marked by an afternoon party given by the Chairman of the Council with an 'appropriate ceremony' in the new Conference Hall.[27] Later, in March, the Chairman entertained the Prime Minister, Ramsay MacDonald, to luncheon in the Conference Hall, and the Chairman of the Establishment Committee presided over a celebratory dinner.[28] A bronze plaque commemorating the completion of Section D was set up in the new bridge passage.

The new section contained some 300 rooms, bringing the total number in the whole building to about 1,200 (including store rooms). There was now accommodation in County Hall for approximately 3,500 staff, enabling the Council to dispose of a number of scattered offices. However, the transfer of the work of the Poor Law authorities meant that it had to retain the old Spring Gardens building, which was occupied by the Valuation, Estates and Housing Departments.[29] The Fire Brigade and Tramways departments were also housed elsewhere. Thus, even before Section D was complete, there were plans to develop the land across Belvedere Road, and centralize the LCC offices once and for all.

Architectural Description

The North Façade

The main changes to the design of the north elevation and the reasons for them have already been briefly described on page 93. This front (Plate 18a, fig. 41) is nearly half as long again as the Westminster Bridge Road front, but its

---

[c]The names of the contractors who worked on Section D are included in Appendix IV.

Fig. 41. Central section of the north façade of County Hall. The shields in the frieze show, from left to right, the arms of Hampstead, Hackney, Lambeth, Fulham and Finsbury

pavilions are almost exactly the same distance apart as their southern counterparts. All of the extra width is taken up in the rusticated walls which run to the corners of the building east and west of the northern pavilions. Because the northern roadway is at basement level, the basement storey here is treated as part of the façade, making it the tallest of the four façades at County Hall, and the resulting proportions are much more harmonious than those of the Westminster Bridge Road front.

The lowest storey falls within the 'plinth level' of the whole building and is faced with grey granite which is extended up to first-floor level within the pavilions. This is the only front where the granite gains an architectural presence beyond its role as a plinth designed to deal with the awkwardness of a sloping site. The nature of the stone has influenced the detail of the entrances at the base of the pavilions. Two square-headed arches, for vehicle access, are each flanked by two lower tunnel-like entrances for pedestrians in a pleasing composition, combining good proportion with strong modelling (Plate 18b). Less successful is the treatment of the three central entrances leading to the Conference Hall and Public Control rooms, whose presence is marked by voussoirs (fig. 41). Above the plinth the façade rises in Portland stone, detailed in a very similar way to the earlier work. At cornice level a frieze of coats of arms completes the list of London boroughs represented in this way at County Hall (Plate 18c). This frieze and the other architectural sculpture on Section D were carved by C. H. Mabey.[d]

The roof above the north façade has the usual two rows of dormers but departs from the arrangement on the other fronts in having one window above another on both levels. Elsewhere (except in the Members' Courtyard) the upper row has only half the number of dormers. Great stone chimney stacks rise through the roof, matching those of the earlier building, but only for reasons of symmetry, since in Section D only rooms on the Principal Floor have fireplaces.

In the absence of Ernest Cole, the sculptural groups for the four pavilions on Section D were carved by Alfred Hardiman (see page 65). Intended to be representative of the departments that were to occupy the new building, they take the form of four heroic nude or semi-nude figures – two male and two female – three of whom are supporting children (Plate 31c,d). The iconography may be less obscure than Cole's, but the themes of the groups are not self-evident. That on the river front is 'Open Spaces', and the two on the north front are 'Education'

(west pavilion) and 'Healing' (east pavilion). It is not known what the seated male on the Belvedere Road front represents.[e31]

'Open Spaces' was the cause of some embarrassment to the Chief Officer of Public Assistance, who occupied the second-floor room immediately behind it. In June 1933 he complained to the Establishment Committee of the effect produced by the presence outside his window of the seven-foot high 'piece of statuary comprising two figures in the nude – an infant supported by an adult male, both facing the river'. Not only did it interfere with his view, it disturbed his visitors:

notwithstanding the artistic merit of the statuary in the aspect for which it was worked, the appearance of this arresting and, from the reverse, meaningless figure in its full height in such proximity and with the consequential exaggeration of outline – particularly, for example, of the glutaeus maximus – provokes comment and is likely to continue to do so, with such frequency as to prove tedious to myself and to destroy in large measure the amenities of my room.

He wanted eight of the panes of clear glass replaced by stained-glass panels designed 'to portray in symbolic manner that part of the Council's care of the poor and needy' which came within the ambit of his department.[32] A list of suitable subjects was drawn up, and it was proposed to have the work designed and made by students at the Central School of Arts and Crafts, but the scheme was never carried out.[f] Instead, panes of frosted glass were installed, which have since been removed.

The Plan

Externally, there was little change to the pre-war design, with the exception of the additional public vehicular access, and the alteration to the corner pavilions on the north front. Internally, however, the changes were more substantial, although the organizational principle of the building remained the same. The Principal Floor was for the use of Members and departmental chiefs, the floors above for general offices, the ground floor was open to the public (being mainly taken up by the counters of the Public Control Department), while the basement and sub-basement were for storage and maintenance. However, a very much larger part of the Principal Floor was devoted to committee rooms than in Knott's earlier scheme (folded drawing AIII). In addition, the 'drum' containing the Conference Hall, Education Library and Vehicle Licensing Hall made significant changes to the workings of the

[d]The boroughs represented on the north front are, from east to west: Lewisham, Woolwich, Stepney (1931), Hampstead (1931), Hackney (1924), Lambeth (1922), Fulham (1927), Finsbury (1931), Shoreditch, St. Pancras and Deptford. Only those with dates had been granted official coats of arms by 1933. For the remainder Mabey was required to carve the seals of the councils. Four panels, two at each end of the frieze, were left blank for subsequent carving and remain blank.[30]

[e]In 1933 the editor of *Town and Country Planning* asked the Clerk for a photograph of the statue of 'Town Planning' on the northern front of County Hall, only to be told that the 'significance of the statuary ... is general rather than particular, and that there is no statue specifically symbolic of "Town Planning".'

[f]The subjects suggested were: St Martin dividing his cloak with the beggar; monks feeding the poor at a monastery gate; King Lear on the heath; the Good Parson from Goldsmith's *Deserted Village*; Oliver Twist asking for more; and a modern tramp.[33]

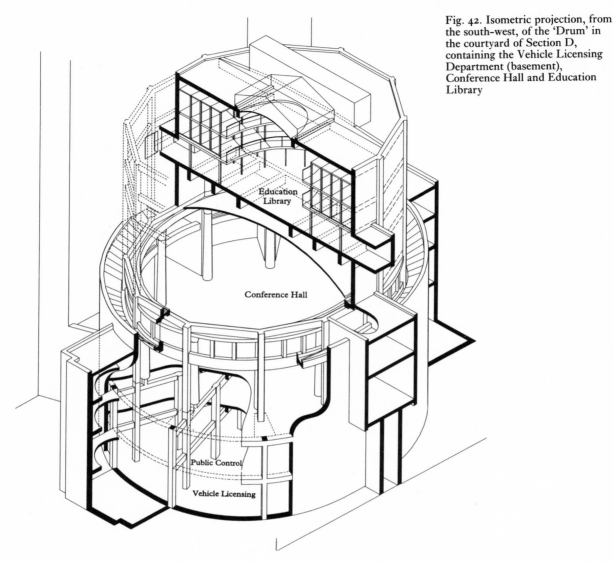

Fig. 42. Isometric projection, from the south-west, of the 'Drum' in the courtyard of Section D, containing the Vehicle Licensing Department (basement), Conference Hall and Education Library

plan throughout the Principal Floor. A bridge passage, lit by small round skylights, was built from the centre of the Main Committee Room, passing through Block 12 – the northernmost block of the 1922 building – and leading into the new Conference Hall (Plate 42d). Thus circulation was improved, but at the cost of making room 129 – the Main Committee Room – part of a through route. For this reason room 129 ceased to function as a committee room and was reserved for the use of Members and their visitors.[34] Together with adjoining rooms 128 and 130, it became known as the Ceremonial Suite. The Conference Hall itself became part of the circulation space when not in use for meetings or cinema performances – hence its role also as a portrait gallery.

The other major change to the plan was the addition of offices on the courtyard side of the corridors. There was insufficient room to carry this around the existing Block 12, but along the north, east and west sides of the court-yard, offices are distributed in a way which presages the post-war 'infill' in the Members' Courtyard and H court-yard.

The staircases, too, are treated more freely, opening up a corner space of light and movement (Plate 32c) to contrast with the long and rather boring corridor plan which the original scheme had bound the later phase to follow. Fire doors added in the 1960s to meet new regulations have to a large extent destroyed this sense of flowing space.

Simple but significant architectural advantages were gained internally from the decision to move the northern pavilions inwards. Instead of two rather small rooms at the corners, each with a grand window but awkward in plan and proportion, as occurs in the Westminster Bridge Road pavilions, there were now four 'pavilion rooms', each properly planned and proportioned. While the arrangement is clearly an improvisation within the general lines of Knott's earlier plans for Section D, the ensemble

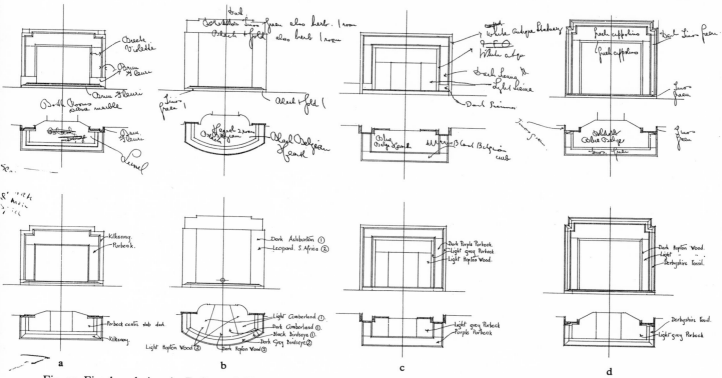

Fig. 43. Fireplace designs by E. Stone Collins for Committee Rooms in Section D, showing (above) the earlier designs and choice of marbles, and (below) the revised designs using mainly English materials
a For room 142, where Kilkenny and Purbeck replaced Breche Violette and Brun Fleuri
b For rooms 145 and 152, where Ashburton, Birdseye, Cumberland, Leopard (from South Africa) and Hopton Wood replaced Black and Gold, Tinos Green and Black Belgian
c For room 158, where Purbeck and Hopton Wood replaced Sienna, Blue and Black Belgian, and White Statuary
d For room 164, where Derbyshire Fossil, Hopton Wood and Purbeck replaced Greek Cippolino, Tinos Green, and Blue Belgian

has been made to work because the corner staircases (D and E) have been re-designed. On the Principal Floor rooms 143 and 153 interrupt the corridors running north and west into the corners, which are diverted into the staircase landings. By thus annexing part of the corridors Knott has increased the width of the two corner rooms, making them wider than any other room in the building, apart from the Main Committee Room. Indeed these two rooms are among the finest in County Hall, and reflect the freedom in planning created by the new arrangement (Plates 33c, 34a, folded drawing AIII).

The Principal Floor

Most of the detailed design work for the interior decoration of Section D was undertaken by Collins, after Knott's death. On the Principal Floor there is no radical change of style, but Collins's designs have a greater suavity and a slightly more modern feeling. This is particularly apparent in his Art Deco chimneypieces, which are made from English 'marbles' – Hopton Wood, Derbyshire fossil, Purbeck, Sussex, and others – and are subdued in tone with browns, greys and dark greens predominating (fig. 43). The use of native marbles was presumably a consequence of the Council's insistence on British materials; Collins had originally designed the chimneypieces for imported marbles in a brighter range of colours.[35g] The main rooms on this floor have enriched plaster ceilings and full-height oak panelling. A number of rooms have carved decoration by Alfred H. Wilkinson. The oak panelling and false plaster vaulting in the corridors are, of course, copied after Knott's original designs.

On the Belvedere Road front are two committee rooms (155 and 158) and one room for committee chairmen (164).

[g]At one stage the three eighteenth-century chimneypieces installed in rooms 127, 160 and 161 in 1933, were to have been used in Section D.[36]

Each room has an individually designed chimneypiece, that in 164 having a particularly 'moderne' profile. Latterly these rooms were used for offices and most of their original light-fittings have been removed.

The large square corner room behind the Belvedere Road pavilion (153) was designed to function as a luncheon room as well as a committee room (Plate 34a),[37] and is equipped with a servery in room 154. In the west wall of 153 are three sets of double doors, two of which communicate with room 152. This allows the two rooms to be used *en suite* during social or ceremonial occasions. Above the doors are carved wooden panels incorporating in one case the arms of the Borough of Lambeth, in another those of the LCC, and, in the centre, a clock (Plate 29b). These panels, together with the frieze and the architraves around the doors, were designed and carved by Wilkinson.[38] The ceiling is decorated with a large circular plaster wreath enriched with anthemions and floral motifs. All the original wall and ceiling lights have been preserved.

The range of committee rooms along the north front forms a handed sequence comparable to that along the central portion of the Belvedere Road front, although it 'breaks down' in the two pavilion rooms (152 and 145). The east end of 152 is partly screened off by two short projections with detached piers, creating a vestibule between the main part of the room and the doors into 153 (Plate 34b). In 145 the equivalent space serves as a public gallery to the large committee room in the north-west corner. Apart from this, and some minor variants in the

detailing of the woodwork, the two rooms are handed and have identical chimneypieces and decorative plasterwork. The original light fittings in 145 have been replaced. Rooms 151 and 146 are the smallest of the committee rooms along this front: both have typical Collins fireplaces and retain their original light fittings. The larger rooms 150 and 147 are self-contained, having no direct access to adjoining rooms, but each has two sets of double doors, opening on to the corridor, dressed internally with broken segmental pediments. They do not have fireplaces. By 1986 room 150 had been partitioned to make two rooms.

In the centre of the north front the corridor widens out to form the Crush Hall, the transition being marked by shallow arches, marble columns and a tessellated marble floor (Plate 33a). On the south side of this space doors open into the Conference Hall and on the north side a ceremonial staircase leads down to the main north entrance, which is protected by a bronze internal porch (Plate 32a). As this entrance is at basement level the staircase has to rise through two substantial storeys. Built of stone, it has a handsome bronze balustrade (Plate 32a,b) which is returned across the edge of the landing. The Crush Hall itself was a rather modest arrangement with similar problems to the Belvedere Road entrance, for it served as a public entrance on special occasions and was also part of the Principal Floor corridor on a daily basis.

The large north-west corner room (143) behind the pavilion on the river front was designed to replace room 129 as the main committee room (Plate 33c). The press

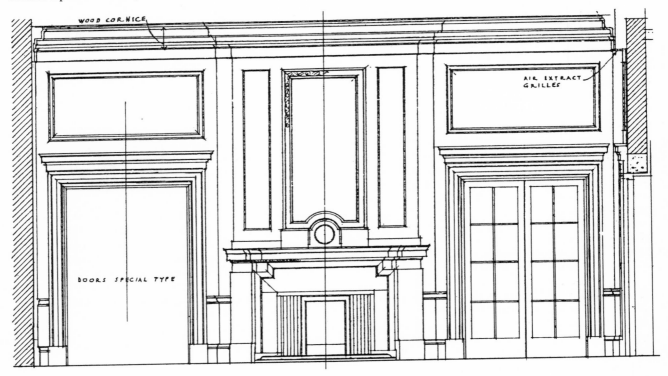

Fig. 44. Room 142. Working drawing for panelling and chimneypiece, 1931

and public gallery – for which room 145 was curtailed – occupies a niche on the east side, angled in towards the centre of the room, and reminiscent of a box in a theatre. The gallery has a separate entrance from the corridor and its own independent room number (144). It is furnished with tiers of benches fitted with folding flaps which can be raised for note-taking. In the committee room itself all that remains of Collins's original furniture is the Chairman's bench, the rest having been replaced in the 1960s. The original elegant ceiling lights survive, but the wall lights do not. Double doors in the south wall of the committee room connect with a finely panelled and finished retiring-room (142) whither Members adjourned for private discussions (Plate 34d, fig. 44).

A similar sequence was created along the river front, with a public gallery, committee room and retiring-room occupying rooms 141, 140 and 134 respectively. The retiring-room was formed in part out of a room in the 1922 building which had been used for a servery. Later, when the committee room (Plate 34c) was turned over to office use, the public gallery in room 141 was partitioned off and the seating removed. The former committee room, which retains its original light fittings, has a coffered ceiling. The two double doors opening into the corridor have broken segmental pediments embellished with palmettes. In the south wall two round-headed doorways lead into the former retiring-room. This room has a small square chimneypiece, with a carved overmantel panel and integral clock, and the ceiling is enriched with a Greek-key motif.

The Drum

This elliptical tower, containing the former Licensing Hall, Conference Hall and Education Library (Plate 38d, figs 40, 42), was devised as a way of accommodating these additional and diverse elements into the scheme without disrupting the overall plan. It is a clever and on the whole a satisfactory solution to the problem. The external walls are faced with white glazed bricks, like most of the courtyards at County Hall, and this gives the whole structure a style reminiscent of Constructivist architecture. The discrepancy between the Conference Hall interior and this exterior, however, is every bit as extreme as that between the Council Chamber and its outward form (Plates 21, 33b, 38c,d).

At the heart of this block is the Conference Hall (Plate 33b), accessible from the south by way of the bridge passage and the former Main Committee Room, and from the north through the Crush Hall. The Conference Hall is elliptical in plan, rising through two storeys, with a shallow domed roof. At one end is a removable stage and dressing-room accommodation and at the other a projection room at gallery level above a store. A hoist hatch is concealed in the centre of the floor, giving access to a chair store at ground-floor level below. The twelve columns ringing the main space are made of concrete on steel stanchions, and finished in lapis-lazuli blue scagliola,

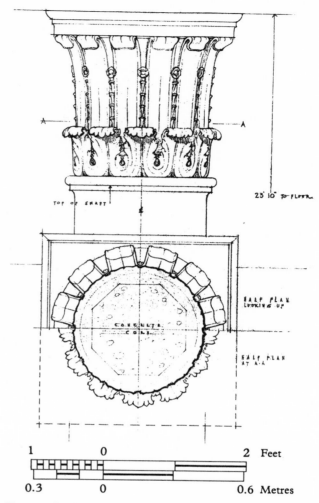

Fig. 45. Conference Hall. Working drawing for the plaster capitals to the columns, 1932

with black bases and gilded capitals (fig. 45), while the entablature they support was originally a buff colour picked out in light purple. Between them are set single-storey top-lit alcoves for hanging the collection of Chairmen's portraits. Neatly concealed in the partitions between these alcoves are the structural columns which support the Education Library. Just inside the north entrance is a memorial to Emma Cons, the first woman Alderman on the LCC (Plate 46a). Presented to the Council in 1930, this is a plaster cast of a bronze portrait in bas-relief of Miss Cons by Sir William Goscombe John.[39]

The Conference Hall is not a very comfortable or gracious public space and it seems to have suffered some acoustic problems, nothing apparently having been learnt from similar difficulties experienced in the Council Chamber.

At basement level, and directly accessible from the northern roadway, was the Licensing Hall, a practical and stylish piece of 1930s glazed tilework in white, grey, blue and black, with hardwood fittings, to which the faceted oval form gave added interest (Plate 36d). This was destroyed when the area was refurbished in 1963, and, after vehicle licensing was centralized in Swansea in the early 1970s, the space was remodelled by the GLC as a staff training centre.[40]

Above the Conference Hall is the galleried Education Library, with space for 100,000 books. Like so much of the Education Department's accommodation, the library was up-to-date in design and concept (Plate 35a). On plan it is a twelve-sided ellipse linked by bridges to the cross corridors at fourth-floor level (fig. 46). Twenty rows of bookstacks are arranged at right angles to the external walls on three levels: the entrance level plus two levels of galleries. Stairs on the long axis of the ellipse – on the east and west sides – lead to these galleries. Each quadrant of the plan is served by a book lift within the bookstacks. In the roof there is a shallow dished skylight of green and clear glass (fig. 47). A large glass chandelier, which could be lowered on a winch, was originally suspended from the centre of this skylight, but after being broken in a fall, was not reinstated. The gallery fronts were originally green, with steel and bronze railings, and the steel bookstacks were enamelled in dark blue with flecks of black. This Art Deco colouring scheme has since been replaced by white paint throughout.

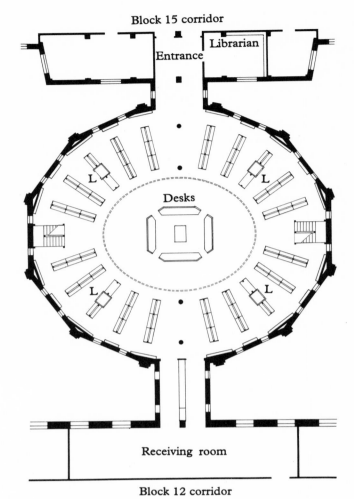

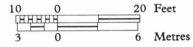

Fig. 46. Education Library. Plan at entrance (fourth-floor) level. L book lifts

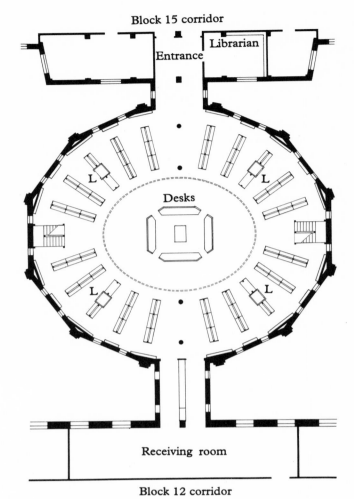

Fig. 47. Education Library. Plan of the glazing in the skylight

CHAPTER IX

The New County Offices – North and South Blocks

By the early 1930s the LCC was well on the way to completing its headquarters building, but with the expansion of the Council's local government responsibilities its staff was increasing at a rate which outpaced the building programme. In April 1930 the Establishment Committee asked the Clerk, the Architect and the Valuer to report generally on the need for further accommodation after the completion of Section D, and specifically on the possibility of developing the east side of Belvedere Road for this purpose.[1]

Growth of the Council's Staff

The passing of the Local Government Act of 1929, under which the LCC took over the Poor Law administration (see page 92), had added very considerably to the burden of extra work, and in 1932 new duties in the field of planning were laid on the Council by the passing of the Town and Country Act. As the LCC's responsibilities for public housing increased, so did the staff of the Valuation Estates and Housing Department; while under G. H. Gater's brilliant administration the Education Department had been expanded and was occupying much of Section D.

When County Hall was originally planned a total staff complement of under 3,000 had been anticipated. By 1934, when the Chief Officers reported on the need for additional accommodation, there were 4,112 central office staff, supported by a smaller army of 300 'housekeepers, messengers, male cleaners, engineering operative staff and chainmen, and 175 charwomen'. Of the permanent staff, 3,726 worked in County Hall itself.[2]

By replanning Section D with offices on both sides of the corridors, and by using parts of the basement and the seventh-floor attic for offices, the Council had been able to accommodate more staff at County Hall than had originally been allowed for. But the building was overcrowded, and an additional 15,000 square feet were required to deal with this problem alone. A further 40,000 square feet would be needed for the Valuer's Department, which still occupied the old Spring Gardens building.

The location of the medical examination rooms was also causing concern. Between 1921 and 1930 the number of schoolchildren examined each year had nearly doubled, from about 12,500 to 23,500, and by the time new space was allocated in Section D, the number of visitors had reached 37,665, or nearly 70,000 if accompanying relations and friends were included. It was hoped that the new extension would provide for, and to a large extent isolate, this function of the Council. (In the end, however, the medical examination rooms were not transferred.) If existing overcrowding was to be alleviated and accommodation provided at County Hall for the 'out-housed' departments, a total of 82,500 square feet of additional space would be required.[3]

Land on the east side of Belvedere Road

Although the proposed site on the east side of Belvedere Road was already partially in the Council's ownership, its potential was affected by the need to take into account various proposals for road-widening and improvements generally. The most important of these was for a new Charing Cross road bridge, which had been engaging the attention of London town planners and improvers since the beginning of the century. There were variants of this scheme, but in outline it involved the removal of the railway station and the replacement of the rail bridge by a high-level road bridge. This would be part of a magnificent new boulevard extending from Trafalgar Square to the Surrey side of the Thames, which, in the words of the Lutyens Report of 1942, was 'seen as the geographical hub of the Metropolis'.[4] Though the line of the new road was considerably to the north of County Hall, it affected plans for the whole area as far north as Waterloo Bridge.

One of the objectives of this plan was to relieve Rennie's Waterloo Bridge, which had been proving inadequate for the increased traffic flow through Kingsway. But once the LCC decided in 1932 to provide a four-lane replacement for Waterloo Bridge,[5] the scheme for a new bridge at Charing Cross fell into abeyance, though it featured in the 1943 *County of London Plan*.[6] It was, of course, seen as part of the projected rebuilding of the South Bank, which also had its effect on the LCC's thinking about the extension of County Hall, and was to be a major element in post-war redevelopment.

Another factor to be taken into account was a proposed traffic scheme for Westminster Bridge Road and York Road, for which, by 1932, the Council had already acquired over two acres of land opposite County Hall.[7] It did not own all the north side of Westminster Bridge Road between York and Belvedere Roads, however, and obtaining possession of the other buildings there presented problems. The caterers J. Lyons & Company had a tea shop at the Belvedere Road corner, and would have to be compensated, probably with another site in the same area.

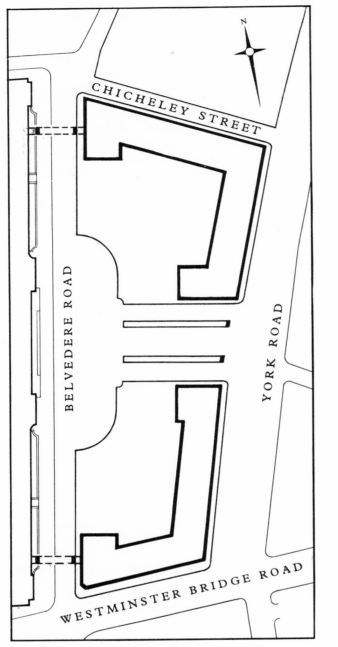

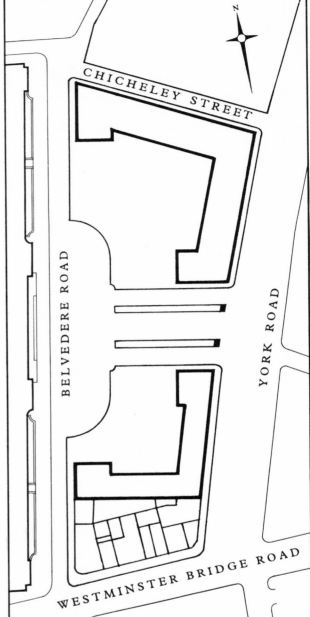

a Preferred scheme extending from the old line of Chicheley Street to Westminster Bridge Road, showing the bridges originally intended to link County Hall to the new offices

b Alternative scheme stopping short of Westminster Bridge Road where the existing properties did not belong to the Council

Fig. 48. The New County Offices (North and South Blocks). Outline plans of the development as originally proposed in 1930–1

(Isidore Salmon, the firm's Chairman and Managing Director, was still an LCC Member, so the matter needed tactful handling.) The New Inn public house at No. 254 Westminster Bridge Road would probably require similar compensation. Between these two buildings stood a branch of the National Provincial Bank, which had recently bought the freehold of properties on the west corner of Westminster Bridge Road and York Road with the intention of rebuilding there. The Bank had also made an agreement with the GPO to sublet part of its new premises as a branch post office.

Early Proposals

The new offices project was discussed in January 1931 by a group of senior officers – including the Clerk (Sir Montagu Cox), the Valuer (Frank Hunt), and the Architect (G. Topham Forrest) – who had before them an outline plan for the development drawn up by the Architect's Department.[8]

The suggested development (fig. 48a) consisted of two L-shaped blocks following the Chicheley Street-York Road-Westminster Bridge Road edge of the proposed site, each block having short return ends facing into a new large courtyard or *place* which addressed the main building across Belvedere Road. Passing between the two blocks, under a linking bridge, was a new entrance to County Hall from York Road. There had been concern for some time about the deleterious effect of the narrow Belvedere Road on the main entrance to County Hall, and it made sense for any extension to combine road widening with civic improvement. Two other bridges, at the north and south ends of Belvedere Road, connected the new building to the old. Although revised, the essential form of the new development as laid down in this early plan was never significantly changed nor seriously challenged.[a]

For the meeting in January 1931 the Architect's Department had ready two versions of the scheme, the second (fig. 48b) showing how the layout might be adapted to a curtailed site excluding the properties along Westminster Bridge Road which the Council did not own. The Valuer pointed out that the frontage here would eventually be rebuilt as part of a road-widening scheme, but this improvement was still some years off and he doubted if anything could be done to bring it forward. He thought the north front of the proposed development should be 'squared up', to align with the north front of Knott's building, and Chicheley Street moved further north as part of the Charing Cross Bridge scheme. It was felt that the northern half of the site would be adequate for the Council's immediate needs, and that the southern half should be developed in such a way that the upper floors could be let out as offices, to be repossessed as the need arose. The whole of the ground-floor front along York Road should be shops. Since no Chief Officers would be housed in the new blocks they were to be plain office buildings. The Council should offer the National Provincial Bank accommodation in the new building in exchange for the freehold of its important corner site.[10]

It was in these terms that the officers reported to the Establishment Committee the following May, but shortly afterwards all building plans had to be abandoned in the face of the national economic crisis of August 1931.[11]

The scheme was not formally considered again until 1934, when a report was prepared for the Establishment Committee reviving the 1931 proposals in an amended form. One of the changes was the 'squaring up' of the north end and the re-alignment of Chicheley Street, as previously suggested by the Valuer. It was now proposed that the north and south blocks should be linked together by an 'open architectural screen' embodying two enclosed bridges (one at sixth-floor level), and that the east side of the *place* or courtyard 'intervening between the new building and the central portion of County Hall' should be laid out as 'a flat elliptical crescent, 460 feet in width'. The point of the crescent-shaped lay-out was to 'ensure a spacious and impressive effect'. Some of the site was set aside for gardens, to be made 'additionally attractive' by the planting of trees. The question of what to do with the problematic frontage along Westminster Bridge Road was left open.[12] At this time the proposed extension was known officially as the New County Offices, and it was not until after the war that the nomenclature North and South Blocks was adopted.

Choosing an Architect

When the revised scheme was sent to Committee in October 1934 the question was raised whether the new offices should be designed by the Council's Architect or thrown open to a public competition. Hitherto all the planning and design work had been carried out 'in house'. Further consideration of the scheme was therefore adjourned while Gater, who was now the Clerk, reported on the implications of holding a competition.[13] It was 'undoubtedly desirable', he said, that the merit of the design and layout of the new building should be beyond question, and he thought that a competition (or the appointment of an eminent outsider) would best secure public confidence. But there were some serious practical objections, not least the impossibility of indicating the exact site, since the Council did not own all the land. Furthermore, a competition would certainly delay the start of work on the building, which might lead in turn to problems with the National Provincial Bank, who had given up their corner site on the understanding that the Council would provide them with accommodation as soon as possible.[14] The solution, hinted at by Gater and adopted by the Council, was to bring in an eminent Consultant Architect to be 'associated with the general planning and design of the building as developed by the Council's architect'.[15]

The man chosen for this role was Sir Giles Gilbert Scott, who had already advised the LCC on architectural

---

[a] In 1935 a more up-to-date solution in the form of a skyscraper was suggested, somewhat light-heartedly, by Alan Chorlton, M.P. In a letter to Herbert Morrison, he asked why not emulate Stockholm Town Hall – 'the finest post-war municipal building' – and erect a thirty-storey tower on the lines of 'a New York multi-storey office'.[9]

and town planning matters. Scott's appointment, and his fee of £4,000, were approved by the Council in December 1934.[16] The fairly narrow limits of his responsibility are made clear in a letter he wrote to the Clerk:

I shall be able to act as consultant, provided I have not got to prepare a design for the elevation ... I have seen the plans prepared by the L.C.C. Architect's Department, and I think it would be possible for me to modify these and get the necessary drawings prepared by the Architect's Department, so as to save my having to do them.

My supervision will naturally have to extend to the detail drawings, even down to the full size sections of mouldings, but it will be more in the nature of amending than creating.

Scott's duties as President of the RIBA prevented him from assuming more than the usual obligations of a consultant architect; he would not, therefore, be doing as much as he had at Battersea Power Station, where he 'redesigned and detailed the whole of the exterior'.[17] Subsequently, however, he agreed that he and the Council's Architect were to have joint design responsibility for the exterior of the buildings. As regards planning, Scott's role was that of a consultant only, and he had no responsibility for the construction.[18]

Within the LCC's Architect's Department the development, planning and designing of the new offices was largely in the hands of Frederick Hiorns (1876–1961), a former senior assistant under Riley who had risen to the rank of assistant architect. Neither Topham Forrest, nor his successor as Architect to the Council in 1935, E. P. Wheeler, appear to have had more than nominal responsibility for the work.[b] Hiorns himself had been in charge of the design and construction of buildings for the Council since 1926, and in evidence to the House of Commons in 1935 he defended the layout and plan of the new offices in a way that clearly indicates him as their author.[20] Over twenty years later, at the age of eighty-two, Hiorns was to recall the origins of the designs in a letter to the *Architects' Journal*, intended in part to counter the then prevailing impression that the elevations had been largely the work of Scott:

When the London County Council acquired the York Road Site, I was invited to a small, 'all-party', meeting of three Leaders (with Sir George Gater, the Clerk) and was asked if I would personally undertake the design and carrying-out of an extension building, corresponding in length with the County Hall itself. This I was glad to agree to do ... Later – in the working drawing stage – a confirmatory opinion was obtained from Sir Giles Scott, with some modifications of detail that were valuable. But the general design was not altered.[21]

This meeting must have taken place sometime between Gater's promotion to Clerk in 1933, and Scott's appointment in December 1934.

At the end of May 1935 a report went before the Establishment Committee which incorporated Scott's main recommendations. These were, firstly, the addition of curved two-storey wings connecting the central and end blocks of the building on the Belvedere Road side and occupying the space which had been provisionally allotted for gardens; secondly, the omission of the open architectural screen or colonnade between the two blocks, and with it the proposed high-level bridge; and, thirdly, the replacement of Hiorns's roof, with its two storeys of attics above the main cornice, by a roof containing only a single storey.[22] The only one accepted by the Committee was the omission of the screen and high-level bridge.[23] There is an undated drawing for the screen and the bridge among Scott's papers (Plate 39a) suggesting that he did at least attempt to find a satisfactory treatment for this feature before recommending its total excision.[24]

Scott also advised that the LCC should take the opportunity provided by the building of the new offices to improve traffic circulation near County Hall:

I fully appreciate that it is important to avoid delay with the new building, but the lay-out of roads in the vicinity is faulty, and future road improvements should not be made impossible by building work being done now ....

Westminster Bridge Road is a main thoroughfare, and it is crossed twice within 100 yards by York Road and Belvedere Road, necessitating two traffic policemen and frequent hold-ups. Motor buses are sent on a detour round St. Thomas's Mansions in an attempt to relieve the congestion.

These problems could be solved by turning Belvedere Road into a private road where it passed between County Hall and the new buildings, and by making a 'traffic circus' at the junction of Westminster Bridge and York Roads.[25] Both suggestions were adopted after the war, the closing of Belvedere Road in 1948, and the traffic roundabout as part of the Island Block development in 1970.[26]

Acquisition of the Site

The proposed extension covered three-and-three-quarter acres, of which more than half was already in the Council's possession. The National Provincial Bank had agreed to sell their recently acquired site on the corner of Westminster Bridge and York Roads to the LCC on condition that it was allowed to lease back part of the new offices. Thus the Council was able to extend the first phase of building round the south-east corner of the site, as it was unable to do at the corresponding northern end. Under an Act passed in June 1935, the Council obtained compulsory purchase powers, together with authority to stop up parts of Belvedere Road and Guildford Street, and to move Chicheley Street further north.[27] Some properties were

---

[b]In an obituary of E. P. Wheeler (1874–1944), a cultured and retiring man who spent his whole working life with the LCC, Hiorns made a point of praising his former boss for setting himself 'to change the questionable system, hitherto all too common in official Departments, whereby the authorship of work is exclusively ascribed to the Departmental Head'.[19]

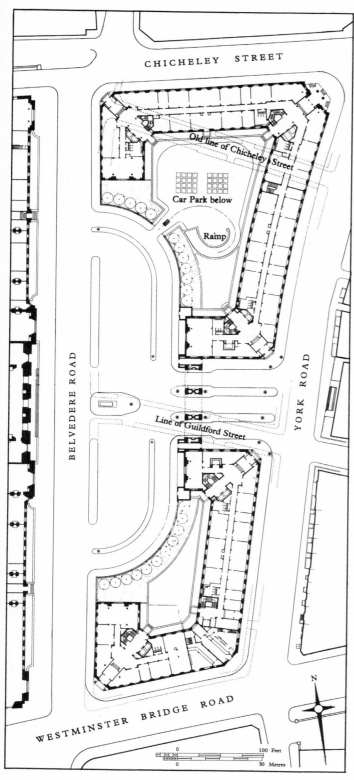

Fig. 49. Ground-floor plan of the New County Offices (North and South Blocks) as finally approved by the Council in 1936 but only partially built

acquired under existing Council powers such as slum-clearance and highway-improvement.[28] The difficulty of obtaining actual possession of all the land immediately was the reason why the scheme could not be completed under a single contract, and was only partially finished at the outbreak of the Second World War.

The Final Design

The Council approved the scheme in July 1935, although the elevations had still to be finalized. The Establishment Committee reported only that they would be 'on generally plain lines expressed in Portland stone with a red tiled roof'.[29] A detailed adjustable model was, however, available showing not only the recommended scheme but also Scott's preferred version, which included features already rejected by the Committee, chiefly the curved quadrant wings (Plate 39b).[30]

The new offices were planned as eight-storey blocks, two floors being fitted into the mansard behind a parapet, with additionally one basement floor for dry storage. At fourteen feet the ground storey was rather higher than the others in order to accommodate the Bank and retail uses. The internal planning, which dispensed with light-wells, was 'double-banked', that is, the offices were arranged on both sides of a central corridor (fig. 49).[31] Hiorns had recommended this arrangement as providing the 'maximum of effective office area for the minimum of occupied land' while ensuring the 'maximum amenity outlook and access of sunshine' that seemed possible in the circumstances.[32]

In December 1935 the working drawings for the super-structure were sent to Scott, who had been making sketches for the elevations in November and now suggested improvements.[33] Scott's principal modification to the design was to repeat the grand architectural order of the two pavilions at the return ends of the two blocks, which faced each other along Belvedere Road, on the two central pavilions flanking the new entrance from York Road. Scott not only repeated this element but, as the Architect's Report said, wished to add further modifications 'to this now monumentally embellished ensemble ... i.e., one-storey projecting pavilions, breaks, rusticated corners and applied pylon motifs at the 6th floor corner returns'.[34] He also suggested replacing the two-storey curved wings which had already been rejected by the Council with one-storey wings of identical form. Since the Committee had objected to two-storey wings on the grounds of expense and obstruction of the space needed for access to an underground car park, Hiorns advised against the single-storey wings. This apart, he recommended approval of the drawings as modified by Scott. As working drawings progressed throughout the following year, Scott continued to make suggestions. All concerned matters of detail, and chiefly involved tinkerings of the sort which many architects of 'refined classicism' at that time found difficult to resist.[c] The changes to the elevational treatment were finally approved by the Council in July 1936.[36]

Construction

Because of the uncertainties over the site, the original construction contract was only for the central portion of the new offices either side of the new entrance from York Road – northwards as far as the old line of Chicheley Street, southwards up to and including the corner with Westminster Bridge Road (see fig. 50). The building programme was split into three contracts, in a similar way to the original County Hall programme. Foundations, steel framing and superstructure were designed separately to allow work to start while the details of the elevations were still under consideration by the architects. The contract was nominally under the direction of the Council's Architect, E. P. Wheeler, but in recognition of Hiorns's role in developing the plan and the design he was named as the 'associated architect'. Engineering work was handled by the Council's Chief Engineer, T. Peirson Frank, two assistants in his department, H. Firth and F. M. Fuller, being apparently responsible for design work on the foundations.[37]

The foundations were begun in the spring of 1936 and the superstructure in the summer of 1937. Both were built by Higgs & Hill and cost £31,600 and £436,000 respectively. The steel frame, which cost £46,500, was executed by Redpath Brown.[38] The external walls were faced with Portland stone, above a granite plinth, and the roofs covered with reddish Italian tiles – the same combination of materials as Knott had used. Some of the granite salvaged from old Waterloo Bridge was incorporated in the piers of the triple-arched bridge connecting the two blocks – a sentimental gesture in no way compensating for the Council's controversial demolition of Rennie's masterpiece.

The new offices were 'completed' in 1939, being occupied during the course of the year, but an opening ceremony planned for July, seems to have been abandoned.[39] The final costs were £287,113 for the acquisition of land, and for buildings £537,176. An additional and grim extra was £18,348, spent on wartime provisions, such as blackout and the equipment of air raid shelters for the whole County Hall complex.[40]

Architectural Description and Comment

The LCC's own opinion of its new offices is revealed in the text of a press release drafted in September 1938. The buildings had been designed to accord harmoniously with Knott's work, but no attempt had been made to copy it. While 'generally following tradition', the new offices had 'a definitely modern flavour'.[41] To Nikolaus Pevsner, writing in 1952, they showed the 'typical later approach of the epigones of Edwardian Imperial glories: no change of heart, but under a willy-nilly influence of the coming Modern Movement a reduction in moulding and ornaments, and a more straightforward emphasis on verticals and horizontals' (Plates 40–41).[42]

The 1938 press release drew attention to certain points of interest in the design:

The offices and communication corridors are treated internally with extreme severity, but an attempt is made to give a special character and interest to the vestibules of the various entrances, the external doors of which latter will be of bronze. These and other features, where decorative treatment is involved, are intended to show the high quality still possible in the traditional handicrafts of this country.[43]

This is not just lip service to the ideals of Swinton and other early Members: the suave yet severely detailed entrance vestibules still look well after half a century of use (Plate 41c,d). Very characteristic of the period are the 'moderne' staircase balustrades and the light-fittings, the decorative plasterwork of the ceilings, and the treatment of the walls, which are lined with travertine marble and Ancaster stone in light and dark shades of brown. The floors are paved in 'Perrycot' Portland stone. Each vestibule has two stone panels carved in low relief by J. B. Spiro with Thames-side scenes and some rather sinister birds (Plate 41b).

Externally the decoration was concentrated on the two pavilions facing Knott's building and around the entrances. Scott was particularly concerned with the detailing of the pavilions and it was he who designed the large ornamental bronze windows with their elaborate swan-neck pediment feature (Plate 39c). These, together with the bronze doorways in York Road (Plate 41a), and the heavy curved boundary railings on the west side of the building, were made by J. Starkie Gardner Limited. E. J. and A. T. Bradford and F. P. Morton carved the four stone panels set in the single-storey projections at the base of the pavilions. These show heraldic devices and various wide-ranging allusions to London and the Empire, and to the work of the Council (Plate 40b,c).

Another sculptor, A. J. Oakley, designed and carved the capitals of leaping fish for the ten free-standing columns of Portland stone which guard the entrances from York Road. The columns are fourteen feet high and carry bronze lanterns (Plates 40a,d, 41a).

[c]Hiorns's notes on an interview with Scott in September 1936 give an example of the matters discussed by the two architects: 'The stone string at 1st floor level to be somewhat modified in section and the stone courses immediately below to the depth of the window heads to be increased (in height) by 9″, the rusticated courses below correspondingly adjusted, and the projection of courses slightly increased ... As regards the main cornice, Sir Giles suggests a slight modification in the section of the top members and a plain capping to the parapet above. He also considers that a reduction in the diameter of the columns is called for, and a variation in the capital'.[35]

The axis of the layout was originally emphasized by a Portland stone plinth and a flagstaff in the centre of the courtyard. The upper surface of the plinth was fitted with floodlighting for ceremonial occasions (Plate 39d).[44] Both the plinth and the island on which it stood were demolished as part of a post-war 'traffic rationalization'.[45]

In 1966 Pevsner's unfavourable view of the Hiorns-Scott buildings was echoed by Ian Nairn, who dismissed them as 'fawning, curry-favour extensions'.[46] Nearly a quarter of a century later, however, their cool neo-Georg-

ian classicism and architectural good manners are held in somewhat higher esteem. The central portion of the building, with its imposing and carefully detailed pavilions, is a handsome composition, but the necessary symmetry of the ensemble has been seriously compromised by the LCC's unfortunate post-war decision not to complete the buildings in accordance with the original Hiorns-Scott designs. Under recent proposals for the development of County Hall (see pages 121–2) these buildings would not survive.

Sketch of the bronze and iron gates at the foot of the Ceremonial Stairs made by Singers

CHAPTER X

The Second World War and Post-War Development

The effect of the Second World War on the work of the LCC was very much greater than that of the Great War. Since 1919 the LCC's responsibilities for hospitals and care of the elderly and sick had increased; under the emergency legislation it was to act as the co-ordinating authority for London, and as ideas for post-war planning developed, it became the major partner in shaping rebuilt London. These two roles were to bring another round of staff increases, with consequent extensions to County Hall.

At the end of the Second World War the LCC was faced not only with the need to complete the blocks on the east side of Belvedere Road (fig. 50), but also to reinstate considerable areas of damage to County Hall itself. The building had been involved in over thirty 'incidents', nineteen of which occurred within its precincts.[1] The most serious was on the night of 19–20 September 1940, when a high explosive bomb made a hole 30 feet deep and as many feet across in the Members' Terrace, shattering all the windows and causing a good deal of internal damage (Plate 42a). Though 200 people were working in the building at the time, there were only two fatalities. As *The Times* reported:

In the council chamber most of the windows were blown out and the chairman's seat leaned forward to where it had been pushed by a massive door blown in on it. The dome over the entrance to the chamber was smashed and the carpet beneath strewn with glass ... Many of the staff continued at their work after the explosion, carrying on by the light of torches because of the black-out curtains having been destroyed.[2]

Although the damage affected about 160,000 square feet of office space, more than two thirds of this was soon brought back into use after temporary repairs.[3]

The 1940 bombing affected the Crescent particularly badly and had also destroyed staff dining-rooms and kitchens on the sixth and seventh floors. Space for these functions had to be found elsewhere, and other accommodation was rendered temporarily unusable. Considerable structural repairs were required and those still outstanding in the Crescent in 1950 involved the taking down of:

over 50% of the existing stone and brick walling ... to varying levels, in some cases down to the top of the first floor windows, together with the major portion of the attic storey, the main entablature, and over 50% of the stone columns to their bases.[4]

The process of reinstating war damage was a prolonged one, not being completed until the late 1960s, and was carried out in parallel with plans for completing the County Offices (now known as North and South Blocks – see below) and the schemes for setting out the adjoining part of the South Bank.[5]

Post-war Schemes for the South Bank

After Labour's election victory in 1934 the Council had taken steps to acquire the parts of the South Bank between County Hall and Waterloo Bridge which it did not already own, intending to replace the industrial and commercial premises there with a modern town planning scheme – including a riverside park and cultural buildings. This was part of their attempt to put into practice the provisions of the 1932 Town and Country Planning Act. The acquisition of the land was a slow and difficult process which brought out several defects in the Act, and no firm development plans were made before the war.

In response to Lord Reith's request in March 1941 for Reconstruction Plans,[6] the LCC commissioned the *County of London Plan*, prepared by J. H. Forshaw, Architect to the Council from 1941 to 1946, and Sir Patrick Abercrombie, Professor of Town Planning at University College, London. Forshaw's predecessor, Frederick Hiorns, who had retired on grounds of age, after two years as Architect to the LCC, was thanked warmly by the authors for his 'very valuable pioneer work'. The *Plan* appeared in 1943, and was followed by the *Greater London Plan* in 1944.

In addition to the general principles laid down to guide post-war reconstruction and redevelopment generally, which affected the development of the area round County Hall, the authors made specific proposals. They collected together and rationalized the various projects which had been developed within the LCC and outside it, and incorporated these into their plan for the South Bank. They called for the replacement of Hungerford Bridge – Charing Cross Railway Bridge by a road bridge and the construction of a tunnel to take trains beneath the river, while the South Bank was to become a 'great cultural centre'.[7]

After the war the LCC brought in the distinguished architect, Charles Holden (1875–1960), as planning consultant. The choice was not so much theirs as that of the Ministry of Public Building and Works, who were interested in using the South Bank for government offices. Holden was preparing plans for the whole South Bank from Westminster Bridge to Bankside, and his brief from

the LCC in 1947 was to act as architectural and planning consultant for the general layout of the area. His studies were to be based on approximate schedules of accommodation for the various buildings proposed, including the layout and massing of buildings, access and traffic arrangements, provision for the parking of vehicles, general directions as to the type of building materials to be used, 'and all other matters which the Consultant may with the concurrence of the Architect ... of the Council ... deem necessary to be included'.[8]

While generally accepting the Abercrombie-Forshaw road layouts, Holden felt their detailed proposals were flawed, observing, in his Report to the LCC of June 1948, that it appeared that 'the area had been planned piecemeal, more with a view to disposal of sites than to beneficial co-ordinated planning', and asking for 'a free hand in replanning the area'. In fact, his proposals to integrate the existing County Hall buildings into his layout involved making physical modifications to them. He thought the river-front Crescent the worst part of the composition, suggesting the addition of an attic storey and parapet built up on the existing wall, with a second attic storey rising on top of that, but set back six feet. The flèche would be re-erected at the lower level. His reason for proposing these changes was simple. He wanted County Hall to resemble the buildings he was hoping to see erected to its north along the river:

From the architectural point of view the harmony and scale in the buildings along the Riverfront would be greatly enhanced: for the existence of a high pitched roof with the inconvenient accommodation resulting is out of character with the nature and spirit of modern frame construction.

He then set about replanning the layout of sites and internal roads, suggesting that Belvedere Road to the north of County Hall be realigned and widened, both for reasons of improved access to the proposed office buildings and to give a better view of County Hall. The LCC's officers pointed out, however, that this would mean reducing the length of the proposed extension to North Block along Chicheley Street by 65 feet, with a consequent loss of office space. Yet there was no sign that they regretted the architectural implications of the idea. On the contrary, they agreed that this change would result in 'a more dignified and architecturally satisfactory entrance to Belvedere Road from County Hall Courtyard' – the new name used by the LCC officers for the southern stretch of Belvedere Road which had been closed in 1948.[9]

So began the disintegration of Hiorns's pre-war plan, in which the internal façades of the returns to the North and South Blocks were seen as a means of focusing attention on the Belvedere Road entrance to County Hall, and of making a *place* there. The post-war planning schemes of Holden and Robert Matthew, Architect to the LCC from 1946 until 1953, were to turn the extension of North Block along Chicheley Street away from the County Hall buildings, and address it to what was anticipated to be a

much more exciting group to the north. The *County of London Plan* provided for office development to the north of County Hall as far as Hungerford Bridge, with a park laid out along the river front. Theatres and concert halls were to be further north next to the approach to Waterloo Bridge. These planners therefore felt justified in thinking that the north façade of North Block ought to have a strong architectural relationship with this area, and that the County Hall Courtyard was of secondary importance.

In time this plan influenced the decision to hold the Festival of Britain Exhibition on the South Bank, a festival first mooted in 1943 as a centenary celebration of the Great Exhibition of 1851. The original scheme was for an international affair to be held in Hyde Park, and even when it was made a strictly national event, the South Bank site, of only thirty acres, was opposed in many quarters as being too small. But the site had two advantages. Firstly, the LCC had decided to build a concert hall there in any case, so providing a major facility at no expense to central government, who were to finance the Festival. Secondly, it had a strong advocate in Herbert Morrison (1888–1965), the best known pre-war leader of the LCC, now Lord President of the Council, who was in charge of setting up the Festival of Britain. The South Bank site was selected in 1949.

Post-war Accommodation Problems

A decision about permanent war damage reinstatement was deferred in the autumn of 1947, when it was felt that the Ministry of Health, responsible for financing the repairs, was unlikely to provide the necessary funds immediately. Nevertheless, the Architect was instructed to proceed with all preparatory work in readiness for more favourable times. Temporary repairs continued since additional accommodation was needed for a number of reasons, one of them being the demolition of No. 23 Belvedere Road, for the South Bank Scheme, which displaced 200 staff.

Space was also needed because some departments were expanding, in particular those of the Architect, the Valuer, and the Director of Housing. Also to be considered was the old question of centralization of staff, of whom about ten per cent were housed away from County Hall. There were still 300 at Spring Gardens, the lease of which would expire in 1958, and not only would renewal be costly, but the buildings would remain, in the opinion of the Chief Officers, 'not very suitable for office purposes'.

A report prepared early in 1950 distinguished between the short term problem of the best way to utilize the existing space at County Hall, and the long term one of providing additional accommodation to meet the needs of the increased staff and the transfer from Spring Gardens.[10]

When the County Hall competition was held in 1907, space standards had been put at something over 100 square feet per person, but over the years this had fallen. Lower standards were being recommended generally in government circles. A mean of 80 square feet per person was adopted in the 1950 report, producing the equivalent of an increase in floor area in the building of over 57,000 square feet, enough to house 720 extra staff.

Much of the building was 'poorly provided with natural light', but the adoption of strip lighting was a means of eliminating a distinction between actual and useful floor area which had been employed until that time. By artificially lighting this formerly 'dead' space, a further gain of 21,000 square feet was made.

But the long-term problems could not be solved by arithmetic and electricity alone. In addition to the 300 staff at Spring Gardens, 200 staff occupied temporary offices on the Principal Floor, the jealously guarded province of Members and Chief Officers.[11] Much of the extra accommodation could have been provided by the reduced space standards, but for the extensive war damage which was still to be repaired. Replanning the main building according to lower space standards was, in any case, meant to be a short term measure.

Thus, the completion of the North and South Blocks, which had been indefinitely postponed in 1938, became almost inevitable, although an immediate start was out of the question. There were government restrictions on office building, but informal talks with the Ministry indicated that the LCC would be given sympathetic consideration as soon as economic and industrial conditions improved.[12] Though the Chicheley Street site was needed in the short term as a car park for the Festival of Britain, the extension to the North Block represented the most significant piece of accommodation, providing room for 750, and for that reason alone was most attractive to the Council. The North Block stopped well short of the realigned Chicheley Street, leaving space for another 85,000 square feet, while the South Block already extended around the corner on to Westminster Bridge Road, leaving only 30,000 square feet to be built there, which would accommodate 300 staff. Thus, an estimated 1,050 spaces for officers would be provided by the new buildings, and 1,013 were needed.

Costs were put at £902,000 for the North Block Extension and £503,500 (including £125,000 for land acquisition) for the South Block Extension. The building time was estimated at thirty-eight and thirty-three months respectively. For war damage reinstatement the cost was estimated at £785,000, the major part of which would be paid for by the War Damage Commission, and the time at thirty-nine months. A provisional timetable suggested that the North Block should be completed between 1952 and 1956, and the other works between 1957 and 1961, after the North Block Extension had been occupied.[13] At the beginning of August 1950 the Council passed estimates for the work in full with a liability on capital account of £1,280,000 for the extensions to North and South Blocks, excluding land acquisition, and approved £737,500 for war damage reinstatement.[14]

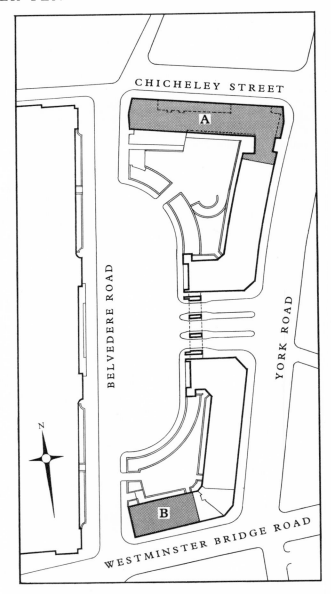

Fig. 50. North and South Blocks as built, 1936–1963. Post-war sections are indicated by stippling. A North Block Extension (1955–8); B South Block Extension (1960–3)

The Completion of North Block

By the spring of 1952, although the Ministry had not given permission for the Council to proceed, a modification of the pre-war scheme had been prepared by the Architect's Department. The project, nominally under the control of the Architect, Robert Matthew, was being run by Edwin Williams (1896–1976), an architect who had worked for Sir Guy Dawber, and then on the Festival Hall together with Matthew himself, Leslie Martin, and Peter Moro.[15] Williams was a senior member of the Building Regulations

Division, who had been appointed Senior Architect for the County Hall extensions, a post he held under successive Architects to the LCC, including the two successors to Matthew, (Sir) Leslie Martin (1953–5) and (Sir) Hubert Bennett (1955–71).[a] Other members of the team were C. H. Bates, R. A. Laker and C. G. Shankland.

Hiorns's pre-war plan had to be modified, for the decision to widen Belvedere Road reduced the space available and there was now a requirement for about 8,000 square feet for a branch of the Westminster Bank.[17] Moreover, the Council architects were keen to promote their own ideas. They needed to convince the Establishment Committee to go along with them, and produced a report with this in mind. They presented three alternatives to the Hiorns plan, rather confusingly known as schemes 3, 4 and 5. Having noted that the 1930s plan envisaged the North and South Blocks completing an 'architecturally related precinct', with road barriers at the Westminster Bridge Road and Chicheley Street ends of Belvedere Road, they went on:

The shortening of the North wing . . . with enhanced possibilities in the development of the adjoining land between County Hall and Charing Cross Viaduct and the widening of York Road, now present an opportunity to explore less formal and more flexible arrangements for satisfying accommodation requirements.[18]

Scheme 3 was a truncated version of the Hiorns block, its end pavilion missing to allow the widening of Belvedere Road, and with a capacity for 707, rather than 838 staff. Scheme 4 was designed to restore all the accommodation of the block, and more. As the report continued:

the elevational freedom would allow of greater freedom in construction, internal planning, and arranging the accommodation economically and flexibly.

The extra cost of scheme 4 over scheme 3 was estimated at only £50,000, largely because different methods of construction and thinner detailing would be cheaper. But the building would have risen eleven storeys to parapet level, twenty-five feet higher than the North Block adjoining it.

Scheme 5, preferred and recommended by the Architect, depended on sleight of hand. If the Committee were to rescind their decision to shorten the block in accordance with Holden's plan, which had anyway been much altered, it would be possible to provide the full accommodation at a reduced height. This was ostensibly a return to Hiorns's scheme, retaining his layout and section, but omitting his architecture, which would be replaced by something 'fresh, distinctive and contemporary'.

When the Establishment Committee eventually reported to Council, in the summer of 1954, they presented only two schemes for consideration. One was the abbreviated Hiorns project (scheme 3), the other a new design for a stylistically modern building which kept the cornice line of the earlier work but tucked an extra storey into an immensely tall roof. Accommodation in this second scheme was for 760 staff compared with 707 in the first.[19] The more up-to-date scheme was chosen and shortly afterwards the Ministry gave its go-ahead for work to begin.

The tender of Gee Walker & Slater Limited was, at £659,331, the lowest received for building the extension and was approved by the Council at the end of November 1955.[20] Problems arose over tenders for steelwork, all ten firms tendering the identical sum of £50,238 19s. 3d., and the LCC decided to recommend to central government that the matter be referred to the Monopolies Commission.[21]

The South Bank and the County Hall site were not completed according to Holden's grand design. Already modified by Robert Matthew and Leslie Martin, in the intervening years it had been lost sight of. Shell redeveloped their own land without much relation to the rest of the area, and further problems arose over the site for the National Theatre, with repercussions on the development of County Hall.

The National Theatre had its origins as the Shakespeare Memorial National Theatre, and for many years its promoters tried to get it built in South Kensington, with Lutyens as architect. After Lutyens's death in 1944, both architect and site were changed, the foundation stone being moved in 1951 to the new site just to the north of County Hall, on the present location of Jubilee Gardens.[22] The new alignment of Chicheley Street was altered to take account of this, and laid out at a slight angle to the north front of County Hall, to allow oblique views of the theatre when built. By the time the site for the National Theatre was moved once more, Chicheley Street had been laid out on this new axis, as had the extension to North Block. Both were set, like broken bones by an incompetent surgeon, according to mistaken principles. A slight aesthetic lameness can be detected to this day.

The extension to North Block was completed in the early spring of 1958, and was not well received (Plate 44). The architectural critic J. M. Richards was particularly harsh, describing it as 'this senseless cliff of solid-looking stonework', a 'most unfortunate design' and a 'compromise that falls between all possible stools'.[23] Outlining the respective cases for completing the 'Giles Scott' scheme and building something quite different, Richards blamed Council Members for forcing a compromise, apparently unaware that Matthew and Martin had both recommended such a move in the early 1950s. Indeed, to Richards the compromise went further than just the building, marring the LCC's reputation for an 'architectural policy which in the last ten years has brought so much credit to them, and has been admired all over the world'.

[a]Williams, who had hoped to succeed Forshaw in 1946, had expectations of designing the Festival Hall, for which he ended up as site architect.[16]

He saw the building as being 'in several practical ways less satisfactory even than the Scott building which was its starting-point'. Many of the fashionable architectural devices employed do indeed impinge upon the convenience of the building in use. Loadbearing columns had not 'freed the plan', as modern architecture demanded they should, but merely cluttered it up by being too close to the walls, which themselves had the appearance of loadbearing structures. The offices (Plate 44d) are worse lit than those of the Hiorns-Scott building, partly because of the adoption of rectangular windows and the peculiar treatment of the end walls. But, as Richards pointed out, this under-lighting is only partly due to the refusal, 'presumably for stylistic reasons', to provide larger windows, 'it is chiefly due to the width of the building being far too great'.

Richards was an advocate of the 'stylistic unity' theory proposed by Holden and his followers, assuming that the North Block was to become part of the larger South Bank rather than the County Hall precinct. In defence of the option for a 'modern' solution to the extension block, he claimed this function for it:

It had the additional role of providing the background to the new South Bank development and should conform to it in style, which there was then every reason to hope would be a frame-and-cladding rather than a masonry style. Although the end elevation of the Ralph Knott wing also faced the new site, this was due later to be partly blanketed by the National Theatre.

Fortunately, the anticipated 'blanketing' of the impressive northern façade of County Hall never occurred, leaving clearly visible one of the best elevations on the South Bank. This would certainly not now be seen as an embarrassment, and with the current public image of the Modern Movement, perhaps the position has been reversed, at least for the time being.

The completion of the North Block was significant in a practical way, for it was suggested to the Council in 1957 that it presented an opportunity to re-group the office staff in a more modern arrangement.[24] The original system placed Heads of Department on the Principal Floor, easily accessible to Members and conveniently located for attending committee meetings, while the staff of their departments were organized vertically above them in the building. This system logically called for a building that could expand vertically with a growing organization, but of course this was impossible, and departments found themselves scattered in many parts of the County Hall and its extensions. The Council therefore decided to change the system and allocate accommodation so that each department and its Chief Officer would be together.

The Completion of South Block

The 1950 building programme had assumed that the completion of North Block would provide enough space for the decanting of staff while war damage repairs were carried out, as well as for the centralization of office staff when the lease of Spring Gardens expired. The increasing numbers of central office staff, which had reached 6,568 by 1957, now made this impossible, so it was suggested in that year that the South Block be completed. If started immediately there was a good chance the building could be finished by the early months of 1962.[25]

It was accepted by the Council that the new wing alongside Westminster Bridge Road would have to accommodate both an extension to the existing Post Office as well as a new tea-shop for J. Lyons, who would be displaced. The inclusion of the tea-shop was advocated by C. G. Shankland, one of the architects working on the scheme, as 'good comprehensive planning' in view of the future increase of office workers attracted to the new South Bank.[26] Two designs were prepared for the completion of South Block, one a simple truncation of the 1930s scheme, providing 250 places, and the other an L-shaped plan, again to a shorter length than the original, which brought the total up to 320. It was recognized that an extra seventy places were not going to solve the LCC's accommodation problem, and since the smaller scheme – thought by the architect to be the more satisfactory – was estimated to cost about fifteen per cent less per place, it was adopted.[27]

In the new scheme the block facing Belvedere Road had a simpler treatment than that proposed in the original New County Offices scheme, and for reasons of economy the short return along Belvedere Road was omitted. The cost per place was higher than that of the North Block Extension because of the need to continue the design of the existing South Block along Westminster Bridge Road. It was recognized that no architectural solution was 'practicable which would enable a departure from this form which is basically more expensive than a modern building employing new techniques'. The main expense would be the work in Portland stone which would have to consist of solid slabs with setbacks to carry the cornices and mouldings through the elevation; apart from the extra cost of the stone itself, this involved heavier and more expensive construction and steelwork.[28]

Tenders for foundations were received in July 1960, and the contract was won by the Demolition & Construction Company Limited, at £33,029 7s. 5d. W. J. Simms, Sons & Cooke, Limited, were awarded the main building contract with a price of £379,056, and finished the building early in 1963.[29]

It was intended that the opportunity would be taken to re-plan the courtyard, by removing the plinth and replacing it with a fountain – a programme first mooted in 1949.[30] The plan also provided for an increase in the number of car-parking spaces. In the event, the idea of a *place* with gardens in front of County Hall was abandoned. The plinth was demolished, the fountain was never built, and the courtyard became a car-park.

From the time of the South Block Extension, the Council seems to have thought of County Hall merely in terms of square feet of office space. Buildings designed subsequently were no longer intended as expressions of the Council's belief in its political or social roles. The involvement of the Royal Fine Art Commission with the Island Block project, which is discussed below, is indicative of the Council's new attitude. The RFAC saw themselves as stepping in to prevent the building becoming too obtrusive, almost to defend London from a Council which

had once seen itself as setting the standards for urban development in the capital.

Addington Street Annexe

Before work on the South Block Extension was begun, the Council agreed to a recommendation by the Establishment

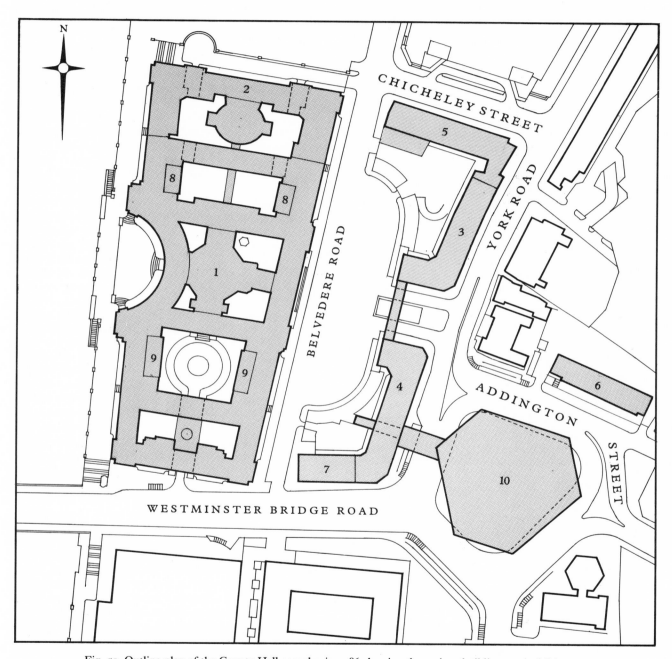

Fig. 51. Outline plan of the County Hall complex in 1986 showing the various buildings and additions.
1 Main Building (1913–22); **2** Main Building (Northern Front) (1930–33); **3, 4** North and South Blocks (1936–9); **5** North Block Extension (1955–8); **6** Addington Street Annexe (1960); **7** South Block Extension (1960–3); **8** Infill building, H courtyard (1970–3); **9** Infill building, Members' Courtyard (1972–4); **10** Island Block (1970–4)

Committee for the provision of more temporary office space, to the east of York Road, in Addington Street. During the 1930s the LCC had been negotiating with the Ecclesiastical Commissioners for the purchase of land between York Road and Belvedere Road for their extension scheme, and were forced to take Addington Street off the Commissioners' hands at the same time. A redundant school and some cottages, scheduled for demolition, stood on the site, and the future of the area from a town planning point of view was uncertain. In March 1960 the Council decided to build a prefabricated four-storey structure on the site to help with the decanting problems while war damage repairs were going ahead. The building was finished in the autumn of 1960, providing space for 340 staff at an estimated cost of £118,750. It was expected to have a serviceable life of seven years, but was still in use in 1986.[31]

Though modest in size, and not generally reviewed in architectural publications, the Addington Street extension was seen by at least one critic as a fine example of modern design (Plate 45a). Ian Nairn thought it displayed 'just the sort of sober richness and care over details that would transform most office blocks – yet without any pretensions or appliqué aesthetics'. Written in 1964, his observations also reflect a boredom in architectural circles with the pompous commercial classicism of the 1930s. He called it 'an enormous relief from the exhausted style' of the Hiorns-Scott building.[32] His words recall the misgivings about classicism generally as a modern idiom, expressed by Halsey Ricardo at the time of the competition, over fifty years earlier.

The Creation of the GLC

In 1965 the LCC was replaced by the GLC, an event which, despite the delegation of many powers to the London Boroughs, was to mean the recruitment of more staff, and even more pressure on space at County Hall.

By a sad irony, the passing of the LCC coincided with that of one of its most distinguished Members. Herbert Morrison had been one of the strongest opponents of the creation of the GLC, and his death in early March 1965 was the occasion of a poignant ceremony. Morrison's body was cremated, and he had asked in his will that his ashes 'be scattered into the high tide of London's river from the terrace of County Hall where I was privileged to render several years of happy service to the people of London'.[33] This deed was performed by the Leader of the Council, Sir Isaac Hayward (1884–1976), a few hours before the LCC's final meeting. As the tide was low at the time, Morrison's ashes were scattered from the LCC fireboat *Firebrace*, which had set out from the Festival Pier.

War Damage Reinstatement

Though much discussed, the repairs to war damage at County Hall were deferred because they did not offer the immediate gains in accommodation that new building did. However, some of the most substantial internal changes were made to County Hall in connexion with war damage reinstatement. These involved the 'refurbishment' of the Chairman and Members' accommodation overlooking the Thames in the Crescent (Plate 43c), and ultimately the removal of the contents of the Members' Library to Clerkenwell, and its use as offices. The staff restaurant and kitchens were moved from the sixth and seventh floors to a position beneath the Members' Terrace. Plans for this move, which made a gain of 20,000 square feet of office accommodation, were approved in 1964, and the new restaurant opened two years later, in July 1966.[34] *The Times* described the new restaurant 'suite' in somewhat exaggerated terms as 'encompassing the whole length of the building and a range of vision as fine as any in London', and went on to itemize a foyer, 324–seat cafeteria (Plate 43b), two 90–seat waitress service restaurants, a senior officers' restaurant seating 60, a snack bar and a 'beautiful gallery coffee lounge with seats in riverside picture window recesses'.[35] The severe granite wall, relieved only by a few 'arrow-loops', which faced the public embankment walk in front of the Members' Terrace, was replaced with a full-height strip of sheet glass screened by net curtains, thus providing the new coffee lounge with a panoramic view of the Thames (Plate 42b). This alteration to the river front was not universally welcomed, arousing, in particular, the ire of the Victorian Society.

A further modernization was the redecoration of the Belvedere Road entrance hall in 1968. Knott's severe design, planned with visions of the mob storming the Ceremonial Staircase, gave way to a comfortable lobby where the mob could await the attentions of authority 'in a modern, friendly and efficient atmosphere'.[36] Carpeting appeared in place of mosaic, and the marble chimneypieces disappeared behind curtaining. Staff were discouraged from using the redecorated entrance, and Hector, the County Hall cat, was removed as being *infra dig*.[37] Some ten years later, it was discovered that the marble fireplaces had disappeared for ever, as, of course, had Hector.

One South Bank cat did rather better. In 1948 George VI, reading of the South Bank development, had expressed concern for the fate of the two Coade stone lions on the Lion Brewery, which was being demolished at the time. The LCC loyally agreed to preserve the lions, and in 1951 they were exhibited at the Festival of Britain. The larger lion was subsequently removed to York Road, and after a brief sojourn at Waterloo Station in the early 1960s, was installed in its present position atop the pedestal on the corner of Westminster Bridge in 1966.[b]

The Island Block

The efforts of the LCC to centralize their staff, while sometimes approaching their goal, had never actually

---

[b]The smaller lion, after spending many years in the County Hall store, was removed to the Rugby Union Headquarters in Twickenham in 1972.[38]

achieved it. Each new plan, projected to resolve the dilemma once and for all, had been overwhelmed by an ever-growing central office staff, a problem which continued under the GLC.

In 1967 and 1968 the Establishment Committee reported that a third of central office staff were in scattered accommodation, and dusted off the now familiar arguments for bringing everyone together. They invited a firm of management consultants to advise on the problem, and were disconcerted to be told that decentralization was the answer – that some 2,000 staff working at County Hall could be sent to work outside central London. The Committee rejected this advice, preferring to take advantage of proposals to build the long-awaited roundabout at the junction of York Road and Westminster Bridge Road, and giving instructions that a scheme be prepared for an office building on the traffic island at the centre of the roundabout. This was announced to the press in February 1968.[39]

The first Island Block design was for a 'triple-octagon tower block of 15 storeys, 170 ft high', containing 154,000 square feet of offices, estimated to cost £3,020,000 and providing room for 1,540 people. The Council approved this design early in 1969, but the Royal Fine Art Commission was opposed to it, asserting that the area was sensitive to high buildings. The Establishment Committee, though they felt that there were no views in the vicinity that a tower could spoil, agreed to modify the plans.[40]

Work on site began on 4 December 1970, and the building was officially opened on 21 October 1974 (Plate 45b-d). The block was designed by R. A. Laker, J. E. Knight and W. Sutherland, under Sir Roger Walters as Architect to the Council. Trollope & Colls were the main contractors. The structure of the building is situ-cast concrete faced with 'grit blasted calcinated flint panels which should minimise the irregularities of weathering', according to the architects. The cost of the building was £3,623,647. Ancillary works, including landscaping and alterations to the South Block, added a further £226,773. The cost per square foot was very high, mainly because of the restricted nature of the site, which made construction difficult, and the high level of servicing.[41]

As built the Island Block provides the same accommodation as the earlier project would have done, with a hexagonal plan rising from the basement through seven storeys, the last three of these stepped back. Isolated by the swirl of heavy traffic and by the deep light well which surrounds its lower storeys, the building has no entrance at ground level and is connected to the rest of County Hall by means of subways and a bridge across York Road from South Block. The main entrance is from the Belvedere Road Courtyard via an ingeniously contrived escalator up to the bridge (Plate 45c), so that the visitor arrives directly on the 'second floor' of the Island Block. There is a roof garden on the top of the building, though it is unused. Internally the spaces are arranged as large open

offices on the *burolandschaft* (landscaped artificially controlled deep office space) principle and the whole building was a sealed environment, fully air-conditioned with automatic solar-control blinds. These bright orange blinds were controlled by solar cells on the roof, but problems were found in tuning the system so that rapidly changing weather conditions did not cause them to be rolling and unrolling themselves throughout the day.

When it was opened, the Island Block contained the Valuation and Housing Departments. These two departments had to be easily accessible to the public, hence the complicated escalator and bridge arrangement, though some users found its open plan as confusing as the corridors of the original building. Some architectural critics saw the idea as a clever use of otherwise dismal urban space, and the building itself as a realization of this idea to a high architectural standard. 'Not many buildings', wrote David Rock, 'are taking advantage of the sophistication in internal environmental techniques and it needs a client body like the GLC to advance such techniques'. He thought the stepped-back floors gave 'a simple Teutonic solution to the design problem'.[42] When the building was opened Edward Jones agreed that 'a much above-average working environment has been achieved', even though 'the initial programmatic difficulties will not disappear'. But he was also interested in the wider implications of the development, noting that the new building housed approximately a quarter of the total 8,500 office staff working for the GLC at the South Bank headquarters. Before the adoption of the *burolandschaft* principle of office planning, the two per cent daylight factor would have necessitated a tower of Centre Point proportions on that site.[43]

Infill Buildings

Coincident with the building of the Island Block were two schemes that gained more space by filling in parts of the two large internal courtyards – the Members' Courtyard and H courtyard to the north of the Council Chamber. These provided for 496 and 250 people respectively, at the space standard of 80 square feet per person, and were built using curtain wall construction. The cost for both schemes was estimated at £754,000. Altogether, the three developments pushed central office accommodation from 6,500 to 8,800 places.[44]

These infill structures are utilitarian in design, with no deference to Knott's work which surrounds them (Plates 42c,d, 43a). While this is excusable in the northern area, it is indefensible in the magnificent Members' Courtyard. Although the two infill blocks were built within two years of each other – that in H courtyard in 1970-3, that in the Members' Courtyard in 1972-4[45] – they are much further apart than that in style. Owing to its green-tinted spandrel panels and clear glass, the former looks like a product of the 1950s, whereas the black glass and glazing bars of the

Members' Courtyard infill reflect much more accurately the fashion in curtain wall design then prevailing.

In 1973 feasibility studies were made for expansion northwards. *The Times* reported the proposals as being for 'a building of moderate bulk which might house a new council chamber and would certainly include members' accommodation and space for the public to meet members and officials'.[46]

Nothing came of these proposals, and within a few years central government had taken away some of the Council's functions, a process culminating in the abolition of the GLC.

Working at County Hall

County Hall developed a distinctive character, that, as in all buildings, grew out of the nature of the work carried on there and the collective personality of the Members and staff, and which was also partly determined by its design. The immense size of the building tended to the development of isolated communities within it. Many such 'villages' existed in County Hall, the inhabitants of which knew of each others' existence, and sometimes ventured into each others' territory, but tended to maintain an independence of character. This was partly based on the differing work done in the various departments, and to some extent on the architecture of the building itself. The Architect's Plan Room, for example, deeply embedded in the sub-basement, was in recent memory a distinct and almost monastic community, where silence prevailed, and visitors were rare.

Recollections are inevitably personal and varied, but certain features do emerge from those of the former Members and officers that help to convey a sense of the unique atmosphere of County Hall when it was the centre of a London-wide local authority.

The scale of the building and its internal layout were the features which, not unnaturally, made the greatest impression upon the councillors, their officers, and those members of the public who had reason to visit it. The size of County Hall did not appeal to all, and ten years after its official opening Sir Harry Haward, a former Comptroller of the LCC, thought that a number of Members still felt some regret at leaving Spring Gardens where, although the offices were 'mean and uninspiring ... there was an intimate character about the Chamber and its lobby which is entirely lacking in the vast building across the river'.[47] To Herbert Morrison its magnitude was not inappropriate, however, for he regarded the 'massive building' of County Hall as an expression of the power of municipal government in London and 'a highly organised workshop of public administration' which gave the impression of modernity.[48] The staff who worked there also reacted to the building's scale in different ways. One found that 'the great building ... always seemed to me to lack the charm of the great Victorian town halls', while

another regarded its size as 'oddly liberating by reason of the anonymity it bestowed'.[49]

It was the lengthy corridors which did much to convey the sense of scale of the building and contributed a great deal to its distinctive personality. They ran for five-and-a-quarter miles, and much time could be spent simply walking from one room to another along 'those echoing corridors with highly polished floors ... leading for hundreds of yards' and 'in places extending as far as the eye could see'. Due allowance had to be made for the time which was required to make a journey within the building in order to arrive at a meeting on time. The consequences of a misjudgment were not entirely pleasant, for 'Late-comers had to pound, breathless, along the slippery parquet of the identically panelled corridors, frantically trying to find the right door'. Such unwelcome experiences could make a lasting impression. A former officer recalled that 'After twenty years, I still have the occasional bad dream when I am hurrying through those endless corridors, up stairs with no top, in lifts that don't work, in tunnels (there is one) that turn into dwindling caves and potholes, always late for something very important'. Even an experienced Member heading for a familiar destination on the Principal Floor 'had to allow at least ten minutes, once inside County Hall, to be punctual for a meeting'. The corridors were apparently 'interminable' and even 'formidable', but they did have some helpful features, among them 'the deep window sills along one side ... which gave the assurance one could stop and juggle around with one's papers before reaching one's destination'.

The corridors were partly to blame for the problems which many encountered in finding their way around County Hall, for although their arrangement was a logical one, it was not readily understood. There was, moreover, an inherent difficulty of orientation within the building. One Member found that this caused him considerable problems 'until I was advised that the trick was to open a door and get a view of the river'. The numbering of the rooms also had a logic to it, but it did not survive intact, due to the subdivision of rooms and the creation of new ones as the pressure upon accommodation increased. That the population of County Hall had risen considerably was very apparent to an officer returning there in 1968 after an absence of eighteen years, to find that 'the building was crammed full of people ... there were printers in the roof space and scientists in the sub-basement'. The effect of the greater numbers employed within the building was that 'alterations and adaptations were constantly being carried out in one part or another, with the result that the numbering of the rooms ... became chaotic, especially when old cross-corridors were closed and new ones opened'. In addition, departments were reorganized and relocated within the building, disturbing the original arrangements. The Survey of London was particularly mobile, having nine sets of offices within thirty years, two of them outside County Hall. The combined result of such reorganization, the layout and room numbering was that it required 'months or years to fully understand how rooms had been subdivided (and not always logically renumbered) and why cross corridors would wind off apparently to nowhere'. Even after many years of service, one officer 'would sometimes come across a tiny room off a cross corridor which I had not known to exist'.

The consequence was that it was by no means easy for visitors to find their way within the building. Indeed, this rather understates the situation, for, as one Member reported, it was 'not surprising to find a visitor completely lost'[50] and an officer later recalled that 'many were the lost souls one encountered on a journey in County Hall'. The difficulties were experienced by the diarist of *The Times* who, in 1966, attempted to keep an appointment with 'the holder of a high office' and so began a search which led 'down passages, measureless to man ... Upstairs and down, round corners, finding numbers on doors apparently planned as part of a game of snakes and ladders ... [until] by guessing and good luck, we found the promised room'. The conclusion drawn from this evidently memorable adventure was that 'The designers of the Cretan labyrinth and the Hampton Court maze would treat the County Hall men as their peers'.[51]

What of the rooms themselves? The chief ones, on the Principal Floor, were generally much appreciated. One Leader of the GLC recalled, with evident pleasure, his 'magnificent suite of offices ... in the curved section of the river frontage'. A change of post or rank often meant a change of room, however, and perhaps a change of aspect. A Member who served on the LCC and GLC for twenty years experienced a range of the accommodation which County Hall offered to Members, from 'a lovely front room with a river prospect' to 'a rather sinister internal room with a half-concealed entrance'. The Council Chamber and Conference Hall were regarded as fine rooms, 'well designed, comfortable and convenient for Members, but much too high' and both 'were acoustically a disaster'. The visitors' galleries in the Chamber were 'too high up, too remote and very uncomfortable' and the view of the Members which they afforded 'was chiefly confined to seeing the not infrequently bald tops of their heads'. The space allocated to the press was also less than satisfactory, for by the 1950s they were placed 'at the back of a bank of members' seats, so that a stranger would not have known a reporter from a member'. Strictly speaking, the Principal Floor was restricted to the use of the Members and their staff and those senior officers who had business there. There were exceptions to this rule, one being that the Members' Library could also be used by officers. It represented 'a civilised refuge, with a desk at which to ruminate and make notes for speeches' and a quiet spot 'where one could research and write in peace'. The sanctity of the Principal Floor was gradually eroded; it was no longer maintained in the early 1970s and by the early 1980s had been completely abandoned.

The impression created by offices elsewhere in County Hall depended partly upon their aspect. One officer found himself working with a section 'housed in one large and inconvenient room on the ground floor, at the south end of the crescent, with an outlook largely obscured by the sub-structure of the members' terrace'. Those rooms facing the river were to be preferred, for obvious reasons. 'The view from the fourth-floor offices was always beautiful on late winter afternoons when the lights came on along the Victoria Embankment.' Their occupants could also appreciate one of the few benefits of London's polluted atmosphere, which was the 'exceptional beauty of the sunsets, on occasion, behind Big Ben, going down in a haze of mauve, purple, indigo'. One drawback of the rooms on the riverfront was 'the strong winds, especially in the winter months'. Indeed, much of the building suffered with 'related problems of heating and ventilation'. This applied to the older parts and to the later multi-storey infill rooms on the east and west sides of the Members' Courtyard and H courtyard which had large windows. They therefore became rather hot in summer, for 'the internal sun-blinds provided were of little use', and cold in winter, when 'the air-conditioning system ... led to trouble, because at times the occupants of one floor would block up the vents on account of draughts, thereby creating even colder air-flows for those in the rooms above or below them'. Even the small offices in the original building were less than ideal, especially those which were long and narrow 'so that two people sitting by the window had good light, while the more junior staff tended to have less light further into the room'. The position of a room relative to the catering facilities also affected the equanimity of its occupants. One officer, whose room was in the basement directly below the canteen, could identify a 'fish day' long before lunchtime arrived. The pungency of the odours was much reduced when the new staff restaurant complex was opened in 1966. Even apart from the cooking facilities, County Hall did have a distinctive smell, which, once experienced, 'was never to be forgotten'. The floor polish and the disinfectants used contributed largely to it and the drains also played an important part in the 'unique and subtle blend' of smells 'which pervaded many of the corridors'. There were some seasonal variations and 'on very hot days the drain element tended to predominate'.

Individual impressions of the building as a place of work varied, but in general they were favourable. Although the grandeur of the principal areas did not extend to the offices, it was felt to be a 'pleasant rather than unpleasant building to be employed in'. The ceremonial areas were at their most splendid when they were decked out in municipal flowers for the entertainment of a visiting head of state, though the annual Chairman's Reception also gave an opportunity for 'exotic floral displays'. An officer who had worked there for almost forty years remembered it as 'pleasant, comfortable and convenient ... a building to be proud of', while for one elected Member County Hall 'was the "second best club in London" yielding place only to the House of Lords!'

CHAPTER XI

The Future of County Hall

In April 1986, under the legislation abolishing the Greater London Council, the ownership of County Hall passed to the London Residuary Body (LRB), an organization created expressly to oversee the transfer of functions and property to successor bodies, such as the London Boroughs, and the London Fire and Civil Defence Authority. Like other assets not officially needed or transferred, County Hall was to be sold. Not surprisingly, the disposal and future use of so prominent a building attracted a good deal of interest, both in the press and among members of the public.

Proposals for retaining the building as the offices of a public body, thereby reducing the need for substantial alterations, received considerable attention, even though they were unlikely to find favour with a government which had abolished the GLC. Political opponents of abolition were especially keen to see as little change as possible, in the hope that a future government might reinstate the building as the headquarters of a new London-wide authority. The Inner London Education Authority (ILEA), the Association of London Authorities, and the London Charitable Trust – a group formed especially for the purpose – all considered making offers to purchase County Hall. One local government use proposed was a combined base for the ILEA, the London Fire and Civil Defence Authority and the London Waste Regulation Authority.[1] The ILEA, which was originally intended to survive its parent body, was a serious contender for at least part of the complex. The possibility of using County Hall for government offices was also canvassed. Lord St John of Fawsley favoured the relocation there of the Department of the Environment, as this would allow the demolition of its Marsham Street offices, which he described as 'one of the most hideous structures in London and indeed in the kingdom'.[2] One proposal would have turned County Hall into a headquarters for the Metropolitan Police; another recommended its conversion to a prison.[3] Envious eyes were cast on the building from across the river, at least one M.P. suggesting to the government that it might be used for Members' accommodation.[4] A grander and more appropriate role was envisaged by those who felt that the building would make a fitting meeting-place for the European Parliament, or a headquarters for the European Community.[5]

The County Hall complex, whose future was being so hotly discussed, comprised some areas of open space used by the public, as well as a variety of buildings, not all of which were of architectural importance (fig. 51). Those of interest included Knott's 'riverside building', the Scott-Hiorns North and South Blocks, and, from the town-planning point of view, the riverside terrace, and Jubilee Gardens. The Gardens occupied the site of the LCC's first purchase on the South Bank, and in 1951 the area had been used for part of the Festival of Britain site.

The press foresaw considerable difficulties in finding a suitable buyer for what the *Financial Times* described as both 'the jewel in the property portfolio' and 'the most vexatious asset to sell'.[6] The London *Evening Standard* was making the same point when it half-jokingly suggested that a sale notice might read:

Very important property covering $6\frac{1}{2}$ acres, premier position, nine floors, 900 rooms, 12 miles of corridor, marble council chamber, pillared conference hall, kitchens, bars, cafeterias, restaurants, car parks, mod cons at every turn. Suit goodness knows who.[7]

To the usual difficulties of dealing with a large and famous building in a prominent position had to be added the extra dimension of opposition to the sale, both in Parliament and from the London Borough of Lambeth, and the planning problems thrown up by the proposal to use Waterloo Station as a London terminus for Eurotunnel traffic.

In order to establish possible alternative uses for the building, in the hope of enhancing its marketability, the LRB submitted more than a dozen applications to the local planning authority, the London Borough of Lambeth, in October 1986. These included requests for a decision as to whether the use as offices of any of the buildings involved 'development' and therefore required planning permission; planning applications for office use for them all; and applications for a change of use for the listed 1922 Main Building to hotel use, and to mixed hotel and residential use.[8] No decision having been made during the statutory period by the reluctant Borough Council, the LRB appealed to the Secretary of State for the Environment, who called a Public Inquiry.[9]

At this Inquiry, which opened in April 1987, particular attention was paid to the fact that the Main Building is listed Grade II*, and that County Hall is within a conservation area. The question of whether the existing use of the Main Building should be preserved was also addressed. Citing the Department of the Environment's own general guidelines – that the 'best use for a historic building is obviously the use for which it was designed'[10] – the spokesman for English Heritage urged the desirability of keeping the Main Building as the headquarters of a public or quasi-public authority, 'the nature of whose activities would be likely to ensure the preservation and continued use of such important features as the Council Chamber and ambulatories, the Conference Hall, the Education Library and the principal committee rooms'. Conversion to hotel or residential use would require the introduction of domestic services and other changes threatening the fabric of this 'great civic monument'. In any case, no decision should be taken over the future of the Main Building until detailed plans had been submitted.[11] Lambeth Council was concerned that the proposed development would conflict with existing planning guidelines, as laid down in the Greater London Development Plan and the Waterloo District Plan, by increasing private office development, thereby putting strain on local transport and car-parking arrangements, and by threatening public access to the riverside.[12]

The Inspector, David Keene Q.C., allowed the office applications for the subsidiary buildings, but rejected all four planning applications seeking a change of use for the Main Building. Any office use other than by a local authority would constitute 'development' requiring a planning permission. He also took the view that the main purpose of County Hall 'had been a governmental one albeit confined to London, but with the distinct characteristics of an elected government use', and that in 'balancing the competing need to retain County Hall for London governmental use against the need for office use' he thought that the Main Building ought to continue in local government use. The Inspector concluded that the outline applications for change to residential and hotel use could not be granted without the submission of detailed information to allow the implications for the listed building to be assessed. The problem of inadequate parking space also had to be resolved before consent could be granted for conversion for residential purposes.[13]

The Inquiry's findings and the Secretary of State's decisions were made public on 20 October 1987. The Secretary of State, Nicholas Ridley, accepted that a change to general office use needed a planning application, but he did not agree with his Inspector's finding that there was 'an overriding need' for local government use to continue. Ridley therefore granted outline planning permission for County Hall to be used for general offices, and he also stated that with the submission of proper detailed plans, neither hotel nor residential use would be unacceptable. Although concerned about the lack of parking space, he was more worried that the application was not detailed enough to allow a proper assessment of its likely impact on an important listed building. He therefore refused consent for residential and hotel use.[14]

The Secretary of State's decision was challenged in the courts by Lambeth, the ILEA and others on the one hand, and the LRB on the other. The point ultimately to be resolved was whether the Secretary of State was legally bound by his Inspector's 'competing need test' – the desirability of preserving an existing use weighed on its planning merits against the need and desirability of the proposed new use – and although the House of Lords eventually decided, in July 1990, that he was not so bound, the delay caused by these legal actions proved embarrassing.[15]

The implication of the Secretary of State's decision was that hotel and residential use were not ruled out. Soon after the original announcement of the results of the Inquiry the LRB asked the well-known estate agents, Richard Ellis and Partners, to find a purchaser. In the prevailing favourable economic climate, they were able to attract over 300 inquiries, from which some twenty serious applicants emerged. Potential developers had to be assessed not only on their size and viability, and the amount of money bid, but also on the likelihood of their schemes receiving planning approval.[16]

Twelve developers finally submitted proposals for the building, and four were selected for further consideration. From these the scheme prepared by the American architectural practice of Skidmore, Owings & Merrill for the County Hall Development Group, was chosen by the LRB in June 1988.[17] The underbidders' names were not officially released, but a few of the other schemes were discussed in the architectural press. One was by the Building Design Partnership (BDP) in association with the Heery Group, another by Aukett Limited for the Thamesside Development Corporation.[18]

The Heery-BDP scheme proposed considerable environmental improvement for the whole South Bank area. This included the creation of a public park between County Hall and the National Theatre to provide a landscaped setting for the major buildings on the South Bank, the relocation of Charing Cross Station across the river at Waterloo East, and the building of a new square in front of Waterloo Station. County Hall itself was to be split vertically into lettable units, though the Principal Floor would be retained intact. The Conference Hall and Education Library were to house a National School of Contemporary Dance. The Island Block and the Addington Street Annexe would be demolished and several local roads re-routed underground. North and South Blocks were to be replaced by new offices.[19]

The Thamesside Development Corporation also proposed to demolish the North and South Blocks, but planned to retain the Island Block, refurbished as high-quality commercial offices. Public open space was to be enhanced by the landscaping of Jubilee Gardens, while County Hall itself was to be given as public a use as possible, as a hotel and arts centre. The arts centre would include a Saatchi Gallery, housing the private collection of over 700 works of modern art, built up by Charles Saatchi and his wife.[20]

The County Hall Development Group found strong Anglo-Japanese backing to fund the costs of development, which the Property Correspondent of *The Times* estimated at £950 million in February 1989. British investors were said to have put up half the capital for the development and the Japanese the other half.[a21]

The Group's architects, Skidmore, Owings & Merrill, had proposed the retention of most of Knott's Main Building and the conversion of its southern end into a 400 bedroom hotel and business centre, incorporating conference and exhibition facilities. The Members' Courtyard would form the main entrance to the hotel, with additional entrances in new stone-faced blocks with which it was intended to replace the 1970's glass infill walls. The northern end, from Block 2 northwards, would be converted to over 300 residential units arranged around a new enlarged courtyard reminiscent of an Oxford college quadrangle, the intervening range (Block 12) being demolished (Plate 48a). To provide a clear garden space it was proposed to dismantle the Education Library and reassemble it below the Conference Hall, and to floor over the whole courtyard at third-floor level with a raised terrace above the Conference Hall.

All other County Hall buildings were to be demolished. A new office building, the Belvedere Centre, including a shopping mall, would be erected on the sites of North and South Blocks, between Belvedere and York Roads. The Addington Street Annexe was to be replaced by the octagonal Addington Centre, a considerably larger and more magnificent building, and the Island Block by a great traffic circus (Plate 48b). The centre of this circus would be graced by a circular island with a central column, similar in scale to Nelson's Column, surmounted by a statue, representing, it was suggested by the *Daily Telegraph*, either Florence Nightingale or the Prime Minister, Margaret Thatcher.[22]

The scale of the proposed development inspired some hostile criticism, Gavin Stamp describing the Belvedere Centre as 'one of the most cynical and greedy over-developments of a sensitive central London site I have seen'.[23] The Royal Fine Art Commission, too, was unhappy with the size of the Belvedere Centre, which the Chairman, Lord St John of Fawsley, called a 'monstrous white elephant of an office building' whose bulk and height would dominate Knott's riverside building and 'cast a giant shadow in front of it'.[24] Marcus Binney, on the other hand, thought the Group's scheme for restoring and re-using Knott's 'Edwardian baroque masterpiece' could 'hardly be bettered', and he welcomed the demolition of the 'hideous' Island Block, 'resembling nothing so much as an overblown three-pin plug'. But the architecture of the Belvedere and Addington Centres disappointed him, the former being likened to a giant slab of shiny gelatine 'partially wrapped in those paper cutouts which open up to provide an endless repetition of a single motif', and the latter to the 'largest pill box ever constructed'.[25]

The successful consortium applied to Lambeth Borough Council for planning permission in February 1989, before the appeal from the original Public Inquiry was concluded. When Lambeth again failed to decide the application within the prescribed statutory period of eight weeks, the County Hall Group and the LRB applied to the Secretary of State, who called a second Public Inquiry, under John Taylor, Q.C., which opened in September 1989.[26] The Inspector reported in March 1990, expressing dissatisfaction with the bulk of the Belvedere Centre, as well as with some lesser matters, such as pedestrian access to the traffic island, and he recommended that the applications should be rejected. But in July 1990, the then Secretary of State, Chris Patten, gave the Group three months to produce acceptable revisions which would meet the Inspector's criticisms.[27]

A revised scheme had been expected in early autumn, at which time the Group should have completed the contract for the purchase of County Hall – scheduled for 1 October 1990. But the Inspector's call for a reduction in the size – and therefore lettable space – of the Belvedere Centre had effectively threatened the profitability of the whole scheme at a time when the property market was severely depressed and finance difficult to raise. In the circumstances the consortium was unable to proceed with the completion of the purchase on time. It tried unsuccessfully to persuade the LRB to agree to defer the completion date, and it attempted to renegotiate the selling price, offering to buy County Hall for around half the sum originally agreed. The LRB, under an obligation to maximise the return from County Hall, refused the new offer, and on 8 October 1990 the County Hall Development Group called in the receivers.[28]

At the time of writing (December 1990) the LRB is looking for a new buyer for County Hall, but it has decided to continue with the planning application for the Skidmore, Owings & Merrill scheme, subject to some modifications.[29] The new Secretary of State, Michael Heseltine, has announced the re-convening of the Public Inquiry under John Taylor in January 1991 to consider how the Inspector's criticisms have been resolved. This Inquiry is still in progress at the time of going to press.

The LRB moved out of County Hall in August 1990, having occupied the building for just over four years, during which time they also acted as landlords to a variety of successor bodies. Another more unusual role was as location agents for various film and television companies, and County Hall has been captured in a number of different guises, providing a recognisable background in everything from feature films to television commercials. The *cognoscenti* will have recognised the building as KGB headquarters, a Parisian night club, a British court-room,

---

[a]The members of the original consortium were New England Properties, London & Metropolitan, Lazard Brothers, and TR Property Trust. They were joined by National Provident Institution, Sir Robert McAlpine & Sons, Gulliver Property Unit Trust, and the pensions funds of the BBC, Vauxhall, Rank Xerox and Rolls-Royce, together with a Japanese group including the Shimizu Corporation.

and even viceregal Delhi.[b] Not all the roles were worthy of County Hall, but these glimpses will serve to amplify public knowledge of a great London interior.[30]

Hôtel deVille into Hotel Proper?

The idea of turning the building into a hotel was not a new one. Indeed, the possibility was raised in 1892 – long before the present complex had even been conceived – in a pamphlet entitled *The Doom of the County Council of London*. Though satirical in tone, the writer reflects a very clear concern among Moderate (Conservative) public opinion about the threat posed by the LCC, pointing out how much the Council had achieved in its first three years of office, 'on what it has attempted and declared its wish to accomplish'. Written from an extreme Moderate position, the fantasy imagines an LCC which, by 1911, had

achieved its various objectives, including that of building a new County Hall – in Trafalgar Square. Amongst other powers, it had been given that of policing London and as a result had built up an army of 30,000 men. With this force in hand the Council had taken over Parliament and the House of Lords, where the ineffectual 'Lord Tulipstalk' – Rosebery – was in their thrall. The Progressives ruled from an Hôtel de Ville built on the site of the National Gallery, gathering about them the powers of a centralized state and taking over all public services. The end result was a triumphant revolution by the Moderates, after which:

the tramways and omnibuses, and the docks were sold to private companies, and the proceeds applied to the reduction of the municipal debt ... while the Hôtel de Ville became the property of a Limited Liability Company, and was transformed into an hotel proper, which was largely patronised by wealthy American visitors.[31]

[b]Among the productions for which County Hall was used as a location are the feature films *Buster*, *Golden Eye* and *Scandal*, and the television productions *Mountbatten – the Last Viceroy*, *A Perfect Spy*, *Poirot* and *The Red Monarch*.

County Hall: Terms of the Competition as set out in
Instructions to Competing Architects and *Replies to Competing Architects*

These documents, which were issued to would-be competitors by the LCC, are reproduced in Alexander Koch's book, *London County Council Hall Final Competition*, a Special Number of *British Competitions in Architecture*, 1908. The following selection from the *Instructions*, and the *Replies* which amplified them, are here reproduced from Koch.

Instructions to Competing Architects

The London County Council, being desirous of erecting a new County Hall and Offices, has determined to invite architects to submit designs for the building which it is proposed to erect on a site bounded by the River Thames, Belvedere Road, Westminster Bridge, and the Council's works department offices and depot as shown on the accompanying block plan. *(See Mr. Riley's suggested plan* ... [included in the *Instructions*, see fig.4 on page 21].)

1. The competition will be divided into two stages, viz.: (*a*) the preliminary; (*b*) the final. The preliminary stage will be open to architects of any nationality.

2. In the preliminary stage the professional assessors will select in private not less than ten, nor more than fifteen designs. The authors ... together with eight architects invited by the Council, will compete in the final stage.

4. The designs of the successful competitors will be returned on the completion of ... the preliminary stage, to enable their authors to compete in the final stage.

5. Each architect submitting a design for the final stage ... will receive an honorarium of two hundred guineas (£210).

6. [Deals with the appointment of Shaw and Riley as assessors for the preliminary stage.]

7. [Deals with the appointment of a third assessor to act only in the final stage] ... This assessor, who will be nominated by the competitors in the final stage ... will be required to give an undertaking that he did not participate in the preliminary stage. ...

8. It is the intention of the Council to assign to the author of the design placed first ... the work of carrying out his design, and the Council has decided that Mr. W. E. Riley, the official architect, shall have discretionary power in all matters relating to internal economy, building construction, and stability. The successful architect shall obtain all the information he requires upon the site, making the necessary estimates, preparing all the necessary sketches, working drawings, detail drawings and specifications, subject to the Council's approval in all matters which, in the opinion of the official architect, should be brought to it for decision ... [He] shall ... exercise in conjunction with the official architect, general and usual superintendence of works. ...

9. For these services the successful architect and the Council's official architect will be remunerated on the basis of the usual five per cent. on the total cost of the completed building ... this commission ... will be divisible between the two architects in the proportion of nine-tenths to the successful architect, and one-tenth to the Council's official architect.

12. A clerk of works or clerks of works will be employed to superintend the work at the expense of the Council. [W. H. Hookham was appointed clerk of works, assisted by A. H. Castle and W. B. Johnson.]

15. Designs will be excluded from the competition –
(*a*) If sent in after the time fixed for receiving the designs, etc.
(*b*) If considered by the assessors as not in strict accordance with the instructions.
(*c*) If they do not provide substantially the accommodation asked for.
(*d*) If the area shown exceeds the limits of the site.
(*e*) If the assessors should determine that the probable cost of the buildings will materially exceed the outlay stated.
(*f*) If any competitor attempts to make known his identity or to influence the decision personally, either through any member of the Council or the assessors.

16. The drawings submitted in the preliminary stage ... will be returned under seal to their respective authors after the award, and, with the exception of the assessors, no one else (pending the final award) will be permitted to see the drawings ... during the time they are in the keeping of the Council.

17. The successful competitors in the preliminary stage ... can amend or redraw their designs for the final stage. ...

18. Three calendar months will be allowed from the date the drawings are dispatched to the successful architects in which to complete their matured schemes, at the end of which time both the eight ... invited architects and those ... [successful] in the preliminary competition must deposit their final designs. ...

19. The accepted design will become the property of the Council, which reserves to itself the right of exhibiting the other designs sent in for the final stage of the competition. ...
NOTE. – The designs, etc., for the preliminary stage ... **must be delivered to the Council on or before noon on Tuesday, 27th August, 1907.**

24. The land edged green on block plan will be reclaimed foreshore. An embankment wall will be constructed by the Council ... Competitors will be required to include in their schemes a design for the superstructure of this embankment wall which is to be of granite. ...

27. A sketch plan of the proposed first floor is attached, which shows a suggested arrangement of the accommodation ... but it is to be regarded as merely a suggestion which competitors may modify in any way they desire.

28. A schedule of provisional requirements is included, giving the several departments to be accommodated, their approximate positions in the general scheme, the names and numbers of the rooms, etc., and their approximate areas. ...

30. In considering the designs, the greatest importance will be attached to simple and convenient planning, and it is essential that all parts of the building should be amply lighted. The construction is to be of fire-resisting material throughout.

33. The choice of materials to be used for the building will be left to the discretion of the competitors.

34. The sum of £850,000 is considered sufficient to provide a substantial structure suitable for the Council's purpose, exclusive of embankment superstructure....

35. The site will be covered with a concrete raft....

36. Each competitor must accompany his design by a short typewritten descriptive report ... giving all information that may be considered necessary ... to fully explain his design.

37. This report is to be accompanied by a typewritten schedule ... giving the areas of the accommodation apportioned to each department on each floor....

38. Open fire-places are to be provided in the principal rooms, in addition to which the whole of the building is to be heated by radiators. A system of mechanical ventilation is also to be provided....

40. The competitors are to tint the areas on each floor allocated to the various departments as shown in the schedule of tints indicated on the sketch plan....

41. Each plan is to have clearly marked thereon the areas of all the rooms, and also a schedule of the areas apportioned to each department in the bottom left hand corner.

42. Each design must be accompanied by a declaration, signed by the competitor, stating that the design is his own work, and that the drawings have been prepared under his own supervision, in his own offices, and by his own staff.... [Declaration to be enclosed in a sealed envelope supplied by the Council.]

SCHEDULE A.
List of drawings.

The whole of the drawings in the preliminary stage of the competition are to be drawn to a scale of 16 feet to 1 inch, with the exception of the site plan showing the block plan of the new building in relation to the immediate surroundings drawn to a scale of 40 feet to an inch.

Preliminary stage of the competition.

Plans of each floor, elevations of the three principal façades [the north front was not required], sections, one longitudinal, one cross through the building, showing internal courts, etc.

No perspective drawings are to be submitted in either stage of the competition.

Additional drawings for the final stage of the competition.

Sections through council chamber and main staircase. Scale 8 feet to 1 inch.

Detail of a portion of one of the façades. Scale 2 feet to 1 inch.

All the plans with the exception of the block plan to be drawn on paper 52 inches by 30 inches, and mounted on strainers with a 2 inch margin.

All the drawings sent in to be in dark brown or black ink, in line only and in geometrical projection, but the plans and sections should have the sectional parts filled in solid.

In elevations, no washes, shading or hatched shadows for the purpose of embellishment will be permitted other than flat washes in the openings.

Strict compliance with these restrictions will be enforced.

SCHEDULE B.

[Outline of agreements between the LCC and the Ecclesiastical Commissioners over lighting angles in Belvedere Road.]

SCHEDULE C.

[A long schedule of the accommodation to be provided. As regards the Members' accommodation this is surprisingly brief and general – almost vague, but very detailed and exacting as regards departmental requirements, giving rise to the impression that the convenience of the officers rather than that of the Members was the prime consideration in planning the building. A total of 389,652 square feet was called for, of which 16,000 was for the 'general use of members'. This did not, of course, include Council Chamber, meeting rooms and offices.]

Replies to Competing Architects.

18th May, 1907.

To form part of the Instructions issued in February, 1907.

29. Is the number of floors fixed by the Superintending Architect? – The number of floors will probably depend on the planning.

50. Is accommodation to be provided on every floor for charwomen, and if so, is such accommodation to include w.c.'s, &c.? – Yes. W.c.'s for charwomen are not required on every floor, but such provision should be made near charwomen's common room.

58. Is it necessary to provide a general dining-room or other dining-room with necessary kitchen, &c., for use of members and staff, and if so, are they to be separate? – Provision should be made to seat a maximum of approximately 500 of staff ... Any space for general use of members (dining or other) should be separate from that for the staff. It is to be provided within the 16,000 square ft. for general use of members.

60. The plans seem to imply that the main entrance for the Councillors is from Belvedere Road. Is any provision to be made for their carriages and motor-cars? – The position of the main entrance is left at this stage to the discretion of the competitors. It would be advisable to make provision for vehicular access to Main Entrance.

63. Should there be a smoking room for gentlemen and a retiring room for ladies besides the necessary cloak rooms? – The area for these rooms is included in the 16,000 square ft. for use of members.

81. May steps and landings to the water level project beyond the face of the Embankment wall? – It is undesirable that there should be any projection beyond line of Embankment wall marked on plan.

84. Will the new terrace formed by the reclamation of the foreshore be for the use of the public, or only for the members and employees of the County Council? – Pedestrian access for the public to the Embankment should be provided. The "Members' terrace" within the plan is intended for representatives only.

95. Is the library for reference purposes only, or will it be used as members' reading-room? – There is to be a reading-room as well as a library, and the areas at this stage are left to the discretion of the competitors....

112. Will the public be admitted to committees? – No, except by invitation of the committee.

The County Hall Competition, 1907–8:
List of Competitors and Published Designs

The County Hall competition produced a total of 107 designs – 99 in the preliminary stage, plus those of the eight architects invited into the second stage. The designs of the fifteen architects or architectural partnerships who won through to this stage and those of the invited architects were all published. But of the other 84 designs only 23 were published, and as no complete list of entries appears to have survived, if, indeed one was ever made, the identity of most of the competitors remains unknown.

The original competition drawings were returned to the competitors, and it is remarkable that so few of them have come to light. A complete set for H. Percy Adams & C. H. Holden's entry, which was not published, are in the RIBA Drawings Collection, as are some for Beresford Pite's. Two of C. Stanley Peach's elevations are in the possession of Stanley Peach & Partners. A full set of plans for Knott's winning design, with the required elevations and sections, are in the GLRO.

All the known competitors are listed below, together with an indication where their designs were published (if at all). The principal source of information about the competition entries is Alexander Koch's *London County Council Hall Final Competition* which came out shortly after the result was announced in February 1908 (*K*). This reproduces all twenty-three designs in the second stage, plus six unsuccessful designs from the first stage. The four principal journals of the architectural and building press – *The Architect & Contract Reporter* (*A*), *The British Architect* (*BA*), *The Builder* (*B*), and *The Building News* (*BN*) – all published a selection of the competition entries between 1907 and 1909. Inevitably there was a lot of overlap, but each journal published one or more designs from the first stage which the others ignored. The published designs often included perspectives, although these were specifically excluded from the competition itself. Nineteen competitors exhibited their designs at the Royal Academy (RA) in 1908 or 1909.

Invited Architects

1. John Belcher: (*K*), (*BN*)
2. William Flockhart: (*K*), (*A*), (*B*), (*BN*), (RA)
3. Ernest George & Yeates: (*K*), (*BN*)
4. H. T. Hare: (*K*), (*A*), (*B*), (*BN*)
5. T. G. Jackson: (*K*), (*A*), (*B*), (*BN*)
6. E. L. Lutyens: (*K*), (*BN*), (RA)
7. E. W. Mountford: (*K*), (*A*), (*BN*)
8. Nicholson & Corlette: (*K*), (*BN*), (RA)

Architects successful in Preliminary Competition

9. R. F. Atkinson: (*K*), (*A*), (*B*), (*BN*), (RA)
10. Hippolyte J. Blanc: (*K*), (*B*), (RA)
11. G. Washington Browne: (*K*), (*B*), (RA)
12. T. Davison: (*K*), (*BA*), (*BN*)
13. M. J. Dawson: (*K*)
14. J. B. Fulton: (*K*), (*B*), (*BN*)
15. O. R. Gardner & S. Woods Hill: (*K*), (*BN*)
16. William Haywood: (*K*), (*B*), (*BN*), (RA)
17. Houston & Horne: (*K*), (*BA*)
18. Jemmet & McCombie: (*K*), (*B*)
19. Ralph Knott: (*K*), (*A*), (*BA*), (*B*), (*BN*), (RA)
20. Marshall Mackenzie & Son: (*K*), (*B*)
21. Russell & Cooper: (*K*), (*A*), (*B*), (*BN*), (RA)
22. Warwick & Hall: (*K*), (*A*), (*B*), (*BN*), (RA)
23. C. Young & E. W. Poley: (*K*), (*BN*)

Architects unsuccessful in the Preliminary Competition

24. H. Percy Adams & C. H. Holden
25. A. Cantoni, of Paris and Milan
26. Cressy & Keighley: (RA)
27. Alfred S. W. Cross: (*BN*), (RA)
28. Crouch, Butler & Savage: (*BN*)
29. J. E. Dixon-Spain & A. C. Allen: (*A*)
30. Gibbs & Flockton: (*BA*)
31. Groll, Wallis, Huntley & Treacher: (*BA*)
32. Edwin T. Hall: (*A*), (*BN*), (RA)
33. Stanley Hamp: (*K*), (*BA*), (*BN*), (RA)
34. W. Ernest Hazell & H. Paul Willoughby: (*A*)
35. R. Allsebrooke Hinds & Jules Deperthes: (*K*)
36. Horsley, Naylor & Pearce: (*BA*)
37. Alex. Koch & J. Herbert Belfrage: (*K*)
38. H. V. Lanchester & E. A. Rickards: (*BA*), (*B*), (RA)
39. Percy Lovell & Hubert Bulman: (*A*)
40. Nicol & Nicol: (*A*)
41. 'Monsieur Normand', of Paris
42. C. Stanley Peach: (RA)*
43. Beresford Pite: (*BN*)
44. Edward Turner Powell
45. Arthur & Walter Reid & East: (*K*), (*A*), (*BA*)
46. C. H. Reilly: (*BN*), (RA)
47. Salmon, Son & Gillespie: (*BA*)
48. Adrian Gilbert Scott: (*B*), (RA)
49. William Stewart: (*BA*)
50. Treadwell & Martin: (*K*), (RA)
51. Harold A. Woodington: (*K*)

*A modified version of Peach's design, dated 1908, by the noted perspectivist, S. D. Adshead, was published in the *Liverpool Architectural Sketch-Book* (1910).

APPENDIX III

Works by Ralph Knott

The following list, compiled mainly from Knott's obituary notices and Charles Marriott's *Modern English Architecture* (1924), includes all Knott's known buildings and designs for buildings.

From 1908 his work other than at County Hall was jointly credited to the partnership of Ralph Knott and E. Stone Collins.

Dated works

County Hall, London, 1908–29.

No.21 Upper Grosvenor Street, Westminster; new house, 1908–9, and stable at the back (now No.27 Culross Street), 1911.

Mallord House, Mallord Street, Chelsea Vale; new house for the artist Cecil A. Hunt, 1911.

No.1 Upper Grosvenor Street, Westminster; refronting and internal reconstruction, 1911–12.

No.18 Upper Brook Street, Westminster; new house, Knott and Collins being responsible for the plans but not the elevation, 1913–16.

No.20 Wood's Mews, Westminster; rebuilt as part of the reconstruction of No.18 Upper Brook Street, 1914–17.

Daily Mail '£200 cottage', 1917.

Administration Buildings for the Northern Ireland Parliament Buildings, Stormont, Belfast (in association with Arnold Thornely), 1923; not built.

Country House at Kingswood, *c.*1923; perspective and plans published, but may not have been built.

Sports Pavilion, Grove Park, London SE; for the City of London School (attended by both Knott and Collins), 1925.

Speaker's House, Northern Ireland Parliament Buildings, Stormont, Belfast, 1927–8.

Works of uncertain date

'Domestic buildings in Sussex'; unidentified, before 1908.

Actors' Orphanage, Langley, Buckinghamshire; observation wards.

Black Horse Ridge, Birdlip, Gloucesterhire; unidentified work.

Branksome Cliff, Bournemouth, Dorset; unidentified work.

Chasely House, Rugeley, Staffordshire; unidentified work at a late-eighteenth-century house.

Office/factory building for W. T. Henley's Telegraph Company Limited, Gravesend, Kent.

Garthynghared, near Dolgellau, Gwynedd; unidentified work probably on the interiors, which have affinities with some rooms at County Hall.

Overdene, Busbridge Lane, Godalming, Surrey; unidentified work. Overdene is one of three virtually identical adjacent houses erected *c.*1905

York House, Twickenham; conversion to municipal offices.

Competition designs

Bristol Central Reference Library, 1902 (with Collins).

Malvern Free Library, 1904 (with Collins).

Lambeth Municipal Buildings, 1905 (with Collins).

London County Council, County Hall, 1907–8.

Bethnal Green Municipal Buildings, 1907 (with Round).

Devonport Municipal Buildings and Guildhall, 1913 (with Collins).

Select List of Major Contractors and Suppliers for County Hall (Main Building), 1909–1933

The following information is based on the Contracts files in the GLRO (class AR/CB/2), and the detailed reports to Council by the Establishment Committee printed in the Council Minutes.

Many of the firms described in this list as 'of London' had only an office or showroom there, the works being elsewhere. This was no hindrance to their employment on Sections A, B and C of the main building, but in the changed economic circumstances of the late 1920s and early 1930s – when Section D was built – the Council wanted off-site work to be carried out within the 'London district' and contractors to give preference to local workmen.

Acme Flooring & Paving Company (1904) Ltd of London
  Portions of the wood block flooring (all Sections).
Albany Forge, Wainwright & Waring
  Ironwork for gates, grilles and balustrades (Section D).
Albion Art Foundry
  Bronze grilles and galleries in Council Chamber.
George Alexander of Chelsea, sculptor
  Wood carving in the Principal-Floor Committee Rooms and on the Lady Members' Staircase, benches and chairs in the Council Chamber; also modelled bronze work in the Council Chamber (Sections A, B and C).
Ames & Hunter (later Ames and Finnis) Ltd of London
  Sub-contractor for supplying and fixing roof-tiles and grates (all Sections).
Art Pavements & Decorations Ltd of London
  Mosaic and terrazzo pavements in the Belvedere Road and Westminster Bridge Road entrance halls.
Atlantis Engineering Company Ltd of London
  Bronze capitals for the columns and pilasters in the Council Chamber.
Automatic Sprinkler Company of London and Manchester
  Sub-contractor for sprinklers (Section D).
George P. Bankart of Bromsgrove
  Sub-contractor for plasterwork; also supplied lead gutters and rainwater heads (Sections A, B and C).
F. J. Barnes of Stone Quarries, Isle of Portland
  Sub-contractor for Portland stonework (Sections A, B and C).
Bath & Portland Stone Firms Ltd of London and Bath
  Sub-contractor for Portland stonework (all Sections).
Bath Cabinet Makers' Company Ltd of London and Bath
  Furniture for the Principal Floor, including furniture for the Main Committee Room.
Gilbert Bayes of St. John's Wood, sculptor
  Modelled the bronze horses' heads and lion-head mooring rings on the embankment wall, and the Knott memorial plaque.
Birmingham Guild Ltd of London and Birmingham
  Sub-contractor for decorative bronze and other metal work in Section D; also bronze curtain-rods and supports in the Council Chamber and the bronze 'Bar of the House'.
Boekbinder & Sons (London) Ltd
  Decorative plasterwork, including plasterwork in the Council Chamber (Sections A, B and C).

F. Braby & Company Ltd of London
  Sub-contractor for copperwork.
British Luxfer Prism Syndicate Ltd of London (Luxfer Ltd)
  Sub-contractor for steel lantern lights (Sections A, B and C). Supplier of gates, grilles and balustrades, and galleries and book-shelves in the Education Library (Section D).
British Vacuum Cleaning & Engineering Company Ltd of Fulham
  Suppliers of vacuum cleaning plant (Section D).
Bromsgrove Guild Ltd
  Decorative bronze and other metal work, including lamp standards, balcony railings on Ceremonial Stairs and window guards over staff entrances (Sections A, B and C).
The Buffalo Forge Company Ltd of London
  Heating and ventilation system for the Council Chamber and the Main Committee Room.
Ernest Cole, sculptor
  Figure sculptures on the exterior of Sections A, B and C.
Cooper, Wettern & Company Ltd of London
  Sub-contractor for granite work (Sections A, B and C).
Crittall Manufacturing Company Ltd of London and Essex, and its subsidiary, the Crittall Freeman Bronze Company Ltd
  Decorative bronze and other metal work including bronze main doors in Belvedere Road, and the Members' Entrance doors (Sections A, B and C).
Richard Crittall & Company Ltd of London
  Sub-contractors for heating, hot water supply and heat for cooking (Sections A, B and C).
Crompton & Company Ltd of London and Chelmsford
  Sub-contractors for electrical work.
Davey, Paxman & Company Ltd of London and Colchester
  Six marine type multi-tubular boilers (Sections A, B and C).
A. D. Dawnay & Sons Ltd of Battersea and Tyneside
  Contractor for the constructional steelwork (Section D).
Dorman, Long & Company Ltd of London and Middlesbrough
  Contractors for portions of the constructional steelwork (Sections A, B and C).
Dorman & Smith Ltd of London
  Sub-contractors for the main and sub-main switchboards (Section D).
Doulton & Company of Lambeth
  Sanitary work (Sections A, B and C).

J. L. Emms of Hammersmith
Sub-contractor for lead work, including cast lead gutters and rainwater heads (Sections A, B and C).

Exchange Telegraph Company Ltd of London
Supply and installation of electric 'annunciators' in the lobbies and surrounding rooms to show business in progress in the Council Chamber.

Express Lift Company Ltd of Southwark
Passenger, goods and service lifts (Sections A, B and C).

Faraday & Son Ltd of London
Four electroliers for the Council Chamber.

Farmer & Brindley Ltd of Westminster
Sub-contractor for the decorative marble work, including marble chimneypieces (Sections A, B and C).

Fennings & Company Ltd of Hammersmith
Sub-contractor for part of the granite work (Sections A, B and C).

John Freeman, Sons, & Company Ltd
Sub-contractor for the granite work for the northern extension of the embankment wall, and for part of the granite work on Sections A, B and C.

W. J. Furse & Company Ltd of London and Nottingham
Sub-contractor for lightning conductors (Section D).

Galsworthy Ltd of London
Gates, grilles, balustrades and other ironwork (Section D).

Gee, Walker & Slater Ltd of London and Derby
Main contractors for Section D.

E. Gibbons & Sons of Stockwell
Sub-contractors for York stonework (Sections A, B and C).

J. Gibbons Ltd
Gates, grilles and balustrades and other ironwork (Section D).

Gillett & Johnson of Croydon
Installation of synchronised clocks.

W. T. Glover & Company Ltd of London and Manchester
Sub-contractor for main and sub-main cables (Section D).

G. N. Haden & Sons Ltd of London
Sub-contractor for heating and hot-water systems.

Alfred F. Hardiman, sculptor
Figure sculptures on the exterior of Section D.

Alexander Hawkins & Sons of London
Electric lighting and power (Section D).

F. & H. F. Higgs Ltd of Loughborough Junction
Principal contractors for the foundations, including the concrete raft and retaining walls.

Hobbs, Hart & Company Ltd of London
Suppliers of all locks (Sections A, B and C).

Holland & Hannen and Cubitts Ltd of London
Principal contractor for the superstructure (Sections A, B and C).

Hollis Brothers Ltd
Portions of the wood-block flooring (Sections A, B and C).

Henry Hope & Sons Ltd of London and Birmingham
Steel window-casements (all Sections).

J. Jeffreys & Company Ltd of Teddington
Heating arrangements throughout the whole building, including the hot water supply and the supply of heat for cooking, and vacuum cleaning system for Section C.

E. C. & J. Keay Ltd of London and Darlaston
Contractors for portions of the constructional steelwork (Sections A, B and C).

Keystone Varnish Company of Hull
Paints and varnishes (Sections A, B and C).

J. A. King & Company Ltd of London
Pavement lights (all Sections).

Korkoid & Ruboleum Tile Company of London
Laying 'Ruboleum' in the 'ambulatory'.

La Brea Asphalte Company of London
Sub-contractor for asphalt work (all Sections).

Laurence, Scott & Electromotors Ltd of London and Norwich
Electric motors (Section D).

W. Lucy & Company Ltd
Sub-contractor for the supply and fixing of steel shelving (Sections A, B and C).

Charles H. Mabey of Vauxhall, sculptor
Architectural stone carving, including the heraldic shields on the river and northern fronts, the capitals for the columns on the river and Belvedere Road fronts and the carved trophies above the main entrances. Some decorative wood carving in the lobbies. Also made architectural models of County Hall.

H. H. Martyn & Company
Gates, grilles, balustrades and other ironwork (Section D).

Morris Singer & Company of London, sculpture founders (see also William Morris and Company (Westminster) Ltd and J. W. Singer & Sons)
Sub-contractor for cast lead gutters and rainwater pipes and heads (Section D).

William Morris & Company (Westminster) Ltd
Bronze cases for the radiators in the Members' Entrance and Council Chamber.

Morrison & Mason Ltd of Glasgow
Contractors for northern extension of embankment wall.

Newton Fire Extinguisher Company Ltd of London
Sub-contractor for the sprinkler installation (Section D).

F. A. Norris & Dutton Ltd of London
Sub-contractor for heating and hot water (Section D).

Pennycook Patent Glazing & Engineering Company of London
Sub-contractor for patent glazing.

Pirelli & Company Ltd of London
Portions of the electrical works (Sections A, B and C).

Price & Reeves Ltd of London
Contractor for the main portion of the embankment wall.

H. Pooley & Son Ltd of Clerkenwell
Weighbridges (Section D).

Shanks & Company Ltd of London and Scotland
Sanitary fittings (Section D).

W. B. Simpson & Sons of Clapham
Sub-contractor for wall and floor tiling (Sections A, B and C).

J. W. Singer & Company of Frome, sculpture founders (see also Morris Singer & Company)
Decorative bronze and other metal work, including gates across the Ceremonial Stairs, and the horses' and lions' heads on the embankment wall (Sections A, B and C).

Stella Conduit Company Ltd
Steel conduits and cast-iron boxes for electrical installations (Sections A, B and C).

Strode & Company Ltd of London
Decorative bronze and other metal work, including wrought-iron gates at the Westminster Bridge Road entrance, bronze balconies for windows in entrance lobby and copperwork for the flagstaff.

United Stone Firms Ltd
Sub-contractor for the Portland stonework (Sections A, B and C).

Vertigan & Company Ltd of London
  Sub-contractor for parts of the wood-block flooring (Sections A, B and C).
Waddell & Wilson
  Sub-contractor for the supply and fixing of steel shelving (Sections A, B and C).
Charles Wall Ltd of London
  Contractor for the substructure – basement and sub-basement – and portions of the constructional steelwork (Sections A, B and C).
Waygood Otis Ltd of Clapham
  Electric passenger lifts in all Sections, also electric book lifts in the Education Library.
J. Westwood & Company Ltd of Millwall
  Contractors for portions of the constructional steelwork (Sections A, B and C).

A. & S. Wheater & Company Ltd of London
  Sub-contractor for non-decorative plasterwork (Sections A, B and C).
Whitaker, Hall & Owen of London
  Consulting engineers for the constructional steel work (all Sections).
J. Whitehead & Sons Ltd of Kennington
  Supplied and fixed Roman marble for the Belvedere Road and Westminster Bridge Road entrance halls (Sections A, B and C). Supplied and fixed Hopton wood stone pavings and fixed polished limestone work in the north entrance hall of Section D.
Alfred H. Wilkinson, sculptor
  Stone carving in entrance halls and Members' Library; wood carving in Section D committee rooms

References

ABBREVIATIONS

A.C.R.   *The Architect & Contract Reporter*

A.J.   *The Architects' Journal*

APR   Drawings in the Greater London Record Office, formerly in the Architect's Plan Room at County Hall

A.R.   *The Architectural Review*

AR/CB   London County Council Architect's Department: Records of Council Buildings (Construction and Maintenance), in the Greater London Record Office

B.N.   *The Building News*

CL/ESTAB   London County Council Records of Staffing, Management, Accommodation, and Organizational Matters, in the Greater London Record Office

D.N.B.   *Dictionary of National Biography*

Estab. Com.   London County Council Establishment Committee

Gibbon and Bell   G. Gibbon and R. W. Bell, *History of the London County Council 1889–1939*, 1939

GLC   Greater London Council

GLC *Mins*   Greater London Council, *Minutes of Proceedings*

GLRO   Greater London Record Office

Koch   Alexander Koch (ed.), *London County Council Hall Final Competition*, Special Number of *British Competitions in Architecture*, 1908

LCC   London County Council

LCC/MIN   London County Council, Council and Committee Minutes and Papers, in the Greater London Record Office

LCC *Mins*   London County Council, *Minutes of Proceedings*

P.O.D.   *Post Office Directories*

PRO   Public Record Office

RIBA   Royal Institute of British Architects

RIBAJ   *Journal of the Royal Institute of British Architects*

CHAPTER I (pp. 1–5)

The London County Council and the Need for a County Hall

1. *The Times*, 22 March 1889, p.4e.
2. Herbert Morrison, *How Greater London is Governed*, 1935, p.40.
3. William A. Robson, *The Government and Misgovernment of London*, 1939, pp.22–4: Kenneth Young and Patricia L. Garside, *Metropolitan London: Politics and Urban Change 1837–1981*, 1982, p.23.
4. This paragraph is based on David Owen, *The Government of Victorian London*, 1982, pp.23–39,47–155 *passim*.
5. Young and Garside, *op.cit.*, pp.28–33: Robson, *op.cit.*, pp.66,71–3.
6. Frederic Boase, *Modern English Biography*, vol. 1, 1892, pp.1050–1: *The Times*, 5 Sept. 1889, p.4f.
7. John Davis, *Reforming London: The London Government Problem 1855–1900*, 1988, pp.64–5,71–3,76–95: Gibbon and Bell, pp.65–9: Owen, *op.cit.*, pp.108–14: Young and Garside, *op.cit.*, pp.30–1: Robson, *op.cit.*, pp.71–9.
8. Young and Garside, *op.cit.*, pp.53–7.
9. Gibbon and Bell, pp.72–4,76: Davis, *op.cit.*, pp.103–4,107.
10. Gibbon and Bell, p.74: Davis, *op.cit.*, pp.176–84,195–8: Young and Garside, *op.cit.*, pp.86–101.
11. *The Times*, 1 Feb. 1889, p.9b.
12. Owen, *op.cit.*, pp.207–8.
13. Young and Garside, *op.cit.*, p.60.
14. *The Times*, 5 Sept. 1889, p.4f.
15. Gibbon and Bell, pp.84–5: Davis, *op.cit.*, pp.118–19.

16. Young and Garside, *op.cit.*, pp.61–3: Gibbon and Bell, pp.92,668.
17. Davis, *op.cit.*, pp.115–20.
18. Ken Young, *Local politics and the rise of party: The London Municipal Society and the Conservative intervention in local elections 1894–1963*, 1975, pp.47–9,57–61.
19. *Ibid.*, pp.41–2,91,96–7.
20. Young and Garside, *op.cit.*, p.343.
21. Gibbon and Bell, pp.367–8.
22. James Gillespie, 'Municipalism, Monopoly and Management...', in Andrew Saint, ed., *Politics and the People of London: The London County Council 1889–1965*, 1989, pp.106,110–11.
23. Gibbon and Bell, pp.182,203.
24. H.J.Laski, W.I.Jennings and W.A.Robson, eds., *A Century of Municipal Progress, 1835–1935*, 1935, p.468.
25. Gibbon and Bell, p.658.
26. Herbert Morrison, *How London is Governed*, 1949, p.77.
27. Robert Vigars, MS 'Recollections of County Hall 1988', in possession of the Survey of London.
28. Robson, *op.cit.*, pp.330–2,388–402.
29. W. Eric Jackson, *Achievement: A Short History of the London County Council*, 1965, pp.71–4,109–17.
30. Cited in K.B.Smellie, *A History of Local Government*, 2nd ed., 1949, pp.193–4.
31. Young and Garside, *op.cit.*, p.296.
32. Young, *op.cit.*, p.197.
33. Young and Garside, *op.cit.*, pp.307–9: Frank Smallwood, *Greater London: The Politics of Metropolitan Reform*, 1965, pp.87–97: Helen Jones, 'Conservatives and the LCC after 1934', in Saint, *op.cit.*, pp.247–8.

34. Donald L. Foley, *Governing The London Region: Reorganisation and Planning in the 1960's*, 1972, pp.27–33: *Report of the Royal Commission on Local Government in Greater London*, 1960, cmnd.1164: *London Government and the London Boroughs*, Report to Ministry of Health and Local Government, 1962.
35. Young and Garside, *op.cit.*, pp.315–17,343.
36. Foley, *op.cit.*, pp.33,35: S.K.Ruck and Gerald Rhodes, *The Government of Greater London*, 1970, pp.154–7.
37. GLC *Mins*, 1977, pp.281–2.
38. Sir Frank Marshall, *The Marshall Inquiry on Greater London*, 1978, pp.105–14.
39. Ken Young, 'Governing Greater London: The Background to GLC Abolition and an Alternative Approach', in *The London Journal*, vol.10, 1984, p.71: *Parliamentary Debates, House of Commons*, vol.126, 4 Feb. 1988, cols.1178–9.

CHAPTER II (pp.6–13)

The Acquisition of the Site

1. *Survey of London*, vol. xx, 1940, pp.66–7.
2. *The Times*, 1 Feb. 1889, p.9b; 6 Sept. 1889 (Letter from W.M.Acworth), p.9f.
3. David Owen, *The Government of Victorian London*, 1982, pp.159–61,170.
4. *Ibid.*, pp.41–2.
5. *The Times*, 22 March 1889, p.4e.
6. *Ibid.*, 25 Jan. 1890, p.8a.
7. *The Fortnightly Review*, Feb. 1892, p.172: LCC *Mins*, 6 Dec. 1904, p.3021 (37).
8. LCC/MIN/12,626, 4 March 1889.
9. *The Times*, 10 July 1889, p.8b: LCC/MIN/12,626, 14,29 March 1889: LCC *Mins*, 9 July 1889, p.544 (9).
10. *The Times*, 23 April 1890, p.10e: LCC *Mins*, 2 Aug. 1889, p.674 (6); 27 Oct. 1908, p.717 (7/1).
11. *The Times*, 19 April 1905, p.12a.
12. LCC/MIN/12,626, 28 June 1889.
13. *Ibid.*, 31 Jan. 1890.
14. LCC *Mins*, 4 July 1893, pp.694–8 (7).
15. *Ibid.*, 4 July 1893, p.698: *The Times*, 5 July 1893, p.13b.
16. *The Times*, 28 June 1893, p.12d; 2 Aug. 1893, p.11g.
17. LCC *Mins*, 14 July 1896, p.807 (7).
18. *Ibid.*, 2 March 1897, p.224 (16).
19. *Who Was Who*, vol. III, 1929–40: *The Times* 18 Jan. 1937, p.14d.
20. *Who Was Who*, vol. III, 1929–40: *The Times*, 2 May 1901, p.7b.
21. LCC/MIN/12,740, 11 May 1900 (3).
22. *The Times*, 28 Nov. 1900, p.8b.
23. *Ibid.*, 21 July 1902, p.3e.
24. *Ibid.*, 15 Oct. 1902, p.10d; 22 Oct. 1902, p.10b.
25. LCC/MIN/12,741, 13 Nov. 1900 (3).
26. *Ibid.*, 11 Dec. 1903 (3).
27. A.R. Bennett, *Proposals for London Improvements*, 1904: AR/CB/2/76, cuttings about Bennett's scheme from *The Morning Leader* (9 Jan. 1905), *The Daily Mail* (6 Jan. 1905), *The Daily News* (7 Jan. 1905), and *The Sphere*.
28. *A.C.R.*, 13 Jan. 1905, p.32.
29. Gibbon and Bell, pp.234–8.
30. LCC/MIN/10,385, 26 Feb. 1893 (1), report by Valuer.
31. LCC *Mins*, 21 March 1893, pp.329–30 (24/2).
32. *The Times*, 15 July 1896, p.10a.
33. Sir Percy Harris, *Forty Years in and out of Parliament*, 1947, p.50.
34. LCC *Mins*, 25 Oct. 1898, p.1215 (32).
35. *The Times*, 15 Oct. 1902, p.10e.
36. *Ibid.*, 22 Oct. 1902, p.10b.
37. LCC *Mins*, 9 Feb. 1904, pp.149–50 (12).
38. Arthur Cawston, *Street Improvements in London*, 1893, pp.68–71.
39. AR/CB/2/76, cutting from *The Pall Mall Gazette*, *c.*1905.
40. AR/CB/2/76, cutting from *The Westminster Gazette*, 29 Nov. 1904.
41. LCC *Mins*, 26 Jan. 1909, p.83 (25/21–2).
42. *Ibid.*, 18 June 1907, p.1240 (16).
43. *The Westminster Gazette*, 19 April 1905, p.26: *The Times*, 19 April 1905, p.12a.
44. LCC *Mins*, 18 April 1905, pp.1479–81 (18): *London Municipal Notes*, vol.1, n.s., 6 May 1905, p.141.
45. GLRO, London County Buildings Bill 1906. Bills, Petitions, Minutes &c, and Evidence.
46. *Ibid.*, GLC L&P Deeds Docket No.38070. Agreement of Purchase – John Whately Simmonds & anor. and the LCC, 14 July 1905.
47. LCC *Mins*, 10 Oct. 1905, p.1156 (27/13); 19 Dec. p.2264 (39/19).
48. *Ibid.*, 9 Oct. 1906, p.714 (8).
49. *Survey of London*, vol. XXIII, 1951, p.62.
50. J. Foster Petrie, 'Maudslay, Sons and Field as General Engineers', in *Trans. of the Newcomen Society*, vol. XV, 1936, pp.39–61.
51. Chas. E. Goad, *Insurance Plan of London*, vol. X, 1886.
52. LCC *Mins*, 20 July 1909, p.243 (27/12).
53. *Ibid.*, 9 Oct. 1906, p.714 (28/8).
54. *The Builder*, 10 June 1882, p.723; 2 Dec. 1882, p.714.
55. LCC/MIN/4585, 5 April 1906 (16): LCC *Mins*, 24 July 1906, p.368 (38/6).
56. *The Builder*, 22 Oct. 1881, p.512.
57. Peter Brotherhood Catalogue *c.*1920, (copy in the Science Museum Library): LCC *Mins*, 24 July 1906, p.368 (38/6).
58. GLRO, London County Buildings Bill 1906, evidence by Henry Holloway to House of Commons Committee, 30 April 1906.
59. GLRO, London County Buildings Bill 1906. Evidence to the House of Commons Committee, 30 April 1906. House of Lords Committee, 26,27 June 1906: Patricia Spencer-Silver, 'George Myers, 1803–75, Stonemason, Builder, Contractor', in *Construction History*, vol.5, 1989, pp.47–57.
60. LCC *Mins*, 10 July 1906, p.187 (39): GLRO, GLC L&P Deeds Docket No.38054. Arbitration award dated 28 March 1908.
61. LCC *Mins*, 11 April 1922, p.460 (16); 18 April 1905, p.1478 (18).

CHAPTER III (pp.14–25)

The County Hall Competition

1. 'Rising Rates and Spendthrift Palaces', in *Truth*, 27 April 1905, pp.1062–3.
2. William Kent, *John Burns, Labour's Lost Leader*, 1950.

3. John Burns, 'London, the Cinderella of the Cities, A Hall for the County Council and a New Embankment', in *The Pall Mall Magazine*, Oct. 1905, pp.403–8.
4. *See* Susan Beattie, *A Revolution in London Housing: LCC Housing Architects & their Work, 1893–1914*, 1980.
5. LCC *Mins*, 31 Jan. 1899, p.91 (7); 21 March 1899, p.369 (7).
6. LCC/MIN/6326, 13 March 1899 (4), Riley's application for LCC post: *Who Was Who*, vol. III, 1929–1940: *The Builder*, 19 Nov. 1937, p.917: *RIBAJ*, vol. XLV, 24 Jan. 1938, p.317.
7. Andrew Saint, *Richard Norman Shaw*, 1976, p.345 *et seq*.
8. *RIBAJ*, *loc.cit.*
9. *The Builder*, 19 Nov. 1937, p.917.
10. Beattie, *op.cit.*, pp.89,97.
11. AR/CB/1/166, file on RIBA Committee on Official Architecture, 1913–15, Riley to Herbert Wills, 25 March 1915.
12. Saint, *op.cit.*, pp.346–350.
13. RIBA Fellowship application, 19 Oct. 1920; RIBA biography files: *The Times*, 19 Jan. 1961, p.17c: *Isle of Wight County Press*, 21 Jan. 1961: *RIBAJ*, March 1961: LCC *Mins*, 21 Jan. 1939, p.6 (12).
14. LCC/MIN/4648, 19 June 1902 (13).
15. *Ibid.*, 20 March 1902 (16).
16. GLRO, London County Buildings Bill, evidence to House of Lords Committee, 26 June 1906, pp.145,175.
17. AR/CB/2/82, 18 March 1908, Riley to Koch, draft.
18. AR/CB/2/124, 14 April 1908, notes of discussion of Adjourned Report of the Estab. Com., comment by Rev.F.Hastings.
19. *B.N.*, 21 April 1905, p.563.
20. LCC/MIN/4659, 18 May 1905 (15), Riley to Cleland.
21. AR/CB/2/80, 1 June 1905 and 15 Feb. 1906, reports by Riley to Estab. Com.
22. Quoted in Saint, *op.cit.*, p.351.
23. Saint, *op.cit.*, p.346.
24. LCC/MIN/4666, 26 April 1906 (26), RIBA to Clerk, 3 April 1906.
25. *Ibid.*, 10 May 1906 (19), report by Riley.
26. LCC/MIN/4585, 3,10,17 May 1906, pp.665,691,717.
27. LCC *Mins*, 24,31 July 1906, pp.368 (38/7), 410 (14).
28. LCC/MIN/4585, 19 July 1906 (30); 26 July 1906 (9): LCC/MIN/4667, 26 July 1906 (9), report by Riley.
29. LCC *Mins*, 24,31 July 1906, pp.368 (7), 410 (14).
30. LCC/MIN/4668, 25 Oct. 1906 (14), report by Riley.
31. LCC/MIN/4586, 18 Oct. 1906 (12), 25 Oct. (19), 15 Nov. (10), 22 Nov. (29–30), 29 Nov. (14–15), 13 Dec. (13): LCC/MIN/4669, 22 Nov. 1906 (28–30), 29 Nov.(14), 13 Dec. 1906 (13).
32. LCC *Mins*, 18 Dec. 1906, p.1602 (26/20); 22 Jan. 1907, p.21 (4).
33. LCC/MIN/4585, 26 July 1906 (9).
34. *The Builder*, 5 Jan. 1907, p.24; 12 Jan. 1907. p.27.
35. LCC/MIN/4586, 13 Dec. 1906 (15).
36. LCC/MIN/4666, 10 May 1906 (19), report by Riley: LCC/MIN/4672, 18 April 1907 (23), Letter from RIBA; 25 April 1907 (10) Shaw to Clerk.
37. LCC/MIN/4672, 18 April 1907 (23), RIBA to Clerk.
38. *Ibid.*, 25 April 1907 (10), Shaw to Clerk.
39. *RIBAJ*, vol. XIV, 15 June 1907, pp.542–51 *passim*.
40. LCC/MIN/4585, 26 July 1906 (9): LCC/MIN/4666, 10 May 1906 (19), report by Riley.
41. *RIBAJ*, vol. XIV, 15 June 1907, *loc.cit.*
42. LCC/MIN/4586, 9 May 1907 (16).
43. *A.R.*, vol. XII, Oct. 1902, p.126.
44. *The Builder*, 11 May 1907, p.575.
45. *A.R.*, vol. XX, July–Dec. 1906, p.24.
46. Many of these were reproduced in Koch.
47. LCC *Mins*, 18 Feb. 1908, p.337 (19/11).
48. AR/CB/1/168.
49. AR/CB/2/80, 1 June 1905, report by Riley.
50. LCC *Mins*, 31 July 1906, p.411 (14); 19 Feb. 1907, p.422 (36/19): LCC/MIN/4586, 31 Jan. 1907 (15), 7 Feb. 1907 (20).
51. AR/CB/2/80, 28 Nov. 1905; 15 Feb. 1906, report by Riley.
52. Koch, p.7.
53. Hussey, *op.cit.*, p.141.
54. Koch, pp.4–5.
55. Gibbon and Bell, pp.100–1.
56. *The Times*, 7 Feb. 1907, p.5c.
57. AR/CB/2/81, 9 April 1907; 9 May 1907: LCC/MIN/4586, 19 June (2), report by Riley.
58. LCC *Mins*, 18 June 1907, p.1243 (16).
59. *Ibid.*, 22 Feb. 1910, p.380 (51/15); 11 Oct. 1910, p.564 (33/19); 6 Dec. 1910, pp.1322–3 (24/11); 13 Dec. 1901, pp.1444–5 (40/21); 24 Jan. 1911, p.81 (34/10–11).
60. AR/CB/2/81, 4 July 1907, draft report by Riley.
61. *Ibid.*, 4 July 1907, report by Clerk.
62. LCC *Mins*, 23 July 1907, pp.340–1 (22/12).
63. *Ibid.*, 8 Oct. 1907, p.652 (51/15): LCC/MIN/4587, 3 Oct. 1907 (14).
64. LCC/MIN/4676, 7 Nov. 1907 (7): LCC/MIN/4587, 30 Jan. 1908 (6), reports by Assessors.
65. LCC *Mins*, 4 Feb. 1908, pp.197–8 (22): *The Times*, 5 Feb. 1908, p.19c.
66. *The Builder*, 29 Nov. 1902, p.506: Malvern Library, Public Library Committee Minutes, 29 April 1904, p.102: *B.N.*, 8 April 1904, p.535: *The Builders' Journal and Architectural Engineer*, 27 April 1904, p.205.
67. *B.N.*, 7 Feb. 1908, p.207. Knott executed a perspective, section and plan of Aston Webb's design for the Victoria and Albert Museum for exhibition at the Royal Academy in 1907. This fine drawing is reproduced in Gavin Stamp, *The Great Perspectivists*, 1982, p.19.
68. PRO, RG11/84, ff.31v.-32r.: *P.O.D.*: *D.N.B.*
69. *The Builder*, 9 Feb. 1901, p.138.
70. AR/CB/2/124, 13 Feb. 1908, Riley to Belcher.

CHAPTER IV (pp.26–48)

The Final Design

1. *B.N.*, 31 Jan. 1908, p.199.
2. *The Builder*, 8 Feb. 1908, p.137.
3. Koch, pp.2–6.
4. *B.N.*, 21 April 1905, b/w pp.562–3 (another version was published in the *The Pall Mall Magazine*, Oct. 1905, p.405): Koch, p.7: AR/CB/2/124, 17 March 1908, Koch to Riley.
5. *A.C.R.*, 7 Feb. 1908, p.90.
6. *See* Koch, pp.100–3, for his own design. In addition to his book, the main sources are: *A.C.R.*, 7 Feb. 1908, pp.90–4,96–7; 14 Feb. 1908, pp.106–8,112–3: *B.N.*, 7 Feb. 1908, pp.201–3,206–7: *The Builder*, 8 Feb. 1908, pp.137–140,152–3; 15 Feb. 1908, pp.169–172,185: *A.R.*, vol. XXIII, March 1908, pp.156–60. Other designs were also published

as follows: *The Builder*, 18 Jan. 1908, b/w pp.70–1, Lanchester & Rickards perspective and plans; 23 Jan. 1909, p.90, C.H.Reilly perspective and plan: *B.N.*, 15 Nov. 1907, pp.676–7, C.H.Reilly plan.

7. Koch, p.95.
8. Christopher Hussey, *The Life of Sir Edwin Lutyens*, 1950, p.141.
9. *B.N.*, 7 Feb. 1908, p.200.
10. *A.R.*, vol. XXIII, March 1908, pp.156–60: Koch, pp.60–3.
11. *The Builder*, 15 Feb. 1908, p.169.
12. *Ibid*, 8,15 Feb. 1908, pp.138,170; *B.N.*, 7 Feb. 1908, p.200.
13. *The Builder*, 18 Jan. 1908, b/w pp.70–1 (Lanchester & Rickards design); 15 Feb. 1908, p.172.
14. *Ibid.*, 12 Sept. 1908, pp.282–3.
15. *The British Architect*, 25 Oct. 1907, pp.189,194–5,198–9; 1 Nov. 1907, pp.226–7.
16. *B.N.*, 15 Nov. 1907, p.673.
17. Drawings by Stanley Peach in possession of Stanley Peach & Partners.
18. *B.N.*, 7 Feb. 1908, p.201.
19. *A.C.R.*, 14 Feb. 1908, p.108.
20. *The Builder*, 12 Sept. 1908, pp.282–3.
21. Adams & Holden's competition drawings are in the RIBA Drawings collection, AHP/AD [9] 1–12.
22. *A.C.R.*, 7 Feb. 1908, p.90.
23. *The Builder*, 8 Feb. 1908, p.137.
24. *A.R.*, vol. XXIII, March 1908, pp.156–60.
25. *B.N.*, 7 Feb. 1908, p.200.
26. Koch, p.8.
27. LCC/MIN/4676, 14 Nov. 1907 (13).
28. *A.C.R.*, 7 Feb. 1908, p.90.
29. AR/CB/2/124, 12 Feb. 1908, E. Stone Collins to W.E.Riley.
30. *British Competitions in Architecture*, vol. II, part 3, no.15.
31. CL/ESTAB/2/243, Collins to Montagu H. Cox, c.1929.
32. AR/CB/2/125, 18 Sept. 1908, notes of meeting between Knott and Riley.
33. Postcard, 8 July 1911, from Julian Leathart to his colleagues in Knott's office. Original in the possession of Mr. J.A.Leathart, who kindly lent it to the Survey of London.
34. Gavin Stamp, 'Indian Summer', in *A.R.*, vol.159, June 1976, p.370.
35. *The Builders' Journal and Architectural Engineer*, 30 July 1913, p.105: Colin Cunningham, *Victorian and Edwardian Town Halls*, 1981, pp.240–1.
36. LCC *Mins*, 3 June 1919, p.621 (8/3).
37. LCC/MIN/4673, 19 June 1907 (2).
38. LCC *Mins*, 4 Feb. 1908, p.198 (22).
39. AR/CB/2/127, 20 April 1909, report, Riley to J.D.Gilbert.
40. *A.R.*, vol. XXIII, March 1908, p.159.
41. Sir Percy Harris, *Forty Years in and out of Parliament*, 1947, p.50.
42. AR/CB/2/124, 14 April 1908, notes of discussion in Council.
43. Told to Anthony McIntyre in 1988 by Sir John Summerson.
44. *The Builder*, 8 Feb. 1908, p.137.
45. *A.C.R.*, 7 Feb. 1908, p.91.
46. AR/CB/2/81, 7 Feb. 1908, notes of meeting.
47. AR/CB/2/124, 14 Feb. 1908, notes of meeting.
48. *Ibid.*, 25 Feb. 1908, notes of meeting.
49. *Ibid.*, 27 Feb. 1908, report by Riley and Knott.
50. *Ibid.*, 26 March 1908, order of Estab. Com.
51. AR/CB/2/83, 2 July 1908, report by Knott and Riley: LCC *Mins*, 7 July 1908, p.97 (33/6).
52. AR/CB/2/83, 14 July 1908, notes on Council debate.
53. *The Times*, 28 Aug. 1908, p.8e.
54. AR/CB/2/125, 18 Sept. 1908, notes by Riley on meeting with Knott.
55. *Ibid.*, 18,30 Sept. 1908, notes of meetings between Riley and Knott.
56. *Ibid.*, 18 Sept. 1908, notes of meeting between Riley and Knott.
57. *Ibid.*, 4 Feb. 1909, meeting between Assessors and Knott.
58. *Ibid.*, 16 Oct. 1908, notes of meeting between Riley and Knott.
59. C. and A. Williams-Ellis, *The Pleasures of Architecture*, 1924, p.122.
60. AR/CB/2/84, 25 Jan. 1909, notes on Knott's Plans.
61. AR/CB/2/125, 2 Feb. 1909, meeting of the Assessors; 1 March 1909, Shaw to Riley.
62. *Ibid.*, 4 Feb. 1909, meeting between Knott and Assessors.
63. *Ibid.*, 15 Feb.–29 March 1909, *passim*.
64. *Ibid.*, 25 March 1909, notes by Riley.
65. AR/CB/2/88, 28 May 1910, note by Ginham.
66. AB/CB/2/125, 15 Feb. 1909, meeting between Ginham and Shaw; 19 Feb. 1909, meeting between Riley and Webb; 1 March 1909, Shaw to Riley.
67. AR/CB/2/88, 20 July 1910, meeting between Riley and Webb.
68. AR/CB/2/125, 1 March 1909, Shaw to Riley.
69. *B.N.*, 12 May 1909, b/w pp.113–4.
70. LCC *Mins*, 6 April 1909, pp.878,880 (20).
71. *Ibid.*, 7 Dec. 1909, p.1283 (13).
72. *The Builder*, 10 Sept. 1910, b/w pp.290–1: *B.N.*, 29 April 1910, p.586; 6 May 1910, p.622.
73. AR/CB/2/88, 11 July 1910, memo; 14 July 1910, report by Knott and Riley: LCC *Mins*, 19 July 1910, p.267 (20).
74. AR/CB/2/88, 20 July 1910, meeting between Riley and Webb; 13 Oct. 1910, report by Assessors: LCC *Mins*, 15–16 Nov. 1910, p.1062 (11).
75. LCC *Mins*, 11–12 April 1911, p.1029 (23).
76. *B.N.*, 15 Nov. 1907, p.647.
77. Told to Hermione Hobhouse by Lord Reilly, C.H.Reilly's son.
78. AR/CB/2/128, c.Oct 1909, meeting between Riley, Knott, and Salmon.
79. RIBA, MS coll. M/189, Knott to Leathart, 23 Nov. 1916.
80. AR/CB/2/125, 13 Nov. 1908, meeting between Riley and Knott.
81. *A.R.*, vol. XXIII, March 1908, p.159.

CHAPTER V (pp.49–56)

The Building of County Hall 1909–1922

1. AR/CB/2/85, 21 July 1909, meeting between Riley and Knott.
2. LCC *Mins*, 27 Oct. 1908, pp.788–9 (44).
3. *The Times*, 16 Jan. 1909, p.8e; 15 Sept. 1909 (*Engineering Supplement*), p.15e: AR/CB/2/86,88, 7 Oct. 1909, 8 June 1910, notes by Riley: Ralph Knott and W.E.Riley, 'The New London County Hall', in *RIBAJ*, 27 Jan. 1923, p.170.
4. Knott and Riley, *loc.cit*.
5. AR/CB/2/86, 16 Sept., 15 Dec. 1909, Knott to Riley.
6. AR/CB/2/241, p.223.
7. GLRO, LCC Index to General Contracts, vol.2, 1908–1922, p.43, Contract no.4089.

8. AR/CB/2/245, Raft Foundations & Retaining Wall – Arbitration F.& H.F.Higgs & LCC 1909–1914: LCC *Mins*, 27 Jan. 1914, p.146 (14).

9. AR/CB/2/245, Raft Foundation & Retaining Wall – Arbitration F.& H.F.Higgs and LCC 1909–1914.

10. Knott and Riley, *op.cit.*, p.173: *Survey of London* vol. XXIII, 1951, p.64: *The Architects' & Builders' Journal*, 25 May 1910, p.515: Information kindly supplied by Christine Jones of the Museum of London.

11. LCC, *Opening Ceremony at the New County Hall, on Monday, 17 July 1922*, Ceremonial Pamphlet, 1922, pp.31,34.

12. AR/CB/2/86–87, Knott/Riley correspondence, Oct. 1909–Jan. 1910.

13. AR/CB/2/86, 7 Oct. 1909, notes by Riley.

14. AR/CB/2/88, 16 June 1910, report by Knott and Riley.

15. AR/CB/2/89, 24 Nov. 1910, report by Riley.

16. AR/CB/2/93, 20 Nov. 1911, note by Riley.

17. AR/CB/2/91, 20 March 1911, Knott to Riley.

18. LCC *Mins*, 25 July 1911, pp.336–7 (16/1).

19. AR/CB/2/93, 5 Dec. 1911, reply to Council question.

20. *Ibid.*, 7 Dec. 1922, notes by Riley.

21. *Ibid.*, 12 March 1912, reply to Council question.

22. AR/CB/2/94, 14 May 1912, notes by Riley.

23. *Ibid.*, 3 June 1912, notes by Riley.

24. AR/CB/2/93, notes by Riley on meeting of 7 Dec. 1911: AR/CB/2/94, 24 May 1912, table of buildings prepared by Riley; 3 June 1912, notes by Riley.

25. AR/CB/2/94, 13 June 1912, notes by Riley; 9 July 1912, notes by Riley.

26. *Ibid.*, 16 July 1912, notes by Riley.

27. AR/CB/2/98, 11 Feb. 1913, notes by Riley.

28. AR/CB/2/107, 6 May 1914, cutting from *The Star*.

29. LCC, *County Hall Laying of Foundation Stone of the New Hall on Saturday, 9 March 1912*, Ceremonial Pamphlet, 1912.

30. LCC *Mins*, 4 March 1913, pp.554–6 (24).

31. AR/CB/2/242, p.123.

32. AR/CB/2/102, 19 Dec. 1914, Capital Estimates 1914–15.

33. *The Times*, 21 Dec. 1911, p.3d.

34. R.W.Postgate, *The Builders' History*, 1923, p.401 *et seq.*

35. LCC/MIN/4730, 21 May 1914 (11), report by Riley.

36. LCC *Mins*, 26 Nov. 1912, p.1300 (36/13).

37. AR/CB/2/93, 7 Dec. 1911, notes by Riley: AR/CB/2/100, 15 Jan. 1914, Progress Report by Knott and Riley.

38. LCC *Mins*, 26 Nov. 1912, p.1300 (36/13); 17–18 Dec. 1912, p.1588 (49).

39. AR/CB/2/100, 10 Feb. 1914, notes by Riley.

40. AR/CB/2/241, p.215: GLRO, LCC Index to General Contracts, vol.2, 1908–1922, p.256: LCC *Mins*, 14 July 1914, p.166 (1).

41. AR/CB/2/166, 14 July 1915, Holloway to Lloyd George.

42. AR/CB/2/104, 3 March 1916, notes by Riley.

43. LCC/MIN/4738, 4 March 1915, Progress Report by Chief Engineer.

44. AR/CB/2/104, 14 Dec. 1915, notes by Riley.

45. LCC/MIN/4739, 18 March 1915, report by Knott and Riley: LCC/MIN/4742, 10 June 1915 (13), Holland & Hannen and Cubitts to the Clerk.

46. LCC/MIN/4748, 7 Feb. 1916, H.Llewelyn-Smith to Clerk.

47. AR/CB/2/104, 2 March 1916, notes by Riley.

48. Knott to Leathart, 23 Nov. 1916, letter in possession of Mr. J.A.Leathart.

49. *D.N.B.*: AR/CB/2/105, 6 Dec. 1916, Knott to Riley.

50. AR/CB/2/105, 8,23 Feb. 1917, notes of meetings between W.T.Saddler and W.Pott, and Pott and Riley.

51. *Ibid.*, 1 March 1917, Riley to Estab. Com.

52. *The Times*, 25 May 1917, p.3a.

53. *Ibid.*, 15 Oct. 1917, p.5c; 2 Nov. 1917, p.8b; 6 Feb. 1918, p.3f.

54. AR/CB/2/106, 15 Nov. 1918, Clerk to Riley.

55. LCC/MIN/4760, 11 Oct. 1917, Riley to Estab. Com.

56. *The Times*, 11 Jan. 1919, p.11f.

57. AR/CB/2/106, 17 May 1919, Riley to the Valuer.

58. LCC *Mins*, 15 April 1919, pp.405–6 (16): AR/CB/2/106, 26 May 1919, Knott and Riley to Estab. Com.

59. AR/CB/2/140, 12 Feb. 1919, notes of meeting between Bird, Pott, Ruthen, and Riley.

60. *See* Ken Young and Patricia L. Garside, *Metropolitan London: Politics and Urban Change 1837–1981*, 1981, pp.128–34, for a discussion of these issues.

61. AR/CB/2/140, 12 Feb. 1919, notes of meeting between Bird, Pott, Ruthen, and Riley.

62. AR/CB/2/106, 5 June 1919, Clerk to Estab. Com.

63. LCC/MIN/6276, 8 July 1918 (18). Riley was due to retire on 12 October 1918.

64. *Ibid.*, 28 July 1919 (47), a memorial to the Committee from staff of the Architect's Department.

65. LCC *Mins*, 14 Oct. 1919, pp.1192–3 (22).

66. AR/CB/2/242, p.436, 17 July 1919 (2).

67. LCC *Mins*, 14 Oct. 1919, pp.1192–3 (22).

68. AR/CB/2/110, 15 March 1921, Progress Report by Knott and Riley.

69. *The Evening News*, 4 Oct 1921.

CHAPTER VI (pp. 57–69)

Architectural Sculpture and Decorative Treatment

1. AR/CB/2/242, p.255, 25 March 1915 (14): AR/CB/2/144, March 1915, schedule of decorative works; 30 March 1915, Knott to Riley.

2. Nicholas Taylor, 'Sir Albert Richardson: A Classic Case of Edwardianism', in Alastair Service, *Edwardian Architecture and its Origins*, 1975, p.450.

3. Colin Cunningham, *Victorian and Edwardian Town Halls*, 1981, p.190.

4. Information on mural painting at the period has been provided by Dr. Clare Willsdon, of the University of Glasgow.

5. AR/CB/2/144, 30 March 1915, Knott to Riley; 13 April 1915, Report by Riley; 16 April 1915, note.

6. APR, AD6/02, Drawing for the Main Committee Room.

7. AR/CB/2/84, 12 Dec. 1908, Riley to Ginham, List: English Heritage, London Division, copy of report by the Clerk and Architect to the Historical Records sub-com., 16 July 1909.

8. AR/CB/2/242, p.198, 2 May 1914 (13): APR, CD2/03.

9. AR/CB/2/108, 20 Aug. 1920, Knott to Riley.

10. APR, CD2/06.

11. AR/CB/2/242, p.460, 20 Nov. 1919 (24).

12. AR/CB/2/118, 23 Jan. 1923, report.

13. George P. & G.E.Bankart, *Modern Plasterwork Design*, and *Modern Plasterwork Construction*, c.1907.

14. Duncan S. James, *A Century of Statues, The History of the Morris Singer Foundry*, 1984.
15. *A.R.*, Aug. 1927, pp.84–5: Crittall Freeman Bronze Ltd, *Catalogue*, 1926.
16. LCC *Mins*, 9 May 1922, p.562 (42).
17. AR/CB/2/86, 16 Sept. 1909, Knott to Riley; 9 Oct. 1909, Riley to Engineer; 15 Dec. 1909, Knott to Riley.
18. Gordon Honeycombe, *Selfridges*, 1984, p.158.
19. AR/CB/2/144, March 1915, schedule of decorative works.
20. Susan Beattie, *The New Sculpture*, 1983, p.51: M.H.Grant, *Dictionary of British Sculptors*, 1975, p.154: Benedict Read, *Victorian Sculpture*, 1982, pp.222,234. Will of James Mabey, modeller, died 20 Oct. 1883, names his brother C.H.Mabey, sculptor as executor. Charles H. Mabey Sen., of 4 Stonehill Mansions, Streatham, died 17 Feb. 1912. Charles H. Mabey Jun. died 1 June 1965, at Worthing.
21. LCC *Mins*, 7 Dec. 1909, p.1283 (13); 13 May 1919, p.509 (30/25); 9 May 1922, p.562 (42/4); 27 Jan. 1931, p.90 (34/26): GLRO, LCC Contract No.6758.
22. LCC/MIN/4753, 9 Nov. 1916, report by Riley.
23. AR/CB/2/145, 14 Nov. 1916, Minutes of Special Sub-committee of Estab. Com.
24. AR/CB/2/146, 28 Aug. 1919, Order for Architect; 9 Oct. 1919, Memo by Chairman: AR/CB/2/179, 27 Feb. 1923, Reply to question by P.H.Reed.
25. AR/CB/2/144, 25 May 1915, Debenham to Riley; 27 Jan. 1916, Knott to Riley. The LCC coat of arms was granted in 1914, College of Arms, ref.177/115.
26. AR/CB/2/146, 13 Oct. 1921, report.
27. *Charles Ricketts: Self Portrait*, compiled by T.Sturge Moore, ed. Cecil Lewis, 1939, p.275n.
28. AR/CB/2/145, 10 April 1917, A.H.Mackmurdo to Clerk. Mackmurdo had been given authority by Cole to take care of his affairs.
29. *Charles Ricketts...*, p.270.
30. Much personal information about Cole has been kindly provided by the artist's niece, Mrs H.Lusby.
31. *Charles Ricketts...*, p.275n.
32. AR/CB/2/146, 3 July 1919, joint report by the Architects.
33. *Ibid.*, 11 April 1921, joint report by the Architects.
34. *Ibid.*, 3 Aug. 1921, Cole to the Clerk: Information on the Induni family was kindly supplied by their descendants, Mrs Margaret White and Mrs Josey Parkhouse.
35. AR/CB/2/146, 17 March 1921, notes by Riley.
36. *Ibid.*, 24 March 1921, postcard from 'Lowie Cole'.
37. *Ibid.*, 14 April 1921, notes by Riley.
38. *Ibid.*, 10 Aug. 1921, Binyon to Knott.
39. *Ibid.*, 26 April 1921, Clausen to Knott.
40. *Ibid.*, 6 Oct. 1921, Report by Knott and Riley.
41. *Ibid.*, 14 Nov. 1921, Dr. Laurie Cole to Clerk.
42. Information kindly supplied by Cole's niece, Mrs. Lusby.
43. CL/ESTAB/2/49, Notice of Question to Council on 11 May 1920.
44. AR/CB/2/146, 13 July 1923, Riley to Clerk.
45. *Country Life*, 19 Oct. 1918, pp.328–30: AR/CB/2/144–146, *passim*.
46. Charles Marriott, *Modern English Architecture*, 1924, p.109.
47. *Survey of London*, vol. XL, p.323, fig.77: AR/CB/2/174, 10 Nov. 1930, report by Collins and Topham Forrest.
48. *Exhibition of Designs for Mural Painting for the the Decoration of Schools and Other Institutions*, Crosby Hall, London, 1912. Dr. Clare Willsdon kindly drew attention to this reference.

49. AR/CB/2/100, 29 Nov. 1913, Garnett to Riley, enclosing part copy letter from Ricardo.
50. AR/CB/2/99, 17 June 1913, Knott to Riley.
51. *Ibid.*, 22 July 1913, report by Knott and Riley.
52. AR/CB/2/144, 10 Feb. 1916, Education Committee, Central School Advisory Sub-committee (response from Knott).
53. AR/CB/2/146, 19 July 1921, notes by Riley of meeting between Hubert Greenwood, Swinton, Knott, and Riley.
54. *Ibid.*, 12 Dec. 1921, 26 Jan. 1922, reports by Knott and Riley: LCC *Mins*, 9 May 1922, p.562 (8/9).
55. AR/CB/2/174, 4 Dec. 1930, Report by Collins. Wilkinson was paid £1,273.
56. *A.R.*, vol. LIII, Feb. 1923, pp.37–9,103.
57. *The Studio*, vol.85, 1923, p.100.
58. *A.R., op.cit.*, pp.37–9.
59. AR/CB/2/146, 5 Dec. 1922, Knott to Riley; 21 June 1923, report by Architects.
60. *Ibid.*, 25 Oct. 1923, Clerk to C.Sims, Keeper of the Royal Academy.
61. *Ibid.*, 17 Nov. 1923, Henry Tonks *et al* to Chairman.
62. *The Times*, 9 Feb. 1924, p.6b.
63. *Ibid.*, 19 Feb. 1924, p.10d; 22 Feb. 1924, p.8b (letter from Arthur Hinch).
64. AR/CB/2/106, 6 Jan. 1920, F.Giannini to Lord Downham.
65. *Ibid.*, 29 Jan. 1920, Estab. Com. order; 19 Feb. 1920, Giannini to Clerk: AR/CB/2/107, 3 March 1920, Knott to Riley: AR/CB/2/110, 19 May 1921, Knott to Riley.
66. This section is based on a full account of the GLC Heritage Collection compiled in 1986 by Derek Holdaway, copies of which are available in the City of London Art Gallery and the Greater London Record Office.
67. *Who Was Who*, vol. III, 1929–40: *The Times*, 18 Jan. 1937, p.14d.
68. GLRO, George Swinton, 'Note on Portraits of the Chairmen of the London County Council', 12 June 1933.
69. LCC *Mins*, 28 Nov. 1922, p.668 (12); 24 April 1923, p.581 (35/51).
70. GLRO, Swinton, 'Note on Portraits ...'
71. *Ibid.*
72. J.Lomax and R.Ormond, *John Singer Sargent and the Edwardian Age*, catalogue of exhibition at the National Portrait Gallery, 1979, Nos. 42 and 62.
73. GLRO, Swinton, 'Note on Portraits ...'
74. 3 & 4 Geo. 6, c.xv, LCC (General Powers) Act 1940, Section 4.

CHAPTER VII (pp.70–91)

London's Hôtel de Ville: The 1922 Building

1. LCC *Mins*, 16 May 1922, p.624 (16); 17 Oct. 1922, p.360 (16/1): *The Times*, 7 July 1922, p.8f; 15 July 1922, p.11a; 17 July 1922, p.10b.
2. LCC *Mins*, 7 June 1921, p.784 (21/2).
3. LCC *Mins*, 8 July 1919, p.812 (31/1): AR/CB/2/116, 11,12 July 1922, notes by Hiorns.
4. *Architectural Association Journal*, vol. XXIII, no.257, July 1908, p.202.
5. LCC *Mins*, 11 April 1922, p. 460 (16): A. and C. Williams-Ellis, *The Pleasures of Architecture*, 1924, p.223.

6. *The Times*, 17 July 1922, p.15b.
7. *A.R.*, vol.52, Sept. 1922, pp.59–73.
8. LCC, *Opening Ceremony at the New County Hall, on Monday, 17 July 1922*, Ceremonial Pamphlet, 1922, p.17.
9. C.H.Reilly, 'The London County Hall', in *Country Life*, 22 July 1922, pp.89–91.
10. *The Architect*, 4 Aug. 1922, p.79.
11. *The Builder*, 14 July 1922, pp.52–5.
12. *The Evening Standard*, 27 Oct. 1924.
13. CL/ESTAB/2/3, 21 July 1931, report by Architects.
14. LCC, *Opening Ceremony ...*, Ceremonial Pamphlet, 1922, p.17: R.Knott and W.E.Riley, 'The New London County Hall', in *RIBAJ*, vol. XXX, 27 Jan. 1923, p.180.
15. AR/CB/2/88, Sept. 1910, letter from F.C.Clarke.
16. *The Times*, 17 July 1922, p.15g.
17. AR/CB/2/109, 22,25 Feb. 1921, letters between Riley and Knott.
18. Reginald Blunt, 'The London Society at the County Hall', in *The Journal of the London Society*, no.58, Dec. 1922, p.5.
19. LCC *Mins*, 9 May 1922, p.562 (42).
20. *Ibid.*, 9 May 1922, p.562 (42/8).
21. APR, AD4/02.
22. *Ibid.*, AD46/12: LCC *Mins*, 24 Jan. 1922, p.62 (41).
23. AR/CB/2/112, 4 Oct. 1921, Knott or Collins to Riley.
24. Charles Marriott, *Modern English Architecture*, 1924, pp.108–9.
25. Knott and Riley, *op.cit.*, p.179.
26. AR/CB/2/112, 13 Sept. 1921, Riley to Clerk: LCC *Mins*, 24 Jan. 1922, p.63 (43).
27. *The Builder*, 14 July 1922, p.54.
28. AR/CB/2/180, 23 Oct. 1913, report by Riley and Knott.
29. LCC *Mins*, 9 May 1922, p.562 (42/5).
30. *Ibid.*, 9 May 1922, p.562 (42/6).
31. *The Architects' & Builders' Journal*, 12 Feb. 1913, p.167: AR/CB/2/100, 23 Oct. 1913, note by Riley.
32. LCC *Mins*, 11 Nov. 1921 , p.413 (40).
33. *The Times*, 17 July 1922, p.16a.
34. *The Daily Express*, 30 Oct. 1922, p.7: AR/CB/2/90, 1 Dec. 1910, Riley to Knott; 3 Dec. 1910, Knott to Riley; 20 March 1911, Riley to Knott.
35. AR/CB/2/116, Mrs Kate C. Smith to Chairman: *The Times*, 25 July 1922, p.15e; 26 July 1922, p.15e; 27 July 1922, p.15e; 28 July 1922, p.8c.
36. AR/CB/2/180 *passim*.
37. AR/CB/2/90, 1 Dec. 1910, Riley to Knott.
38. Williams-Ellis, *op.cit.*, p.224.
39. Gibbon and Bell, p.119.
40. GLRO, LCC Contract No.6758.
41. APR, AD5/02, AD3/03: AR/CB/2/106, 1 Dec. 1919, Knott to Riley; 11 March 1920, report by Knott and Riley.
42. LCC *Mins*, 28 Nov. 1922, p.668 (12).
43. *The Builder*, 14 July 1922, p.54.
44. LCC *Mins*, 9 May 1922, p.562 (11): APR, AD4/02.
45. AR/CB/2/146, 22 Jan. 1922, report by Architect.
46. AR/CB/2/99 (2), 22 July 1913, report to Estab. Com.: AR/CB/2/100 (5), 23 Oct. 1913, report to Estab. Com.: AR/CB/2/242, p.144.
47. LCC *Mins*, 4 July 1922, p.95 (79/8).
48. *Ibid.*, 24 Oct. 1967, p.601; 9 July 1968, p.380 (2); 27 July 1973, p.391 (16/3).
49. APR, M/AD1–AD7.
50. *Ibid.*, AD20/37.

51. *Ibid.*, M/AD7/06, M/AD7/08, M/AD7/09: *A.R.*, vol.62, 1927, p.85.
52. APR, M/AD20/12, M/AD37A/03.
53. Blunt, *op.cit.*, p.6.
54. APR, M/CD/01.
55. CL/ESTAB/2/19, 30 Oct. 1945, report on Library.
56. GLRO, Library File 449, R.A.Bell to Historical Records and Buildings Committee, and *passim*.
57. Rupert Gunnis, *Dictionary of British Sculptors 1660–1851*, rev. ed. [n.d.], p.111: *Survey of London*, vol. III, 1912, p.99.
58. APR, M/AD6/01–4, AD/07.
59. LCC *Mins*, 4 July 1922, p.93 (58).
60. APR, AD6/05, CD2/06.
61. Blunt, *op. cit.*, p.5.
62. Eric W. Jackson, *Achievement: A Short History of the London County Council*, 1965, p.8: Gibbon and Bell, pp.79–80: Gloria Clifton, 'Members and Officers of the LCC, 1889–1965', in Andrew Saint, ed., *Politics and the People of London: The London County Council 1889–1965*, 1989, p.8.
63. *A.R.*, vol.62, Aug. 1927, pp.84–5.
64. LCC *Mins*, 25 Jan. 1921, p.77 (68): APR, BD3/04.
65. APR, BD3/04–5.
66. *Ibid.*, CD2/02–03: AR/CB/2/242. p.198.
67. APR, CD2/06.
68. LCC *Mins*, 7 Feb. 1933, p.215 (36/16).
69. *Ibid.*, 26 May 1908, p.1214 (7): AR/CB/2/118, 23 Jan. 1923, report.
70. APR, CD2/04.
71. AR/CB/2/115, 23 July 1922, note by Hiorns.
72. AR/CB/2/146, 14 April 1921, notes by Riley: AR/CB/2/110, 21 April 1921, notes by Riley. Old furniture purchased by the LCC included a Hepplewhite bookcase.
73. AR/CB/2/146, 27 Oct. 1921, report of Furnishing Sub-Committee.
74. *The Builder*, 14 July 1922, p.54.
75. AR/CB/2/102, 11 Dec. 1914, meeting between Riley and Knott.
76. *The Builder*, 14 July 1922, p.54.
77. LCC, *Opening Ceremony at the New County Hall, on Monday, 17 July 1922*, Ceremonial Pamphlet, 1922, p.17: LCC *Mins*, 9 May 1922, p.563 (39/49); 4 July 1922, p.93 (35/54).
78. LCC *Mins*, 26 Jan. 1915, p.90 (36/22); 22 Jan. 1924 p.79 (33/61).
79. *Ibid.*, 8 Nov. 1955, p.592 (27/3).
80. *The story of the Staff Chapel at London's County Hall*, produced by the Chapel Trustees, [1966], pp.4,8.
81. *The Illustrated London News*, July 1922: Knott and Riley, *op.cit.*, pp.165–88.
82. LCC, *Opening Ceremony ...*, Ceremonial Pamphlet, 1922, p.26.
83. *Ibid.*, pp.26,30.

CHAPTER VIII (pp.92–102)

The Northern Front

1. LCC *Mins*, 24 July 1928, p.227 (16): AR/CB/2/165, 5 Nov. 1914, note by Riley.
2. AR/CB/2/112, 27 Oct. 1921 (35), Estab. Com. meeting.

3. AR/CB/2/163, 2 Nov. 1922, notes by Riley: LCC *Mins*, 3 July 1923, p.984.
4. LCC *Mins*, 24 July 1928, p.227 (16).
5. GLRO, LCC Contracts, vol.1, pp.221,234: LCC *Mins*, 20 May 1930, p.928 (5).
6. LCC *Mins*, 11 Feb. 1930, pp.272–3 (32); 15 April 1930, p.740 (31).
7. *Ibid.*, 13 July 1920, p.125 (30); 2 Nov. 1920, p.703 (37); 14 Dec. 1920, p.1008 (20): AR/CB/2/166, 11 Nov. 1920, notes by Riley.
8. AR/CB/2/166, 30 Sept. 1922, report by Riley.
9. AR/CB/2/167, 26 June 1924, order of Estab. Com.
10. *Ibid.*, 6 Aug. 1924, notes by Riley: LCC *Mins*, 15 April 1930, p.740 (31).
11. AR/CB/2/168, 5 May 1927, Section D sub-committee report: AR/CB/2/169, 12 July 1928, Estab. Com. report: LCC *Mins*, 24 July 1928, pp.226–7 (16).
12. AR/CB/2/169, 12 July 1928, Estab. Com. report.
13. LCC *Mins*, 24 July 1928, p. 227 (16): AR/CB/2/169, 22 Aug. 1928, Knott to Riley.
14. LCC *Mins*, 30 Oct. 1928, p.447 (11): AR/CB/2/169, 25 Sept. 1928, notes of meeting between Knott, Riley, Clerk, and others.
15. AR/CB/2/169, 26 Nov. 1928, Knott to Riley.
16. *Ibid.*, 6,17 Dec. 1928, letters between Riley and Knott.
17. *Ibid.*, 17 Jan. 1929, Riley to Knott.
18. *Ibid.*, 22 Jan. 1929, Knott to Riley.
19. LCC *Mins*, 29 Jan. 1929, p.89 (8).
20. *Ibid.*, 21 July 1931 p.194 (34/16); 21 June 1932, p.90 (23/1): AR/CB/2/174, 15 June 1932.
21. CL/ESTAB/2/4, 21 Feb. 1929, report by Clerk.
22. CL/ESTAB/2/10, 11 July 1929, report by Education Officer to the Education (Books and Apparatus) Sub-Committee.
23. *Ibid.*: *The Teachers World*, 9 March 1922.
24. AR/CB/2/169, 23 July 1929, notes by Hiorns: CL/ESTAB/2/10, 29 Oct. 1929.
25. AR/CB/2/169, 5 Nov. 1928, notes by Hiorns on meeting between Riley, Knott and Hall (Knott's engineer).
26. LCC *Mins*, 15 April 1930, p.740 (31): AR/CB/2/233,244: GLRO, Architect's Department contract A2573; *Completion of County Hall*, LCC Pamphlet, 1933.
27. LCC *Mins*, 31 Jan. 1933, p.99 (28/7).
28. *A.J.*, 1 Feb. 1933, p.175: *The Times*, 2 March 1933, p.9a.
29. LCC Pamphlet, *Completion of County Hall*, 1933.
30. AR/CB/2/244, Section D contracts, Nov. 1930: LCC *Mins*, 27 Jan. 1931, p.90 (34/26).
31. AR/CB/2/174, 10 Nov. 1930, 18 June 1931, Estab. Com. reports: CL/ESTAB/2/49, W.L.Hare to Clerk, 28 March 1933, and reply, 7 April 1933.
32. Copy of report by Chief Officer of Public Assistance to Estab. Com., in possession of Survey of London.
33. AR/CB/2/174, 19 Dec. 1933, Francis Spear (Central School of Arts and Crafts) to the Chief Officer of Public Assistance.
34. LCC *Mins*, 7 Feb. 1933, p.215 (36/17).
35. APR, DD25/03, DD25/06.
36. CL/ESTAB/2/3, 13 Oct. 1932, Collins to Estab. Com.: LCC *Mins*, 7 Feb. 1933, p.215 (36/16).
37. APR, DD2/25, DD3/16,21.
38. AR/CB/2/244, Section D contracts, Dec. 1930: *A.J.*, 1 Feb. 1933, p.176.
39. LCC *Mins*, 21 Jan. 1930, p.56 (32/21).
40. APR, DD4/04: LCC *Mins*, 21 May 1963, p.383 (33/7); 19 Nov. 1963, p.746 (25/5).

The New County Offices – North and South Blocks

1. AR/CB/2/181, 3 April 1930, Est. Com. Order.
2. *Ibid.*, 5 Oct. 1934, draft report by Clerk, Architect, and Valuer.
3. *Ibid.*, joint report by Clerk, Architect, Engineer, and others.
4. *London Replanned, The Royal Academy Interim Report*, 1942, p.6.
5. LCC *Mins*, 16 Feb. 1932, pp.211–17 (9): for an account of the battle over demolition *see* Hermione Hobhouse, *Lost London*, 1971, pp.228–30.
6. J.H.Forshaw and Patrick Abercrombie, *County of London Plan*, 1943, pp.131–4.
7. CL/ESTAB/62, 12 July 1932, memo from Improvements Comm. to Estab. Com.: LCC *Mins*, 8–9 Feb. 1927, pp.195–6 (26); 15 Feb. 1927, p.227 (8).
8. AR/CB/2/181, 8 Jan. 1931, note of interview between Clerk, Architect, Valuer, and others.
9. AR/CB/2/182, 3 June 1935, Chorlton to Morrison.
10. AR/CB/2/181, 8 Jan. 1931, notes of meeting between Clerk, Architect, Valuer, and others.
11. *Ibid.*, 1934, joint report by Clerk, Architect, and Valuer.
12. *Ibid.*, 5 Oct. 1934, draft report by Clerk, Architect, and Valuer.
13. *Ibid.*, Oct. 1934, draft report by Clerk.
14. *Ibid.*
15. LCC *Mins*, 30 July 1935, p.185 (20).
16. *Ibid.*, 18 Dec. 1934, p.845 (53/6).
17. RIBA Library, Scott Papers, (ScGG/254/1), Scott to the Clerk, 28 Nov. 1934.
18. *Ibid.*, Scott to the Clerk, 11 Dec. 1934.
19. *RIBAJ*, April 1944, p.158.
20. AR/CB/2/181, draft Proof of Evidence of F.R.Hiorns in the House of Commons.
21. *A.J.*, 22 May 1958, p.769.
22. AR/CB/2/182, 30 May 1936, joint report by Clerk, Engineer, Architect, and Valuer.
23. CL/ESTAB/2/66, 20 June 1935, Estab. Com. order.
24. RIBA Drawings Collection, ScGG, WhE and HiF [1], 4.
25. CL/ESTAB/2/66, 24 May 1935, Scott to Clerk: RIBA Drawings Collection, ScGG, WhE and HiF [1], 1–2.
26. AR/CB/2/213.
27. 25 & 26 Geo. 5, c.iii, London County Council (General Powers) Act 1935: Royal Assent 6 June, 1935.
28. AR/CB/2/181, 25 Oct. 1934, Estab. Com. memo.
29. LCC *Mins*, 30 July 1935, pp.185–8 (20).
30. AR/CB/2/182, 20 June 1935, Estab. Com. Order.
31. LCC *Mins*, 30 July 1935, pp.185–8 (20).
32. AR/CB/2/181, 22 Feb. 1935, memo by Hiorns.
33. AR/CB/2/182, 19 March 1936, report by Architect: RIBA Drawings Collection, ScGG, WhE, and HiF [1] *passim*.
34. AR/CB/2/183, 19 March 1936, report by Architect.
35. *Ibid.*, 18 Sept. 1936, notes by Hiorns.
36. LCC *Mins*. 21 July 1936, pp.102–3 (18).
37. *Architectural Design and Construction*, Oct. 1939, p.370: LCC *Mins*, 31 Jan. 1939, p.6 (12/1): AR/CB/2/181, 9 Feb. 1935, interview between Firth, Fuller, Hiorns, and Moodie.
38. LCC *Mins*, 18 Feb., 1936, p.119 (17); 8 Dec. 1936, p. 520 (21); 6 July 1937, p.27 (23): *Architectural Design and Construction*, Oct. 1939, p.370.

39. AR/CB/2/184, 8 Feb. 1939, Wheeler to Higgs and Hill, and undated draft by Clerk: LCC *Mins*, 31 Jan. 1939, p.7 (12/3). Accounts of the new offices appeared in *Architectural Design and Construction*, Oct. 1939, pp.367–71: *The Builder*, 20 Oct. 1939, pp.586–8: *A.J.*, 2 May 1940, pp.457–62.
40. AR/CB/2/184, answer to question in Council on 6 Feb. 1940.
41. AR/CB/2/183, draft description of 13 Sept. 1938.
42. Nikolaus Pevsner, *The Buildings of England, London, except the Cities of London and Westminster*, 1952, p.274.
43. AR/CB/2/183, draft description of 13 Sept. 1938.
44. *A.J.*, 2 May 1940, pp.461–2.
45. CL/ESTAB/2/27, 13 May 1949, Clerk to Architect.
46. Ian Nairn, *Nairn's London*, 1966, p.117.

CHAPTER X (pp. 110–119)

The Second World War and Post-War Development

1. W.Eric Jackson, *Achievement: A Short History of the London County Council*, 1965, Chap. 4.
2. *The Times*, 20 Sept. 1940, p.2a.
3. LCC *Mins*, 4 Nov. 1947, p.659 (22).
4. CL/ESTAB/2/73, 17 Jan. 1950, joint report by Clerk, Chief Engineer, Architect, Solicitor, and others, para.18.
5. GLC *Mins*, 30 Jan. 1968, p.37 (24).
6. Charles Stuart, ed., *The Reith Diaries*, 1975, p.274.
7. *The Times*, 10 July 1943, p.5f.
8. CL/ESTAB/2/26, June 1948, South Bank Development, Scheme by ... Charles Holden.
9. *Ibid.*, 30 Nov. 1948, joint report by Chief Engineer and other Chief Officers.
10. CL/ESTAB/2/73, 17 Jan. 1950, joint report by Clerk, Chief Engineer, Architect, Solicitor, and others, para.18.
11. *Ibid.*, April 1952, D.J.Moxley to Edwin Williams (draft).
12. *Ibid.*, 24 March 1950, Ministry of Health to Sir Howard Roberts.
13. *Ibid.*, joint report by Clerk and Chief Officers *ut supra*.
14. LCC *Mins*, 1 Aug. 1950, pp.497–9 (26).
15. *Building*, 11 June 1974. p.70.
16. LCC *Mins*, 31 Oct. 1961, p.668 (8): AR/CB/2/214, 13 March 1958, note of meeting on South Block Extensions and War Damage Reinstatement.
17. CL/ESTAB/2/73, n.d., draft report by Architect.
18. *Ibid.*, c.April 1952, draft report by Architect.
19. LCC *Mins*, 13 July 1954, pp.449–50 (30).
20. *Ibid.*, 22 Nov. 1955, pp.660–1 (23).
21. *The Times*, 11 May 1955, p.6c.
22. John Elsom and Nicholas Tomalin, *The History of the National Theatre*, 1978, p.94.
23. *A.J.*, 17 April 1958, pp. 565–9.
24. LCC *Mins*, 17 Dec. 1957, p.758 (12).
25. AR/CB/2/214, 23 May 1957, report by Clerk, Chief Engineer, Architect, and Valuer.
26. *Ibid.*, 13 March 1958, note of meeting on South Block Extensions and War Damage Reinstatement.
27. *Ibid.*, 2 Dec. 1958, memo, Clerk to Architect.
28. *Ibid.*, 17 Feb. 1959, report by Clerk and other Chief Officers.
29. AR/CB/2/215, 9 July 1960, report by Chief Engineer; 12 April 1961, joint report by Clerk and Architect.
30. CL/ESTAB/2/27, 13 May 1949, memo by Clerk: AR/CB/2/215, 12 April 1961, joint report by Clerk and Architect.
31. LCC *Mins*, 8 March 1960, p.168 (33); 19 July 1960, p.533 (34).
32. Ian Nairn, *Modern Buildings in London*, 1964, p.19.
33. Bernard Donoughue and G.W.Jones, *Herbert Morrison: Portrait of a Politician*, 1973, p.561.
34. LCC *Mins*, 14 July 1964, pp.749–50 (39).
35. *The Times*, 4 July 1966, p.13c.
36. LCC *Mins*, 19 Dec. 1967, pp.768–9 (11/2).
37. *The Times*, 26 April 1968, p.10g.
38. English Heritage, London Division, LCC HB File 232: *The Times*, 17 Nov. 1948, p.2d: LCC *Mins*, 16 Nov. 1948, pp.701–2 (15); 8 March 1966, pp.141–2 (9).
39. LCC *Mins*, 27 Feb. 1968, pp.133–4 (22).
40. *The Times*, 20 Feb. 1970, p.3c: LCC *Mins*, 25 March 1969, pp.239–40 (30).
41. *A.J.*, 2 Oct. 1974, pp.795–814.
42. *Built Environment*, Aug. 1972, p.297.
43. *Ibid.*, Nov. 1974, pp.546–7.
44. LCC *Mins*, 25–6 March 1969, p.239 (30).
45. *Ibid.*, 7 July 1970, p.445 (20); 4 May 1971, pp.227–8 (31).
46. *The Times*, 14 Nov. 1973, p.21e.
47. Sir Harry Haward, *The London County Council From Within*, 1932, p.50.
48. Herbert Morrison, *How Greater London is Governed*, 1935, pp.38,43.
49. Unless otherwise attributed, the material in this section is from memoirs kindly supplied to the Survey of London by C.D.Andrews, Tony Banks, William Bell, Peter Bezodis, Louis W. Bondy, Kenneth Campbell, Sir Hugh Casson, Charles Corcoran, Lady Denington, O. Wright Holmes, L.W.Hudson, Walter Ison, David G. Moore, Lord Plummer, the late Lord Ponsonby of Shulbrede, Betty Puddifoot, Francis Sheppard, John Smith, Countess Spencer, Sir James Swaffield, Robert Vigars.
50. Margaret Cole, *Servant of the County*, 1956, p.33.
51. *The Times*, 26 Nov. 1966, p.9g.

CHAPTER XI (pp. 120–123)

The Future of County Hall

1. *The Times*, 3 April 1986, p.2; 21 Oct. 1987, p.2: *The Guardian*, 14 Dec. 1987, p.5; 8 April 1988, p.5.
2. *Parliamentary Debates, House of Lords*, vol.495, 11 April 1988, col.915.
3. *Ibid.*, vol.482, 11 Dec. 1986, col.1246: *The Guardian*, 9 April 1988, p.18.
4. *Parliamentary Debates, House of Commons*, vol.121, 26 Oct. 1987, col.18.
5. *The Local Government Chronicle*, 10 June 1986, p.26: *The Evening Standard*, 5 Aug. 1986, p.14.
6. *The Financial Times*, 6 May 1988, p.8.
7. *The Evening Standard*, 12 Dec. 1984, p.20.
8. London Borough of Lambeth, Town Planning Committee (17 Nov. 1986), report submitted by DTPED and others (TP 101/86–87).
9. *The Times*, 4 Feb. 1987, p.2.

10. Department of Environment, Circular 8/87, p.6, para.20.

11. English Heritage, London Division, Lambeth file LAM 13 (B), Proof of evidence, Dr Philip Whitbourn, May 1987.

12. London Borough of Lambeth, Town Planning Committee (16 Nov. 1987), report submitted by DTPED and others (TP 53/87–88).

13. *The Times*, 18 Aug. 1989, p.27, Law Report: *The Independent*, 30 Aug. 1989, p.24, Law Report: London Borough of Lambeth reports (TP 101/86–87, TP 53/87–88).

14. Department of the Environment to Linklater & Paines, 20 Oct. 1987, announcing Secretary of State's decision, p.5: Secretary of State for the Environment, decision notice, 20 Oct. 1987.

15. *Voluntary Voice*, June 1989, p.5: *The Independent*, 30 Aug. 1989, p.24, Law Report: *The Times*, 11 May 1990, p.38: *Local Government Review*, 14 July 1990, pp.548–50.

16. *The Financial Times*, 6 April 1988, p.8; 8 May 1988, p.8.

17. London Residuary Body Press Release, June 1988: *The Evening Standard*, 30 June 1988.

18. *Building Design*, 15 July 1988, p.7; 23 Sept. 1988, pp.19–20.

19. *Ibid.*, 23 Sept. 1988, p.19; 14 Oct. 1988, p.13 (letter from Nicholas Terry, Managing Director of Heery International).

20. *Ibid.*, 23 Sept. 1988, p.20: *The Evening Standard*, 12 Aug. 1987, p.18.

21. *The Times*, 1 Feb. 1989, p.20.

22. *County Hall Development Group: The Proposals*, 1988: *The Daily Telegraph*, 10 Feb. 1989, p.8.

23. *The Independent*, 8 Nov. 1989, p.23.

24. *Parliamentary Debates, House of Lords*, vol.504, 2 March 1989, cols.1142–4: *The Daily Telegraph*, 3 March 1989, p.15.

25. *The Sunday Telegraph*, 26 March 1989, p.19.

26. Department of the Environment News Release (347), 20 June 1989.

27. *The Times*, 25 July 1990, p.2.

28. *Ibid.*, 2 Oct. 1990, p.21; 9 Oct. 1990, p.20: *The Evening Standard*, 3 Oct. 1990, p.21; 4 Oct. 1990, p.18: *The Financial Times*, 9 Oct. 1990, p.12; 10 Oct. 1990, p.10: *The Independent*, 9 Oct. 1990, p.8.

29. Information kindly supplied by John Howes of the London Residuary Body.

30. Information kindly supplied by Keith Breathwick and other members of the London Residuary Body Establishments and Accommodation staff.

31. Anonymous, *The Doom of the County Council of London*, 1892.

Index

The symbols in the left-hand margin distinguish those persons who have worked, or are thought to have worked, on the County Hall buildings, and the authors of unexecuted designs:

^a architect or engineer who worked on design of CH buildings, and architects who entered the CH Competition
^b contractor who built or supplied materials for CH buildings
^c craftsmen or artists who worked on CH buildings

Abercrombie, Sir Patrick 110
^bAcme Flooring & Paving Co. Ltd 129
^aAdams, H. Percy, & Holden, C. H. 35, 127, Pl. 4a
Addington Centre, proposed 122, Pl. 48b
Adelphi 9, 10
Adelphi Terrace House 38
Admiralty Arch 8, 25, fig. 2
Adshead, S. D. 127n.
^cAlbany Forge, Wainwright & Waring 129
^cAlbion Art Foundry 129
Aldwych see Kingsway Improvement Scheme
^cAlexander, George 59, 63, 75, 77, 81, 82, 83, 129, Pls 13c, 17b, 26b, 28d
Alma-Tadema, Sir L. 69, 76
^bAmes & Hunter (later Ames & Finnis) Ltd 129
Anderton, F. R. 70, Pl. 11
Architect, Official 19, 20; see also W. E. Riley
Architect & Contract Reporter 9
Architectural Association Journal 70
Architectural criticism of County Hall: Riley's design 16–17; Knott's original design 23, 35, 41, 43; **Main Building** 70–1, 75–7 passim, 118–19; New County Offices 108–9; North Block Extension 113–14; Addington Street Building 116; Island Block 117; re-development scheme 121–2
Architectural perspectives 19–20
Architectural Review 19, 20
Architectural salvage 57, 59, 87, 88, 90
Architectural sculpture see stone carving and statuary
Arnold, Sir Arthur 68
^cArt Pavements & Decorations Ltd 76, 80, 129
Art Workers' Guild 16
Arts and Crafts movement 15
Assessors 17, 18, 19, 23, 51, 57, 125, Pl. 3d; report of 23, 26, 39, 41; alterations to Knott's design 42–7; plan for CH 45, fig. 19a
^aAtkinson, R. Frank 31, 35, 127
^bAtlantis Engineering Co. Ltd 129
^aAukett Ltd 121
^bAutomatic Sprinkler Co. 129
Avery Hill Training College, Eltham, onyx columns from 87

Baker, Herbert 21
^cBankart, George P. 59, 129
Banks, Tony 69, Pl. 47d
Barlow, Francis 83
Barnard's Inn 7

^bBarnes, F. J. 129
Bassae order 73
^aBates, C. H. 113
^cBath Cabinet Makers' Co. Ltd 83, 89, 129, Pl. 24c
^bBath & Portland Stone Firms Ltd 129
Battersea Power Station 106
^cBayes, Gilbert 49, 59, 129
Bayes, Walter John 59, 66
Beachcroft, Melvill 7, 10
Beck & Lee 15
^aBelcher, John 18, 20, 25, 31, 127; & Joass 73n.
Bell, Reginald 4, 80
Bell, Robert Anning 82, fig. 34
Belvedere Centre, proposed 122, Pl. 48b
Belvedere Road 11, 13, fig. 3, Pl. 3a; east side 11, 13; development of 103–9, 110–11, 114, 116, figs 48–51; north end 111; Nos 3–9 (odd) 11; Nos 15, 17 11; No. 23 (Bartram's Wharf) 9, 111; wharves 11–12, fig. 3
Belvedere Road Courtyard see **County Hall, New, Building, County Hall Courtyard**
Benn, Sir John 62, 68
Bennett, Alfred R., scheme for County Hall 9
^aBennett, Sir Hubert 113
Beresford-Hope, C. T. 87
Bethnal Green Municipal Buildings competition (1907) 38, 128
Binney, Marcus 122
Binyon, Laurence 63
Bird, James 55, 89, Pl. 11
Birdlip, Gloucestershire 128
^cBirmingham Guild Ltd 129
Birmingham Town Hall 57
Bishop's Acre 11, fig. 3
Blackwall Tunnel 3, 15
Blake, W. E., Ltd 53
^aBlanc, Hippolyte J. 26, 127
Blashill, Thomas 6, 15
Blomfield, Reginald 18
Blunt, Reginald 75, 81, 83
Boateng, Paul Pl. 47d
^cBoekbinder & Sons (London) Ltd 129
Boston, Massachusetts, public library 57
Boulnois, E. 7
Boundary Street Estate 15
^bBraby, F., & Co. Ltd 129
Braden, Miss 66n.
^cBradford, E. J. & A. T. 108, Pl. 40b, c

Brangwyn, Frank 57
Bristol Reference Library competition (1907) 25, 37, 128
[b]British Luxfer Prism Syndicate Ltd 129
[b]British Vacuum Cleaning & Engineering Co. Ltd 129
Brock, Sir T. 57
[c]Bromsgrove Guild Ltd 53, 59, 75, 76, 129, fig. 26a, b, *sketch*
     p. 48, Pls 7c–e, 16c, 20a
Brooke, Henry 4
Brooks, H. Jamyn 6n., Pl. 2b
Brotherhood, Peter 11, 13, 14, fig. 3
[a]Browne, G. Washington 26, 127, fig. 7b
[b]Buffalo Forge Co. Ltd 129
Building Design Partnership (BDP) 121
Building Research Centre 77
Burn, Rodney 66
Burnet, J. J. 38
Burns, Rt. Hon. John 6, 10; views on design of County Hall
     14; library given to LCC 82–3
Burolandschaft office planning 117

Campbell, Kenneth xvii
[a]Cantoni, A., of Paris and Milan 127
Cardiff City Hall and Law Courts 57
Carlos Place, Mayfair (No. 13) 65
Caröe, W. D. 38
Casson, Sir Hugh xvii
[a]Castle, A. H. 125
Cawston, Arthur, schemes for South Bank 10
[c]Central School of Arts & Crafts 53, 66, 97
Charing Cross Road Bridge 7n., 93, 103, 105, 110
Charing Cross Station 9, 121
Chelsea Town Hall 57
Chicheley Street 105–6, 111–14 *passim*, figs 48–51
Chorlton, Alan 105n.
Christ's Hospital, Newgate Street 7
City of London, Corporation of 1, 2, 6; School 25
Clark, J. Cosmo 66n.
Clausen, Sir George 63
Cleland, J. W. 17, 23
Cobb, Sir Cyril 62
Cockerell, Sydney 17
Cohen, Alfred 9
Colcutt, T. E. 19
[c]Cole, Ernest 57, 62–5, 71, 97, Pl. 30; opinions on his work 63,
     65; statuary, subjects of 63, 65
Cole, Laurie (*née* Manly) 62–3
Collard, 'Old' fig. 15b
Collier, Hon. John 68, Pl. 46d
[a]Collins, Ernest Stone 15, 25, 42, 54, 128, figs 43, 44, 101, Pls
     32–4, 35a; CH competition, involvement in 37–8; succeeds
     Knott 93–5; designs for CH 99–102 *passim*
Collins, William 83
Collins, Sir William 68
Competition for new County Hall: advertised 20; Assessors'
     report on 23, 42–3; competitors 18, 23, 25, 26–35 *passim*,
     127; *Instructions to Competing Architects* 18, 19, 20–2,
     26, 125–6; exhibition of entries 26; Halsey Ricardo's
     opinion of 41, 48; terms of 18, 20–2; RIBA intervention
     17–20; Riley's attitude 17, 18–20; results of 23–25; unsuc-
     cessful entries 26–35, figs 7–12, 17b, Pl. 4
Cons, Emma, memorial to 101, Pl. 46a
Conservative Party 3, 4, 5; organization in London 3
Cooper, Edwin *see* Russell & Cooper

Cooper, Wettern & Co. Ltd 129
Corlette *see* Nicholson, Sir Charles
Cornwall, Sir Edwin 11, 68
Cotton, Sir Evan 65
County Hall, New, controversy over need for 5, 6
     design for: 6, 14; proposal for in-house design 16–17, fig. 4;
     Knott's winning design 25, 35–7, figs 5, 13, 14, 16, 17a,
     18a, 24; Assessors' changes to 39–42; development of 42–
     7, figs 25, 26, Pl. 5; influence of unsuccessful designs 26–
     47 *passim*
     new uses for 120–3; public inquiry 120–2; sale of 121–2;
     schemes for redevelopment 121–2, Pl. 48
COUNTY HALL, New, Building
     Addington Street Annexe 115–16, fig. 51, Pl. 45a
     Ambulatory 76, 80, fig. 32, Pl. 20b, c
     Architect's Plan Room xviii, 118
     architectural stone carving and statuary *see* stone carving and
          statuary
     Assembly Hall *see* **Conference Hall** and Public Hall
     'Bear and the Beehive' chimneypiece 83, Pl. 27d
     Belvedere Road entrance hall 66, 67, 70, 71, 75, **76**, 80, 100,
          116, fig. 28, *sketches* pp. 56, 109, Pls 13b, c, 19, 27c
     Belvedere Road Front 26, 35, 41, 47, 63, 65, 75, **76–7**, fold-
          out drawing BIII, fig. 16, Pl. 13; statuary for 63, 65
     Block 12 87, 122, fig. 25, Pl. 9c
     Bridge passage 92–3, 97, fig. 40, Pl. 42d
     Ceremonial Entrance 75, 76, *sketch* p. 56, Pl. 13c; *see also*
          Belvedere Road entrance hall
     Ceremonial Staircase 56, 66, 76, 116, *sketches* pp. 48, 109,
          Pls 19b, 20a
     Ceremonial suite *see* Main Committee Room
     Chief Officers' Rooms 88, figs 37, 38; *see also* individual
          rooms
     chimneypieces, historic 57, 59, 83, 88, fig. 25, Pl. 27d; in
          Members' Rooms and public areas 57, 67, 80, 81, 82, 83,
          99–101 *passim*, 126, figs 25, 28, 36a, 37, 43, 44, Pls 22–3,
          24b, 25a, b, 27, 29c, d, 34d, 36a; in officers' rooms 88–9,
          90, figs 37, 38, Pl. 37c
     clocks 130, sketch 56; moved from Old CH 87
     committee rooms, requirements for 22, 126; siting of 53;
          decoration of 57, 59; use of old chimneypieces in 57, 59,
          87, fig. 25; visited by George V 70; *see also* **Principal
          Floor Rooms** Nos 134, 135–9, 140–7, 151–3, 158, 159–
          163, 164, 167–8, 169, 170–1, 172–3, 175–7, 180–4
     Conference Hall 97–8, 101, 119, 121–2, figs 40, 42, 45, Pls
          28d, 33b, 38d
     conference rooms *see* **Principal Floor Rooms** Nos 170, 171
     corridors 90, 118, Pls 26a, c, d, 36b, c; double-banking of
          93, 103, 107, Pl. 36b, c; principal floor corridors 66, 76,
          80–1, 118, Pl. 26a, c, d
     Council Chamber 22, 54–5, 59, 71, **77–80**, 110, 119, figs
          14, 31, 32, fold-out drawing BII, *frontispiece*, Pls 21, 28a;
          acoustics 77; alternative schemes 41–2, 44–5, figs 18, 19;
          seating 89, fig. 39; ventilation of 77, 81, 90, fig. 39
     County Hall Courtyard 106, 109, 111, 113, 114, 117, Pls 39d,
          40e
     courtyards, infilling of 75, 92, 98–9, 117–19, Pls 42c, d, 43a
     Crescent, riverside 52, 61–2, 71, **73**, 110, fold-out drawing
          BI, Pls 5c, 10, 12a, b, 42a; changes to plan of 45–7, figs
          18, 19; frieze 61–2; Holden's opinion of 111; *see also*
          Members' Terrace, **Principal Floor Rooms** Nos 115,
          116, 119–24, 131
     Crush Hall 100–1, fig. 40, Pls 32b, 33a

County Hall, New, Building (Contd.)

decorative treatment 57–67, 75–89, 99–102

'Drum' 93, 97–8, 101–2, figs 40, 42, Pl. 38d

Embankment wall **49**, 54, 59, fig. 3, Pls 8b, 9b, 31a, b, e

fire-doors 98

flèche 35, 73, 111, fig. 29, Pl. 12c

foundation stone 52–3, Pl. 7

galleries, press and public 76–7, 83, 100–1, 119, figs 31, 32, 35, 36, Pls 21, 24a, c, 33c

heating and ventilating 90–1, 119, 126, fig. 39

Island Block 106, 115, **116–17**, fig. 51, Pl. 45b–d

kitchens 90, 110, 116

laboratories 90, Pl. 37a

Lady Members: Entrance 75, 87, Pl. 26b; Rooms *see* **Principal Floor Rooms** Nos 188–9

lavatory towers 75

Library: Education **95**, 97, **101–2**, 121–2, figs 40, 42, 46, 47, Pls 35a, 38d; Education (Block 12) 90, Pl. 35b; Members' 22, 26, 41, 44, 70, **80**, 95, 126, fig. 33, Pls 23a, 29c; *see also* **Principal Floor Room** No. 114; Pedagogical Lending 95

lifts 130, 131, Pls 28b, 32d

lighting, natural 31, 71, 73, 75, 77, 93, 111–12, 117, 119

Main Building (1922 and 1933) 71–91, fold-out drawings A, B, Pls 1, 10b, c; architectural sculpture 57–65, 95–7; character of 118–19; communities within 118; completion of 51, 52, 54, 70, 95; construction 49–54, 95, fig. 22, Pls 1, 6b, c, 8a–c, 9a–c; delay in completion 48, 51–6; drains 119; film location, use as 122–3; finding way 76, 118–19; opening of 70, 95, Pl. 10a; plan of 71–3, 92–3, foldout drawings AI–III; post-war redevelopment 110–1; re-use of 121–2; residential use for 120–2; roof 51, 54, 73, Pls 9a, 38a; site Pls 2c, d, 3a, b; tender procedures 51–3

Main Committee Room 70, **83**, 90; *see also* **Principal Floor Rooms** Nos 128–30

Medical Examination Rooms 103; *see also* Competition for new County Hall: *Instructions to Competing Architects*

Medical Supplies Room 90, Pl. 35c

Members' Carriage Drive 71, 75, 80, fig. 30, Pls 14b, d, 15, 38b

Members' Cloakrooms 80, 83; *see also* **Principal Floor Room** No. 179

Members' Courtyard 45, 57, 59, 61, 75, 80, 117–18, 119, 122, figs 19a, b, 30, Pls 16, 17, 42c

Members' Entrance 38, 45, 47, 61, 62, 70, 71, **75**, **80**, figs 17, 19a, b, *sketch* p. 69, Pls 17, 28c, d

Members' Reading Room 70; *see also* **Principal Floor Room** No. 115

Members' Rooms: Chairman's 81–2, Pls 24d, 43c; Vice-Chairman's 81; Whips' 81

Members' Terrace 21, 44, 70, **81**, 110, 126, Pls 12a, b, 16a, 42a, b, d, 47c; colonnade for 45, 47, figs 18a, 19; granite lions for 57n.

'Minerva' 62, 82

New County Offices (North and South Blocks) 95, **103–9**, 114, 121–2, figs 48, 49, 50, 51, Pls 39, 40, 41; construction 108

North Block Extension 112–14, 121–2, figs 50, 51, Pl. 44

North Entrance Pl. 32a

Northern Front, Exterior 23, 42, 54, 62, 71, **92–102**, 111, 114, figs 40, 41, Pls 18a, 38d

Northern Front, Interior (Section D) 97–9, figs 40, 42, Pls 32, 33, 34, 35, 36d

Octopus Room 90, Pl. 37d

office floors 89–90, fig. 38, fold-out drawing AI, Pls 36b, 37c, 43a, **Room Nos 201** Pl. 37c, **448** Pl. 43d

panelling:
  'enriched leather' 80
  Indian laurel 80
  oak, in corridors 80–1, Pl. 20a, c, d; rooms 81–3, 87–9, 99, 100, figs 35–6, 37, 44; treated with potash 87; linen-fold 90
  silk tapestry 87
  softwood 83–7, 88, fig. 37

Pavilion blocks 27, 45, 47, 73, 75, 83, 87, 93, 97–8, fig. 17a, Pl. 30; sculptural decoration of 63–5, figs 27, 24, Pl. 30a

Picture gallery 92–3, 98; *see also* **Conference Hall**

plasterwork, ceilings 81, 83, 87, 99, 108, 129, figs 35, 36; capital 101, fig. 45; coloured 81

Post-war refurbishment 81, 116, Pl. 43b, c

Principal Floor, Main Building 22, 41, 56, 68, 70, 75–8, 97–101, 112, 114, 118–19, fold-out drawing AIII; future of 121; restricted use of 112, 119; working in 118–19

Principal Floor Rooms: Nos. **103A** 89; **104** 88; **105** 88, fig. 37; **106A**, **107** 89; **108** 88, fig. 37; **109** 88, 89; **112–13** 89; **114** 82–3, fig. 33, Pls 23a, 29c; **115** 81–2, Pls 25c, 27a, 43c; **116A**, **116** 81; **118** 83, Pl. 27d; **119** 81; **120** 81, Pl. 24d; **120–4** 81; **128** 83, fig. 35, Pl. 24b; **129** 57, 71, 83, 87, 98, 100, figs 35, 36b, Pl. 24a–c; **130** 83, figs 35, 36a; **131** 81, 87; **132** 81–2; **133** 81, 87, Pl. 27b; **134** 81, 101; **135** 87; **136** 87, Pl. 25b; **137–9** 87; **140** 101, Pl. 34c; **141** 101; **142** 101, figs 43a, 44, Pl. 34d; **143** 99, 100, Pl. 33c; **144** 101, Pl. 33c; **145** 100, 101, fig. 43b; **146**, **147**, **150**, **151** 100; **152** 100, fig. 43b, Pl. 34a, b; **153** 62, 99, 100, Pls 29b, 34a; **154** 100; **155** 99–100, **158** 99–100, fig. 43c; **159–63** 87; **164** 99–100, fig. 43d; **165** 88, Pl. 25a; **167** 87; **168** 87, Pl. 23b; **169** 83, 87; **170–1** 83; **172–6** 83, 87; **177** 83, 87, Pl. 22b; **179** 83; **180–3** 87; **184** 87, 89; **185** 88; **187** 88; **188** 87, Pl. 27c; **189** 87; **190** 88; **192** fig. 37 (caption); **193–4** 88; **195** 89; **196** fig. 37 (caption); **197** 88; **198–9** 89

Public Hall 22, 25, 26, 31, 35, 37, 41–2, 92–3, fig. 4; *see also* **Conference Hall**

radiator 77, 91, *sketch* p. 69, Pl. 28d

Record Room 75, 90

refreshment rooms 70, 81, 126; *see also* **Principal Floor Rooms** Nos 131, 132, 133

rifle range 90

Riverside Front 42–7, 73, 90, fold-out drawing BI, figs 5, 13, 16, Pls 5, 9b, 10b, c, 12, 42a, b; statuary for 62–5, figs 23, 24, 27, Pl. 30a, b

sculpture, named groups: **external** 'Creation of Eve' 65, Pl. 30a; 'Hero' 65; 'Love' 65; 'Expulsion from Eden' 65; 'Good Samaritan' 65; 'Thames' 65; 'Motherhood' 65; 'World Beyond' 65, Pl. 30c; 'Benevolence and Humanity' 65; 'Open Spaces' 97, Pl. 31d; 'Education' 97, Pl. 31c; 'Healing' 97; **internal** 'Justice' 80; 'Nemesis' 80, Pl. 29d; 'Mercury' 80; 'Truth' 82; *see also* stone carving and statuary

Section D *see* **Main Building**, Northern Front, and individual **Principal Floor Rooms** Nos 140–164

South Block Extension 114–5, 121–2, figs 50, 51

Staff Chapel 76, 90, Pl. 37b

staff entrances 71, 73, 75, 116

staff restaurants 53, 66, 90, 110, 119, 126, Pl. 36e; new 116, 119, Pls 42b, 43b

County Hall, New, Building (Contd.)
    staircases 80, 82, 87, 98–9, Pls 26d, 32a–c, 41d, 44b; *see also* Ceremonial Staircase
    statuary *see* sculpture, named groups; stone carving and statuary
    stone carving and statuary 47, 57, 59–65, 66, 75, 76, 77, 80, 82, 97, 108, figs 23, 24, 27, 28, 41; *sketch* p. 56; *frontispiece*, Pls 12b, 14d, 16a, 17a, 18c, 27c, 29c, d, 30, 31, 40a–d, 41a, b
    sub-basement 51, 90, 118
    Vehicle Licensing Hall 97, 101–2, figs 40, 42, Pl. 36d
    vehicular access 21, 47, 71–2, 97, 126
    Voting Lobbies 68, 77, **80**, fig. 32, Pl. 22a
    Waiting rooms *see* **Principal Floor Rooms** Nos. **118, 174**
    War Memorial 76, fig. 32
    weathervane 73, fig. 29, Pl. 12c
    Westminster Bridge Road entrance halls 66, **80**, Pls 15b, 29d, 36a
    Westminster Bridge Road Front 25, 73, **75**, figs 5, 17, 30, Pls 8b, c, 9b, 14, 29d, 36a; decoration of 62; statuary for 65
    wood carving 59, 66, 77, 80, 81, 83, 87, 90, 99, 100, figs 35, 36, 39, Pls 26b, 29b, 37b
County Hall, Old, Spring Gardens 1, 6, 7, 8, 10, 14, 56, 95, 103, 111, 112, figs 1, 2, Pl. 2a, b; comparison with other town halls 14; first meeting of LCC at 3, 6n, 8; Council Chamber at 77, 80, Pl. 2b; as site for rebuilding 7–8, 10; chimneypieces from 87; clocks from 87
County Hall Development Group 121–2
County of London Plan (1943) 4, 103, 110–11
Cox, Sir Montagu 105
*a*Cressy & Keighley 127
Critchley, William 15
Crittall, Richard, & Co. Ltd 91, 129
*c*Crittall Freeman Bronze Co. Ltd 70, Pls 13c, 17b
*c*Crittall Manufacturing Company Ltd 59, 129
*b*Crompton & Co. Ltd 129
*a*Cross, Alfred S. W. 19, 127
Crosse & Blackwell 11; works 13, fig. 3, Pls 2d, 3a
*a*Crouch, Butler & Savage 127
Culross Street, No. 27 128

Dane, W. Surrey 82–3
*b*Davey, Paxman & Co. Ltd 90, 129
Davison, Thomas 31, 127
*b*Dawnay, A. D., & Sons Ltd 95, 129
*a*Dawson, Matthew J. 31, 127, fig. 23
de Souza, Sir Walter 87
Debenham, Sir Ernest 62
*b*Demolition & Construction Co. 114
*a*Denington, — fig. 15a
Denington, Dame Evelyn Joyce Pl. 47a
*a*Deperthes, Jules *see* Hinds & Deperthes
Devonport Municipal Buildings and Guildhall competition 38, 128
Devonshire, 8th Duke of 7
Dickinson, W. H. 68
Dicksee, Frank 69
*a*Dixon-Spain, J. E., & Allen, A. C. 127
*b*Dorman, Long & Co. Ltd 129
*b*Dorman & Smith Ltd 129
*b*Doulton & Co. Ltd 59, 129
Dove, F. L. 50, 53

Dresden Town Hall 73n.

Ecclesiastical Commissioners 9, 11–13, 116; estate of fig. 3
Ellis, Richard, & Partners 121
Electra House, Moorgate 73n.
Embankment 9, 14, 21, 31, 33, 35, 41, 43, 47, 54, 126; *see also* **County Hall, New, Building**: Embankment Wall
Embankment Gardens Generating Station 20
ʿEmms, J. L. 130
English Heritage 120–1
Environment: Dept of 120; Secretary of State for 120, 121, 122
Euston Square: Amalgamated Approved Building Societies, 73n.; Weights & Measures Office 16
Evening Standard 120
Exchange Telegraph Co. Ltd 130
*b*Express Lift Co. Ltd 130

*b*Faraday & Son Ltd 130, Pl. 28a
*c*Farmer & Brindley Ltd 59, 130
Farrer, T. H. (1st Baron) 6, 9
*b*Fennings & Co. 130
Festival of Britain 111, 112, 113n., 120
Field, Horace 18
Financial Times 120
Firebrace 116
*a*Firth, H. 108
Firth, J. B. 2–3
*a*Fitzmaurice, Maurice 49, 52
Float Mead 11, fig. 3
*a*Flockhart, William 18, 31, 42, 127
Food, Ministry of 55
Ford, Ford Madox 57
*a*Forrest, George Topham 56, 95, 103, 105, 106, Pl. 11
Forshaw, J. H. 110
Four Acres 11, fig. 3
Frampton, G. J. 82
*a*Frank, T. Peirson 108
*b*Freeman, John, Sons & Co. Ltd 130
*a*Fuller, F. M. 108
*a*Fulton, J. B. 127
Furniture 83, 89, 101, Pls 26d, 28e
*b*Furse, W. J., & Co. Ltd 130
Furzedown House, Streatham, chimneypieces from 59, 89

*b*Galsworthy Ltd 130
*a*Gardner, O. R., & Hill, S. Woods 127
*c*Gardner, J. Starkie, Ltd 108
Garnett, William 65
Garthynghared, Gwynedd 128
Gater, G. H. 95, 103, 105, 106
Geddes, Patrick 65
*b*Gee, Walker & Slater Ltd 95, 113, 130
Geffrye Museum 59, 90
George V 1, 52, Pl. 10a
George VI (Duke of York) 70, 116, Pl. 10a
George, David Lloyd 54, 55
*a*George, Ernest 18, 31; & Yeates 127
Gibbon & Bell 4, 80
*b*Gibbons, E., & Sons 130
*b*Gibbons, J., Ltd 130
*a*Gibbs & Flockton 127
Gibson, J. S. 19

Gilbert, J. D. 9, 41
Gilbert, John 9n.
Gillespie *see* Salmon, Sons, & Gillespie
[b]Gillett & Johnson 130
[a]Ginham, Percy 16, 38, 45
Glanfield, E. 15
[b]Glover, W. T., & Co. Ltd 130
Gomme, Laurence 19, 23
Goodhart-Rendell, H. S. 38
Goswell Street, chimneypieces from 87n.
[a]Granger, William Frazer 38, fig. 15a
Greater London Council 1, 2, 5, 67–8, 69, 116, 118; Director-General 22n.
Greater London Development Plan 121
Greater London Plan 1944 4, 110
Greenwood, Hubert 63
[a]Groll, Wallis, Huntley & Treacher 127
Guildford Street 106, fig. 49
Guthrie, R. C. 66n.

Hacker, Arthur 69
[b]Haden, G. N., & Sons Ltd 91, 130
[a]Hall, Edwin T. 127
Hall, H. E. *see* Warwick & Hall
[a]Hamp, Stanley 127
Hampstead Heath, Vale of Health 66–7, Pl. 29a
Harcourt: George 69; Sir William 2
[c]Hardiman, Alfred F. 62, 65, 97, 130; works by Pl. 31c, d
[a]Hare, H. T. 18, 25, 42; scheme for County Hall 31, 39, 41, 42, 75, 127, figs 8a, 17a
Harris: Sir Henry 10, 68; Percy 41, 52, 92
Hastings, Rev. Frank 23, 25, 43, 45
Haward, Sir Harry 118
[b]Hawkins, Alexander, & Sons 130
Hawkins, H. Weaver 66; works by Pl. 29a
Hayward, Sir Isaac 116
[a]Haywood, William 127
[a]Hazell, W. Ernest, & Willoughby, H. Paul 127
Health, Ministry of 55, 111, 112
Hector (the County Hall cat) 116
Heery Group 121
Henley, W. T. 128
Herkomer: Herman 68; Sir Hubert 68
Heseltine, Michael 122
[b]Higgs & Hill 108
[b]Higgs, F. & H. F., Ltd 49, 130
[a]Hinds, R. Allsebrooke, & Deperthes, Jules 26, 127, fig. 9a
[a]Hiorns, Frederick 15, **16**, 89, 106–8, 110; works by Pls 39, 40
[b]Hobbs, Hart & Co. Ltd 130
[a]Holden, Charles H. 35, 110–11, 127, Pl. 4a
[b]Holland & Hannen and Cubitts Ltd 53, 54, 55, 130
[b]Holliday & Greenwood 53n.
[b]Hollis Brothers Ltd 130
Holloway, Sir Henry 54
[b]Holloway Brothers 11–13, 19, 92; premises of 23, 37, 41, 42, **54**, 92, 95, fig. 3
[a]Hookham, W. H. 125
[b]Hope, Henry & Sons Ltd 130
Horder, Morley 38
Horsley, Gerald 18
[a]Horsley, Naylor & Pearce 127
Horsnell, A. C., perspective by *frontispiece*
[a]Houston & Horne 127

Howard, Norman 66n.
Hume, Sir George Pl. 22a
Humphreys, G. W. 90, Pl. 11
Hungerford Bridge 110–11
Hunt: Cecil 38; Frank 105; J. Rider & Co. 51; & Stewart 13
Huskinson, E. 22
Hutton, Sir John 68

Image, Selwyn 62
[c]Induni 59, 63n.
Inner London Education Authority (ILEA) 5, 120, 121
Italian Government, gift of marble from 67, 76

Jack, Richard 68–9
[a]Jackson, T. G. 18, 127
[b]Jeffreys, J., & Co. Ltd 9, 130
[a]Jemmet & McCombie 42, 75, 127, fig. 8b
Jephson, H. L. Pl. 20c
John, William Goscombe 101
[a]Johnson, W. B. 125
Jones, Edward 117
Joseph, N. S., Son, & Smitham 9
Jubilee Gardens 113, 121

[b]Keay, E. C. & J., Ltd 130
Keene, David 121
Kenyon, George 37
[b]Keystone Varnish Co. 130
[b]King, J. A., & Co. Ltd 130
Kingsway Improvement Scheme 8, 15–16, 17, 19, 23, 57; competition 20, 25
Kingswood, house by Knott at 128
[a]Knight, J. E. 117
[a]**Knott, Ralph** xvii–xviii, 16, 54, 89, 90, 92, 128, fig. 6, *frontispiece*, Pls 5b, 11, 16c, 17c, 19b, 20a, 27a–c, e; wins competition 25, scheme for CH 25, 35–8, 70, figs 5, 13, 14, 16, 17a, 18, 19, 27; career and works 25, 38, 38n., 128; association with E. S. Collins 37–8; office 38, 54, fig. 15; changes to design of CH 42–7, 95, figs 18, 19, 40, 42, Pl. 5a–c; attitude to architectural salvage 57, 59; to craftsmen 59, 66; to materials 67, 70, 77, 81; to students' work 65–7; relations with R. C. Norman 41; relations with Riley 51, 52, 56, 93; relations with Cole 63; dies 93; memorial to 59, 93, Pl. 17c; *see also* **County Hall, New**
[a]Koch, Alexander 21, 26, 35; & Belfrage, J. Herbert 127
[b]Korkoid & Ruboleum Tile Co. 130

[b]La Brea Asphalte Co. 130
Labour Party 3, 4, 5, 55
[a]Laker, R. A. 113, 117
Lambeth, borough and parish of 11, 120–2 *passim;* arms of 62n., 100; Municipal Buildings competition 25, 128; Works Dept. 11, fig. 3
[a]Lanchester, H. V. 19; & Rickards 31, 35, 75, 127, fig. 10; Stewart & Rickards 57
Langley, Actors' Orphanage 128
[b]Laurence, Scott & Electromotors Ltd 130
Lavery, Sir John 69
Leaming, John, & Sons 51
[a]Leathart, Julian R. 38, 59, fig. 15b; work by Pl. 31a
Lee, Henry J. 66n.
Lethaby, William 16; views on CH 17
Liberal Party 3; electoral victory 22

Lidgett, Rev. J. Scott 55
Liley, William 66n.
Lincoln's Inn Fields 8; chimneypieces from 57, 59, 87
Lion Brewery 116
Liverpool Cathedral competition 19
Livingstone, Ken Pl. 47d
Llewellyn, Sir Richard 68; Sir William 69
Local Government Act: 1888 1, 2, 3; 1899 2, 3
Local Government in England and Wales (1945) 4
Local Government in London, Royal Commission on 1922–3, (Ullswater) 3, 55
London Authorities, Association of 120
London Building Acts 21
London Charitable Trust 120
London County Buildings Bill (1906) 11, 13, 14, 19
London County Council: formation of 1, 2; functions of 3, 4; concern about public image 6; interest in improvement 10, 15; compared with Parliament 22, 119; moves in to CH 56; Act, Annual 69; architectural policy 113; area governed by 2, 5, 55; replacement of 5, 116; *Doom of* 123
   bookplate: LCC Members' Library 82, fig. 34, Burns' collection 82–3
   Chairman 3, 6, 81, 95; seat 77; Reception 119
   Chief Officers 22, 59, 88–9, 105, 112, 114, Pl. 11; Architect 103, 111; Clerk 15, 19, 23, 88, 89; Deputy Clerk 88, room occupied by fig. 37 (caption); Engineer 15, responsible for design of embankment wall 49; Librarian 56; Valuer 103
   Committees: Council Chamber and Offices, appointment of 6–7; Education 66, 83, 87; **Establishment** 6, 7, 8, 10, 14, 16–20, 23, 59, 63, 66–8, 70, 89, 92, 95, 97, 105–7, 113, 115, 117; report to, on competition 18; approves changes to CH design 42–7 *passim*, 51–3; meets at CH 56
   Historical Records Committee 9, 57, 82
   Departments of, demands of 22, 126
      Architect's: 4, 14–16, 42, 56, 90, 111, Pl. 44d; designs for CH 16–17, fig. 4, 105–6, 112–18, figs 48–51; General Construction section 16; Housing of the Working Classes Branch 15
      Comptroller's 56; Education 22, 56, 95, 103; Fire Brigade 15–16, 89, 95; Housing 111, 117; Public Assistance 97; Public Control 15, 22, 93, 97; Supplies 89; Tramways 89, 95; Valuation, Estates & Housing 89, 95, 102, 111, 117; Works 9, 14, 23
   Historic Buildings Panel 57
   Leaders, of the Council and of the Opposition 3, 81
   Members': accommodation 118–19, 125–6; aeroplanes 53; numbers of 3
   portraits *see* Portrait Collection, LCC, *and* individual chairmen
   relations: with central government 55; with other London authorities 1–4 *passim*
   staff: accommodation, need for 1, 3, 6, 7, 53, 55, 92, 95, 102, 110–12, 114, 116; organization of 20–2, 114; fig. 4; decentralization proposed 117; growth of 53, 119; *see also* Chief Officers
   Staff Arts & Crafts Society 16
   Staff Assocation 90
   Staff Christian Union 90
London Fire & Civil Defence Authority 120
London Government Act (1963) 5
London Metropolitan Boroughs, arms of 62, 97, fig. 41, Pl. 18c
London Municipal Reform League 2, 6, 22; *see also* Progressive Party

London Municipal Society 3, 22, 55; *see also* Moderate Party
London Residuary Body 5, 120–2, moves out of CH 122
London School Board 2, 3, 22, 23, 67, 95
London Society 81
London Waste Regulatory Body 120
Lorimer, Robert 18
*a*Lovell, Percy, & Bulman, Herbert 127
Lubbock, Sir John 6, 68, Pl. 46d
Lucas Brothers 13
*b*Lucy, W., & Co. Ltd 130
*a*Lutyens, Edwin L. 18, 21, 38; scheme for CH 26, 31, 127, figs 7a, 8c; Report (1942) 103
Lyons, J., & Co. 53, 103, 114

Mabey, Charles Henry 61
*c*Mabey, Charles Henry, Junior 59, 61, 65, 75, 80, 97, 130; firm makes County Hall model 45, 47, Pl. 5c; work illustrated Pls 12b, 14d, 18c
Mabey, James 61
Macartney, Mervyn 18
McCombie *see* Jemmet & McCombie
MacDonald, R. Falconer 19; *see also* Read & MacDonald
MacDonald, Ramsay 95
McDougall, Sir John 68
McEvoy, Ambrose 69
*a*Mackenzie, Alexander Marshall, & Son 26, 127
McKim, Mead & White 57
Madonna di Vico, church of 44
Mallord House, Chelsea 38, 128
Mallows, Charles E. 10, 18, 19
Malvern Free Library competition (1904) 25, 37, 128
Manchester Town Hall 57
Manship, Paul 63
Marrable, Frederick 6, Pl. 2a
Marriott, Charles 65, 76
Marshall, Sir F. 5
*a*Martin, Sir Leslie 112, 113
*b*Martyn, H. H., & Co. 130
Mary, Queen (wife of George V) 52, 70, Pl. 10a.
Master Builders' Assocation 53
Materials: British 73, 92, 99, 129, fig. 43; general 126, 129–131; suitable xvii, 70
   Brickwork 51, white glazed 71
   Bronze 49, 59, 70, 75, 76, 77, 80, 100, 102, 108, 129–30 *sketches* pp. 48, 69, 109, Pls 13c, 17b, c, 19b, 20a, 28a, c, d, 31a, b, 39c
   Cement, Keene's 81
   Flooring materials 76, 80, 89, 100, 129–31 *passim*
   Granite 49, 54, 70, 97, 108, 125, Pl. 38b
   Iron, ornamental 75, 76, 129, 130, fig. 26, *sketch* p. 109, Pls 16c, 19b, 28b
   Lead 129, 130, Pl. 14c
   Marble 56, 67, 76, 77, 80, 81, 99, 108, 130, 131, fig. 43
   Oak: black 77; *see also* **County Hall, New, Building**: Panelling
   Scagliola 101
   Stone 116; Ancaster 108; Portland 56, 70, 73, 75, 100, 107, 108, 109, 114, 129, 130
   Tiles, red 70, 73, 107, 108
   Tilework glazed 102, Pls. 36d, 38b
*a*Matthew, Robert 111, 112, 113
Maudslay, Son & Field 11, Pl. 6a
May, E. J. 18

Metropolitan Asylums Board 2, 3, 67, 92
Metropolitan Board of Works 1–3 *passim*, 5, 6, 15, 67
Metropolitan Municipal Reform Association 2
Metropolitan Police 4, 120, 123
Middlesex County Council 67
Millbank: Nos 25 & 29, chimneypieces from 87n., fig. 25; Estate 15; Prison 7
Models: architectural 45, 47, 61, 107, Pls 5c, 39b, 40d, 48b; for bronze ornaments 59, 61; *see also* Alexander, George *and* Mabey, C. H., Junior
Moderate Party 3, 6, 10, 22, 52, 123; *see also* Municipal Reform Party
Mond, Sir Alfred 55
Monkswell, 2nd Baron 68
Montford, P. R. 57
Moor Place, Much Hadham 48
Moro, Peter 112
Morrell, Frances Pl. 47d
*c*Morris: Art Bronze Co., 59n.; William, & Co. (Westminster) Ltd 59, 130; Singer & Co. 59n., 130, Pl. 17c; *see also* Singer, J. W.
Morrison, Herbert (1st Baron Morrison of Lambeth) 1, 105n. 111, 116, 118
*b*Morrison & Mason Ltd 54, 130
Morten, Frederick 11
*c*Morton, F. P. 108, Pl. 40b, c
*a*Mountford, E. W. 18, 31, 37, 127
Municipal Corporations Act 1835 1, 4
Municipal Reform Party (Conservatives) 3, 4, 22, 23, 35–6, 41, 52, 55, 66, 77, 89, 92; attempt to abandon CH competition 23; attempt to reduce expenditure on CH 26; policies of 22–3; electoral victory in 1907 22–3
Munitions, Ministry of 54–5
Mural painting 57, 65–7, Pl. 29a
Murphy, Jane Pl. 47d

Narraway, William E. Pl. 47a
National Telephone Co. 11
National Theatre 113–14, 121
New Delhi 7n., 38
Newgate Prison 7
Newton, Ernest 16, 18
*b*Newton Fire Extinguisher Co. Ltd 130
*a*Nicholson, Sir Charles 18; & Corlette 35, 38, 127, fig. 12
Nicholson, Sir William 69
*a*Nicol & Nicol 127
Nightingale, Florence, proposed statue of 122
Norman, Montagu (1st Baron) 41
Norman, Philip 41
Norman, Ronald Collet 41, 43, 44, 45, 50, 52, 55, Pl. 46c; supports Knott's scheme 41, 47–8
*a*Normand, Monsieur, of Paris 127
*b*Norris, F. A., & Dutton Ltd 29, 91, 130
Northampton Polytechnic, Clerkenwell 65

*c*Oakley, A. J. 108, Pl. 40d
Orchardson, Sir William 69
Orpen, William 69
Ouless, William 69
'Overdene', Godalming 128

Paris, Hôtel de Ville 14, 57
Parkes, Kineton 59

Parliament Street 7
Paton, Hubert 59
Patten, Chris 122
*a*Peach, C. Stanley 35, 127
Peckham, chimneypieces from 87n.
Pedlar's Acre 11, fig. 3
*b*Pennycook Patent Glazing & Engineering Co. 130
Philpot, Glyn 69
*b*Pirelli & Co. Ltd 130
Pitchforth, R. V. 66n.
*a*Pite, Beresford 38, 73, 127
Pitt, Lord Pl. 47b
Poley, W. *see* Young, Clyde, & Poley
Pollock, Courtney 59
Pomeroy, F. W. 57
Ponsonby of Shulbrede, 3rd Baron Pl. 47c
*b*Pooley, H., & Son Ltd 130
Portrait Collection, LCC 68–9, 80, 92–3, 101, Pls 46b–d, 47
*a*Powell, Edward Turner 127
Poynter, Edward 69
Prague, Municipal House 80n.
*b*Price & Reeves Ltd 49, 130
Progressive Party 3, 6, 10, 22, 52, 55, 77; *see also* Liberal Party

Quantity Surveyors 51

Read, Herbert 19; & MacDonald 13
*b*Redpath Brown 108
*a*Reid, Arthur & Walter, & East 26, 127
*a*Reilly, C. H. 35, 47, 70–1, 75, 127, fig. 20
Reith, 1st Baron 16, 110
Rhodes, Cecil, memorial to, Cape Town Pl. 31e (caption)
Ricardo, Halsey 17n., 20, 31, 35, 41, 48, 65
Richards, Sir James (J. M.) 113–14
Richmond, Sir William 68
Rickards, A. E. *see* Lanchester & Rickards
Ricketts, Charles 62
Ridley, Nicholas 121
*a*Riley, W. E., character 15, Pl. 3d; as architect to LCC 14–16; design for CH 16–17, 26, 35, Pl. 3c; opposition to competition 17, 17n., 20, 25; as 'Official Architect' 17–18, 19, 20, 38–9, 38n., 41; as Assessor 17, 19, 20, 23; role disliked by RIBA 18–20; proposes changes to Knott's Plan 42–7; relations with Knott 38, 48, 51–2, 56, 93; opinion of Cole's work 63, 65; attitude to students' work 66–7; influence on design of Conference Hall 92–3; retirement 56, 93–5; *see also* Assessors
Ritchie, C. T. 2, 6
Rivière, Britton 69
Robinson, Richard 23, 69
Robson, William 4
Roman boat 49–51
Rosebery, 5th Earl of 1, 3, 6, 7, 68, 123
Rothenstein, William 66
Roumieu & Aitchison 13
Round (Knott & Round) 38n., 128
Royal Academy 65, 66, 69; architecture room at 19–20; President of 68
Royal Aquarium 8
Royal College of Art 62, 65, 66
Royal Fine Art Commission 115, 117, 122
Royal Institute of British Architects 15, 17; protest about competition 18–20

*a*Russell, S. B., & Cooper, E. 31, 35, 127, fig. 9b
Russell, Walter 69

Saatchi, Charles 121
St. John of Fawsley, Baron 120, 122
St. Paul's Churchyard 7
St. Thomas's Hospital 9, 14
Salmon, Sir Isidore 51–4, 104
*a*Salmon, Son & Gillespie 31, 33, 35, 127, fig. 11, Pl. 4b
Sargent, John Singer 57, 69, Pl. 46b
*a*Scott: Adrian Gilbert 31, 127, Pl. 4c; Giles Gilbert, 105–8, fig. 49, Pls 39, 40a, e
Sebag-Montefiore, R. M. 53
*a*Shankland, C. G. 113, 114
*b*Shanks & Co. Ltd 130
Shaw, Richard Norman 41, 51, Pl. 3d; relations with LCC 16–17; support for Riley 17, 19; assessor for CH competition 18, 18n.; views on 18, 19; views of Knott's design 41n., 45; involved in changes to design 42–7, 44n., 70, 73; *see also* Assessors
Shell U.K. Ltd 113
*a*Shoosmith, Arthur Gordon, ('Shoo') 38, fig. 15a
*a*Simmonds, John Whateley (Simmonds & Morten) 11
*b*Simms, W. J., Sons & Cooke Ltd 114
*b*Simpson, W. B., & Sons 130
Sims, Charles 66
*c*Singer, J. W., & Sons 59, 76, 130; works by Pls 19b, 31a, b, e; *see also* Morris Singer
Site for New County Hall 6, 23, 123; search for 7–11; purchase of 11–13; cost of 10, 13; South Bank site 9–13, fig. 3
Sitwell, Sir George 7
*a*Skidmore, Owings & Merrill 121–2, works by Pl. 48
Skyscraper, proposed for CH 105n.
Slade: Professors 67; School of Art 66
Smith, Edward 23, 51–2
Society for the Protection of Ancient Buildings 16
Solomon, Solomon J. 69
South Bank xvii–xviii, 4, 9–13, Pls 2c, d, 3a, b, 6; as site for CH 9–13; embanking of 10; effect of CH on 9, 70; post-war redevelopment of 103, 110–14
South Bank Lion 116
South Eastern Technical Institute 16
Southwood, 1st Viscount 82
Spicer, Sir Evan 69
*c*Spiro, J. B. 108, Pl. 41b
Spring Gardens *see* **County Hall, Old**
Stamp, Gavin 122
Steamboat service 22–3
Steer, Wilson 57
*b*Stella Conduit Co. Ltd 130
Stevens, Alfred 59, 62
Stevenson, J. J. 18
*a*Stewart, William 127
Stockholm Town Hall 66, 105n.
Stokes, Leonard 18
Stormont, Speaker's House 128
Strang, William 69
Strikes 52–3
*c*Strode & Co. 75, 130, Pl. 28b
Students, work on CH 57, 65–7
Survey of London 41, 118
*a*Sutherland, W. 117
Swaffield, Sir James 22

Swinton, Capt. George 7, 8, 9, 18, 23, 65–7, 82, 89, 92, 108, Pl. 46b; creates LCC portrait collection 68–9

Tanner, Henry 38, 53
Tannoy system 77
Tasker, Sir Robert Pl. 22a
Taylor, John 122
Temple Bridge 9
a'T.F.T' fig. 15a
Thames Conservators 9, 10, 11
Thamesside Development Corporation 121
Thatcher, Margaret, proposed statue of 122
The Times xvii, 20, 110, 118, 119, 121; letters to 6, 8, 43–4, 67, 77
Tite Prize 25, fig. 6
Thornycroft, Hamo 59
Tonks, Henry 66
Torrance, Andrew 10, 68, Pl. 22a
Totterdown Fields Estate 15, 37
Town and Country Planning Act (1932) 103, 110
Trafalgar Square, site for County Hall 7–8, 123, fig. 2
*a*Treadwell & Martin 127
*b*Trollope & Colls 53n.
Truth 14
Twickenham: R.U.F.H.Q. 116n.; York House 128

*b*United Stone Firms Ltd 131
Upper Brook Street, No. 18 128
Upper Grosvenor Street: No. 1 128; No. 21 38, 128
Upper Marylebone Street, chimneypieces from 87n.

Vauxhall Bridge 19
*b*Vertigan & Co. Ltd 131
Victoria & Albert Museum 25, 57
Victoria Embankment 7, 9, 23, 119
Victoria Memorial 7–8, 57, 63n.
Victorian Society 116
Villiers Street, black oak from 77

*b*Waddell & Wilson 131
*b*Wall, Charles, Ltd 51, 53n., 131
*b*Wallis, G. E., & Sons 53n.
*a*Walters, Sir Roger 117
Wandsworth, architectural salvage from 90
War damage: to CH 55, 81, 110, Pl. 42a; reinstatement of 112, 114, 116; Commission 112
War: Great, effect on CH 54–6, 57, 59; Second World, effect on LCC 108, 110
*a*Warwick & Hall 31, 39, 42, 127, fig. 8d
Waterloo: Bridge 9, 103, 108, 110–11; District Plan 120; Station 116, 120, 121
Watson, Spencer 68
Watt, G. Fiddes 69
Watts, G. F. 68
Watts, Leonard 68
*b*Waygood Otis Ltd 131
Webb, Sir Aston 18, 19, 41, 45, 73, 75, Pl. 3d; elected Third Assessor 23, 37; office 25, 35, 57; involvement with Knott 25, 37; *see also* Assessors
Welby, 1st Baron 68
Westminster Bank 113
Westminster Bridge 10, 116; Flour Mills 11, Pls 2c, 6a

Westminster Bridge Road 11–13, 23, 103–5, 112–14, 117, figs 3, 48–51, Pls 3b, 8c, 9b, 14a; traffic in 103, 106, 117, 122; National Provincial Bank 104–5; Coronet Public House 11, Pl. 3b; No. 254 104

Westminster Gazette 10

Westminster Improvement Area 23

Westminster School of Art 66–7

[b]Westwood, J., & Co. Ltd 131

[b]Wheater, A. & S., & Co. Ltd 131

Wheeler, E. P. 106, 108

[a]Whitaker, Hall & Owen 95, 131

White, Sir Edward 52

[b]Whitehead, J., & Sons Ltd 131

Whitmore, C. A. 7

[c]Wilkinson, Alfred H. 66, 75, 80, 82, 99, 100, 131, Pls 27c, 29b, d

[a]Williams, Edwin 112–13

Williams-Ellis, Clough 44, 70, 77

Wills, Herbert 19

Wise, Valerie Pl. 47d

Wood, McKinnon 68

Woodd & Ainslie 25

[a]Woodington, Harold A. 127

Wood's Mews, No. 20 128

Works: Office of 54–5; Ministry of Public Buildings & 110

Wyllie, Harold 42–3, Pl. 5a

York Road 103–6, 107, 108, 116, 117, 122, figs 48–51

[a]Young, Clyde, & Poley, E. W. 35, 127

PLATES

County Hall under construction. Aerial view looking north in the spring of 1921

2

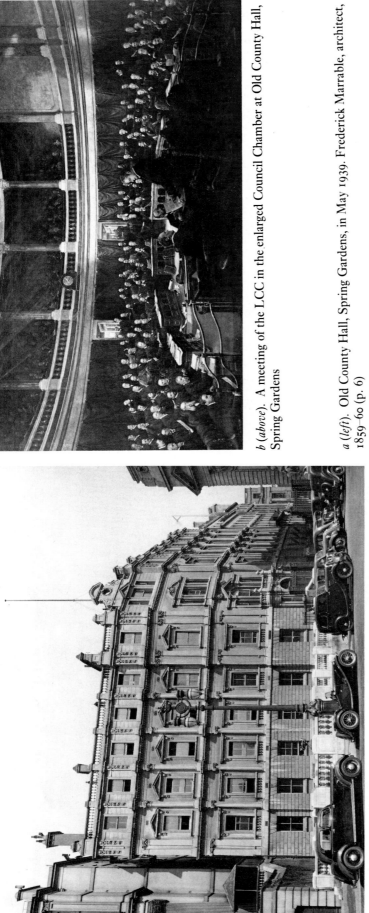

b (*above*). A meeting of the LCC in the enlarged Council Chamber at Old County Hall, Spring Gardens

a (*left*). Old County Hall, Spring Gardens, in May 1939. Frederick Marrable, architect, 1859–60 (p. 6)

c (*above*). County Hall site from Westminster Bridge in 1906. Westminster Bridge Flour Mills on right (p. 11)

d (*right*). County Hall site from the north-west in November 1908. Crosse and Blackwell's factory on left (p. 13)

3

b. County Hall site: shops and houses along north side of Westminster Bridge Road in 1905 (p. 11)

d. The Assessors – from left to right, W. E. Riley, Aston Webb and Norman Shaw – judging the competition entries. Ralph Knott's winning design is on the table

a. Belvedere Road looking north in June 1909. Crosse and Blackwell's factory on left (p. 13)

c. Design by W. E. Riley for the County Hall site, 1905 (p. 16)

4

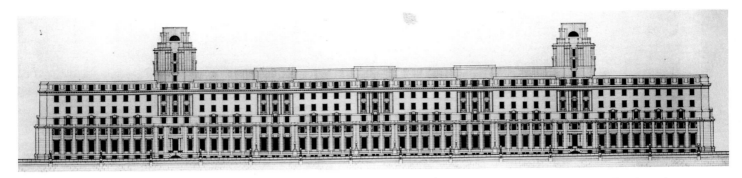

a. P. Adams and C. H. Holden, architects. Competition drawing, by Holden, of the river front elevation (p. 35)

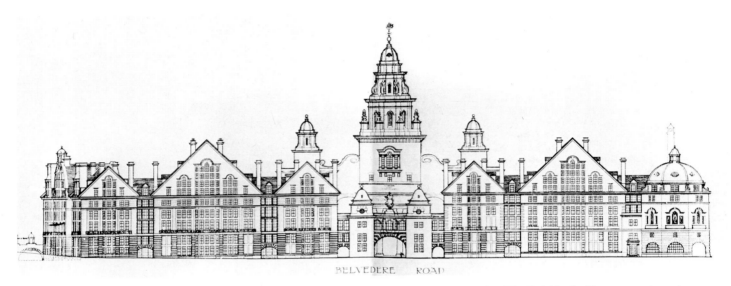

b. Salmon, Son & Gillespie, architects. Elevation to Belvedere Road published by *The British Architect*, 1907 (p. 31)

c. Adrian Gilbert Scott, architect. Perspective published by *The Builder*, 1908 (p. 31)

SOME OF THE UNSUCCESSFUL COMPETITION DESIGNS

a. Painting by Harold Wyllie illustrating the amended design approved by the LCC in 1908 (p. 42)

b. Knott's perspective, exhibited in 1910, showing his preferred treatment of the river front colonnade (p. 45)

c. Model, made by C. H. Mabey, showing the revised design approved by the LCC in April 1911 (p. 47)

THE DEVELOPMENT OF KNOTT'S DESIGN

a. The site looking north from the Westminster Bridge Flour Mills in July 1909. Maudslay's former premises in foreground (p. 11)

b. Reclamation of the foreshore, view looking north in February 1910

c. Foundations of Section A under construction, looking south

a. Site with the foundation-stone ceremony marquee in 1912, looking south

b. The foundation-stone ceremony, 9 March 1912

c–e. Ceremonial mallet, spirit-level and plumb-bob commissioned for the occasion from the Bromsgrove Guild of Applied Arts (p. 53)

LAYING THE FOUNDATION-STONE (p. 52)

8

a. Site looking south on 19 July 1912. Work in progress on Section A

b. View from Westminster Bridge on 25 September 1914. The three-legged cranes were known as 'Scotsmen'

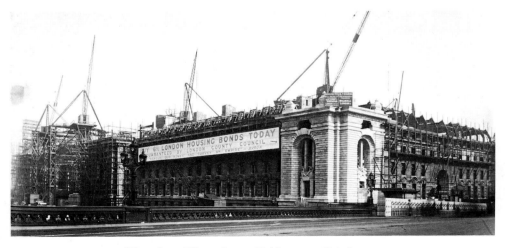

c. View from Westminster Bridge on 9 October 1920

COUNTY HALL UNDER CONSTRUCTION, 1912–20

a (right). Roof structure along Belvedere Road front in May 1920

b (below). View from Westminster Bridge in October 1921

c. The north end of Section C (Block 12) in May 1930

COUNTY HALL UNDER CONSTRUCTION

a. George V and Queen Mary at the opening ceremony, 17 July 1922. The Duke of York (later George VI) and Princess Mary are on the King's right (p. 70)

b. County Hall from Victoria Embankment in 1922

c. County Hall from the north-west *c.* 1933

MR. A. R. DYER, A.M.I.C.E. (Chief of Fire Brigade).

MR. W. C. C. SMITH, O.B.E. (Asylums Engineer).

SIR JAMES BIRD, J.P. (Clerk of the Council).

SIR ROBERT BLAIR, LL.D. (Education Officer).

MR. FRANCIS R. ANDERTON, M.A., J.P. (Chairman of the London County Council).

MR. G. W. HUM-PHREYS, C.B.E. (Chief Engineer and County Surveyor).

MR. G. TOPHAM FORREST, F.R.I.B.A. (Architect to the L.C.C.).

MR. FRANCIS R. ANDERTON, who was elected Chairman of the London County Council last March, is a member of the Municipal Reform Party, and represents South Hammersmith. He is a Justice of the Peace. The Vice-Chairman (elected at the same time) is Mr. H. C. Gooch, of whom we have unfortunately been unable to obtain a portrait. He became Chairman of the Education Committee last year. Miss Henrietta Adler, who was elected Deputy Chairman in March, represents Central Hackney. She is a Progressive. The Architect of the new County Hall, Mr. Ralph Knott, is a partner in the firm of Knott and Collins. He was for eight years in the offices of Sir Aston Webb. Mr. G. Topham Forrest is Superintending Architect of Metropolitan Buildings and Architect to the London County Council. Sir James Bird has been Clerk of the Council since 1915, and was knighted in 1918. He was formerly on the staff of the Metropolitan Board of Works. Sir Robert Blair has been Education Officer of the Council since 1904. He was formerly an inspector of the Scottish Education Department, and afterwards Chief Inspector of Technical Education in Ireland. He was a member of the Mosely Education Commission to America in 1903, and has published, among other works, "Some Features of American Education." Brig.-General Philip Maud, Chief Officer of L.C.C. Parks and Open Spaces, retired from the Army in 1910, but rejoined, on the General Staff, when war broke out in 1914, and became a Brig.-General in 1918. He entered the Royal Engineers in 1889, and in 1897-8 served on the North-West Frontier of India. In 1902-3 he was in charge of the British East Africa and Abyssinia Boundary Survey. Mr. Arthur Reginald Dyer has been Chief Officer of the London Fire Brigade since 1919. He was formerly on the engineering staff of the British Westinghouse Electric and Manufacturing Co., England and Pittsburgh, U.S.A.

DR. W. HAMER, F.R.C.P. (Medical Officer of Health).

BRIG.-GENERAL P. MAUD (Parks Department).

MR. D. P. ANDREWS (Solicitor to the L.C.C.).

MR. F. W. MACKINNEY (Stores Chief Officer).

MR. H. F. KEENE, O.B.E. (Asylums Officer).

MR. V. BROWNE (Parliamentary Officer).

MR. C. D. JOHNSON (Comptroller).

MISS HENRIETTA ADLER, J.P. (Deputy Chairman of the L.C.C.).

MR. J. OLLIS (Public Control Department).

MR. RALPH KNOTT (Architect of the New County Hall).

MR. A. L. C. FELL, C.B.E. (Tramways General Manager).

Ralph Knott and the Chairman and Chief Officers of the LCC at the time of the opening of County Hall in 1922

a. The Crescent and Members' Terrace looking north in December 1922

b. Central bays of the Crescent in 1922. Stone carving by C. H. Mabey

c. The flèche in 1989

RIVERSIDE FRONT (p. 73)

a. View from the north-east in 1973

b (*above*). The central bays and main entrances in 1923

c (*right*). The main entrance *c*. 1930. The ceremonial bronze doors, designed by Knott with enrichments modelled by George Alexander, were made by Crittalls

BELVEDERE ROAD FRONT (p. 75)

14

b (*above*). Members' Carriage Drive *c.* 1923 (p. 75)

d (*left*). Centre of Westminster Bridge Road front and entrance to Members' Carriage Drive in 1963. Stone carving by C. H. Mabey

a (*right*). Westminster Bridge Road front from the south-east in 1988 (p. 73)

c (*below*). Design by Knott for lead rain-water head, 1915. One of two types used at County Hall

b (above). Southernmost bay on the east side looking into entrance hall

a (left). Looking south towards the main gate

MEMBERS' CARRIAGE DRIVE IN 1988 (p. 75)

a. Working drawing for the south side, 1912

c (above). Design by Knott for cast-iron lamps for the Members' Courtyard and the Members' Terrace, 1922. The lamps were made by the Bromsgrove Guild

b (left). Looking west in 1922

MEMBERS' COURTYARD (p. 75)

a. North side and Members' Entrance in 1929

c (*above*). Bronze memorial to Ralph Knott on the east podium flanking the Members' Entrance, unveiled in 1932. Designed by Gilbert Bayes, 1931, executed by Morris Singer (p. 93)

b (*left*). Members' Entrance *c.* 1923. The bronze doors were made by Crittalls, the enrichments modelled by George Alexander

MEMBERS' COURTYARD (p. 75)

a. View from the north-east in 1986

c (*above*). The unofficial arms of the Borough of Deptford. One of eleven heraldic plaques carved by C. H. Mabey (p. 97)

b (*left*). Vehicle entrance in 1933

NORTHERN FRONT (pp. 93, 95)

a. Entrance Hall, Belvedere Road, looking south-east in 1960 (p. 76)

b. Ceremonial Staircase and Gates from the Entrance Hall in 1990. The bronze and wrought-iron gates, designed by Knott, were made by J. W. Singer of Frome (p. 76)

20

a. Ceremonial Staircase looking west in 1922. The bronze balustrading, designed by Knott, was made by the Bromsgrove Guild

c (*above*). Entrance to Council Chamber at the top of the Ceremonial Staircase in 1960. The malachite vases were bequeathed to the LCC by a former Member (H. L. Jephson) in 1914

b (*left*). South-east ambulatory in 1990 (p. 76)

The Council Chamber, looking west towards the Dais in 1938 (p. 77)

22

a. Ayes (North) Lobby, looking east in 1986 (p. 80). The portraits on the walls are of former Chairmen of the LCC. Over fireplace, Sir George Hume (1926–7), right, Sir Robert Tasker (1930–1), left, Sir Andrew Torrance (1901–2)

b. Committee Room (177), looking south in February 1923 (p. 87)

a. Members' Library (room 114), looking south in February 1923 (p. 82)

b. Room 168, looking north-west in 1921 (p. 87)

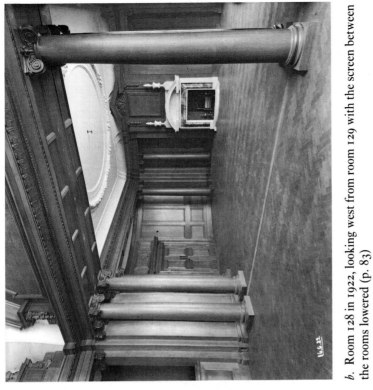

a. Main Committee Room (129) under construction in 1921, looking east

b. Room 128 in 1922, looking west from room 129 with the screen between the rooms lowered (p. 83)

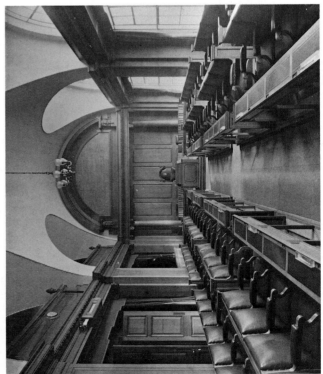

c. Main Committee Room (129) with seating in place and screen raised, looking west in 1922 (pp. 83, 89)

d. Chairman's Room (120) in 1922 (p. 81). Remodelled in the 1960s

b (above). Room 136 in 1921. Originally designed, in 1915, as a committee room (p. 87)

a (above left). Room 165, in occupation of the Chief Education Officer, December 1936 (p. 88)

c (left). Members' Reading Room (115), looking north-east in 1923 (p. 82). Remodelled as the Chairman's Reception Room in the 1960s (see Plate 43c)

26

a (left). Working drawing of 1913, showing panelling and treatment of single-door openings
b (right). Carving by George Alexander at the top of the Lady Members' Stair-case in 1986 (p. 87)

c (below left). Corridor in Block 12, looking west in February 1933
d (below right). Postbox and pigeon-holes for Members' mail in 1986

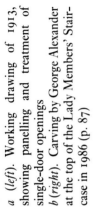

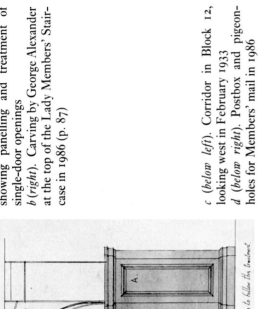

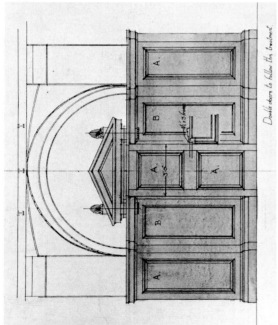

PRINCIPAL FLOOR CORRIDORS (p. 80)

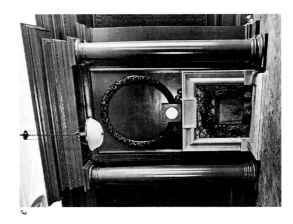

FIREPLACES

a. Room 115, *removed* (pp. 81, 82)

b. Room 133, *destroyed* (p. 81)

c. Entrance Hall, Belvedere Road, *removed* (p. 67)

d. Room 118, 'Bear and Beehive' (p. 83)

e. Room 188, *partly dismantled* (p. 87)

All except *d* designed by Ralph Knott

a (*above*). Lamp-fitting (purchased from Faraday & Son) and ceiling details in the Council Chamber in 1986

b (*right*). Lift cage in 1923. Decorative ironwork, designed by Knott, made by Strode & Co., Art Metal Workers

d (*above left*). Bronze radiator in the Members' Entrance. The same design, by George Alexander, was also used in the Council Chamber (p. 77)
e (*above right*). LCC office coat-stand

c (*left*). Bronze doors in Members' Entrance in 1990

DETAILS

a (*above*). The Vale of Health, Hampstead Heath. Lunette painting for the Principal Floor corridor by students of the Westminster School of Art from a cartoon by H. Weaver Hawkins (p. 66). *Not installed*

b (*left*). Wood carving by A. H. Wilkinson over central door in room 153 (p. 100)

d (*above*). Stone carving ('Nemesis') above fireplace in Westminster Bridge Road west entrance hall. A. H. Wilkinson, sculptor (pp. 80, 82)

c (*left*). Stone carving above fireplace in Members' Library.

DECORATIVE DETAILS

30

a (*above*). 'Creation of Eve': north central pavilion, river front
b (*top right*). Untitled: south-west pavilion, river front
c (*right*). 'World Beyond': south-east pavilion, Westminster Bridge Road front

SCULPTURE BY ERNEST COLE (pp. 62–5)

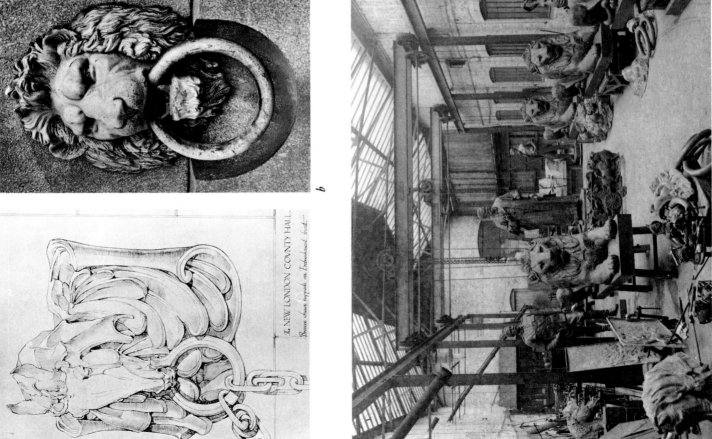

a, b. Ornamental bronze chain-supports and mooring-rings on the embankment wall, modelled by Gilbert Bayes, made by J. W. Singer (p. 59)

c, d. 'Education' and 'Open Spaces'. Sculpture by A. F. Hardiman on Section D (p. 97)

e (left). Foundry of J. W. Singer and Sons, Frome, *c.* 1910, with the lion's-head mooring rings for County Hall on the floor. The lions couchant gardant, being cast at the same time, were modelled by J. M. Swan for the Cecil Rhodes Memorial in Cape Town

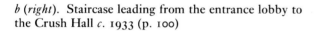

a. North Entrance lobby in 1990 (p. 100)

b (*right*). Staircase leading from the entrance lobby to the Crush Hall *c.* 1933 (p. 100)

d. E lift lobby, Principal Floor, in 1933

c. D staircase in 1990 (p. 98)

SECTION D INTERIORS. Designed by E. Stone Collins

b (*above*). Conference Hall *c.* 1933

a (*top left*). Crush Hall, looking west *c.* 1933, entrance to Conference Hall on left

c (*left*). Room 143, committee room with public gallery (room 144) in February 1933

SECTION D INTERIORS. Designed by E. Stone Collins (pp. 100–1)

34

a. Room 153, originally a luncheon and committee room, looking west into room 152, *c.* 1933

b. Room 152, originally a committee room, looking west in 1933

d. Room 142, originally a retiring-room, looking north-east in 1986

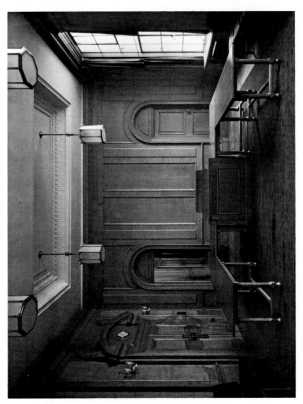

c. Room 140, originally a committee room with public gallery, *c.* 1933, now sub-divided

Section D Interiors. Designed by E. Stone Collins (pp. 100–1)

a (*above*). Education Library in February 1933. E. Stone Collins, architect (pp. 95, 102)

b (*top right*). Education Department, Library and Sample Room, ground floor of Block 12, in 1933 (p. 95)

c (*right*). Medical Supplies Department, room 35, in 1937

b (*above left*). Typical corridor, second floor, in 1990 (p. 90). c (*above right*) Corridor on third floor, Block 12, in 1986

a (*left*). West entrance hall, Westminster Bridge Road, looking north-west in 1988 (p. 80)

d. Vehicle Licensing Hall in 1963 (p. 102)

e. Staff Luncheon Club on sixth floor in 1939

37

b. Staff chapel in 1965 (p. 90)

a. Main laboratory, room 632 (Block 12), looking west in 1954 (p. 90)

d. 'Octopus room' under the Council Chamber in 1921 (p. 90)

c. Room 201, typical office in the 1922 building, in 1990

a. Roofscape looking north along the west side of the Belvedere Road front in 1970. Members' Courtyard on left

b. Contrasting materials: granite and glazed white tiles in Area G in 1990

c. Exterior of the Council Chamber in 1990

d. Exterior of the 'Drum' containing the Conference Hall and Education Library *c.* 1933

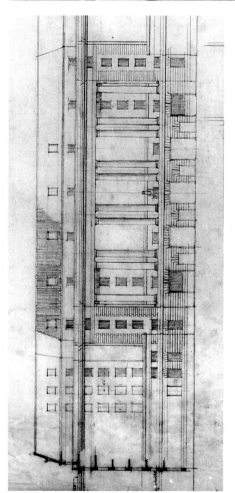

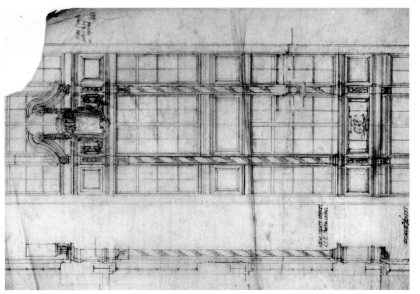

b. Model of the new offices in July 1935 showing Scott's preferred scheme with quadrant wings (p. 107)

d. Perspective view of the intended new offices at night by Stanley H. Smith *c.* 1937

a (*above*). Drawing by G. G. Scott for intended high-level bridge *c.* 1935 (p. 106)

c. Drawing by G.G. Scott for the bronze windows in the two pavilion blocks

NEW COUNTY OFFICES – NORTH AND SOUTH BLOCKS
F. W. Hiorns and Giles Gilbert Scott, architects, 1935–9

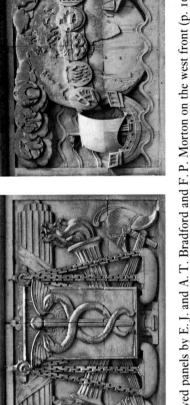

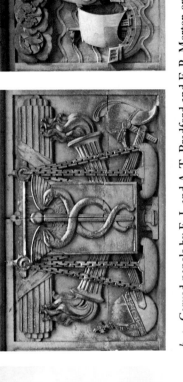

b, c. Carved panels by E. J. and A. T. Bradford and F. P. Morton on the west front (p. 108)

a. North Block from York Road in 1939. Entrance to South Block on left

e. View from the south-west in March 1939, South Block on right

d. Models by A. J. Oakley for the capitals of the stone lantern-columns

NEW COUNTY OFFICES – NORTH AND SOUTH BLOCKS
F. W. Hiorns and Giles Gilbert Scott, architects, 1935–9

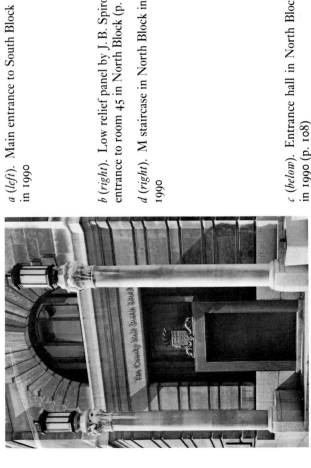

a (*left*). Main entrance to South Block in 1990

b (*right*). Low relief panel by J. B. Spiro over entrance to room 45 in North Block (p. 108)

d (*right*). M staircase in North Block in 1990

c (*below*). Entrance hall in North Block in 1990 (p. 108)

41

42

b (above). The riverside terrace in 1970 showing the exterior of the new staff cafeteria under the Members' Terrace (p. 116)

a (above left). War damage to the Crescent and river front, 18–19 September 1940 (p. 110)

c (far left). Infill block in the Members' Courtyard in 1986 (p. 117)

d (left). Infill block in H courtyard in 1990 (p. 117). The Bridge-Passage was built to link the former Main Committee Room (on right) with the Conference Hall (p. 98)

43

a (*far left*). Offices in one of the Members' Courtyard infill blocks in 1986

b (*left*). New staff cafeteria beneath the Members' Terrace in 1966 (p. 116)

c (*below left*). Chairman's Reception Suite (room 115) in 1970

d (*below*). Chief Planning Architect's room (448) in 1974

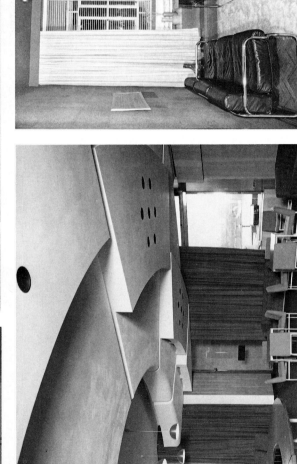

SOME POST-WAR INTERIORS

44

a (top left). Under construction in August 1956, as seen from the arches of the Waterloo railway viaduct
b (top right). L staircase in 1986
c (left). North and west fronts in 1957
d (above). Third-floor offices in the occupation of the Architects' Department in 1960

NORTH BLOCK EXTENSION, 1955–8 (pp. 112–14)

45

b. *Burolandschaft* office planning in the Island Block in 1975

a. Addington Street Annexe (1960) in 1989 (p. 115)

d. The Island Block (1970–4). Exterior from the south in 1975 (p. 116)

c. Escalator connecting Belvedere Road courtyard to the Island Block in 1988 (p. 117)

SOME POST-WAR BUILDINGS

b. Capt. George Swinton, Chairman 1912, Alderman 1922–34, by John Singer Sargent (pp. 7, 69)

a (left). Emma Cons, first woman Alderman of LCC, commemorative plaque in the Conference Hall. Plaster cast from a bronze relief by Sir William Goscombe John

c. Ronald C. Norman, Chairman 1918–19, Alderman 1922–8, by Glyn Philpot (pp. 41, 47)

d. Sir John Lubbock, Chairman 1900–2, Alderman 1892–8, by John Collier

SOME EARLY CHAIRMEN AND ALDERMEN OF THE LCC

a. Dame Evelyn Joyce Denington, Chairman 1975–6, by William E. Narraway

b. David T. Pitt, Lord Pitt of Hampstead, Chairman 1974–5, by Edward I. Halliday

c. Thomas A. Ponsonby, 3rd Baron Ponsonby of Shulbrede, Chairman 1976–7, by Carlos Sancha

d. Tony Banks MP, last Chairman of the GLC, 1985–6, with staff and colleagues, by Jane Murphy. The group on the left includes Paul Boateng and Ken Livingstone, both later MPs, with Frances Morrell of ILEA, and Valerie Wise

SOME CHAIRMEN OF THE GLC

48

a. Artist's impression of the northern, 'residential', courtyard looking south-west. Compare the view, also looking south-west, in Plate 38d

b. Model showing the proposed changes to Knott's Main Building, the new Belvedere and Addington Centres behind, and the traffic circus

COUNTY HALL, REDEVELOPMENT PROPOSALS, FEBRUARY 1989
Skidmore, Owings & Merrill, architects (pp. 121–2)